Legal Analysis Writing Skills

Legal Analysis Writing Skills

Learn Skills, Not Documents

Bradley J. Charles

PROFESSOR

COOLEY LAW SCHOOL

CAROLINA ACADEMIC PRESS

Durham, North Carolina

Library of Congress Cataloging-in-Publication Data

Names: Charles, Bradley J. author
Title: Legal analysis writing skills : learn skills, not documents / by Bradley J. Charles.
Description: Durham, North Carolina : Carolina Academic Press, 2025. | Includes bibliographical references and index.
Identifiers: LCCN 2025006337 | ISBN 9781531033071 paperback | ISBN 9781531033088 ebook
Subjects: LCSH: Legal composition | Bar examinations | Practice of law
Classification: LCC K94 .C34 2025 | DDC 808.06/634—dc23/ eng/20250305
LC record available at https://lccn.loc.gov/2025006337

Carolina Academic Press
700 Kent Street
Durham, North Carolina 27701
(919) 489-7486
www.cap-press.com

Printed in the United States of America

Contents

PART THREE | Storytelling Skills

Acknowledgments

I'm so pleased to tip my hat to a generous tribe of fellow teachers. Distinguished Emeritus Professor Joseph Kimble taught me the truest essence of legal writing: write so your reader will understand and appreciate you. As it pertains specifically to this book, he provided several examples in Chapter 9, Explain Caselaw.

I'll also forever be grateful for the witty, keen, and kind Professor Mark Cooney who contributed to the Opinion Letter and skills of Preview Analysis, Give a Rule Foundation, and Tell a Story.

In terms of just pure teaching ability, there's no one greater than Barb Kalinowski, and it's a privilege to know and associate with her. Many of her ideas inspired several parts of this textbook.

And I also want to acknowledge and thank Professor Richard Henke for his contributions to this text, but also for his kindness and encouragement.

This textbook has benefited greatly from my stalwart and ever-so-smart Research Assistants, Ariana Giurovici and Jordyn Gardner.

Lastly, thank you to the inestimable Professor Chris Trudeau for the ideas and examples in Chapter 10 about applying law. He graciously welcomed me into the legal-writing community in 2008 with an invitation to present with him in his famous "Mind the Gap" presentation at the Legal Writing Institute's biennial conference.

Thank you, all.

PART ONE

The Skills

The three chapters in Part 1 will

- introduce you to the skills (Chapter 1, Learn Skills, Not Documents);
- show them in the context of eight legal documents (Chapter 2, See the Skills in Eight Sample Documents); and
- show you how to identify the parts and skills behind them of any legal document (Chapter 3, Deconstruct Sample Documents).

Chapter One

Learn Skills, Not Documents

1.1 Focus on Learning Skills, Not Documents

Here's what you want to avoid: You begin working in a law firm; they ask you to write a certain document; and you look at it and panic, "I've never learned how to write this document!" Under the conventional way of learning individual documents in law school, that is what happens all too often.

To avoid that, focus on learning the individual, modular skills that you can use flexibly to write any type of analytical document. This flexible approach is a multiplier hack: when you learn one skill in one document, it will serve you in writing a dozen other documents.

And, yes, the skills you'll learn in this textbook apply to the genre of legal documents that require the attorney to explain the law and apply it to a client's situation. We'll call them "analytical" documents. These usually occur in the form of opinion letters, memos, and briefs, but they take on all different shapes and sizes. The key is understanding that they all require applying the same skills.

So this book's approach to learning legal analysis won't rigidly lock you in to just one or two types of documents.

1.2 Don't Read This Book Chronologically

This is a reference manual that you should use in your natural workflow, so you won't read it straight through. Generally, you should begin a writing project by identifying what the end product should look like. In most law-school classes, that'll be one of the sample documents in Chapter 2. Or your professor will give you a sample document. Or you'll find one in your law firm or online.

After you understand what the end product should look like, deconstruct it into parts so you understand what you need to write. Use the taxonomy of skills taught in this textbook to identify the document's parts and the skills behind writing those parts. The annotations to the sample documents in Chapter 2 give you an idea of how to identify the individual parts.

Then, finally, learn about one part of the document at a time and the skill behind it. Learn about it by reading the chapter or portion of the chapter that applies, and then write that part in your document. Then go to the next part. And so on.

So this is more a choose-your-own-adventure book than it is a traditional textbook.

1.3 IREAC Is Foundational

IREAC is so important it gets its own chapter, Chapter 4. But because you'll encounter it in nearly every chapter, you need to know very briefly here at the outset what it means.

IREAC is an evolution of the time-tested IRAC, which you may have heard of. IREAC is simply a reminder to law students and lawyers to write legal analysis in a logical structure. Start by stating the issue. Then state the rule that resolves the issue. Then, if there are any, give caselaw examples of the rule. After that, apply the rules and cases to the client's facts. And, finally, state the conclusion that the analysis led you to. Thus,

I = Issue

R = Rule

E = Example/Explanation from Caselaw

A = Application

C = Conclusion

Sometimes we need to adapt IREAC to a particular document, and some law schools use other permutations of this mnemonic, but they all largely mean the same thing. For instance, you will encounter AREAC, which is identical to IREAC except that you begin by stating an argument instead of the issue. Anyway, you'll get the hang of it.

Okay, with that out of the way, you're ready to get right to the skills.

1.4 These Are the Skills

Below are the modular skills you can use to write any type of analytical document. They're organized by type of skill, and that organization just so happens to reflect how they're organized in this textbook.

Part 1: The Skills

- Learn Skills, Not Documents
- Deconstruct Sample Documents

Part 2: IREAC Skills

- IREAC: Organize all Analysis in IREAC Structure
- **I**REAC: Determine Broad Issues and Arguments
- **I**REAC: Frame the Issue
- I**R**EAC: Give a Rule Foundation
- I**R**EAC: Explain Codified Law
- IR**E**AC: Explain Caselaw
- IRE**A**C: Apply Law
- IREA**C**: Conclude and Recommend

Part 3: Storytelling Skills

- Tell a Story

Part 4: Document Orientation Skills

- Title Documents
- Caption the Document
- Use Document Headings
- Preview the Analysis

Part 5: Citing and Quoting Skills

- Cite and Quote

Part 6: Editing Skills

- Revise and Edit

Good luck on your journey of learning these foundational skills!

Chapter Two

See the Skills in Eight Sample Documents

The eight sample documents in this chapter show all the different ways the modular collection of legal-writing analysis skills can be constituted to create any analytical document.

Perhaps a professor assigned you to read one of them; if so, write one part of the document at a time. The annotations in the sample documents will tell you where to look in the book to learn more about that skill; jump to the skill and chapter, and use it as a reference as you bang out your assignment.

If you're working off of another sample, you need to identify its parts. The skill in Chapter 3 about deconstructing documents will help you with that, but, undoubtedly, the parts in whatever document you're asked to write will be similar to one of the sample documents in Chapter 2. So you can use one of those as a jumping off point.

Here are the eight sample documents you'll find in this chapter:

2.1 Law-School Essay Answer
2.2 Opinion Letter
2.3 eMemo
2.4 Short Office Memo
2.5 Full Office Memo
2.6 Trial-Court Brief (Moving Party)
2.7 Trial-Court Brief (Nonmoving Party)
2.8 Appellate-Court Brief

2.1 Law-School Essay Answer

On the next page, you'll find a sample law-school essay answer.

Here are the document specifications:

Purpose: Analyze how to resolve a client's issue.

Mood: Usually objective, predictive. But it depends on the call of the question.

Structure: IREAC (**I**ssue > **R**ule > Caselaw **E**xample > **A**pplication > **C**onclusion. See Ch. 4)

Audience: Your professor.

Length: Could vary wildly from one sentence to 15 pages.

Final format: Determined by your professor.

Conveyance: Determined by your professor.

To be successful in a claim for intentional infliction of emotional distress (IIED), Craig will need to satisfy four elements. First, he must show that Professor Zet's conduct was intentional or reckless. As with any intentional tort, **the defendant's conduct must have been done with actual intent or substantial certainty to cause harm.** Here, Craig was Zet's student at the Drama School Academy. Zet was especially critical of Craig's work. He mocked and ridiculed him, leading to further ridicule by classmates. This constitutes intentional conduct by Prof. Zet.

IREAC: **Frame the Issue.** Ch. 6. (See Ch. 4 for meaning of IREAC.)

IREAC: **Give a Rule Foundation.** Ch. 7.

IREAC: **Apply Law.** Ch. 10.

IREAC: **Conclude and Recommend.** Ch. 11.

The second element to be proven is that the conduct was extreme and outrageous. **Courts often articulate this by saying it is conduct that exceeds all bounds usually tolerated by decent society. For a person in an authority position to so abuse his power is a classic example of extreme and outrageous conduct.** Indeed, a thematic issue in these cases is a power imbalance between the defendant and the victim, so Prof. Zet's conduct was extreme and outrageous.

IREAC: **Frame the Issue.**

IREAC: **Give a Rule Foundation.**

IREAC: **Apply Law.**

IREAC: **Conclude and Recommend.**

The third element of the claim is a causal connection between the wrongful conduct and the emotional distress. **Causation is satisfied when the injury occurs after the outrageous conduct and would not have happened otherwise.** Since Zet's mistreatment, Craig is suffering myriad physical and psychological symptoms. Zet continued to harass Craig even after Craig informed him of the impact. There is no indication that Craig had any preexisting condition. He began seeing a psychologist only because of the abuse. Causation seems present.

IREAC: **Frame the Issue.**

IREAC: **Give a Rule Foundation.**

IREAC: **Apply Law.**

IREAC: **Conclude and Recommend.**

Finally, the emotional distress must be severe. **Although physical manifestation of emotional harm is not required**, as indicated, Craig has various symptoms. **The caselaw is exacting on this element**, but Craig would seem to satisfy it.

You get the point! Each subissue is analyzed with the methodical IREAC structure explained in Ch. 4.

Overall, the IIED claim is strong.

2.2 Opinion Letter

On the next page, you'll find a sample opinion letter. Use it to get a sense of how to organize its constituent parts and the skills necessary to write it.

Here are the document specifications:

Purpose:	Analyze how to resolve a client's issue.
Mood:	Objective, predictive. (But the same structure could be used to persuade, such as in a cease-and-desist letter.)
Structure:	IREAC (**I**ssue > **R**ule > Caselaw **E**xample > **A**pplication > **C**onclusion. See Ch. 4)
Audience:	The client. But it'll also be shared with attorneys in the firm.
Length:	One to three pages, generally.
Final format:	PDF, hard copy, or both.
Conveyance:	Saved in the firm's electronic filing system, emailed to the client as an attachment, or printed and sent to the client via mail.

Your Firm, LLC

387 Caprese Dr.
Southfield, MI 48075

September 15, 2023

Sadie Zieah
President, LucyCo Manufacturing, Inc.
9834 Commerce Dr.
Wixom, MI 48393

Re: Opinion on Trade-Secret Status of LucyCo's Customer List

Dear Sadie:

It was a pleasure to speak with you last week. When we spoke, you reported that one of your former employees printed out and took LucyCo's password-protected customer list when he left the company. You asked for my opinion on whether that customer list is a trade secret. The answer is no.

Michigan has adopted the Uniform Trade Secret Act, which specifically defines *trade secret*. Under that definition, a trade secret is "information, including a . . . compilation" that both:

(i) [d]erives independent economic value, actual or potential, from not being generally known to, and not being readily ascertainable by proper means by, other persons who can obtain economic value from its disclosure or use[, and]

(ii) [i]s the subject of efforts that are reasonable under the circumstances to maintain its secrecy.

In your case, LucyCo's customer list does not satisfy the *trade secret* definition. This is true even though the list meets the main element by being a compilation of information. The business names, addresses, and contact information on the list are information. And by creating and

1

Caption the Document. See Ch. 14.

Title the Document. 13.2; 13.3.

Letters begin with a salutation.

IREAC: In the opening paragraph, begin with niceties. Then **Frame the Issue** (6.5) and give a brief conclusion (11.2).

IREAC: **Codified Law** (Ch. 8) kicks off this **Rule Foundation** (Ch. 7). Codified law furnishes all the rules for this issue.

IREAC: If there were any caselaw examples, they'd go immediately after the statutory rule and before the Application.

IREAC: **Apply Law**. Ch. 10. After explaining the law, immediately apply it. Start a new paragraph. Begin with a transition and then the ultimate prediction. Then (1) state and argument and (2) prove it with rule-based reasoning (10.3). Because this letter involves only codified law, there is no analogical reasoning to caselaw.

Note: With more complex matters, you'll want to add a section to lay out the facts. That gives your reader, the client, an opportunity to verify and confirm the facts. Because this letter deals with a really straightforward situation, there was no need for a separate fact section. If you did include such a fact situation, you'd use the **Tell a Story** skill. Ch. 12.

IREAC: Note how each paragraph of the **Application of Law** addresses a separate subissue of the law. 10.8(D). The paragraph breaks keep things clear and orderly for the reader. 10.8(F).

IREAC: Observe the rule-based-reasoning techniques of repeating the element's language, using synonyms of the element, and characterizing fact. That connects the analysis to the law and shows the reader that the conclusion is correct. 10.5.

IREAC: **Conclude and Recommend**. Ch. 11. State the global conclusion on the broad issue/question. And then, if appropriate, recommend the next steps for the case.

The **signature block** may be either left justified or, three or four inches from the left margin. Wherever it is, it should line up vertically with the date at the top.

adding to that list year after year, LucyCo has surely compiled this information.

The list probably also satisfies the *maintain its secrecy* sub-element. LucyCo kept the customer list password-protected, and you shared that password with just a few select employees. Thus, LucyCo probably took reasonable efforts to maintain the list's secrecy.

But the customer list does not satisfy the first sub-element, requiring that the information derive economic value from being inaccessible to outsiders. You have confirmed that LucyCo's list contains customer contact information that is widely available at trade shows and in promotional flyers. This contact information is also available to the general public on the customers' own websites. So the information is readily available to the public through proper means and does not satisfy the second element of the *trade secret* definition.

For these reasons, we do not believe that the LucyCo customer list was a trade secret, and we do not believe that litigation (or threats of litigation) would be fruitful. After you've had a chance to digest all this and consider our opinion, please give me a call to discuss the matter. I'm happy to answer your questions and address any concerns.

Thanks again for your trust in me and the firm.

Sincerely,

Your Name

2

Checklist for Opinion Letter

Caption Your Document

At the very top of the letter, did you:

___ include a letterhead with your firm's name and address? (Note: In practice, if you work for a firm, they'll provide this.)

Date

Immediately below the letterhead, did you:

___ include the date you sent the letter? (Note: This may be either left aligned or 3" or 4" to the right of the left margin; wherever it is, it needs to line up vertically with the signature block.)

Addressee

After the date, did you:

___ state the addressee's name, title, and address?

Title Your Document (Subject Line)

Immediately before the salutation, did you:

___ write a subject line that describes the letter's contents? 13.3.

___ begin it with *Re:*? (Note: After the colon, one space, two spaces, or a tab are all acceptable.)

Salutation

At the start of your Opinion Letter, did you:

___ address your client in a professional and realistic manner? (E.g. "Dear Sadie, ...")

___ end the salutation with either a colon (more formal) or a comma (less formal)?

Frame the Issue

In the first paragraph after the Salutation, did you:

___ begin with niceties (optional)?

___ clearly identify the client's legal question (or state it very close to the start)? 6.5.

___ avoid suspense by immediately stating your quick answer to that question? 6.5.

___ provide some factual context, which will help your client point out any misunderstandings and record the facts you relied on in giving your opinion? (Side note: With more complex matters, lawyers state the underlying facts in more detail in a separate section.)

Give a Rule Foundation

When teaching your client the controlling legal rules, did you:

___ synthesize the relevant rules, whether from codified law, caselaw, or both, *before* illustrating them with caselaw? 7.1–7.6(D).

___ teach the reader the rules of law in a logical, step-by-step sequence, and didn't rush it? For example, you started by teaching the broadest rule and ended with the narrowest rule. You taught general rules before teaching exceptions to those rules. 7.1–7.6.

___ if appropriate, refine the issue by focusing the reader on just the elements that are at issue? 7.3.

___ prefer paraphrasing when possible? 7.6(E).

___ avoid technical citations that would perplex a lay client?

Explain Codified Law

When explaining codified law, whether in the Rule Foundation or elsewhere, did you:

___ place codified law before caselaw? 8.2(A).

___ help the reader make sense of codified law by explaining its elements? 8.2(B)–(C).

___ include the essential elements and important contextual information? 8.2(C).

___ where applicable, cohesively synthesize several statutory provisions? 8.2(E).

___ prefer paraphrasing? 8.2(D).

___ quote unique language that cannot be paraphrased? 8.2(D).

___ cite a source for each rule? 17.2–17.3; 17.6.

Explain Caselaw

This sample opinion letter did not involve caselaw. If it did, you would use the guiding principles in Chapter 9, Explain Caselaw. See checklist in 9.11.

Apply Law to Client's Facts

When applying the law to our client's facts, did you:

___ start a new paragraph and use an appropriate transition? 10.3(A).

E.g.:

Here, ...

In our case, ...

In the present case, ...

In Ms. Hanni's case, ...

___ after your transition, write an informative topic sentence announcing your global prediction of how a court would decide our case? (No suspense in good legal writing.) 10.3(B).

___ after the global prediction, clearly state an argument? 10.3(C).

___ after clearly stating an argument, prove the argument with rule-based and analogical reasoning? 10.3(D); 10.5; 10.6. (Analogical reasoning applies only if you included caselaw.)

___ repeat an argument-and-proof combo for each argument? 10.3(E).

___ begin every paragraph after the first one with a clear topic sentence that states a legal argument and doesn't merely rehash law or facts? 10.8(F).

___ pass the two-question test in 10.4(B) to ensure you're actually applying law? See also 10.8(C).

___ weave in counterarguments where appropriate? 10.3(D)(3).

___ signal closure of your analysis? ("Thus, ..." "Therefore, ..." "So ..."). 10.3(F).

Conclude and Recommend (Closing Remarks)

At the end of your Opinion Letter, did you:

___ close with the global conclusion (unless it's too redundant)? 11.3.

___ close with a succinct recommendation? 11.3.

___ follow your recommendation with a quick, respectful, and cordial closing paragraph, with just one sentence (or two)? (E.g., "I hope that this is helpful, Sadie. If you need anything further, I'm happy to help.")

___ invite further interaction?

Complimentary Closing

Did you end the letter by:

___ using a typical closing like sincerely, respectfully, regards, etc.?

___ vertically aligning the closing signature-block closing with the date?

Quoting

Throughout the letter, did you:

___ insert quotation marks around verbatim language if you lifted exact language from another source? Four or more consecutive substantive words from a source constitute a phrase that requires quoting. 18.5(C); 7.6(E).

___ properly format a block quotation? If you've written a block quotation (quotation of 50 words or more), which you should do only sparingly, you've followed conventional rules. 17.8(E).

___ avoid using quotation marks for paraphrased information? If you have paraphrased the court's (or other source's) language, you do not need to insert quotation marks, but you still need to cite the source after the sentence to show your reader where you got the idea from. 7.6(E).

___ cite a source after every quotation? 17.2; 7.6(E).

Use Standard Document Format and Pagination

In setting up the whole document, did you:

___ single-space the text (unique to letters and emails)?

___ use 1" margins on all sides?

___ use a professional font (e.g., Calibri, Times New Roman, Arial, or their ilk)? 18.4(C).

___ include page numbers? 18.4(A).

Revise and Edit

Use Enticing Typography

Throughout the document, did you:

___ ensure that the document's typography (the layout of information, white space) is consistent with professional standards? 18.4.

___ ensure that each *heading* in the same level throughout the document has consistent spacing before and after the heading? Usually put more space before each heading than after it. 18.4(D).

___ use the same amount of space after and before each *paragraph*? 18.4(E).

___ consistently space first-line indents? (Note: You may choose to use a modern block style without indents; in that case, add more line space between paragraphs to set off each paragraph.) 18.4(F).

___ consistently use one or two spaces after a period? 18.4(H).

___ consistently use curved quotation marks and apostrophes (as opposed to straight ones you get when pasting from the internet)? 18.4(I).

Use Guru Grammar

Before submitting the final document, did you:

___ edit the final draft for punctuation and grammar? 18.5.

___ use quotation marks (" ") whenever you lifted exact, verbatim language from a case or statute (with a post-sentence citation)? 18.5(C).

___ avoid quoting/paraphrasing from—or citing to—a case's synopsis or headnotes (which are not part of the court's actual opinion but rather are supplied by the publisher's staff)?

Ensure Rad Readability

Throughout the document, did you:

___ remember that you are a teacher on the page? (Whether writing a short memo, a brief to an appellate court, or a law-school essay answer, great lawyers and law students are always teachers, striving to make the complex as clear and simple as possible. That's very hard to do, but it's always the goal.) 18.6.

___ create new paragraphs to avoid intimidating walls of dense, unbroken text? 18.4(E), (F). The goal is three to five paragraphs per page.

___ write in a confident and direct style while avoiding legalese or unnecessarily inflated language? (In other words, you avoided the lawyer tics and plodding, stilted prose that plague so many of the cases you've read in your casebooks.) 18.6.

___ create a well-organized, cohesive message?

Ensure Sightly Citations

When explaining the law, did you:

___ cite every rule of law the first time you stated it? 17.2.

___ use a full citation the first time you cited a source? 17.3.

___ cite after every sentence in a Case Illustration (except for perhaps the facts) and include a pinpoint page number? 17.2.

___ use *Id.* whenever possible, but only after giving the full citation? 17.3.

___ include "at" and a page number for each *Id.* citation? 17.3; 17.4(A)(2).

___ use a short citation when appropriate? 17.3.

___ include the right content, punctuate it correctly, and get the spacing right for each citation? 17.4–17.6.

Final Edits

Before submitting the document, did you:

___ save it as a PDF?

___ print the document after saving it as a PDF and proofread it one more time, even though you were sick of it? (This step is important because sometimes the format changes in the conversion from a word-processing document to a PDF.)

2.3 eMemo

The term *eMemo* is a shorthand reference for "email memo." What follows on the next page is a sample.

Here are the document specifications:

Purpose: Answer a small legal question.

Mood: Objective, predictive. (But the same structure could be used to persuade, such as in a cease-and-desist letter.)

Structure: IREAC (**I**ssue > **R**ule > Caselaw **E**xample > **A**pplication > **C**onclusion. See Ch. 4)

Audience: Attorneys within the firm and the client.

Length: Anywhere from one to four or five paragraphs. Anything longer would become an office memo.

Final format: An email.

Conveyance: Saved in the firm's electronic filing system and emailed.

Subject line: Opinion on "driving" a vehicle intoxicated (Vivek file)

Mr. Green,

Question

You asked me to research the elements for operating a vehicle while intoxicated and to analyze whether being passed out behind the wheel of a vehicle while its engine is running with its transmission in Neutral is considered driving that vehicle.

Answer

The answer is no. Puntab Vivek, our client, was not driving the car because he was not in actual control of the vehicle, and it did not pose a threat to anyone.

Controlling Law

Under Mich. Comp. Laws Ann. § 257.625 (West 2023), a person "shall not operate a vehicle upon a highway … if the person is operating while intoxicated." For our case, the main issue will be whether Mr. Vivek was "operating" the vehicle. The Motor Vehicle Code defines "operating" as "[b]eing in actual physical control of a vehicle." MCLA § 257.35a.

The Michigan Supreme Court put a finer point on this definition by defining *operating* in terms of the danger of colliding with another vehicle. *People v. Wood*, 538 N.W.2d 351, 353 (Mich. 1995). In *Wood*, a driver was passed out in a vehicle at a fast-food drive-thru. The vehicle's transmission was engaged, but his foot was on the brake.

The Court held that the driver was operating the vehicle, despite not being in actual physical control, because the risk of collision with another vehicle was high: all he had to do was remove his foot from the brake, and the vehicle would be in motion.

Application

In our case, a court is likely to find that Mr. Vivek did not "operate" the vehicle because he was not in actual physical control of the vehicle and there was no risk of colliding with anything else. If the vehicle had been in Drive, like the defendant's vehicle in *Wood*, then our client would have

Title the document. 13.3. For an email, this goes in the subject line.

IREAC: **Frame the Issue**. Ch. 6. This is a one-sentence issue statement in an informal document. 6.5. That's enough.

IREAC: Give the conclusion and preview the analysis. 11.2. Often, we put the conclusion not just at the end of the IREAC packet, but near the beginning of it and in the Application.

IREAC: **Give a Rule Foundation**. Ch. 7. This pieces together the rules that control the broad issue. And note that it focuses the reader on the one subissue.

IREAC: **Explain Caselaw**. Ch. 9. This case write-up illustrates the sub-element at issue, "operating." The topic sentence gets right to the point by defining the element. And the facts, holding, and reasoning are directly on point with no extraneous information (like what the parties argued or court procedure).

IREAC: **Apply Law**. Ch. 10. After explaining the law, immediately apply it. Start with a transition and then the ultimate conclusion. Then prove the conclusion with rule-based reasoning and analogical reasoning.

IRE<u>A</u>C: **Applying Law**. Ch. 10. The application of law to fact continues here with rule-based reasoning by applying the plain meaning of the rule from *Wood*.

posed a risk of collision with another person, vehicle, or object. But our client's vehicle's transmission was not engaged, and his foot was not on the brake—ready to be released and start the car moving at any moment. So it did not pose a threat.

IRE<u>A</u>C: **Applying Law**. 10.6. Note the tight analogy between the present case and *Wood*.

Making the car a risk to others would require two intentional acts that Mr. Vivek was not capable of because he was unconscious. First, he would have had to apply enough pressure on the brake to free the shifter for movement. Second, while holding sufficient pressure on the brake, he would have had to move the shifter into a gear. Then, if those two things had happened, the vehicle could have posed a risk of colliding with someone or something. But that's not what happened in our case. Unlike the threat of harm in *Wood* that was poised to happen at any moment because the vehicle's transmission was engaged, there was no threat of harm in our case.

IREA<u>C</u>: **Conclude and Recommend**. Ch. 11. State the global conclusion on the broad issue/question. And then, if appropriate, recommend the next steps for the case.

Recommendation

If the prosecutor offers a plea deal, we should not take it because Mr. Vivek did not violate the statute.

Please let me know if there's anything else I can help you with.

— Samwise Hughjobite

Checklist for eMemo

Title Your Document

In the email's subject line, did you:

___ use an informative subject line, one that would help a busy boss immediately understand the contents? 13.3.

Salutation

At the beginning of your eMemo, did you:

___ address the recipient in a professional and realistic manner? (E.g. "Karen, you asked me to ....") (Note: The salutation may go before the Question section or within the Question section.)

Use Document Headings

In your eMemo, did you:

___ include five headings: Question, Answer, Controlling Law, Application, and Recommendation? 15.1; 15.2.

___ format the headings with bold? 15.2(B).

Frame the Issue (Question)

In the Question section, did you:

___ begin by clearly identifying which question you were asked to research? 6.5.

___ frame the issue with a bit of law and fact? 6.5.

Preview the Analysis (Answer)

In the Answer section, did you:

___ clearly state the answer to the question? 16.1–16.3.

___ include the main reason for the answer without including too much detail? 16.3.

Give a Rule Foundation (Controlling Law)

When teaching your client the controlling legal rules, did you:

___ if writing multiple subissues, include one global Rule Foundation and, for each subissue, a secondary Rule Foundation? 7.5.

___ synthesize the relevant rules, whether from codified law, caselaw, or both, *before* illustrating them with caselaw? 7.1–7.6(D).

___ teach the reader the rules of law in a logical, step-by-step sequence, and didn't rush it? For example, you started by teaching the broadest rule and ended with the narrowest rule. You taught general rules before teaching exceptions to those rules. 7.1–7.6.

___ if appropriate, refine the issue by focusing the reader on just the elements that are at issue? 7.3.

___ prefer paraphrasing when possible? 7.6(E).

___ avoid technical citations that would perplex a lay client?

Explain Codified Law

When explaining codified law, whether in the Rule Foundation or elsewhere, did you:

___ place codified law before caselaw? 8.2(A).

___ help the reader make sense of codified law by explaining its elements? 8.2(B)–(C).

___ include the essential elements and important contextual information? 8.2(C).

___ where applicable, cohesively synthesize several statutory provisions? 8.2(E).

___ prefer paraphrasing? 8.2(D).

___ quote unique language that cannot be paraphrased? 8.2(D).

___ cite a source for each rule? 17.2–17.3; 17.6.

Explain Caselaw (Controlling Law)

___ Did you include two or three Case Illustrations or one directly on-point Case Illustration? 9.3.

___ Does each Case Illustration have a topic sentence, a citation, the case's facts, the court's holding, and the court's reasoning? 9.4.

Case Illustration > *Topic Sentence*

In the topic sentence of your Case Illustration, did you:

___ transition from the preceding paragraph by showing how the case fits into the big picture? 9.4(A)(1).

___ avoid starting with a source of law? Instead, cite the source after the topic sentence. 9.4(B).

___ state a new point that you have not yet stated in the Rule Foundation? 9.4(A)(2).

___ give a substantive point rather than merely announcing the topic you're going to address? 9.4(A)(3).

___ where appropriate, create an implicit rule from the case where it may not be immediately clear from the specifics of the case how it could apply to the client's matter? 9.4(A)(3)(b).

___ avoid cramming too much information into the topic sentence? Although your topic sentence is a helpful transition/preview for your reader, it can only include so much information.

Case Illustration > *Citation*

Immediately after the topic sentence, did you:

___ cite a case for the source of the topic sentence, whether it be explicit or implicit? 9.4(B); 17.4.

___ follow ALWD or Bluebook rules for formatting the citation? Ch. 17.

___ put the citation in a separate citation sentence? 9.4(B).

Case Illustration > *Case Facts*

When explaining the facts of the precedent case, did you:

___ capture the story to teach your reader what happened in the case you're writing about? 9.4(C).

___ give contextual information that sets the stage for the story? 9.4(C).

___ include the legally significant facts (i.e., the ones used in the court's reasoning)? 9.4(C)(1).

___ avoid unnecessary information like names, dates, party arguments, and lower-court procedure unless they directly relate to your issue? 9.4(C)(2).

___ if writing about a civil case, use informative status words to identify the parties and other "characters" in the story (like *tenant* and *landlord* or *buyer* and *seller*), rather than using their actual names or party designations like *plaintiff* or *defendant*? 9.4(C)(3).

___ if writing about a criminal case, use *the defendant* to refer to the person charged with the crime, which is informative to readers? But for other people, you've tried to come up with informative status words, such as *witness*, *victim*, *accuser*, *arresting officer*, *police officer*, *companion*, *prosecutor*, etc. 9.4(C)(3).

Case Illustration > ***Court's Holding***

When writing about the court's holding in a Case Illustration, did you:

___ give the court's actual decision rather than state a pure rule of law or give only the ultimate procedural outcome like *affirmed* or *reversed*? 9.4(D).

___ state the global holding and any secondary holdings on your issue? 9.4(D).

___ ensure that the holding addresses the narrow issue you're writing about? 9.4(D).

Case Illustration > ***Court's Reasoning***

When summarizing the court's reasoning in a Case Illustration, did you:

___ give *details* about why the court decided the case the way it did? If the court decided multiple *relevant* subissues, you've quickly explained the court's reasoning for each of those subissues, and you've done that in a logical sequence, with signposts to help your reader follow along. 9.4(E).

___ avoid restating the rules the court applied? Rather, put the rules either in the Rule Foundation or in the Case Illustration's topic sentence. 9.4(E).

Case Synthesis

If you've given more than one Case Illustration for a single issue, did you:

___ create coherence among the cases by using the trophy, rubber-band, or paragraph-synthesis method? 9.9(B).

___ apply the checklist in 9.11 for *synthesizing* caselaw?

Apply Law (Application)

When applying the law to our client's facts, did you:

___ start a new paragraph and use an appropriate transition? 10.3(A).

E.g.:

Here, ...

In our case, ...

In the present case, ...

In Ms. Hanni's case, ...

___ after your transition, write an informative topic sentence announcing your global prediction of how a court would decide our case? (No suspense in good legal writing.) 10.3(B).

___ after the global prediction, clearly state an argument? 10.3(C).

___ after clearly stating an argument, prove the argument with rule-based and analogical reasoning? 10.3(D); 10.5; 10.6.

___ repeat an Argument-and-Proof combo for each argument? 10.3(E).

___ begin every paragraph after the first one with a clear topic sentence that states a legal argument and doesn't merely rehash law or facts? 10.8(F).

___ pass the two-question test in 10.4(B) to ensure you're actually applying law? See also 10.8(C).

___ weave in counterarguments where appropriate? 10.3(D)(3).

___ analogize to caselaw in meaningful, strategic places where it helps support a specific point? 10.7(C).

___ analogize to caselaw in meaningful ways by using one or a variety of the nine techniques explained in 10.6(A)?

___ avoid false comparisons? ("Like the *Jones* case, Mary Smith did not ..."—*Jones* is a case, but Mary is a human being.) 10.7(E).

___ avoid organizing your analysis by case? 10.8(D).

___ signal closure of your analysis? ("Thus, ..." "Therefore, ..." "So ..."). 10.3(F).

Conclude and Recommend (Recommendation)

In the Conclusion, did you:

___ state the global conclusion? 11.3.

___ state your recommendation for the case's next steps? 11.3.

___ rehash any of the reasoning? If so, delete it. 11.3.

___ follow your recommendation with a quick, respectful, and cordial closing paragraph, with just one sentence (or two) inviting a willingness to do follow-up work? (E.g., "I hope that this is helpful, Mark. If you need anything further, I'm happy to help.")

Quoting

Throughout the memo, did you:

___ insert quotation marks around verbatim language if you lifted exact language from another source? Four or more consecutive substantive words from a source constitute a phrase that requires quoting. 18.5(C); 7.6(E).

___ properly format a block quotation? If you've written a block quotation (quotation of 50 words or more), which you should do only sparingly, you've followed conventional rules. 17.8(E).

___ avoid using quotation marks for paraphrased information? If you have paraphrased the court's (or other source's) language, you do not need to insert quotation marks, but you still need to cite the source after the sentence to show your reader where you got the idea from. 7.6(E).

___ cite a source after every quotation? 17.2; 7.6(E).

Use Standard Document Format and Pagination

In setting up the whole document, did you:

- ___ single-space the text (unique to letters and emails)?
- ___ use 1" margins on all sides?
- ___ use a professional font (e.g., Calibri, Times New Roman, Arial, or their ilk)? 18.4(C).
- ___ include page numbers? 18.4(A).

Revise and Edit

Use Enticing Typography

Throughout the document, did you:

- ___ ensure that the document's typography (the layout of information, white space) is consistent with professional standards? 18.4.
- ___ ensure that each *heading* in the same level throughout the document has consistent spacing before and after the heading? Usually put more space before each heading than after it. 18.4(D).
- ___ use the same amount of space after and before each *paragraph*? 18.4(E).
- ___ consistently space first-line indents? (Note: You may choose to use a modern block style without indents; in that case, add more line space between paragraphs to set off each paragraph.) 18.4(F).
- ___ consistently use one or two spaces after a period? 18.4(H).
- ___ consistently use curved quotation marks and apostrophes (as opposed to straight ones you get when pasting from the internet)? 18.4(I).

Use Guru Grammar

Before submitting the final document, did you:

- ___ edit the final draft for punctuation and grammar? 18.5.
- ___ use quotation marks (" ") whenever you lifted exact, verbatim language from a case or statute (with a post-sentence citation)? 18.5(C).
- ___ avoid quoting/paraphrasing from—or citing to—a case's synopsis or headnotes (which are not part of the court's actual opinion but rather are supplied by the publisher's staff)?

Ensure Rad Readability

Throughout the document, did you:

- ___ remember that you are a teacher on the page? (Whether writing a short memo, a brief to an appellate court, or a law-school essay answer, great lawyers and law students are always teachers, striving to make the complex as clear and simple as possible. That's very hard to do, but it's always the goal.) 18.6.
- ___ create with either indents or line spacing new paragraphs to avoid intimidating walls of dense, unbroken text? 18.4(E), (F). The goal is three to five paragraphs per page.
- ___ write in a confident and direct style while avoiding legalese or unnecessarily inflated language? (In other words, you avoided the lawyer tics and plodding, stilted prose that plague so many of the cases you've read in your casebooks.) 18.6.
- ___ create a well-organized, cohesive message?

Ensure Sightly Citations

When explaining the law, did you:

___ cite every rule of law the first time you stated it? 17.2.

___ use a full citation the first time you cited a source? 17.3.

___ cite after every sentence in a Case Illustration (except for perhaps the facts) and include a pinpoint page number? 17.2.

___ use *Id.* whenever possible, but only after giving the full citation? 17.3.

___ include "at" and a page number for each *Id.* citation? 17.3; 17.4(A)(2).

___ use a short citation when appropriate? 17.3.

___ include the right content, punctuate it correctly, and get the spacing right for each citation? 17.4–17.6.

Final Edits

Before submitting the document, did you:

___ save it as a PDF?

___ print the document after saving it as a PDF and proofread it one more time, even though you were sick of it? (This step is important because sometimes the format changes in the conversion from a word-processing document to a PDF.)

2.4 Short Office Memo

On the next page, you'll find a sample short office memo.

Here are the document specifications:

Purpose: Analyze how to resolve a client's issue.

Mood: Objective, predictive.

Structure: IREAC (**I**ssue > **R**ule > Caselaw **E**xample > **A**pplication > **C**onclusion. See Ch. 4)

Audience: Attorneys within the firm and the client.

Length: 3 pages but could take up to 6. Anything longer would become a Full Office Memo.

Final format: PDF, hard copy, or both.

Conveyance: Saved in the firm's electronic filing system, emailed as an attachment, or printed and sent via mail.

Caption the Document. 14.1. Vertically align the information after *To, From, Date,* and *Re.*

Preview the Analysis. 16.4. This Overview summarizes all the analysis in this document. That gives the reader context and a roadmap. Because this is a summary of the analysis, it properly follows IREAC structure.

Frame the Issue. Here, the writer frames the subissue so the reader knows which of all the elements is actually at issue—confinement. 5.2; 6.5.

Tell a Story. Ch. 12. Even objective documents like in-house memos require storytelling. Start with context. Then tell the story chronologically, emphasizing the legally relevant facts and giving context for them along the way.

Memo

To: New Attorney
From: Partner
Date: Today's Date
Re: Academy of Motion Picture Arts & Sciences; Donovan Michaels; False Imprisonment

Overview

Donovan Michaels sued the Academy of Motion Picture Arts and Sciences (the Academy) for false imprisonment. Michaels's suit against the Academy will fail because he was not confined. The tort of false imprisonment "consists of 'the nonconsensual, intentional confinement of a person without lawful privilege for an appreciable length of time, however short.'" *Fermino v. Fedco*, 872 P.2d 559, 567 (Cal. 4th 1994) (citation omitted). The only element at issue is whether Michaels was confined because he was not physically restrained. But in California, a person may be confined by fear or unreasonable duress. In the end though, a court would likely hold that Michaels was not confined because the situation was not so severe that his will was overcome, the Academy didn't use anything untoward as leverage to force him to stay, and Michaels wasn't especially vulnerable.

Facts

Actor Donovan Michaels recently filed a $50 million lawsuit against our client, the Academy of Motion Picture Arts and Sciences, for false imprisonment. Michaels is a desperate-to-make-it-big actor. He allegedly has minor roles in two upcoming movies.

The incident occurred at the most recent Academy Awards ceremony. Michaels was told by his publicist that his ticket to the show was "tentatively confirmed." But Michaels and his publicist were unable to locate the ticket before the day of the show. So they assumed that his ticket was being held inside the Dolby Theatre, the venue for the Academy Awards.

1

At the beginning of the red carpet, several signs warned those without tickets that they are guilty of trespass. Michaels proceeded down the red carpet anyway, thinking that his ticket was inside the venue. When Michaels was asked by security guards for his ticket, he explained that his ticket must be at will call. Knowing that there is no will call, and being suspicious of Michaels, the guard took him to the "resolution desk" around 4 p.m.

The resolution desk is located in a suite adjacent to the Dolby Theatre. There is one public entrance in the front. There are several benches and a counter behind which an Academy employee stands.

Tell a Story. Ch. 12.
In these paragraphs, the writer uses signposts to help the reader understand the chronology: *4 p.m., once there, 7 p.m., at some point, later*, etc.

And the writer also gives context along the way (e.g., explaining the resolution desk).

Once there, an Academy employee took Michaels's contact information and photograph. He also questioned Michaels about trespassing on the red carpet. Michaels explained several times that his publicist told him that any actor with any role in a movie that comes out in the year of the Academy Awards gets a ticket to the Academy Awards ceremony. The Academy employee explained that this is a rumor perpetuated by seasoned actors as a ruse on newbie actors.

Michaels finally conceded around 7 p.m. that his naivety was to blame. He apologized for any misunderstanding and asked to leave. The Academy employee told him that he could leave at any time—but that he would be hearing from the Academy attorneys. This prompted Michaels to explain himself further.

Tell a Story. Ch. 12.
How do you know what facts to include? Whether you use them in the Application section below determines whether the facts are significantly necessary and should be included. So write the arguments to know what's relevant. Besides legally relevant facts, include any facts that give contextual understanding to the significantly relevant facts.

At some point, the Academy employee tipped the paparazzi that "someone" was trying to get into the Academy Awards, and he thought he could because of a tiny stunt role in an upcoming movie. Michaels heard the employee make the call and later saw four or five paparazzi standing outside the door of the resolution center holding cameras.

From 7 to 10 p.m., the Academy employee continued to question Michaels about his trespassing and "stupidity" in thinking that he could get tickets. The questioning, which occurred over the counter, was not constant, as the employee had other duties to attend to. During this time, Michaels asked the employee several times to have the paparazzi leave. The employee rebuffed these requests, again saying that he was free to go

2

at any time. Around 10 p.m., the employee said that "he had suffered" enough. He then let Michaels out through the back door of the resolution center, avoiding the paparazzi.

IREAC: This begins with the broad **Issue** (5.2; 6.5) and then a **Rule Foundation.** Ch. 7. The controlling rules come entirely from caselaw because tort law is based in the common law.

Controlling Rules

You asked me to determine if the law will support Donovan Michaels's claim for false imprisonment. In California, the tort of false imprisonment "consists of 'the nonconsensual, intentional confinement of a person without lawful privilege for an appreciable length of time, however short.'" *Fermino v. Fedco*, 872 P.2d 559, 567 (Cal. 4th 1994) (citation omitted). Mr. Michaels's claim will succeed or fail based on his ability to show that he was "confined" at all, which is the only issue in this case.

IREAC: Refine the issue in the Rule Foundation (focus on just "confined"). 7.3. And slip in the conclusion if helpful to your reader. 4.6(D).

Relevant Caselaw

IR**E**AC: **Explain Caselaw.** Ch. 9. Illustrate the rules with caselaw. You'll use the story in the caselaw precedent to analogize in the Application section below.

By following the five-part structure laid out in Ch. 9, the reader can easily understand the case without having to look up the case themselves.

Confinement by unreasonable duress occurs when one's will is overcome. *Parrott v. Bank of America*, 217 P.2d 89, 95 (Cal. App. 2d Dist. 1950). In *Parrott*, bank managers accused a teller of stealing a customer's deposit. The managers held her in a room for questioning. She became hysterical after they questioned her for more than two hours and threatened her with an FBI investigation and to publicly humiliate her. As a result, she confessed to stealing the deposit even though she was innocent. Shortly after the confession, the bank customer found the deposit at home. The teller then sued the bank for false imprisonment.

The court held that the teller was confined during the questioning. *Id.* at 95. In support of this conclusion, the court mainly relied on the fact that an innocent person agreeing to sign a confession is evidence of force. *Id.*

IR**E**AC: **Explain Caselaw.** Ch. 9. Here's a second Case Illustration to illustrate the "confinement" element. Note the substantive topic sentence that teaches the reader the law; it's an implicit rule culled from the facts and the court's reasoning. 9.4(A).

The source of the duress may be when a person uses an invaluable possession as leverage. *Wilson v. Houston Funeral Home*, 50 Cal. Rptr. 2d 169 (Cal. App. 2d Dist. 1996). In *Wilson*, a funeral home director sent a limo to take a family to scheduled burial services. The driver, instead, took the family to a bank where the funeral director demanded full payment even though they previously agreed to payment after the burial services. In the bank, he shouted, "Ain't nobody going nowhere until I get paid." *Id.* at 170. And for 45 minutes he tried to talk the widow into paying him.

3

The court held that the family was confined by unreasonable duress because leaving the bank would have left their deceased loved one to an unknown fate. *Id.* at 174.

The hallmark of confinement by unreasonable duress is fear. *Schanafelt v. Seaboard Fin. Co.*, 239 P.2d 42, 43 (Cal. App. 2d Dist. 1951). The defendant's agent in this case went to the plaintiff's house to repossess furniture that the plaintiff was unable to pay for. The agent parked his car in the driveway to block the plaintiff's car. He was "abrupt and gruff" in demanding that the plaintiff stay put while a utility truck and a crew came to repossess the furniture. *Id.* at 43. The plaintiff could have left on foot, but she "[f]ear[ed] the consequence of contrary action." *Id.* Plus she was pregnant and was worried about consequences to the unborn child. The plaintiff complained to the agent of being hungry, but he wouldn't let her eat, even though he helped himself to food from the neighbor's house. The whole ordeal lasted a bit over three hours.

IREAC: **Explain Caselaw.** Ch. 9. Here's a third Case Illustration to explain the "confinement" element.

The court held that the agent's conduct did amount to confinement because the plaintiff was "effectively prevented" from leaving by the agent's gruff manner, his blocking of the driveway, and the plaintiff's vulnerable status. *Id.*

AREAC: **Explain Caselaw.** Note that attorneys explain all caselaw on a single issue together, consecutively before applying them to the facts. Don't explain a case and then apply it; explain another case and then apply it; and so on. For more, see 10.8(B).

With these three cases as guidance, it appears that California courts determine whether unreasonable duress confines a person by looking at whether (1) fear is used to overcome one's will, (2) valuable possessions are used as leverage, and (3) the plaintiff is in a particularly vulnerable state.

IREAC: When explaining multiple cases, sometimes the primary points are lost. So the writer should "synthesize" the cases. See 9.9(B). (This is the "synthesis paragraph" type.)

Application

In our case, Michaels was probably not confined by unreasonable duress. Michaels's will was not overcome. In fact, the Academy employee said that Michaels was "free to leave." How could anyone reasonably argue that permission to leave would overcome one's will? Yes, that assertion was followed by a statement that the Academy attorney would contact Michaels, but that was merely informing Michaels of the next step; it was not a threat. Such a statement does not create the type of fear that persuades courts to find confinement. Michaels incorrectly assumed that

IREAC: **Apply Law.** Ch. 10. After explaining the law, immediately apply it. Start with a transition and then the ultimate conclusion. Then state an argument ("will not overcome") and prove it with rule-based reasoning and analogical reasoning. 10.3. Note the brief counter-analysis as well (starting with "yes"), which is another way of proving your argument.

4

IREAC: After stating the primary argument in the first paragraph of the Application, the writer presupposed a counterargument and addressed it straight on. See 10.3(D)(3).

he could stay and talk the employee out of turning his information over to the attorneys. So it was Michaels's independent choice to stay.

Michaels will likely argue that "free to leave" did not really mean that. The unspoken subtext, perhaps, was that he would face more trouble if he left without the employee's permission. Michaels's presence for six hours supports this argument, suggesting that "free to leave" really did not mean that Michaels was free to leave. After all, that is almost an entire work day, much longer than the entire Academy Awards ceremony. If the employee's job was to simply collect information of those who allegedly trespassed on the red carpet, he could have done it in about 15 minutes. In light of that, six hours might suggest some force confined Michaels.

IREAC: Every paragraph in the Application begins with a legal argument— never with just fact or just law. See 10.8(C), (F).

Despite these arguments, Michaels still has an uphill battle because the precedent on unreasonable duress sets a very high bar. The victim in *Parrott* was so overcome by threat of FBI prosecution and public humiliation, what the court called force, that she confessed to a crime she did not commit. Michaels, on the other hand, persisted in trying to talk the employee out of turning his name over to the attorneys. So his will was not overcome as he did not confess to trespass just to leave.

IREAC: Here's an analogy to one of the cases. See 10.6; 10.7.

The Academy had no real leverage or even motive to force Michaels to stay in the resolution center. He might argue that the duress came from fearing the negative consequences of having to face the paparazzi. He feared them so much that it was a relief when the employee finally let him avoid the paparazzi by exiting through the back door.

Michaels will likely read much into the employee's statement, "you've suffered enough," which he said right before letting Michaels out. This statement, combined with allowing Michaels to exit through the back entrance, indicates that the employee used his position of authority to control Michaels—similar to the funeral director's leverage in *Wilson*. Perhaps he did it to send a message to others who would try to get onto the red carpet without permission. Or perhaps he wanted to make an example of Michaels.

More likely, though, "you've suffered enough" signals that the employee felt sorry for the joke of calling the paparazzi and sympathized

5

with the stress the paparazzi caused Michaels. But it was just that: stress, and nothing more. It certainly was not unreasonable duress. It is not as though there was an angry mob out front throwing rocks. Such threat of violence could cause unreasonable duress. The threat of severe injury from rocks pales when compared to paparazzi photos or video.

IREAC: Throughout this entire Application, the writer has been using a great mix of rule-based reasoning and analogical reasoning. This paragraph relies heavily on rule-based reasoning, but then the next paragraph supports this with an analogy. See 10.5; 10.6.

Wilson underscores that confinement by unreasonable duress requires a severity that is not present in this case. The mourners in *Wilson*, who physically could have left, stayed in the bank because the funeral director leveraged the burial of their loved one to keep them in the bank. Leaving would have meant foregoing one of our society's most solemn rights: to bury a loved one.

Michaels, on the other hand, would have given up very little—if anything—by braving the paparazzi. Any airtime, even if somewhat negative, could have even helped his career. Many so-called stars, from Paris Hilton to Kim Kardashian, got their starts through publicized scandals. So perhaps there is no such thing as bad publicity. If Michaels was so concerned about the paparazzi, he could have avoided them by covering his head with his shirt or hand. Besides, the chances of this non-newsworthy event making it on air, the Internet, or in print was very slim.

To top it all off, Michaels was not in a particularly vulnerable state. Unlike the teller employee who was questioned and threatened, the pregnant home owner who bought expensive furniture, or the family who just wanted to bury their deceased loved-one, Michaels was in complete control of his situation. He could have walked out the resolution center at any time with very little to lose.

Therefore, Michaels was not confined by unreasonable duress.

IREAC: End each IREAC packet with an internal conclusion. 10.3(F); 11.2.

Conclusion

For the reasons stated above, Michaels was not confined, so the Academy is not liable for false imprisonment. The next step would be to advise our client that suing the Academy for false imprisonment is not wise.

IREAC: **Conclude and Recommend.** 11.3. State the global conclusion on the broad issue/question. And then, if appropriate, recommend the next steps for the case. Do not rehash the arguments here. Keep it simple.

6

Checklist for Short Office Memo

Caption Your Document

Did you:

___ title the document "Memo" at the very top, center and bold it? 14.1.

___ below the title, write the standard office-memo caption of *To:*, *From:*, *Date:*, and *Re:* in that order? 14.1.

___ avoid double-spacing the caption, instead preferring 1.5 spacing or 6 points after each paragraph? 14.1.

___ in the *Re:* line, describe the matter and the client's name? 14.1.

___ vertically align the information after the colons? 14.1.

Use Document Headings

Did you:

___ organize your analysis by inserting the following headings: Overview, Facts, Controlling Rules, Relevant Caselaw, Application, and Conclusion? Ch. 3; 15.2.

___ bold and center each heading or otherwise set it off as a heading? 15.2.

Preview the Analysis (Overview)

In your Overview, did you:

___ ensure that the entire section follows a syllogistic structure from issue, to rule, to application, to conclusion? 16.4(A), (B).

___ identify the issue in the first sentence? 16.4(A)(1).

___ state the pivotal rule of law (prefer paraphrasing, but quote when necessary) in the second sentence? 16.4(A)(2).

___ state a summary of the application of the law to the facts (i.e., it summarizes your main reasoning points) in the third sentence (and maybe fourth and fifth)? 16.4(A)(3).

___ state the conclusion (i.e., predict the outcome) in the final sentence? 16.4(A)(4).

___ limit the Overview to four (or five) sentences?

___ make sure that the paragraph had a logical flow to it? In other words, the conclusion (prediction) in the final sentence seemed logical given what you wrote in the sentences that preceded it.

Tell a Story (Facts)

In your Facts section, did you:

___ include legally significant, background, and emotional facts? 12.2(A).

___ include even unfavorable facts? 12.2(A)(1).

___ begin with contextual information that introduces the parties and the broad issue? 12.2(B).

___ prefer to organize the facts chronologically? 12.2(C)(1).

___ avoid organizing the facts according to which document you got them from? 12.2(C)(1).

___ where appropriate, organize the facts by each character's perception (i.e., where characters disagree on the facts)? 12.2(C)(3).

___ consider using headings for longer, more complex factual statements? 12.2(D)(4).

___ use lots of paragraphs, averaging three to five per page? 12.2(D)(2).

___ use names, not role designations like *plaintiff* or *customer*? 12.2(D)(3).

Give a Rule Foundation (Controlling Rules)

When teaching your client the controlling legal rules, did you:

___ if analyzing multiple subissues, include one global Rule Foundation and, for each subissue, a secondary Rule Foundation? 4.6(E); 7.5.

___ synthesize the relevant rules, whether from codified law, caselaw, or both, *before* illustrating them with caselaw? 7.1–7.6(D).

___ teach the reader the rules of law in a logical, step-by-step sequence, and didn't rush it? For example, you started by teaching the broadest rule and ended with the narrowest rule. You taught general rules before teaching exceptions to those rules. 7.1–7.6.

___ if appropriate, refine the issue by focusing the reader on just the elements that are at issue? 7.3.

___ prefer paraphrasing when possible? 7.6(E).

___ include a citation to binding legal authority for each rule? Ch. 17.

Explain Codified Law

When explaining codified law, whether in the Rule Foundation or elsewhere, did you:

___ place codified law before caselaw? 8.2(A).

___ help the reader make sense of codified law by explaining its elements? 8.2(B), (C).

___ include the essential elements and important contextual information? 8.2(C).

___ where applicable, cohesively synthesize several statutory provisions? 8.2(E).

___ prefer paraphrasing? 8.2(D).

___ quote unique language that cannot be paraphrased? 8.2(D).

___ cite a source for each rule? 17.2–17.3; 17.6.

Explain Caselaw (Controlling Law)

___ Did you include two or three Case Illustrations or one directly on-point Case Illustration? 9.3.

___ Does each Case Illustration have a topic sentence, a citation, the case's facts, the court's holding, and the court's reasoning? 9.4.

Case Illustration > ***Topic Sentence***

In the topic sentence of your Case Illustration, did you:

___ transition from the preceding paragraph by showing how the case fits into the big picture? 9.4(A)(1).

___ avoid starting with a source of law? Instead, cite the source after the topic sentence. 9.4(B).

___ state a new point that you have not yet stated in the Rule Foundation? 9.4(A)(2).

___ give a substantive point rather than merely announcing the topic you're going to address? 9.4(A)(3).

___ where appropriate, create an implicit rule from the case where it may not be immediately clear from the specifics of the case how it could apply to the client's matter? 9.4(A)(3)(b).

___ avoid cramming too much information into the topic sentence? Although your topic sentence is a helpful transition/preview for your reader, it can only include so much information.

Case Illustration > *Citation*

Immediately after the topic sentence, did you:

___ cite a case for the source of the topic sentence, whether it be explicit or implicit? 9.4(B); 17.4.

___ follow ALWD or Bluebook rules for formatting the citation? Ch. 17.

___ put the citation in a separate citation sentence? 9.4(B).

Case Illustration > *Case Facts*

When explaining the facts of the precedent case, did you:

___ capture the story to teach your reader what happened in the case you're writing about? 9.4(C).

___ briefly give contextual information that sets the stage for the story? 9.4(C).

___ include the legally significant facts (i.e., the ones used in the court's reasoning)? 9.4(C)(1).

___ avoid unnecessary information like names, dates, party arguments, and lower-court procedure unless they directly relate to your issue? 9.4(C)(2).

___ if writing about a civil case, use informative status words to identify the parties and other "characters" in the story (like *tenant* and *landlord* or *buyer* and *seller*), rather than using their actual names or party designations like *plaintiff* or *defendant*? 9.4(C)(3).

___ if writing about a criminal case, use *the defendant* to refer to the person charged with the crime, which is informative to readers? But for other people, you've tried to come up with informative status words, such as *witness, victim, accuser, arresting officer, police officer, companion, prosecutor*, etc. 9.4(C)(3).

Case Illustration > *Court's Holding*

When writing about the court's holding in a Case Illustration, did you:

___ give the court's actual decision rather than state a pure rule of law or give only the ultimate procedural outcome like *affirmed* or *reversed*? 9.4(D).

___ state the global holding and any secondary holdings on your issue? 9.4(D).

___ ensure that the holding addresses the narrow issue you're writing about? 9.4(D).

Case Illustration > *Court's Reasoning*

When summarizing the court's reasoning in a Case Illustration, did you:

___ give *details* about why the court decided the case the way it did? If the court decided multiple *relevant* subissues, you've quickly explained the court's reasoning for each of those subissues, and you've done that in a logical sequence, with signposts to help your reader follow along. 9.4(E).

___ avoid restating the rules the court applied? Rather, put the rules either in the Rule Foundation or in the Case Illustration's topic sentence. 9.4(E).

Case Synthesis

If you've given more than one Case Illustration for a single issue, did you:

___ create coherence among the cases by using the trophy, rubber-band, or paragraph-synthesis method? 9.9(B).

___ apply the checklist in 9.11 for *synthesizing* caselaw?

Apply Law (Application)

When applying the law to our client's facts, did you:

___ start a new paragraph and use an appropriate transition? 10.3(A).

E.g.:

Here, . . .

In our case, . . .

In the present case, . . .

In Ms. Hanni's case, . . .

___ after your transition, write an informative topic sentence announcing your global prediction of how a court would decide our case? (No suspense in good legal writing.) 10.3(B).

___ after the global prediction, clearly state an argument? 10.3(C).

___ after clearly stating an argument, prove the argument with rule-based and analogical reasoning? 10.3(D); 10.5; 10.6.

___ repeat an Argument-and-Proof combo for each argument? 10.3(E).

___ begin every paragraph after the first one with a clear topic sentence that states a legal argument and doesn't merely rehash law or facts? 10.8(F).

___ pass the two-question test in 10.4(B) to ensure you're actually applying law? See also 10.8(C).

___ weave in counterarguments where appropriate? 10.3(D)(3).

___ analogize to caselaw in meaningful, strategic places where it helps support a specific point? 10.7(C).

___ analogize to caselaw in meaningful ways by using one or a variety of the nine techniques explained in 10.6(A)?

___ avoid false comparisons? ("Like the *Jones* case, Mary Smith did not . . . ."—*Jones* is a case, but Mary is a human being.) 10.7(E).

___ avoid organizing your analysis by case? 10.8(D).

___ signal closure of your analysis? ("Thus, . . ." "Therefore, . . ." "So . . ."). 10.3(F).

Conclude and Recommend (Conclusion)

In the Conclusion, did you:

___ state the global conclusion? 11.3.

___ state your recommendation for the case's next steps? 11.3.

___ rehash any of the reasoning? If so, delete it. 11.3.

Quoting

Throughout the memo, did you:

___ insert quotation marks around verbatim language if you lifted exact language from another source? Four or more consecutive substantive words from a source constitute a phrase that requires quoting. 18.5(C); 7.6(E).

___ properly format a block quotation? If you've written a block quotation (quotation of 50 words or more), which you should do only sparingly, you've followed conventional rules. 17.8(E).

___ avoid using quotation marks for paraphrased information? If you have paraphrased the court's (or other source's) language, you do not need to insert quotation marks, but you still need to cite the source after the sentence to show your reader where you got the idea from. 7.6(E).

___ cite a source after every quotation? 17.2; 7.6(E).

Use Standard Document Format and Pagination

In setting up the whole document, did you:

___ double-space the text?

___ use 1" margins on all sides?

___ use a professional font (e.g., Calibri, Times New Roman, Arial, or their ilk)? 18.4(C).

___ include page numbers? 18.4(A).

Revise and Edit

Use Enticing Typography

Throughout the document, did you:

___ ensure that the document's typography (the layout of information, white space) is consistent with professional standards? 18.4.

___ ensure that each *heading* in the same level throughout the document has consistent spacing before and after the heading? Usually put more space before each heading than after it. 18.4(D).

___ use the same amount of space after and before each *paragraph*? 18.4(E).

___ consistently space first-line indents? (Note: You may choose to use a modern block style without indents; in that case, add more line space between paragraphs to set off each paragraph.) 18.4(F).

___ consistently use one or two spaces after a period? 18.4(H).

___ consistently use curved quotation marks and apostrophes (as opposed to straight ones you get when pasting from the internet)? 18.4(I).

Use Guru Grammar

Before submitting the final document, did you:

___ edit the final draft for punctuation and grammar? 18.5.

___ use quotation marks (" ") whenever you lifted exact, verbatim language from a case or statute (with a post-sentence citation)? 18.5(C).

- ___ avoid quoting/paraphrasing from—or citing to—a case's synopsis or headnotes (which are not part of the court's actual opinion but rather are supplied by the publisher's staff)?

Ensure Rad Readability

Throughout the document, did you:

- ___ remember that you are a teacher on the page? (Whether writing a short memo, a brief to an appellate court, or a law-school essay answer, great lawyers and law students are always teachers, striving to make the complex as clear and simple as possible. That's very hard to do, but it's always the goal.) 18.6.
- ___ create new paragraphs to avoid intimidating walls of dense, unbroken text? 18.4(E), (F). The goal is three to five paragraphs per page.
- ___ write in a confident and direct style while avoiding legalese or unnecessarily inflated language? (In other words, you avoided the lawyer tics and plodding, stilted prose that plague so many of the cases you've read in your casebooks.) 18.6.
- ___ create a well-organized, cohesive message?

Ensure Sightly Citations

When explaining the law, did you:

- ___ cite every rule of law the first time you stated it? 17.2.
- ___ use a full citation the first time you cited a source? 17.3.
- ___ cite after every sentence in a Case Illustration (except for perhaps the facts) and include a pinpoint page number? 17.2.
- ___ use *Id.* whenever possible, but only after giving the full citation? 17.3.
- ___ include "at" and a page number for each *Id.* citation? 17.3; 17.4(A)(2).
- ___ use a short citation when appropriate? 17.3.
- ___ include the right content, punctuate it correctly, and get the spacing right for each citation? 17.4–17.6.

Final Edits

Before submitting the document, did you:

- ___ save it as a PDF?
- ___ print the document after saving it as a PDF and proofread it one more time, even though you were sick of it? (This step is important because sometimes the format changes in the conversion from a word-processing document to a PDF.)

2.5 Full Office Memo

Beginning on the next page, you'll find a sample full office memo.

Here are the document specifications:

Purpose:	Analyze how to resolve a client's issue. But this format is reserved for matters that are more complex than what you'd analyze in an eMemo or Short Office Memo. The people reading your full office memo will use the analysis to decide what to do with the case.
Mood:	Objective, predictive.
Structure:	IREAC (**I**ssue > **R**ule > Caselaw **E**xample > **A**pplication > **C**onclusion. See Ch. 4)
Audience:	The client and attorneys within the firm.
Length:	Anywhere from 6 to 15 pages or so, but it could take upwards of 20 pages to analyze everything. For anything more than that, consider breaking up the analysis into separate issues and separate documents.
Final format:	PDF, hard copy, or both.
Conveyance:	Saved in the firm's electronic filing system, emailed as an attachment, or printed and sent via mail.

Memorandum

To: Stewart Osman
From: Jerry Aguilar
Date: February 24, 2025
Re: *Peters v. Giles*; 25-1901-CZ; Retaliation

Caption the document. 14.1.

Issue Statement

Under Michigan's Elliott-Larsen Civil Rights Act, which prohibits an employer from retaliating against an employee for filing a discrimination complaint, did the employer retaliate against the employee when she complained that her employer sexually harassed her, and, within eight days of that complaint, the employer took away her office keys, monitored her files, and required her to clean the office?

IREAC: **Frame the Issue.** This issue is framed in the traditional under-does-when style. 6.6(B).

Brief Answer

Probably. A court will more than likely find that Peters has established retaliation. Retaliation requires an adverse employment action that was caused by the employee's complaint of sexual harassment. Giles interfered with Peters's ability to do her job when he took away her office keys and gave her busywork like cleaning the bathroom.

These actions were caused by Peters's complaint because there was a short period of time, eight days, between the filing of the complaint and when Giles acted out against her. Furthermore, Giles exhibited a retaliatory motive when he knowingly violated company policy in treating Giles poorly. Therefore, Giles did retaliate against Peters.

Preview the Analysis with a Brief Answer. 16.4. Start with *Yes*, *No*, *Probably*, or *Probably not*. State the conclusion/prediction. Then give a short statement of the main law. Then summarize the main points of reasoning that support your conclusion.

Statement of Facts

Plaintiff Chloe Peters sued Guss Giles for retaliation in relation to a sexual harassment complaint. Peters was employed at DORA Oil and Gas Exploration, LLC.

Giles is the owner, president, and managing member of the company, and thus became Peters's supervisor. Although Peters primarily performed accounting and administrative assistant tasks, her job responsibilities changed many times throughout her employment. The only other employee that was present in the office, Kathy, had similar responsibilities.

Tell a Story in the Statement of Facts. Ch. 12. Tell the story in logical order, which often is chronological. Because this is an objective document, **stay completely objective**. Do not position or use biased adjectives. And certainly do not make any legal conclusions. For example, do not write: "Rob discriminated against her when he fired her for being pregnant." But write: "Rob fired her."

1

Early in her employment, Giles subjected her to an implied quid pro quo request for sex in exchange for being allowed to use accumulated vacation time. Peters immediately told Giles that his request was inappropriate, but, according to Peters, the inappropriate behavior only escalated from that point forward. Additionally, among other things, Giles groped her on multiple occasions and unsuccessfully attempted to entice her into sexual relations with a client. This behavior culminated when Peters and Giles began what has been characterized as an "affair" between May and September 2024. The affair came to a sudden end when Giles's wife, Tara Giles, discovered it. Tara Giles then sent an email message to Peters, threatening her employment and warning her to stay away from her husband "or else."

Peters has stated that, following Tara Giles's discovery of the affair, Guss Giles initially left her alone and turned his attention to Kathy Smith. However, this quiet period in the office lasted only two weeks, after which Giles began to grab Peters's breasts and make inappropriate comments; approximately ten to twenty such incidents occurred between September and November 2024. Peters once again told Giles that she didn't appreciate his conduct, but he persisted.

Peters further asserted that Giles added housekeeping tasks to her job responsibilities in October and November 2024. Giles required her to clean the office bathroom, water the plants, vacuum, dust, and take the garbage out. Peters's pay and job title remained the same. Giles has explained that he assigned the custodial work to Peters because "with the economy hitting the skids and all, I had decided to save a bit of money by firing Merry Maids." However, Giles admitted that his wife chose Peters, rather than Smith, for this work because his wife hated Peters. Giles offered no explanation for allowing Smith's conduct towards Peters, other than stating that Smith "could have been nicer."

In Giles's deposition, he also admitted that during this time period, he knew that Kathy Smith was using derogatory language toward Peters in the office and writing derogatory notes about Peters on the office whiteboard. Smith's language directed at Peters included "fat f----- cow," "s--- for brains," and "loser."

On November 8, 2010, Peters's attorney sent a letter to Giles. The letter informed Giles that the attorney had been retained to represent Peters in a sexual harassment claim and further stated that Peters had been exposed to unwelcome sexual advances and a hostile working environment at DORA. The letter invited Giles to enter into settlement negotiations.

Eight days later, on November 16, 2024, Peters sent her letter of resignation to Kathy Smith. Peters wrote that the working environment changed after Giles received her attorney's letter. Her office keys had been taken away, she was no longer allowed in office by herself, she was not allowed to eat lunch in the office, her computer files were being monitored, she not allowed to bring her purse into office, she was required to list all tasks that she completed—but not allowed to keep copies of the lists, she was not allowed to bring copies of memos regarding her employment home, and she was treated as a "cancer in the office." The letter stated that Smith had claimed that these "precautions" were being taken because Peters was "sabotaging" the company. Finally, Peters stated that the stress of working at DORA had become unbearable, and that she was resigning "for [her] own well being." This suit followed.

This Discussion section has two IREAC packets, one for each subissue, which are under headings A and B on the following pages. With multiple subissues, tie the IREAC packets together with an Analysis Preview or global Rule Foundation, which this writer did in these first two paragraphs. 4.6(E).

Discussion

You have asked me to evaluate Chloe Peters's retaliation claim in anticipation of the settlement conference. To prevail, Peters must show that her employer took an adverse employment against her because she complained of sexual harassment. She is likely to prevail because her employer dramatically reduced her privileges immediately following her harassment allegations. Therefore, she'll likely prevail.

Preview the Analysis. Ch. 16. This paragraph is an **internal** Analysis Preview for both subissues. State the issue, the main rule at issue, a summary of the reasoning, and the conclusion. 16.5.

The relevant portion of the ELCRA states that an employer "shall not ... retaliate or discriminate against a person because the person has opposed a violation of [ELCRA] ...." Mich. Comp. Laws Ann. § 37.2701(a) (West 2025). The statute does not define *retaliation*, but caselaw does:

After the reader is primed with the Analysis Preview, dive into the details with the **Rule Foundation**. Ch. 7. This *global* Rule Foundation sets the stage for the two subissues analyzed below. 7.5.

> To establish a prima facie case of retaliation, a plaintiff must show: (1) that he engaged in a protected activity; (2) that this

Employment law is an example of where the writer needs to synthesize both statutory rules and caselaw rules to create the full picture of the governing rules. 7.2.

3

> was known by the defendant; (3) that the defendant took an employment action adverse to the plaintiff; and (4) that there was a causal connection between the protected activity and the adverse employment action.

Garg v. Macomb Co. Comm. Mental Health, 696 N.W.2d 646, 653 (Mich. 2005) (citation omitted).

Dispense with elements not at issue in the **Rule Foundation** to focus your reader's attention on what is at issue. 7.3.

Peters can easily satisfy the first two elements. As to the first, protected activity occurs anytime an employee "raise[s] the specter" of a discrimination complaint. *Rymal v. Baergen*, 686 N.W.2d 241, 264 (Mich. Ct. App. 2004). Peters satisfied this element when she had her attorney send a letter on November 8, 2024. This letter specifically alleged that Giles had created a hostile working environment (i.e., discriminatory harassment). And Peters satisfied the second element because all the facts indicate that Giles received and read the letter, and he has not denied that.

The writer wraps up the **Rule Foundation** with a brief roadmap for the rest of the analysis. 7.3.

Thus, this analysis will concentrate on the last two elements of a retaliation claim—the adverse employment action and the causal link between the adverse employment action and the protected activity.

IREAC: **Use Document Headings**, especially when your document has more than one subissue. Ch. 15. This heading serves to announce the issue, the I in IREAC. 6.5(C); 15.3(A).

A. Adverse Employment Actions

Not just any change in the plaintiff's job responsibilities or terms of employment is an adverse employment action:

IREAC: This is a *secondary* Rule Foundation that pertains only to this subissue. 7.5.

> [T]o be actionable, an employment action must be materially adverse to the employee—that is, it must be more than a mere inconvenience or minor alteration of job responsibilities. [T]here must be an objective basis for demonstrating that the employment action is adverse because a plaintiff's subjective impressions are not controlling.

Chen v. Wayne St. U., 771 N.W.2d 820, 839 (Mich. Ct. App. 2009) (citations omitted). Typically, an adverse employment action will take the form of "an ultimate employment decision," such as termination, decreased wages, a lesser title, a material loss of benefits, or diminished material responsibilities. *Pena v. Ingham County Rd. Commn.*, 660 N.W.2d 351, 358–59 (Mich. Ct. App. 2003). However, "other indices that might be unique to a particular situation" may also be considered. *Id.*

4

Employer actions must be objectively adverse. An employee's subjective impression that the new position is less desirable cannot create a materially adverse action. *Wilcoxon v. Minn. Mining & Mfg. Co.*, 597 N.W.2d 250, 258–59 (Mich. Ct. App. 1999). In *Wilcoxon*, the employer asked the employee, following a discrimination complaint, to transfer from Michigan to Illinois to perform the same job. While her precise title and responsibilities would slightly change, her salary would remain the same, and she was explicitly instructed to exercise her judgment in creating and defining the new position.

IREAC: Give examples of the element or rule by explaining caselaw. Note the strong topic sentence to begin this full Case Illustration. 9.4(A). A good topic sentence advances the thought by stating new information. After the topic sentence, give the citation, facts, holding, and reasoning. 9.4

The court found the two positions to be objectively equivalent. *Id.* The employee's subjective impressions that the job was worse for her did not persuade the court. *Id.*

However, restrictions on independent exercise of judgment or increased and ostensibly unnecessary supervision of the employee could be materially adverse actions. *Janusz v. Sterling Millwork, Inc.*, 2006 WL 664217 (Mich. Ct. App. March 16, 2006). In *Janusz*, following a complaint of sexual harassment, the employer made the employee begin punching a time card, and took away her cellular phone, her company car, and her office keys. *Id.* Without giving much reason, the court held that these facts were sufficient to create a question for the jury regarding the alleged adverse employment action, based on their timing and circumstances. *Id.*

IREAC: Note with the Case Illustrations on this page how the writer uses the trophy-synthesis method to show (1) how the cases relate to each other and (2) what each one brings to the table. 9.9(B).

Ensure rad readability. Little transitions like "however" and "also" to begin paragraphs help the reader understand how the cases relate to each other. 18.6(B).

Also, a supervisor's failure to stop offensive communication directed toward a plaintiff by her coworkers, following her discrimination complaint, can constitute an adverse employment action if the offensive communications are found to be sufficiently severe. *Meyer v. City of Center Line*, 619 N.W.2d 182, 189 (Mich. Ct. App. 2000). In *Meyer*, coworkers sent offensive notes to the plaintiff after she complained of discrimination. She allegedly brought the notes, along with other incidents of harassment, to the attention of her supervisor, but he refused to take any action.

Cite Sources of Law. After each topic sentence, the writer has correctly cited the source. And then they cited a source for the court's holding and reasoning. Ch. 17.

The court held that the lower court should have allowed the jury to see the notes and evidence of coworker harassment because a "supervisor's failure to respond to an employee's complaints of harassment in retaliation for the employee's opposition to a violation of the Civil Rights Act can constitute an adverse employment action ...." *Id.* at 189.

IREAC: This is the final case example for this subissue.

5

IREAC: Good writers make understanding the caselaw easy, and that's what this synthesis does. Note the topics of "alter job conditions" and "subjective perceptions." The writer creates cohesion by basing the arguments in the Application on these topics. See 9.9(B)(3).

IREAC: **Explain Caselaw**. Note that attorneys explain all caselaw on a single issue together, consecutively before applying them to the facts. Don't explain a case and then apply it; explain another case and then apply it; and so on. For more, see 10.8(B).

IREAC: **Apply Law** in the Application. It begins with a transition ("In Peters's case"). The first sentence is also the topic sentence where the writer states the conclusion up front. This way, the reader knows how to process the information that follows. 10.3.

The first argument, altering employment conditions, comes from the caselaw illustrations and was highlighted in the synthesis paragraph above.

IREAC: Notice how on this page and the next every topic sentence states an actual argument. Nowhere in the Rule Application does the writer merely state fact or merely state law. They always apply the law. 10.8(C), (F).

This paragraph is also a great example of reasoning by analogy. 10.6.

But the court also said that the coworker harassment must be sufficiently severe. *Id.* at 192.

Together, these cases demonstrate that while subjective perceptions of a job change are insufficient, employer actions that dramatically alter job conditions or fail to address hostile work environments can rise to the level of a materially adverse employment action.

In Peters's case, she will likely succeed in proving that the actions taken by her superiors between November 8, 2024, and November 16, 2024, were adverse employment actions. Like the plaintiff in *Janusz*, Peters's working environment and conditions of employment changed dramatically immediately following her harassment allegations. The confiscation of keys, the increased level of unexplained supervision, and the imposition of somewhat-bizarre work rules are strikingly analogous. Giles could distinguish *Janusz* because that plaintiff lost a company car—which has monetary value and may be seen as a reduction in pay. But still, the unnecessary supervision and lack of keys interfered with Peters's duties, and she does not have to prove a decrease in salary.

Giles might argue that Peters's resignation proves only a subjective impression of adverse actions. However, unlike in *Wilcoxon*, where only the location of work changed, there appears to be an objective basis here for a jury to find that the changes were adverse. Whereas the plaintiff in *Wilcoxon* was transferred to an equivalent position and given the freedom to develop her new role and responsibilities, Peters was subjected to extra (and extraordinary) supervision under circumstances where she was unable to determine what the parameters of her responsibilities even were. The timing and circumstances of events, discussed further below, could lead a jury to conclude that an adverse employment action had taken place.

Because of the uncertain timeline, Peters being assigned to custodial duties and being berated by Kathy Smith offer less support to her assertion that an adverse employment action was taken by DORA. It is almost certain that she was assigned to custodial duties prior to Giles's receipt of her attorney's letter. But if not, requiring Peters to take on the cleaning duties is akin to a reduction in pay and a demotion. Assuming this change occurred after the November 8 letter, a jury would find it materially adverse because it was both a demotion and a pay reduction. It was a

6

demotion because janitorial duties are considered blue-collar work below the dignity of the office staff. And it was essentially a pay reduction because she was asked to spend more hours in the office without more pay. So the same pay divided by more hours means less per hour.

It also appears that Smith started to refer to Peters with derogatory language before receiving the letter. This language cannot be considered mere teasing; it was foul enough to make even a sailor cringe. Even if this behavior started before the letter was received, it could be viewed as an adverse employment action if it intensified after the letter was received. In his deposition, Giles admitted that he did nothing to stop Smith's behavior towards Peters, and it must have been painfully obvious in an office where Smith, Peters, and Giles were the only employees. Just as the supervisor's failure to stop the notes being passed in *Meyer* could support a determination that an adverse employment action had taken place, Giles's failure to act here could do likewise.

IREAC: **Use Document Headings** when the memo has more than one subissue. Use it to remind the reader of the issue's overall conclusion as stated in the Brief Answer. Again, this furnishes the I of IREAC. 6.5(C); 15.3(A).

B. Causation

An employee cannot merely establish a causal link between the events. Instead, she must show that her participation in the protected activity was a "significant factor" in the employer's adverse employment action. *Rymal*, 686 N.W.2d at 257. Circumstantial evidence, including close temporal proximity between events, can establish that the protected activity was a significant factor. *Id.*

IREAC: This secondary **Rule Foundation** (7.5) briefly explains the rules for this one issue. Then the writer illustrates these rules with Case Illustrations beginning in the next paragraph.

On the other hand, a large gap in time between events can preclude such a finding. *Aho v. Mich. Dept. of Corrects.*, 688 N.W.2d 104, 110–11 (Mich. Ct. App. 2004). Courts have found that between three months and five years has been found insufficient to establish a causal connection while time periods of between two weeks and two months have succeeded. *See e.g. McLemore v. Det. Receiving Hosp.*, 493 N.W.2d 441, 443–44 (Mich. Ct. App. 1992) (holding that approximately two months was sufficient); *Moore v. Kuka Welding Sys.*, 171 F.3d 1073, 1078–80 (6th Cir. 1999) (holding that two weeks was sufficient).

IREAC: **Explain Caselaw**. This paragraph nicely demonstrates using the rubber-band method to synthesize multiple cases. One topic sentence bands the cases together. 9.9(B)(2).

IREAC: This paragraph actually contains three Case Illustrations, but they're the "short" style. Sometimes a short Case Illustration is all that is needed. 9.7.

Even when an employer presents a legitimate reason for an adverse employment action, a plaintiff can establish that their harassment complaint was a significant causal factor when there is a sudden change in the employer's actions closely related in time to the complaint. *McLemore*,

IREAC: Because the reader wants to make a more substantive point with this case, a full Case Illustration is in order. 9.2.

7

493 N.W.2d at 443–44. In *McLemore*, a clinical instructor working in a hospital was laid off within two months of filing a gender discrimination complaint. The hospital established that it was in legitimate financial distress and there was no direct evidence presented of a retaliatory motive for the layoff.

However, the court held that a jury could infer a retaliatory motive based on the fact that the plaintiff's supervisors almost immediately began rating her performance as unsatisfactory following the complaint, when her performance had always been acceptable before the complaint. *Id.*

A jury may also infer retaliation when an employee is suddenly isolated from coworkers shortly after a discrimination complaint. *Moore*, 171 F.3d at 1080 (applying Michigan law). In *Moore*, within two weeks of filing a discrimination complaint, the plaintiff found himself suddenly working alone; his supervisor had instructed all of his coworkers to move their toolboxes to another area of the plant and left the plaintiff as the sole employee working in his department. *Id.* During this time, Moore was subjected to more frequent disciplinary write-ups for unimportant matters and unwarranted criticism of his work. *Id.*

The court held that the employer's adverse actions were caused by the employee's complaint. *Id.* In its reasoning, the court mainly pointed to the short two-week span between the complaint and the beginning of the adverse actions.

IREAC: Here's a great topic sentence to begin this **Application** section. The writer states the conclusion up front. This way, the reader knows how to process the information that follows. 10.3.

In our case, Peters stands a good chance of convincing the jury to draw a similar inference regarding the motive behind Giles's actions. The previously discussed changes in Peters's work environment all occurred within one week of the receipt of her attorney's letter. Even those events whose timing is less certain—the assignment of janitorial tasks and the crude language directed at the plaintiff by Smith—certainly occurred within the final two months of Peters's employment. The prolonged time frame that caused Aho's retaliation claim to fail simply will not come into play here. Instead, Peters will succeed or fail in proving causation based on a jury's ability and willingness to infer a retaliatory motive from Smith's and Giles's actions.

IREAC: Did you catch this subtle analogy to the *Aho* case? That analogy bolsters the rule-based reasoning. 10.6.

Giles will attempt to show that his motivation was based on vindicating his wife's jealousy and protecting the legitimate interests of his business.

IREAC: It's wise to predict what counterargument might cut into your primary arguments. State it but then neutralize it. 10.3(D)(3).

8

Giles's claim that the economy "hit the skids" is unrefuted. His economic motivation can possibly explain his firing of the cleaning service and his decision to assign the janitorial tasks to one of his employees. He can equally claim to have been acting to mollify his angry wife. Also, the assignment of janitorial tasks to Peters appears to have occurred before she engaged in the protected activity. However, while all of these factors initially appear to weigh in Giles's favor, they will become a liability when used to provide context for the actions that followed.

There does not appear to be any legitimate economic motive for confiscating Peters's office keys, prohibiting her from bringing her purse into the office, not allowing her to be alone, or any of the other similar actions. Kathy Smith may have alleged that these "precautions" were taken to prevent Peters from "sabotaging" the company—which could be viewed as a legitimate, non-retaliatory motive. However, as of yet, Giles has presented absolutely no evidence to demonstrate that Peters was engaging in any such nefarious activity.

IREAC: This paragraph is all rule-based reasoning; it's simply using common sense to explain why the facts relating to causation prove the element. 10.5. It's convincing because everything points toward the meaning of "causation," the element at issue here.

The only apparent reasons for Smith or Giles to believe that Peters was engaged in "sabotage" would be directly related to the underlying sexual harassment that she was enduring or to the protected activity in which she engaged. Any argument that Giles was not retaliating—he was simply continuing to harass Peters like always—would be unlikely to gain traction with a jury. This leaves the protected activity as the only remaining motive for the alleged acts of retaliation. Just like the fact finders in *McLemore* and *Moore* could draw an inference of a retaliatory motive from the timing and background facts presented in those cases, a jury in Peters's case could, and probably would, do the same.

IREAC: End each IREAC packet with an internal conclusion. 10.3(F); 11.2.

Conclusion

If the facts that Peters has alleged are proven to be true, it is likely that she will prevail in her retaliation claim at trial. However, because her success will be predicated upon the jury's ability to draw several inferences regarding the motivation behind her employer's actions, it is by no means guaranteed. The defendant should be encouraged to settle the retaliation claim, and the plaintiff should be encouraged to be reasonable in her demands.

IREAC: **Conclude and Recommend**: The writer has already explained everything above. Now is the time to merely (1) state the global conclusion and (2) the case's next steps. In this case, the writer is preparing a judge for a settlement conference, so the recommendation is based on that. In other cases, you'd state whether we should take the case, write a letter, make a motion, etc. 11.3.

9

Checklist for Full Office Memo

Caption Your Document

Did you:

- ___ title the document "Memorandum" at the very top, center and bold it? 14.1.
- ___ below the title, write the standard office-memo caption of *To:*, *From:*, *Date:*, and *Re:* in that order? 14.1.
- ___ avoid double-spacing the caption, instead preferring 1.5 spacing or 6 points after each paragraph? 14.1.
- ___ in the *Re:* line, describe the matter and the client's name? 14.1.
- ___ vertically align the information after the colons? 14.1.

Use Document Headings

Did you:

- ___ organize your analysis by inserting the following headings: Question Presented, Brief Answer, Facts, Discussion, and Conclusion? Ch. 3; 15.2.
- ___ bold and center each heading or otherwise set it off as a heading? 15.2.
- ___ use headings in the Discussion section *where necessary* to separate different issues? 15.3.

Frame the Issue (Question Presented)

In your Question Presented, did you:

- ___ frame the issue using the under-does-when format (or whatever format your professor requested)? 6.6.
- ___ enumerate the issue statement if you have more than one? (You'll mirror the same enumeration in the Brief Answer and in the global point headings in the Argument section.) 4.7(D); 5.3(A)(1).
- ___ include just the right amount of information for each part, neither framing the issue too narrowly nor too broadly? 6.6(B)–(D).
- ___ in the facts portion, ensure that they are grammatically parallel? 6.6(B)(4).
- ___ in the facts portion, tell a brief, chronological story including only significantly relevant facts? 6.6(B)(4).
- ___ make the symmetry between the law clause and the question clause clear (i.e., if you stated a rule for negligence, then the question is likewise about negligence)?
- ___ ensure that the entire sentence is readable and hangs together?
- ___ end the sentence with a question mark?

Preview the Analysis (Brief Answer)

In your Brief Answer, did you:

- ___ ensure that the entire section follows a syllogistic structure from conclusion, to rule, to application, to conclusion? 16.4(A).
- ___ begin with a short one- or two-word answer (i.e., "yes," "no," "probably," or "probably not")? 16.4(C)(1).

- ___ state the conclusion/prediction in the first sentence? 16.4(A), (C).
- ___ state the core rule of law (prefer paraphrasing, but quote when necessary) in the second sentence? 16.4(A)(2).
- ___ state a summary of the application of the law to the facts (i.e., it summarizes your main reasoning points) in the third sentence (and maybe fourth and fifth)? 16.4(A)(3).
- ___ state the conclusion (i.e., predict the outcome) in the final sentence? 16.4(A)(4).
- ___ limit the Brief Answer to one or two paragraphs?
- ___ make sure that the paragraph had a logical flow to it? In other words, the conclusion (prediction) in the final sentence seemed logical given what you wrote in the sentences that preceded it.

Tell a Story (Facts)

In your Facts section, did you:

- ___ include legally significant, background, and emotional facts? 12.2(A).
- ___ include even unfavorable facts? 12.2(A)(1).
- ___ begin with contextual information that introduces the parties and the broad issue? 12.2(B).
- ___ prefer to organize the facts chronologically? 12.2(C)(1).
- ___ avoid organizing the facts according to which document you got them from? 12.2(C)(1).
- ___ where appropriate, organize the facts by each character's perception (i.e., where characters disagree on the facts)? 12.2(C)(3).
- ___ consider using headings for longer, more complex factual statements? 12.2(D)(4).
- ___ use lots of paragraphs, averaging three to five per page? 12.2(D)(2).
- ___ use names, not role designations like *plaintiff* or *customer*? 12.2(D)(3).

Give a Rule Foundation (Controlling Rules)

When teaching your client the controlling legal rules, did you:

- ___ if writing multiple subissues, include one global Rule Foundation and, for each subissue, a secondary Rule Foundation? 4.6(E); 7.5.
- ___ synthesize the relevant rules, whether from codified law, caselaw, or both, *before* illustrating them with caselaw? 7.1–7.6(D).
- ___ teach the reader the rules of law in a logical, step-by-step sequence, and didn't rush it? For example, you started by teaching the broadest rule and ended with the narrowest rule. You taught general rules before teaching exceptions to those rules. 7.1–7.6.
- ___ if appropriate, refine the issue by focusing the reader on just the elements that are at issue? 7.3.
- ___ prefer paraphrasing when possible? 7.6(E).
- ___ include a citation to binding legal authority for each rule? Ch. 17.

Explain Codified Law

When explaining codified law, whether in the Rule Foundation or elsewhere, did you:

- ___ place codified law before caselaw? 8.2(A).

___ help the reader make sense of codified law by explaining its elements? 8.2(B)–(C).

___ include the essential elements and important contextual information? 8.2(C).

___ where applicable, cohesively synthesize several statutory provisions? 8.2(E).

___ prefer paraphrasing? 8.2(D).

___ quote unique language that cannot be paraphrased? 8.2(D).

___ cite a source for each rule? 17.2–17.3; 17.6.

Explain Caselaw (Controlling Law)

___ Did you include two or three Case Illustrations or one directly on-point Case Illustration? 9.3.

___ Does each Case Illustration have a topic sentence, a citation, the case's facts, the court's holding, and the court's reasoning? 9.4.

Case Illustration > *Topic Sentence*

In the topic sentence of your Case Illustration, did you:

___ transition from the preceding paragraph by showing how the case fits into the big picture? 9.4(A)(1).

___ avoid starting with a source of law? Instead, cite the source after the topic sentence. 9.4(B).

___ state a new point that you have not yet stated in the Rule Foundation? 9.4(A)(2).

___ give a substantive point rather than merely announcing the topic you're going to address? 9.4(A)(3).

___ where appropriate, create an implicit rule from the case where it may not be immediately clear from the specifics of the case how it could apply to the client's matter? 9.4(A)(3)(b).

___ avoid cramming too much information into the topic sentence? Although your topic sentence is a helpful transition/preview for your reader, it can only include so much information.

Case Illustration > *Citation*

Immediately after the topic sentence, did you:

___ cite a case for the source of the topic sentence, whether it be explicit or implicit? 9.4(B); 17.4.

___ follow ALWD or Bluebook rules for formatting the citation? Ch. 17.

___ put the citation in a separate citation sentence? 9.4(B).

Case Illustration > *Case Facts*

When explaining the facts of the precedent case, did you:

___ capture the story to teach your reader what happened in the case you're writing about? 9.4(C).

___ give contextual information that sets the stage for the story? 9.4(C).

___ include the legally significant facts (i.e., the ones used in the court's reasoning)? 9.4(C)(1).

___ avoid unnecessary information like names, dates, party arguments, and lower-court procedure unless they directly relate to your issue? 9.4(C)(2).

___ if writing about a civil case, use informative status words to identify the parties and other "characters" in the story (like *tenant* and *landlord* or *buyer* and *seller*), rather than using their actual names or party designations like *plaintiff* or *defendant*? 9.4(C)(3).

___ if writing about a criminal case, use *the defendant* to refer to the person charged with the crime, which is informative to readers? But for other people, you've tried to come up with informative status words, such as *witness, victim, accuser, arresting officer, police officer, companion, prosecutor*, etc. 9.4(C)(3).

Case Illustration > ***Court's Holding***

When writing about the court's holding in a Case Illustration, did you:

___ give the court's actual decision rather than state a pure rule of law or give only the ultimate procedural outcome like *affirmed* or *reversed*? 9.4(D).

___ state the global holding and any secondary holdings on your issue? 9.4(D).

___ ensure that the holding addresses the narrow issue you're writing about? 9.4(D).

Case Illustration > ***Court's Reasoning***

When summarizing the court's reasoning in a Case Illustration, did you:

___ give *details* about why the court decided the case the way it did? If the court decided multiple *relevant* subissues, you've quickly explained the court's reasoning for each of those subissues, and you've done that in a logical sequence, with signposts to help your reader follow along. 9.4(E).

___ avoid restating the rules the court applied? Rather, put the rules either in the Rule Foundation or in the Case Illustration's topic sentence. 9.4(E).

Case Synthesis

If you've given more than one Case Illustration for a single issue, did you:

___ create coherence among the cases by using the trophy, rubber-band, or paragraph-synthesis method? 9.9(B).

___ apply the checklist in 9.11 for *synthesizing* caselaw?

Apply Law

When applying the law to our client's facts, did you:

___ start a new paragraph and use an appropriate transition? 10.3(A).

E.g.:

Here, . . .

In our case, . . .

In the present case, . . .

In Ms. Hanni's case, . . .

___ after your transition, write an informative topic sentence announcing your global prediction of how a court would decide our case? (No suspense in good legal writing.) 10.3(B).

___ after the global prediction, clearly state an argument? 10.3(C).

___ after clearly stating an argument, prove the argument with rule-based and analogical reasoning? 10.3(D); 10.5; 10.6.

___ repeat an Argument-and-Proof combo for each argument? 10.3(E).

___ begin every paragraph after the first one with a clear topic sentence that states a legal argument and doesn't merely rehash law or facts? 10.8(F).

___ pass the two-question test in 10.4(B) to ensure you're actually applying law? See also 10.8(C).

___ weave in counterarguments where appropriate? 10.3(D)(3).

___ analogize to caselaw in meaningful, strategic places where it helps support a specific point? 10.7(C).

___ analogize to caselaw in meaningful ways by using one or a variety of the nine techniques explained in 10.6(A)?

___ avoid false comparisons? ("Like the *Jones* case, Mary Smith did not ...."—*Jones* is a case, but Mary is a human being.) 10.7(E).

___ avoid organizing your analysis by case? 10.8(D).

___ signal closure of your analysis? ("Thus, ..." "Therefore, ..." "So ..."). 10.3(F).

Conclude and Recommend (Conclusion)

In the Conclusion, did you:

___ state the global conclusion? 11.3.

___ state your recommendation for the case's next steps? 11.3.

___ rehash any of the reasoning? If so, delete it. 11.3.

Quoting

Throughout the memo, did you:

___ insert quotation marks around verbatim language if you lifted exact language from another source? Four or more consecutive substantive words from a source constitute a phrase that requires quoting. 18.5(C); 7.6(E).

___ properly format a block quotation? If you've written a block quotation (quotation of 50 words or more), which you should do only sparingly, you've followed conventional rules. 17.8(E).

___ avoid using quotation marks for paraphrased information? If you have paraphrased the court's (or other source's) language, you do not need to insert quotation marks, but you still need to cite the source after the sentence to show your reader where you got the idea from. 7.6(E).

___ cite a source after every quotation? 17.2; 7.6(E).

Use Standard Document Format and Pagination

In setting up the whole document, did you:

___ double-space the text?

___ use 1" margins on all sides?

___ use a professional font (e.g., Calibri, Times New Roman, Arial, or their ilk)? 18.4(C).

___ include page numbers? 18.4(A).

Revise and Edit

Use Enticing Typography

Throughout the document, did you:

- ___ ensure that the document's typography (the layout of information, white space) is consistent with professional standards? 18.4.
- ___ ensure that each *heading* in the same level throughout the document has consistent spacing before and after the heading? Usually put more space before each heading than after it. 18.4(D).
- ___ use the same amount of space after and before each *paragraph*? 18.4(E).
- ___ consistently space first-line indents? (Note: You may choose to use a modern block style without indents; in that case, add more line space between paragraphs to set off each paragraph.) 18.4(F).
- ___ consistently use one or two spaces after a period? 18.4(H).
- ___ consistently use curved quotation marks and apostrophes (as opposed to straight ones you get when pasting from the internet)? 18.4(I).

Use Guru Grammar

Before submitting the final document, did you:

- ___ edit the final draft for punctuation and grammar? 18.5.
- ___ use quotation marks (" ") whenever you lifted exact, verbatim language from a case or statute (with a post-sentence citation)? 18.5(C).
- ___ avoid quoting/paraphrasing from—or citing to—a case's synopsis or headnotes (which are not part of the court's actual opinion but rather are supplied by the publisher's staff)?

Ensure Rad Readability

Throughout the document, did you:

- ___ remember that you are a teacher on the page? (Whether writing a short memo, a brief to an appellate court, or a law-school essay answer, great lawyers and law students are always teachers, striving to make the complex as clear and simple as possible. That's very hard to do, but it's always the goal.) 18.6.
- ___ create new paragraphs to avoid intimidating walls of dense, unbroken text? 18.4(E), (F). The goal is three to five paragraphs per page.
- ___ write in a confident and direct style while avoiding legalese or unnecessarily inflated language? (In other words, you avoided the lawyer tics and plodding, stilted prose that plague so many of the cases you've read in your casebooks.) 18.6.
- ___ create a well-organized, cohesive message?

Ensure Sightly Citations

When explaining the law, did you:

- ___ cite every rule of law the first time you stated it? 17.2.
- ___ use a full citation the first time you cited a source? 17.3.
- ___ cite after every sentence in a Case Illustration (except for perhaps the facts) and include a pinpoint page number? 17.2.

___ use *Id.* whenever possible, but only after giving the full citation? 17.3.

___ include "at" and a page number for each *Id.* citation? 17.3; 17.4(A)(2).

___ use a short citation when appropriate? 17.3.

___ include the right content, punctuate it correctly, and get the spacing right for each citation? 17.4–17.6.

Final Edits

Before submitting the document, did you:

___ save it as a PDF?

___ print the document after saving it as a PDF and proofread it one more time, even though you were sick of it? (This step is important because sometimes the format changes in the conversion from a word-processing document to a PDF.)

2.6 Trial-Court Brief (Moving Party)

On the next page, you'll find a sample trial-court brief.

Here are the document specifications:

Purpose: Persuade a court to order the opposing side to do something. This brief would be filed in a state circuit court, which is where a big civil lawsuit begins and felonies are heard. In this brief, the moving party is the defendant. The plaintiff's response brief follows this one in 2.7.

Mood: Persuasive.

Structure: AREAC (**A**rgument > **R**ule > Caselaw **E**xample > **A**pplication > **C**onclusion. 4.6(A) and section 5.3)

Audience: Primarily, the court hearing the matter. Secondarily, the court's staff and opposing counsel.

Length: Very case-specific, though most court rules limit briefs to around 20 or 25 pages.

Final format: PDF, hard copy, or both.

Conveyance: Saved in the firm's electronic filing system, filed with the court, and served on opposing counsel.

Please note that the law may have changed since this textbook was created, so do not rely on these sample briefs for research. Rather, use them as examples of how to write a persuasive state trial-court brief.

Caption the Document. Section 14.2 explains how to properly caption a brief.

State of Michigan
In the Circuit Court for Isabella County

TROY C. TROUT,
Plaintiff, No. 19-4546-NO

v. Hon. Rachel Reneria

J.C.K.W. INC., a/k/a BUFFALO WILD WINGS GRILL & BAR,
Defendant.
_____________________________________/

Everette P. Hasan, III P97842402	Samuel Jackson P4583156
Hasan & Abdul PLLC	Vanderhoff, Gargola PC
Attorneys for Plaintiff	Attorneys for Defendant
273 S. Main St.	150 W. Long Lake Rd.
P.O. Drawer 9928	Troy, MI 48098-6330
Grayling, MI 49738 (989) 555-5232	(248) 555-2800
ehas@hasanabdul.com	johno@vangar.com

_____________________________________/

Title the Document. 13.4.

Defendant's Motion for Summary Disposition

The motion. To write the motion, research the court rules for your jurisdiction and deconstruct sample motions (like you learned about in Chapter 3) to figure out the parts. Based on that, recreate a motion for your issue.

Defendant J.C.K.W. Inc. (a/k/a Buffalo Wild Wings Grill & Bar), moves under Mich. Ct. R. 2.116(C)(10) for an order granting summary disposition in its favor because (1) it owed no duty to protect the plaintiff from an open and obvious danger, and (2) it had no actual or constructive notice of the alleged hazard.

Date and Signature Block. Because the motion is often considered a document that is separate from the brief, you need a date and signature block. Include the information you see here.

November 15, 2022

Respectfully submitted,
Vanderhoff, Gargola PC

Sam Jackson

Samuel Jackson P4583156
Attorneys for Defendant
150 W. Long Lake Rd.
Troy, MI 48098-6330
(248) 555-2800
johno@vangar.com

State of Michigan
In the Circuit Court for Isabella County

TROY C. TROUT,
Plaintiff,

No. 19-4546-NO

v.

Hon. Rachel Reneria

J.C.K.W. INC., a/k/a BUFFALO WILD WINGS GRILL & BAR,
Defendant.
____________________________________/

Everette P. Hasan, III P97842402
Hasan & Abdul PLLC
Attorneys for Plaintiff
273 S. Main St.
P.O. Drawer 9928
Grayling, MI 49738 (989) 555-5232
ehas@hasanabdul.com

Samuel Jackson P4583156
Vanderhoff, Gargola PC
Attorneys for Defendant
150 W. Long Lake Rd.
Troy, MI 48098-6330
(248) 555-2800
johno@vangar.com
____/

Brief Supporting Defendant's Motion for Summary Disposition

Caption the Document. The caption must be identical to all documents you file in the court for this litigation. You should copy the motion's caption and paste it here. See Section 14.2.

Title the Document. See Section 13.4.

Use Document Headings. Ch. 15. Deconstruct sample documents to know which headings to include. Your headings should be consistently formatted for each level. And make sure the spacing before and after them is consistent as well. 18.4(D).

Preview the Analysis. Ch. 16. (See Section 16.4 and 16.4(C)(2) in particular.) This should summarize the entire Argument section. Do that by including a summary of the AREAC parts: argument, rule, caselaw (sparingly), application, and conclusion.

Preview the Analysis. Because there are two issues in this brief, the Introduction summarizes both of them. This paragraph summarizes section II in the Argument section.

Tell a Story. Start with context. Then tell the story chronologically, emphasizing the legally relevant facts and giving context for them along the way. 12.2. Because this is a persuasive document, shape favorable and un-favorable facts by changing their airtime and placement. But always maintain an air of objectivity. 12.4; 12.5.

Cite sources in the Facts. Section 17.7 explains how to create citations to the factual record. It's conventional to put citations to the record in parentheses because it signals these are not primary sources of law.

Introduction

This case arises from Troy Trout's alleged slip and fall on ice outside a Buffalo Wild Wings restaurant. Under Michigan law, Buffalo Wild Wings owes no duty to invitees such as Mr. Trout when a dangerous condition is open and obvious and lacks special aspects. Here, the rainy conditions and alleged black ice were open and obvious because the ice contrasted with the gray sidewalk, and the rain on a cold December day alerted invitees to slippery conditions. And the visible ice had no special aspects because it was avoidable and posed no realistic risk of death or severe injury. Thus, no duty existed, and dismissal is appropriate.

Nor did Buffalo Wild Wings owe a duty when it lacked actual or constructive notice of the danger. It's undisputed that Buffalo Wild Wings did not actually know of an alleged ice patch. And Mr. Trout can offer no evidence suggesting that restaurant employees had sufficient time to learn of an ice patch. In fact, he testified that the ice did not exist when he arrived at the restaurant and that he ate a quick 30-minute meal, meaning that the ice existed for just 30 minutes or less before his fall. Therefore, for this additional reason, the Court should grant summary disposition in Buffalo Wild Wings' favor.

Facts

Troy Trout alleges that on December 17, 2021, he slipped and fell on a "slippery, snowy, inclined walkway covered with black ice" outside Buffalo Wild Wings' restaurant. (Exhibit A, Complaint ¶ 4). That day, Trout went to a local casino with a friend and later stopped at Buffalo Wild Wings to get something to eat. (Exhibit B, Dep. Troy Trout 51–52). He recalls that the temperature was "around 40 degrees" and that there wasn't much snow or ice on the ground. (Dep. Trout 54–55). Trout claims that during the 30 or so minutes he was in the restaurant, it rained, and the wet walkways turned to ice. (Dep. Trout 54, 56, 63).

His friend left the restaurant first and pulled the truck to the front, and Trout walked about four or five steps from the building to the ramp. (Dep. Trout 66). As he was walking down the slightly inclined ramp, he slipped and fell backwards due to the rain. (Dep. Trout 61, 63, 66–67). His friend drove them to the friend's house, where Trout had left his car. (Dep. Trout 68.) Trout drove himself home from there. (Dep. Trout 67).

2

Trout did not re-enter the restaurant to tell anyone what had happened. Nor did he ask his friend to go in and report the alleged fall. (Dep. Trout 71). In fact, he never complained, phoned, or otherwise reported the incident. (Dep. Trout 72–73). Thus, Buffalo Wild Wings was not aware of any slip and fall until Trout filed his complaint just days before the statute of limitations expired, almost three years after the fall.

Tell a Story. The writer is using several paragraph breaks to help the reader, and this also creates more topic sentences to emphasize important information. 12.2(D)(2).

A records review by managers on duty at the time of Trout's alleged fall confirmed that although they served hundreds of patrons, no other person reported any slippery conditions or slip-and-fall incidents on either December 17, 2021, or the day after. (Exhibit C, Aff. William Johnson ¶¶ 4–5; Exhibit D, Aff. Mary Jackson ¶¶ 4–5).

Standard of Review

Summary disposition is proper when the affidavits and documentary evidence presented, viewed in the light most favorable to the nonmoving party, show that there is no genuine issue of material fact and that the moving party is entitled to judgment as a matter of law. Mich. Ct. R. 2.116(C)(10). The party opposing the motion—here, Trout—must "set forth specific facts showing that there is a genuine issue for trial" on any issue raised in the motion. Mich. Ct. R. 2.116(G)(4); see also *Lugo v. Ameritech Corp., Inc.*, 629 N.W.2d 384, 388 (Mich. 2001).

Give a Rule Foundation. Ch. 7. This Rule Foundation is particular to just the standard of review for deciding to grant a motion. See 7.9 to learn how to create one.

Argument

I. Trout's suit must be dismissed because Buffalo Wild Wings owed no duty to protect him from an obvious and avoidable slipping hazard that posed no risk of death or severe injury.

AREAC: State the global argument first in a persuasive point heading. 5.3. (AREAC = Argument, Rule, caselaw Examples, Application, Conclusion. 4.6(A).)

A plaintiff suing for premises liability must establish that the defendant owed the plaintiff a duty. *Case v. Consumer Powers Co.*, 463 Mich. 1, 4, 615 N.W.2d 17, 20 (2000). Michigan landowners owe a general duty to protect invitees from unreasonable hazards on the property. *Lugo v. Ameritech Corp., Inc.*, 464 Mich. 512, 515, 629 N.W.2d 384, 386 (2001). But this duty does not usually extend to dangers that "are known to the invitee or are so obvious that the invitee might reasonably be expected to discover them." *Id.* at 515, 629 N.W.2d at 386. "Whether a danger is open and obvious depends on whether it is reasonable to expect that an average person with ordinary intelligence would have discovered the danger on

Give a Rule Foundation. This is a global Rule Foundation. 7.5. It gives the analytical framework for all the sub-arguments to come under Argument I. Any rules that are particular to just one argument should go at the beginning of that argument section, not here.

The controlling rules here come entirely from caselaw because that's the source of tort law. And observe that you may cite only binding caselaw for rules of law. 7.7.

3

Tie AREAC packets together.
4.6(E). This issue I has three subissues, which you'll find below in sections A, B, and C. Each of those subissues is its own AREAC packet. It's crucial to include a global **Rule Foundation** like you see on this page because it ties all of those packets together and shows how the three subissues relate; it gives crucial context, in other words. 7.5.

casual inspection." *Teufel v. Watkins*, 267 Mich. App. 425, 427, 705 N.W.2d 164, 166 (2005). Thus, the open-and-obvious doctrine generally eliminates a premises owner's duty to warn or protect invitees from conditions that are readily apparent. *Lugo*, 464 Mich. at 515, 629 N.W.2d at 387.

Michigan courts have recognized a narrow exception to this no-duty rule for conditions that remain unreasonably dangerous despite their obviousness: "[I]f special aspects ... make even an open and obvious risk unreasonably dangerous, the premises possessor has a duty to undertake reasonable precautions to protect invitees from that risk." *Lugo*, 464 Mich. at 516, 629 N.W.2d at 386. But this exception applies to "only those aspects that give rise to a uniquely high likelihood of harm or severity of harm if the risk is not avoided." *Id.* at 517, 629 N.W.2d at 387–88. Thus, unless an obvious danger is "effectively unavoidable" or creates "a substantial risk of death or severe injury," no duty exists. *Id.* at 517, 629 N.W.2d at 387–88.

AREAC: State the subargument for the subissue in a persuasive point heading. 5.4. Clearly state the argument as a heading with both the main point or **assertion** you want the court to agree to and then the main **reason** the court should agree. Also note how this argument makes sense because the global Rule Foundation above set it up.

A. Buffalo Wild Wings owed no duty to Mr. Trout because the ice he slipped on posed an open and obvious danger with no special aspects.

AREAC: **Give a Rule Foundation.** Ch. 7. This secondary Rule Foundation is particular to this one argument, this one subissue. Do a combination of paraphrasing and quoting to make the rules readable. 7.5.

Our Supreme Court has recognized that snow, ice, and even black ice are common occurrences during Michigan winters and are thus open-and-obvious dangers. *Kenny v. Kaatz Funeral Home*, 472 Mich. 929, 929, 697 N.W.2d 526, 526 (2005) (peremptorily reversing 264 Mich. App. 99, 689 N.W.2d 737 (2004) and adopting dissenting opinion). Likewise, it is well settled that "[a]n open and obvious accumulation of snow and ice, by itself, does not feature any special aspects." *Robertson v. Blue Water Oil Co.*, 268 Mich. App. 588, 590, 708 N.W.2d 749, 752 (2005) (citing *Mann v. Shusteric Enterprises, Inc.*, 470 Mich. 320, 323, 683 N.W.2d 573, 579 (2004)).

AREAC: **Explain Caselaw.** Ch. 9. This is the first Case Illustration. It fleshes out the rules stated immediately above with the story, and the court's holding and reasoning about that story. Note the helpful and informative topic sentence that gets right to the point.

Michigan's leading case involved facts almost identical to those in the present case—and flatly rejected the argument that black ice does not fall within the open-and-obvious-danger rule. *Kenny v. Kaatz Funeral Home*, 264 Mich. App. 99, 689 N.W.2d 737 (2004) (Griffin, J., dissenting) (the Michigan Supreme Court adopted the dissenting opinion). In *Kenny*, an invitee and her companions exited a car parked in a funeral-home parking lot during a snowstorm. The parking lot was covered by a layer of snow. The invitee saw "three of her companions holding onto the hood of the car for support." *Id.* at 115, 686 N.W.2d at 746. As the invitee walked around

4

the car toward the passenger side, she slipped and fell. She later claimed that she'd slipped on clear "black ice" that was camouflaged by a layer of snow. *Id.* at 116, 686 N.W.2d at 746.

The Michigan Supreme Court held that the patch of snow-covered black ice posed an open and obvious danger with no special aspects, so the funeral home owed no duty to protect the invitee. *Id.* at 122, 686 N.W.2d at 749. The Court reasoned that the invitee, a lifelong Michigan resident, should have been aware of the possibility of slippery ice. Plus, she'd seen her companions using the car for support, which alerted her to the slippery conditions outside the car. *Id.* at 121, 686 N.W.2d at 748.

Since the Supreme Court's *Kenny* decision, the Michigan Court of Appeals has applied the open and obvious doctrine to claims arising from black ice covered with snow. For instance, in *Winters-Mobley v. Leidholdt*, No. 264692, 2006 WL 1419847, at *2 (Mich. Ct. App. May 23, 2006), the court of appeals affirmed summary disposition in favor of a landowner, observing that "our Supreme Court ruled that black ice, by itself is an open and obvious condition." Likewise, in *Taylor v. Original Nick's Country Oven*, No. 266679, 2006 WL 1236772, at *1 (Mich. Ct. App. May 9, 2006), the court held that a restaurant owed no duty to protect a truck driver who slipped on black ice in its parking lot, reasoning that "a person in plaintiff's position would have seen the ice on the pavement" had he been looking. (Unpublished opinions attached as Exhibit D).

Here, the alleged black ice that Mr. Trout slipped on was an open and obvious danger with no special aspects, so Buffalo Wild Wings owed do duty to Mr. Trout. Indeed, the ice in this case was more conspicuous than the snow-covered black ice in *Kenny*, making the hazard even more obvious.

Mr. Trout's testimony confirms that an ordinary person in his position could have observed the black ice on a casual inspection and that an average observer would have noticed that the area was likely slippery. Mr. Trout knew that it had been raining and that there had been freezing temperatures in the days before his slip and fall. And this transpired during December in a northern-Michigan town, where icy, snowy conditions are the norm during winter. Mr. Trout acknowledged this during his deposition, confirming that the condition he encountered was an everyday icy condition that Michigan pedestrians expect:

5

AREAC: **Explain Caselaw**. Ch. 9. It's common in a case illustration to have a paragraph break between the facts and the holding.

AREAC: **Cite** authority. Cite every sentence in a case illustration (except maybe the facts). 9.4(B). This paragraph demonstrates an *Id.* citation with parallel reporters. 17.4(A)(2).

AREAC: **Explain Caselaw**. Note that attorneys explain all caselaw on a single issue together, consecutively, before applying them to the facts. Don't explain a case and then apply it; explain another case and then apply it. For more, see 10.8(B).

AREAC: **Explain Caselaw**. Note the great topic sentence that begins this Case Illustration to put the case in context.

AREAC: **Apply Law**. Ch. 10. After explaining the law, apply it. Start with a transition and then the ultimate conclusion. Then state the first argument and prove it. 10.3–10.6.

AREAC: Here's a good example of **analogizing** to caselaw without repeating too much of the precedent case. The focus must be on the facts of the current case. See 10.6(A)(1), (4).

AREAC: **Apply Law**. Ch. 10. This paragraph largely uses common sense, which is the hallmark of rule-based reasoning, to explain why the black ice was obvious. Note how the writer uses many of the techniques explained in 10.5.

Letting the parties speak for themselves is a persuasive way to make a point, but keep quotations brief. This one is reaching the maximum length of a reader's attention.

Q. As a person that grew up in Michigan, particularly with your outdoor experience, you're aware that Michigan winters have rain and snow and freezing temperatures?

A. That is correct.

Q. And that as you say a typical day in Michigan in December can have freezing temperatures or it can have above freezing temperatures, correct?

A. That is correct.

Q. When that happens, there could be ice found as a result of the freezing and thawing and refreezing of precipitation, right?

A. That's correct.

(Exhibit B, Trout Dep. Tr., at p. 56).

Note the **typography**, which is the layout of the text. The spacing before and after each heading at the same level should be consistent from heading to heading. This heading has about 12 points of spacing before it and 6 after it, and that's the same for headings 1 through 6 in this brief. The amount of spacing before and after is less important than making sure that the spacing is consistent from heading to heading. See 18.4(D) for more about typography.

Given all this, a reasonable pedestrian would have been on the lookout for slippery conditions.

In short, Mr. Trout, like the plaintiffs in *Kenny*, *Winters-Mobley*, and *Taylor*, encountered black ice that was an open and obvious danger. Thus, Buffalo Wild Wings owed no duty to protect Mr. Trout unless that patch of black ice had special aspects that made it unavoidable or likely to cause death or severe injury. As will be explained below, the factual record here contains no evidence suggesting that either was true.

AREAC: A new argument packet starts here for the second subissue, so the writer starts the AREAC structure anew. 4.6; 5.3; 5.4.

B. The obvious ice patch here was avoidable and ordinary, and thus had no special aspects giving rise to a high likelihood or severity of harm.

AREAC: **Give a Rule Foundation**. Ch. 7. Just as you saw at the beginning of Argument A, this secondary Rule Foundation is particular to this one argument. 7.5.

The general no-duty rule applies here because the ordinary, obvious ice patch had no special aspects making it unreasonably dangerous. The Michigan Supreme Court has emphasized that "only those aspects that give rise to a uniquely high likelihood of harm or severity of harm if the risk is not avoided will serve to remove that condition from the open and obvious danger doctrine." *Lugo*, 464 Mich. at 518, 629 N.W.2d at 387–88. And "[a]n open and obvious accumulation of snow and ice, by itself, does not feature any special aspects." *Robertson v. Blue Water Oil Co.*, 268 Mich. App. 588, 592, 708 N.W.2d 749, 752 (2005).

Special aspects exist only when a pedestrian has no choice but to confront the danger or will likely suffer death or severe injury by doing so:

6

> [A] situation might involve, for example, a commercial building with only one exit for the general public where the floor is covered with standing water. While the condition is open and obvious, a customer wishing to exit the store must leave the store through the water. In other words, the open and obvious condition is effectively unavoidable. Similarly, an open and obvious condition might be unreasonably dangerous because of special aspects that impose an unreasonably high risk of severe harm. To use another example, consider an unguarded thirty foot deep pit in the middle of a parking lot. The condition might well be open and obvious, and one would likely be capable of avoiding the danger. Nevertheless, this situation would present such a substantial risk of death or severe injury to one who fell in the pit that it would be unreasonably dangerous to maintain the condition....

Lugo, 464 Mich. at 517, 629 N.W.2d at 387.

Here, neither of the two recognized special aspects was present. First, any risk was avoidable because Mr. Trout had multiple paths available to him. In fact, he testified that he entered and exited the restaurant using two different pathways: "Well, I came out the same door, but not the same pathway." (Exhibit B, Trout 56). And even if there'd been just one pathway, nothing in the factual record suggests that the ice patch was so large that it was unavoidable. Mr. Trout could have simply watched where he was going and walked around it.

Second, a patch of ice does not present a "substantial risk of death or severe injury" like a 30-foot pit in the middle of a parking lot. A long line of Michigan appellate decisions confirms this. *See, e.g., Lymon v. Freedland*, 314 Mich. App. 746, 760, 887 N.W.2d 456, 463–64 (2016), *overruled on other grounds by Est. of Livings v. Sage's Inv. Grp., LLC*, 507 Mich. 328, 968 N.W.2d 397 (2021)) (holding that ice-covered driveway did not pose a risk of death or severe injury); *Corey v. Davenport College of Business (On Remand)*, 251 Mich. App. 1, 6–7, 649 N.W.2d 392, 395 (2002) (holding that ice-covered steps did not present a high likelihood of harm or severity of harm); *Royce v. Chatwell Club Apartments*, 276 Mich. App. 389, 395–396, 740 N.W.2d 547, 551 (2007) (holding that "[t]he risk of slipping and falling on ice is not sufficiently similar to those special aspects discussed in *Lugo* to constitute a uniquely high likelihood

7

Normally, a block quotation of this size would be a really bad idea because they normally do not get read. This paragraph, though, really nails the rule right on the head. And, what's more, this paragraph is quoted in almost all cases dealing with this issue. Altogether, it's okay in this situation to do a block quotation. But try to avoid it when possible. 17.8(E).

AREAC: For each argument, you'll simply repeat the same AREAC parts: persuasive point heading, which is the **argument**; rule foundation, the **rules** governing the subissue; Case Illustrations, the **examples** of the rules; **application** of law; and another **conclusion**. 4.6(A).

AREAC: **Apply the law.** This properly begins with a transition so the reader knows that we're switching gears to applying the law. Then the global conclusion is stated followed by the first subissue (avoidable risk). The language of the element is repeated so the reader knows what issue is being addressed. See 10.3 for organizing the Application.

AREAC: **Explain caselaw.** Two points: First, note how the reader is integrating caselaw examples into the application of law. We usually don't do that, but it works in this situation because it gives the reader the information they need in this moment, and it's obvious how these cases connect to the rules above. Second, short Case Illustrations via parentheticals can be very effective at giving several caselaw examples. 9.7(C).

AREA**C**: An internal or mini-**conclusion** like this ends on a persuasive note. 4.2; 10.3(F).

AREAC: Address obvious **counterarguments** when writing a brief. Often, the counter analysis goes within an argument, but, here, it made sense to make it a separate argument.

A**RE**AC: This **Case Illustration** both states the rule and gives a factual example of it. 9.2.

ARE**A**C: This **roadmapping** of "two reasons" is helpful to orient the reader and make them an active reader. 10.3.

or severity of harm and remove the condition from the open and obvious danger doctrine").

Because the alleged ice did not threaten Mr. Trout with death or severe injury, and because the ice was avoidable, no special aspects existed. Therefore, the open-and-obvious rule applies, and Buffalo Wild Wings owed no duty to Mr. Trout.

C. Mr. Trout's anticipated reliance on *Slaughter* is misplaced because unlike the invisible ice there, the ice here visibly contrasted with the sidewalk's surface.

It's anticipated that Mr. Trout will rely heavily on the court of appeals' decision in *Slaughter v. Blarney Castle Oil Co.*, 281 Mich. App. 474, 760 N.W.2d 287 (2008), to argue that black ice may not be an open and obvious danger. But a careful reading of *Slaughter* reveals that it is readily distinguishable.

In *Slaughter*, an invitee parked her truck in a black asphalt parking lot, stepped out, and immediately slipped on black ice. The court held that the black ice was not open and obvious. *Id.* at 478, 760 N.W.2d at 292. The court believed that the definition of *black ice*—that it is "nearly invisible" or "nearly transparent"—is "inherently inconsistent with the open and obvious danger doctrine." *Id.* at 477, 760 N.W.2d at 292. While acknowledging that black ice can be an obvious danger when visible on casual inspection, the court found that this was not the case in *Slaughter*, where the invitee slipped while getting out of her truck and before having a chance to observe the conditions. There were no clues in *Slaughter* that the black asphalt parking lot was slippery.

The present case is unlike *Slaughter* for at least two reasons. First, Mr. Trout was not getting out of a vehicle and stepping blindly onto invisible ice. Instead, he slipped after walking out of the Buffalo Wild Wings restaurant and while facing the multiple paths available to him. Mr. Trout did not have anything obstructing his vision, such as the opening of a truck's door. He confirmed under oath that there was nothing obstructing his vision. (Exhibit B, Trout 62). He even acknowledged that the restaurant's parking lot had ample lighting. (Exhibit B, Trout 60–61). Nothing blocked his view or prevented him from seeing the ice. (Exhibit B, Trout 62).

8

Second, the alleged black ice here was not "nearly invisible," as was the black ice in *Slaughter*. Unlike the ice on black asphalt in *Slaughter*, the ice in this case was on a light-gray sidewalk. (Exhibit B, Trout 60–61). Ice on a gray sidewalk appears as a much darker color, in contrast to ice on black asphalt, which is contrasted only by a sheen of light.

For these reasons, *Slaughter* is distinguishable and does not support Mr. Trout's anticipated claim that the ice in the present case was invisible. Therefore, the open and obvious rule applies, and Buffalo Wild Wings owed no duty to Mr. Trout.

II. Buffalo Wild Wings owed no duty to Mr. Trout because it lacked actual notice of the alleged ice patch and lacked sufficient time to become aware of it.

Besides the ice being an open and obvious condition with no special aspects, Buffalo Wild Wings owed no duty because it did not have notice of the condition. "[E]ven though invitors have a duty to exercise reasonable care in protecting their invitees, they are not absolute insurers of the safety of their invitees." *Lugo*, 464 Mich. at 515, 629 N.W.2d at 386. Thus, for a plaintiff to prevail on a premises-liability claim, they must establish "that defendant, as a premises owner, possessed actual or constructive notice of the dangerous condition." *Lowrey v. LMPS & LMPJ, Inc.*, 500 Mich. 1, 10, 890 N.W.2d 344, 350 (2016). In other words, the unsafe condition must be "known to the storekeeper" or be "of such a character or [present] a sufficient length of time that [the storekeeper] should have knowledge of it." *Id.* at 10–11, 890 N.W.2d at 350.

If a plaintiff facing a motion for summary disposition fails to "proffer evidence sufficient to demonstrate a question of fact regarding defendant's actual or constructive notice of the hazardous condition," then the landowner is "entitled to summary disposition on this basis." *Id.* at 10–11, 890 N.W.2d at 350.

A persuasive Michigan Court of Appeals decision recognized, on nearly identical facts, that the mere presence of inclement weather does not create constructive notice of an ice hazard. In *Tate v. Milonas Properties*, No. 266054, 2006 WL 1628611, at *1 (Mich. Ct. App. June 13, 2006), an invitee broke her ankle after falling in the defendant's parking lot. The lot appeared wet but not icy. The court held that the property

9

AREAC: Here's a good **analogy** to really bolster the writer's point and persuade the court. 10.6(A)(6).

AREAC: This **conclusion** ties up the argument with a bow. By the way, this is called an "internal" or "mini" conclusion because it's not the overall global conclusion for the entire issue; it's just for this one argument. 4.2; 10.3(F).

Argument II does not have subissues like Argument I above. Therefore, this entire argument will be just one AREAC packet.

AREAC: State the global argument in a **persuasive point heading**. 5.4.

AREAC: **Rule Foundation**. A combination of paraphrasing and quoting is usually the best way to do this. 7.6(E). Note the persuasive choice and shaping of the rules to support the client's position. Yes, all parties operate from the same elements, but attorneys have a choice in how they shape the elements and which guiding rules they include. 7.8.

AREAC: This **Case Illustration** explains the "notice" rule stated above. The strong topic sentence, among other things, helps the reader understand how this Case Illustration relates to the rules above. 9.4(A).

owner did not have actual or constructive notice even though the same conditions were present for at least two hours. *Id.* at *1. And there was no evidence to indicate that anyone notified the property owner of icy conditions. *Id.* In fact, the court relied on the plaintiff's evidence that the conditions were not obvious to prove that the property owner could not have known about the ice. *Id.*

AREAC: **Apply the Law.** Ch. 10.

In the present case, Mr. Trout likewise has not provided—and cannot provide—evidence that Buffalo Wild Wings had actual or constructive knowledge of the conditions. As for actual knowledge, it is undisputed that neither the manager nor any other Buffalo Wild Wings employee received reports of slippery conditions on the day in question. (Exhibit C & D, Affidavits). Nothing untoward occurred, as evidenced by the manager's log-book entries for both the 17th and 18th of December. (Exhibit F, Log-Book Notations).

Nor is there evidence suggesting that Buffalo Wild Wings' employees had constructive notice. According to Mr. Trout, the icy conditions first appeared in the 30 minutes it took him to eat a quick dinner. And after that 30-minute period, according to Mr. Trout, there were no clues to the slippery conditions. (Exhibit B, Trout 63). Trout's testimony also makes clear that any alleged hazard existed for only a short time, giving employees little time or reason to become aware of it:

Q. When you walked out the door did you feel the rain coming down?

A. There was no rain coming out at that time.

Q. So what you're saying is when you walked in it was dry; is that right?

A. That's correct.

Q. And when you walked out, it had rained; is that right?

A. (Shook his head in an affirmative manner.)

(Exhibit B, Dep. Troy Trout 60).

Signposts like this ensure rad readability. 18.6.

What's more, Mr. Trout's own description of the conditions cannot be trusted because he said that it had rained and that the temperatures were in the 40-degree range. (Dep. Trout 54–55). In fact, meteorological records for Mt. Pleasant reflect that on December 17, 2021, the temperature

10

ranged between 21 and 30 degrees, and that there was no precipitation of any kind until 0.04 inches of snow fell between midnight and 2:00 a.m. There was no rain at all until December 18, 2021, when there was "light rain" on and off all day, and the temperature averaged between 30 and 45 degrees. (Exhibit E, Weather-Bank Records).

If Trout could not see the alleged black ice, as he now claims, it is unreasonable to expect Buffalo Wild Wings' employees to discover and treat the area, especially in the very short timeframe that Trout described in his testimony. If two hours in *Tate* wasn't enough time to give constructive notice, then thirty minutes here is patently insufficient. There is simply no indication that Buffalo Wild Wings' employees knew or should have known of the alleged black ice.

AREAC: The analogy in this paragraph helps to bolster the rule-based reasoning above it. 10.6(A)(1).

Because Trout has no evidence that Buffalo Wild Wings had actual notice of the black ice—and also admits that any dangerous conditions would have arisen within a very short time—he cannot establish that Buffalo Wild Wings had actual or constructive notice. Buffalo Wild Wings knew of no defect and had no reason to know of a defect. Given Mr. Trout's lack of proof on this point, summary disposition is appropriate.

AREAC: This argument packet correctly concludes with an internal conclusion. 4.2; 10.3(F); 11.2.

Relief Requested

For the above reasons, Buffalo Wild Wings asks this Court to enter an order granting its motion for summary disposition, dismissing Mr. Trout's claims with prejudice, and awarding it attorney fees and costs as permitted by law.

Conclude and Recommend. For briefs, simply write the relief requested here. You may state in a phrase the overall conclusion, but do not rehash any reasoning. Keep it simple and to the point. 11.4.

November 15, 2022

Respectfully submitted,
Vanderhoff, Gargola PC

Sam Jackson

Samuel Jackson P4583156
Attorneys for Defendant
150 W. Long Lake Rd.
Troy, MI 48098-6330
(248) 555-2800
johno@vangar.com

The date and signature block should be identical to the date and signature block for the motion.

Checklist for Trial-Court Brief

Caption Your Document

Did you:

___ include a caption for both the motion and the brief as two separate documents? 14.2.

___ include the court name at the top, the parties on the left, and the case number and judge on the right? 14.2.

___ format the caption so it looks like a conventional caption? 14.2(C).

___ use consistent typography, especially with the parties, so there are consistent line spaces between the parts? 14.2(B)(2).

___ punctuate the parties correctly? 14.2(B)(2).

Title Your Document

Did you:

___ write a title directly below the caption? 13.4.

___ center and apply bold emphasis to the title? 13.4.

___ apply heading capitalization? 13.4.

___ for the motion's title, include the party making the motion, the word *motion*, and a description of the motion? 13.4(B).

___ for the brief's title, include the motion's title verbatim but added either "Plaintiff's Brief in Support" or "Plaintiff's Response to" before it? (Or "Defendant's" as may be the case.) 13.4(C).

Use Document Headings

In looking at the entire document as a whole, did you:

___ organize your document by inserting the following headings: Introduction, Facts, Standard of Review, Argument, and Relief Requested? 15.2.

___ bold and center each heading or otherwise set it off as a heading? 15.2.

___ use headings in the Argument section *where necessary* to separate different issues? 5.3; 5.4.

Preview the Analysis (Introduction)

In your Introduction, did you:

___ ensure that the entire section follows a syllogistic structure from conclusion, to rule, to application, to conclusion? 16.4(A).

___ state the issue or type of case in the first sentence? 16.4(C)(2).

___ state the conclusion/prediction in the first sentence? 16.4(A), (C)(2).

___ state the pivotal rule of law (prefer paraphrasing, but quote when necessary) in the second sentence? 16.4(A)(2).

___ state a summary of the application of the law to the facts (i.e., it summarizes your main reasoning points) in the third sentence (and maybe fourth and fifth)? 16.4(A)(3).

___ state the relief sought in the final sentence? 16.4(C)(2).

___ limit the Introduction to one paragraph, maybe two?

___ make sure that the paragraph has a logical flow to it? In other words, the relief sought in the final sentence seemed logical given what you wrote in the sentences that preceded it.

Tell a Story (Facts)

In your Facts section, did you:

___ include legally significant, background, and emotional facts? 12.2(A).

___ include even unfavorable facts? 12.2(A)(1).

___ begin with contextual information that introduces the parties and the broad issue? 12.2(B).

___ prefer to organize the facts chronologically? 12.2(C)(1).

___ avoid organizing the facts according to which document you got them from? 12.2(C)(1).

___ where appropriate, organize the facts by each character's perception (i.e., where characters disagree on the facts)? 12.2(C)(3).

___ consider using headings for longer, more complex factual statements? 12.2(D)(4).

___ use lots of paragraphs, averaging three to five per page? 12.2(D)(2).

___ use names, not role designations like *plaintiff* or *customer*? 12.2(D)(3).

___ make your story persuasive? 12.4(B).

Give a Rule Foundation (Standard of Review)

In the Standard of Review section, did you:

___ include the court rule that tells the court how to decide the motion? 7.9(A).

___ include rules from caselaw that favor your client? 7.8; 7.9(A).

___ cite both the court rule and the caselaw rules? Ch. 17.

___ "make it your own" by avoiding plagiarism and clunky block quotations? 7.9(B).

Use Document Headings (Persuasive Point Headings)

Beginning with this section of the checklist, the skills pertain to writing the Argument section.

Throughout the Argument section, did you:

___ clearly state each argument in a persuasive point heading? 5.3; 5.4.

___ properly format each heading as a (1) bolded sentence (2) that is single-spaced (3) with sentence capitalization and (4) ends with a period? 5.4(E).

___ ensure that each point heading is an argument with (1) an assertion and (2) a reason? 5.4(D).

___ ensure that the entire sentence is readable and hangs together?

___ enumerate your headings? 5.4(G).

___ avoid enumerating just one heading at a level (i.e., you can't have a 1. if you don't have a 2.)? 5.4(G).

___ format headings at different levels to give visual clues of the arguments' hierarchy? 5.4(G).

Give a Rule Foundation

When teaching the court the controlling legal rules, did you:

___ if writing multiple subissues, include one global Rule Foundation and, for each subissue, a secondary Rule Foundation? 4.6(E); 7.5.

___ synthesize the relevant rules, whether from codified law, caselaw, or both, *before* illustrating them with caselaw? 7.1–7.6(D).

___ teach the reader the rules of law in a logical, step-by-step sequence, and didn't rush it? For example, you started by teaching the broadest rule and ended with the narrowest rule. You taught general rules before teaching exceptions to those rules. 7.1–7.6.

___ if appropriate, refine the issue by focusing the reader on just the elements that are at issue? 7.3.

___ prefer paraphrasing when possible? 7.6(E).

___ include a citation to binding legal authority for each rule? Ch. 17.

Explain Codified Law

When explaining codified law, whether in the Rule Foundation or elsewhere, did you:

___ place codified law before caselaw? 8.2(A).

___ help the reader make sense of codified law by explaining its elements? 8.2(B), (C).

___ include the essential elements and important contextual information? 8.2(C).

___ where applicable, cohesively synthesize several statutory provisions? 8.2(E).

___ prefer paraphrasing? 8.2(D).

___ quote unique language that cannot be paraphrased? 8.2(D).

___ cite a source for each rule? 17.2–17.3; 17.6.

Explain Caselaw

___ Did you include two or three Case Illustrations or one directly on-point Case Illustration? 9.3.

___ Does each Case Illustration have a topic sentence, a citation, the case's facts, the court's holding, and the court's reasoning? 9.4.

Case Illustration > ***Topic Sentence***

In the topic sentence of your Case Illustration, did you:

___ transition from the preceding paragraph by showing how the case fits into the big picture? 9.4(A)(1).

___ avoid starting with a source of law? Instead, cite the source after the topic sentence. 9.4(B).

___ state a new point that you have not yet stated in the Rule Foundation? 9.4(A)(2).

___ give a substantive point rather than merely announcing the topic you're going to address? 9.4(A)(3).

___ where appropriate, create an implicit rule from the case where it may not be immediately clear from the specifics of the case how it could apply to the client's matter? 9.4(A)(3)(b).

___ avoid cramming too much information into the topic sentence? Although your topic sentence is a helpful transition/preview for your reader, it can only include so much information.

Case Illustration > ***Citation***

Immediately after the topic sentence, did you:

___ cite a case for the source of the topic sentence, whether it be explicit or implicit? 9.4(B); 17.4.

___ follow ALWD or Bluebook rules for formatting the citation? Ch. 17.

___ put the citation in a separate citation sentence? 9.4(B).

Case Illustration > ***Case Facts***

When explaining the facts of the precedent case, did you:

___ capture the story to teach your reader what happened in the case you're writing about? 9.4(C).

___ give contextual information that sets the stage for the story? 9.4(C).

___ include the legally significant facts (i.e., the ones used in the court's reasoning)? 9.4(C)(1).

___ avoid unnecessary information like names, dates, party arguments, and lower-court procedure unless they directly relate to your issue? 9.4(C)(2).

___ if writing about a civil case, use informative status words to identify the parties and other "characters" in the story (like *tenant* and *landlord* or *buyer* and *seller*), rather than using their actual names or party designations like *plaintiff* or *defendant*? 9.4(C)(3).

___ if writing about a criminal case, use *the defendant* to refer to the person charged with the crime, which is informative to readers? But for other people, you've tried to come up with informative status words, such as *witness*, *victim*, *accuser*, *arresting officer*, *police officer*, *companion*, *prosecutor*, etc. 9.4(C)(3).

Case Illustration > ***Court's Holding***

When writing about the court's holding in a Case Illustration, did you:

___ give the court's actual decision rather than state a pure rule of law or give only the ultimate procedural outcome like *affirmed* or *reversed*? 9.4(D).

___ state the global holding and any secondary holdings on your issue? 9.4(D).

___ ensure that the holding addresses the narrow issue you're writing about? 9.4(D).

Case Illustration > ***Court's Reasoning***

When summarizing the court's reasoning in a Case Illustration, did you:

___ give *details* about why the court decided the case the way it did? If the court decided multiple *relevant* subissues, you've quickly explained the court's reasoning for each of those subissues, and you've done that in a logical sequence, with signposts to help your reader follow along. 9.4(E).

___ avoid restating the rules the court applied? Rather, put the rules either in the Rule Foundation or in the Case Illustration's topic sentence. 9.4(E).

Case Synthesis

If you've given more than one Case Illustration for a single issue, did you:

___ create coherence among the cases by using the trophy, rubber-band, or paragraph-synthesis method? 9.9(B).

___ apply the checklist in 9.11 for *synthesizing* caselaw?

Apply Law

When applying the law to our client's facts, did you:

___ start a new paragraph and use an appropriate transition? 10.3(A).

E.g.:

Here, …

In our case, …

In the present case, …

In Ms. Hanni's case, …

___ after your transition, write an informative topic sentence announcing your global conclusion you want the court to agree with? 10.3(B).

___ after the global conclusion, clearly state an argument? 10.3(C).

___ after clearly stating an argument, prove the argument with rule-based and analogical reasoning? 10.3(D); 10.5; 10.6.

___ repeat an Argument-and-Proof combo for each argument? 10.3(E).

___ begin every paragraph after the first one with a clear topic sentence that states a legal argument and doesn't merely rehash law or facts? 10.8(F).

___ pass the two-question test in 10.4(B) to ensure you're actually applying law? See also 10.8(C).

___ weave in counterarguments where appropriate? 10.3(D)(3).

___ analogize to caselaw in meaningful, strategic places where it helps support a specific point? 10.7(C).

___ analogize to caselaw in meaningful ways by using one or a variety of the nine techniques explained in 10.6(A)?

___ avoid false comparisons? ("Like the *Jones* case, Mary Smith did not …"—*Jones* is a case, but Mary is a human being.) 10.7(E).

___ avoid organizing your analysis by case? 10.8(D).

___ signal closure of your analysis? ("Thus,…" "Therefore…" "So…"). 10.3(F); 11.2.

Conclude and Recommend (Conclusion)

In the Conclusion, did you:

___ state the global conclusion? 11.4.

___ state the relief you seek from the court? 11.4.

___ avoid rehashing any of the reasoning? If so, delete it. 11.4.

Quoting

Throughout the brief, did you:

___ insert quotation marks around verbatim language if you lifted exact language from another source? Four or more consecutive substantive words from a source constitute a phrase that requires quoting. 18.5(C); 7.6(E).

___ properly format a block quotation? If you've written a block quotation (quotation of 50 words or more), which you should do only sparingly, you've followed conventional rules. 17.8(E).

___ avoid using quotation marks for paraphrased information? If you have paraphrased the court's (or other source's) language, you do not need to insert quotation marks, but you still need to cite the source after the sentence to show your reader where you got the idea from. 7.6(E).

___ cite a source after every quotation? 17.2; 7.6(E).

Use Standard Document Format and Pagination

In setting up the whole document, did you:

___ double-space the text (including the motion paragraph) but not the caption, signature blocks, or point headings?

___ use 1" margins on all sides?

___ use a professional font (e.g., Calibri, Times New Roman, Arial, or their ilk)? 18.4(C).

___ include page numbers? 18.4(A).

Revise and Edit

Use Enticing Typography

Throughout the document, did you:

___ ensure that the document's typography (the layout of information, white space) is consistent with professional standards? 18.4.

___ ensure that each *heading* in the same level throughout the document has consistent spacing before and after the heading? Usually put more space before each heading than after it. 18.4(D).

___ use the same amount of space after and before each *paragraph*? 18.4(E).

___ consistently space first-line indents? (You may choose to use a modern block style without indents; in that case, add more line space between paragraphs to set off each paragraph.) 18.4(F).

___ consistently use one or two spaces after a period? 18.4(H).

___ consistently use curved quotation marks and apostrophes (as opposed to straight ones you get when pasting from the internet)? 18.4(I).

Use Guru Grammar

Before submitting the final document, did you:

___ edit the final draft for punctuation and grammar? 18.5.

___ use quotation marks (" ") whenever you lifted exact, verbatim language from a case or statute (with a post-sentence citation)? 18.5(C).

___ avoid quoting/paraphrasing from—or citing to—a case's synopsis or headnotes (which are not part of the court's actual opinion but rather are supplied by the publisher's staff)?

Ensure Rad Readability

Throughout the document, did you:

___ remember that you are a teacher on the page? (Whether writing a short memo, a brief to an appellate court, or a law-school essay answer, great lawyers and law students are always teachers, striving to make the complex as clear and simple as possible. That's very hard to do, but it's always the goal.) 18.6.

___ create new paragraphs to avoid intimidating walls of dense, unbroken text? 18.4(E), (F). The goal is three to five paragraphs per page.

___ write in a confident and direct style while avoiding legalese or unnecessarily inflated language? (In other words, you avoided the lawyer tics and plodding, stilted prose that plague so many of the cases you've read in your casebooks.) 18.6.

___ create a well-organized, cohesive message?

Ensure Sightly Citations

When explaining the law, did you:

___ cite every rule of law the first time you stated it? 17.2.

___ use a full citation the first time you cited a source? 17.3.

___ cite after every sentence in a Case Illustration (except for perhaps the facts) and include a pinpoint page number? 17.2.

___ use *Id.* whenever possible, but only after giving the full citation? 17.3.

___ include "at" and a page number for each *Id.* citation? 17.3; 17.4(A)(2).

___ use a short citation when appropriate? 17.3.

___ include the right content, punctuate it correctly, and get the spacing right for each citation? 17.4–17.6.

Final Edits

Before submitting the document, did you:

___ save it as a PDF?

___ print the document after saving it as a PDF and proofread it one more time, even though you were sick of it? (This step is important because sometimes the format changes in the conversion from a word-processing document to a PDF.)

2.7 Trial-Court Brief (Nonmoving Party)

Beginning on the next page, you can read the plaintiff's response to Defendant's Motion for Summary Disposition that you just read in 2.6.

Here are the document specifications:

Purpose: Persuade a court to deny the moving party's motion.

Mood: Persuasive.

Structure: AREAC (**A**rgument > **R**ule > Caselaw **E**xample > **A**pplication > **C**onclusion. 4.6(A); 5.3)

Audience: Primarily, the court hearing the matter. Secondarily, the court's staff and opposing counsel.

Length: Very case-specific, though most court rules limit reply briefs to around 10 or 15 pages.

Final format: PDF, hard copy, or both.

Conveyance: Saved in the firm's electronic filing system, filed with the court, and served on opposing counsel.

Caption the Document. Section 14.2 explains how to properly caption a brief.

Title the Document. See section 13.4(C).

Preview the Analysis. Ch. 16. An analysis preview needs an issue, the governing rule, a summary of how the rule applies to the facts, and the conclusion or relief the party seeks from the court. In other words, follow AREAC structure for an analysis preview. For a strategic document like a brief, this is especially persuasive because it follows the syllogistic structure of pure logic. See Section 16.4(C)(2) for more.

STATE OF MICHIGAN
IN THE CIRCUIT COURT FOR ISABELLA COUNTY

TROY C. TROUT,

Plaintiff, No. 19-4546-NO

v. Hon. Rachel Reneria

J.C.K.W. INC., a/k/a BUFFALO WILD WINGS GRILL & BAR,

Defendant.

Everette P. Hasan, III P97842402	Sam Jackson P4583156
HASAN & ABDUL PLLC	VANDERHOFF, GARGOLA PC
Attorneys for Plaintiff	Attorneys for Defendant
273 S. Main St.	150 W. Long Lake Rd.
P.O. Drawer 9928	Troy, MI 48098-6330
Grayling, MI 49738 (989) 555-5232	(248) 555-2800
ehas@hasanabdul.com	johno@vangar.com

Plaintiff's Response to
Defendant's Motion for Summary Disposition

INTRODUCTION

This matter is a premises liability action brought by Plaintiff, Troy C. Trout, against JCKW, Inc. (Buffalo Wild Wings), arising out of a December 17, 2021, incident, where Troy Trout slipped and fell on an unmaintained icy sidewalk and suffered a syrinx (lesion) to his spinal cord at the C2 level, resulting in paresthesia and myelopathy.

As this court is no doubt aware, a defendant invitor has a duty to maintain a safe premises, but they do not need to warn about or remedy open and obvious conditions. Here, Defendant Buffalo Wild Wings

1

breached this duty by not warning about or fixing the black ice that Mr. Trout slipped on. Black ice is per se not an obvious danger because black ice is hidden, nearly invisible. And the black ice here had the special aspect of being unavoidable because it was on a pathway that was the only way to enter or exit the restaurant.

What's more, there is a genuine issue of material fact as to whether Buffalo Wild Wings should have known that the sidewalk was slippery. There are many conflicting factual accounts about the weather conditions, and a jury should hear the evidence to decide the truth.

Finally, there is at least a genuine issue of material fact regarding whether the fall on black ice caused Mr. Trout's spinal-cord injury. Two doctors have stated in an affidavit that the fall did indeed cause the injury, but the defendant's doctors disagree. A jury should likewise be able to sort this out.

For these reasons, Mr. Trout asks this Honorable Court to deny Buffalo Wild Wings' Motion for Summary Disposition.

STATEMENT OF FACTS

On December 17, 2021, at approximately 11:00 p.m., Troy Trout and a friend, Wayne Davis, went to Buffalo Wild Wings Grill & Bar to have a late dinner. Mr. Davis drove to the restaurant, and upon parking the vehicle, Mr. Trout and Mr. Davis walked into the restaurant. Mr. Trout recalled that, when riding to the restaurant and walking from the car into the restaurant, there was no precipitation in any form (rain nor snow). Mr. Trout and Mr. Davis ate a light dinner at the restaurant from approximately 11:00 p.m. to 11:30 p.m. Mr. Trout testified that, at the most, he may have consumed one beer. Furthermore, he did not consume any alcohol at any time earlier the same day or evening. (Deposition of Troy Trout, 53–58, Exhibit A.)

When Mr. Trout and Mr. Davis got up from their table to leave, Mr. Trout went to the restroom, while Mr. Davis went to the parking lot and pulled the vehicle up near the front entrance. After leaving the restroom, Mr. Trout observed Mr. Davis's vehicle in front of the restaurant and proceeded out of the restaurant toward the vehicle. As Mr. Trout

2

An **analysis preview** summarizes the arguments. In this case, the prevailing rule is procedural, the (C)(10) motion. So that's the rule the attorney explains and applies here in the Introduction. In this paragraph, the attorney addresses the "as a matter of law" element of a (C)(10) dispositive motion. The nonmoving attorney needs to prove that the moving party's position on the elements is wrong.

The writer wisely uses paragraph breaks to signal a new subissue being addressed. 18.4(E). The subissue is the second part of a (C)(10) motion, which is to prove that the parties agree on the facts (i.e., no genuine issue of material fact). Because this is the response brief, they need to prove that there *is* an issue of fact so the case can continue to trial.

This is the conclusion or relief that the party seeks from the court. 16.4(A)(4).

Tell a Story. Ch. 12. Start with context. Then tell the story chronologically, emphasizing the legally relevant facts and giving context for them along the way. Because this is a persuasive document, shape favorable and unfavorable facts by changing their airtime and placement. But always maintain an air of objectivity. 12.4.

Cite sources in the Facts. Section 17.7 explains how to create citations to the factual record. It's conventional to put citations to the record in parentheses because it signals these are not primary sources of law.

exited the restaurant, an employee was present working the door, who told Mr. Trout to "have a good night."

Approximately 10 feet outside of the door of the restaurant, while walking down a paved slope toward the parking lot, Mr. Trout slipped on black ice and struck the back of his head against the pavement. Upon observing the fall, Mr. Davis immediately exited the vehicle and rushed toward Mr. Trout. Mr. Trout indicated that he almost lost consciousness and was gravely concerned because his hands immediately began to feel numb, tingly, and cold. In light of Mr. Trout's prior neck surgery, he was concerned that he may have been paralyzed by the fall. After laying on the sidewalk for some time, Mr. Davis helped Mr. Trout up and asked him if he wanted to go to the hospital. Because of an inability to pay for medical expenses, Mr. Trout asked Mr. Davis to take him home. Mr. Trout hoped that he would feel better the following day.

Unfortunately, Mr. Trout's condition did not improve, and he spent the entire following day in bed, in pain, with constant numbness and tingling in his hands. (Deposition of Troy Trout, 47, 59–67, Exhibit A.)

As a result of the continuing pain, numbness, and tingling in his hands, Mr. Trout was unable to sleep, and after spending one and one half days in bed, the second morning following the fall, he went to the emergency room at Gratiot Community Hospital. He was immediately taken by ambulance from Gratiot Community Hospital to St. Mary's Hospital in Saginaw for purposes of an MRI. (Deposition of Troy Trout, 68–12, Exhibit A.)

STANDARD OF REVIEW

Give a Rule Foundation. This Rule Foundation is particular to just the standard of review for deciding to grant a motion. See 7.9 to learn how to create one.

A motion brought under MCR 2.116(C) (10) should be granted only when "there is no genuine issue with respect to any material fact, and the moving party is entitled to judgment as a matter of law." *Miller v. Purcell*, 631 N.W.2d 760, 762 (Mich. Ct. App. 2001). "Where the burden of proof at trial on a dispositive issue rests on a nonmoving party, the nonmoving party may not rely on mere allegations or denials in pleadings, but must go beyond the pleadings to set forth specific facts showing that a genuine issue of material fact exists." *Quinto v. Cross & Peters Co.*, 547 N.W.2d 314, 317 (Mich. 1996). "A genuine issue of material fact exists when the record,

3

drawing all reasonable inferences in favor of the nonmoving party, leaves open an issue on which reasonable minds could differ." *West v. General Motors Corp.*, 665 N.W.2d 468, 471 (Mich. 2003).

When deciding a motion for summary disposition under this rule, a court must consider the pleadings, affidavits, depositions, admissions, and other documentary evidence then filed in the action "in the light most favorable to the nonmoving party." *Ritchie-Gamester v. City of Berkley*, 597 N.W.2d 517, 519 (Mich. 1999).

ARGUMENT

(1) OPEN AND OBVIOUS: Black ice is per se not an open and obvious danger, and it was not open and obvious here because of the surrounding conditions.

Troy Trout was an invitee. An invitee is owed the highest duty. *Wymer v. Holmes*, 412 N.W.2d 213, 216 (Mich. 1987). An *invitee* is a person "who enters upon the land of another upon an invitation which carries with it an implied representation, assurance, or understanding that reasonable care has been used to prepare the premises, and make them safe for their reception." *Id.* at 216. And, conversely, the landowner owes each invitee a duty "not only to warn the 'invitee' of any known dangers, but to also make the premises safe, which requires the landowner to actually inspect the premises. . . ." *Id.*

However, a premises owner owes no duty to protect or warn invitees against "open and obvious hazards." *Lugo v. Ameritech Corp.*, 629 N.W.2d 384, 386 (Mich. 2001). This is not an exception to the duty, but a part of its definition. *Id.* at 386. "[W]here the dangers are known to the invitee or are so obvious that the invitee might reasonably be expected to discover them, the invitor owes no duty to protect or warn the invitee unless he should anticipate the harm despite knowledge of it on behalf of the invitee." *Riddle v. McLouth Steel Products Corp.*, 485 N.W.2d 676, 681 (Mich. 1992).

Whether a hazard or condition is open and obvious depends on whether "an average user with ordinary intelligence [would] have been

AREAC: **Use Document Headings**. As you'll see in 5.3 and 5.4, begin each argument with a persuasive point heading that clearly states the argument with both the main point or **assertion** you want the court to agree to and then the main **reason** the court should agree. This makes the argument crystal clear.

AREAC: **Give a Rule Foundation**. Ch. 7. This secondary Rule Foundation is particular to this one argument. Do a combination of paraphrasing and quoting to make the rules readable.

AREAC: This paragraph continues the **Rule Foundation** from above. Note how the writer uses transition words and phrases to connect the rules. 7.6(D).

AREAC: In persuasive documents, shape the **Rule Foundation** so the rules subtly favor your reader. 7.8.

AR<u>E</u>AC: **Explain caselaw.** Ch. 9. After explaining the rules, the reader will benefit from seeing them play out in real life: that's the benefit of a Case Illustration. Be sure to include all five parts so the reader doesn't have to look up the case themselves: topic sentence, citation, facts, holding, and reasoning. Be sure to cite after every sentence to make it easy for the court to find the information in the case.

able to discover the danger and the risk presented upon casual inspection." *Corey v. Davenport College*, 649 N.W.2d 392, 394 (Mich. Ct. App. 2015).

Uncovered black ice is per se not an open and obvious danger in Michigan. *Slaughter v. Blarney Castle Oil Co.*, 760 N.W.2d 287 (Mich. Ct. App. 2008). In *Slaughter*, a woman slipped and fell on black ice in a parking lot while getting out of her truck. The court held that the black ice was not an open and obvious danger. *Id.* at 292.

In coming to this conclusion, the court explained that the very definition of *black ice* as being "nearly invisible" or "nearly transparent" is "inherently inconsistent with the open and obvious danger doctrine." *Id.* The court did note, however, that uncovered black ice could be open and obvious if the surrounding circumstances would lead an average person to casually observe that the area would be slippery. *Id.* The court reasoned that because the invitee in this case could not discern the nearly invisible black ice, it was not open and obvious. *Id.*

AREA<u>A</u>C: **Apply Law.** After explaining the law, immediately apply it. Start with a transition (like *here*) and then the ultimate conclusion. Then prove the conclusion with rule-based reasoning and analogical reasoning. 10.3–10.6.

Here, because Mr. Trout slipped on uncovered black ice just like the plaintiff in *Slaughter*, this Court should deny Buffalo Wild Wings' motion and find that the black ice was not open and obvious. Just like the plaintiff in *Slaughter*, Mr. Trout did not observe any precipitation or note that the sidewalk ramp was icy before his fall. Based upon the black ice that existed on the sidewalk and ramp, Mr. Trout discovered after his fall, Mr. Trout believes that freezing rain fell during the one-half hour that he was present in the restaurant. He noted that when exiting the restaurant, it was not raining or snowing, and he did not observe that the sidewalk or asphalt was icy or wet. So the overall circumstances would not have alerted a reasonable person to slippery conditions.

ARE<u>A</u>C: The nonmoving party in this case must prove that there is an issue of fact, so this writer correctly makes that clear in the topic sentence here. 10.8(F). And then they support it with reasoning. 10.5; 10.6.

Furthermore, there is a genuine issue of material fact about whether the black ice was on a gray sidewalk or black asphalt. The difference is crucial to determining this issue because the holding in *Slaughter* was very particular to black ice on black asphalt. Mr. Trout maintains that the ice was on an incline of black asphalt while Buffalo Wild Wings claims that if there was any ice at all it would have been on a gray sidewalk. This is a significant difference that a jury should decide.

5

(2) SPECIAL ASPECTS: The special aspect of having no alternative pathway around the black ice invoked a duty to warn.

AREAC: Here's another persuasive point heading. Each distinct argument needs a persuasive point heading. Imagine from the court's perspective how helpful it is to read a clear articulation of the argument. 5.4.

As Defendant noted in its brief, special aspects of an open and obvious danger could make it an unreasonable risk, giving rise to a duty to remedy or at least warn. *Lugo*, 629 N.W.2d at 386. Of the two types of special aspects, the only one that applies here is whether the black ice was unavoidable.

AREAC: Each argument gets its own **Rule Foundation**, called a secondary Rule foundation. 7.5.

In *Lugo*, a person broke their ankle after stepping in a pothole. The court said that a pothole is not unavoidable when there is nothing obstructing its presence and when it's a common condition in Michigan. *Id.* at 387.

AREAC: This short Case Illustration does the trick of explaining the rule. 9.7.

Black ice may be avoidable when alternative pathways around it exist. *Walker v. Kilpatrick*, No. 293626, 2011 WL 711146 (Mich. Ct. App. Mar. 1, 2011). In *Walker*, the court found that an invitee who slipped on a driveway could have avoided the icy patches by walking on the snowy lawn. *Id.* at *5. The court reasoned, "While doing so may have been mildly inconvenient, public policy requires that people take reasonable care for their own safety." *Id.*

AREAC: When possible, use two or three cases to illustrate the rule or element at issue. 9.3.

In our case, this Court should find that Buffalo Wild Wings owed a duty to Mr. Trout because the black ice was unavoidable. There was only one way to enter and exit the building, and that one pathway was a sidewalk. That sidewalk is where Mr. Trout slipped. There was no alternative path.

AREAC: **Apply Law**. This begins with a strong rule-based argument. 10.5.

This is unlike the pothole in *Lugo* because the pothole was in the middle of a large, wide-open parking lot. Here, the dangerous black ice covered the only way out of the restaurant. And it's even unlike the black ice in *Walker* because, here, there was not just no other "mildly inconvenient" alternative—there was no alternative at all.

AREAC: **Apply Law**. This analogy to caselaw bolsters the rule-based reasoning above. 10.6(A).

Mr. Trout noted that while the restaurant employed an individual who monitored activities at the entry/exit door, and that this employee advised Mr. Trout to have a good evening, this employee failed, in any way, to remedy the dangerous inclined sidewalk or advise Mr. Trout of the existence of the black ice.

6

AREA**C**: **Conclude.** A simple conclusion ties up the argument with a nice bow. 11.2.

AREAC: A new AREAC argument packet begins here. Ch. 4, 4.6(A).

A**R**EAC: **Give a Rule Foundation.** This Rule Foundation is really brief because only one rule is needed to define this element. 7.5.

AR**E**AC: This Case Illustration fleshes out this rule by giving an example of the element through a story. 9.2. This appears to not have a topic sentence, but that's because the reader simply wants to illustrate the rule in the opening sentence/paragraph.

ARE**A**C: **Apply Law.** This begins with the conclusion you want the judge to agree to. 10.3.

ARE**A**C: **Apply Law.** A quick apples-to-apples analogy. 10.6(A)(1).

AREA**C**: **Conclude.** A simple conclusion ties up the argument with a nice bow. 11.2.

Just like you saw with the other three arguments, this one also uses AREAC structure. The Rule is actually stated in the point heading: no genuine issue of material fact. And the rest of the section is really about analyzing the facts. Adapt the AREAC structure to the argument and the landscape of the law. See 4.5.

Furthermore, the inability to observe the black ice is corroborated by testimony of Wayne Davis. Attached as Exhibit F is an Affidavit of Wayne Davis describing his inability to observe the dangerous condition of the sidewalk/entranceway.

For these reasons, as a matter of law, the black ice was unavoidable.

(3) NOTICE: Buffalo Wild Wings did not know that the sidewalk was slippery because it had been raining, and the temperatures were above freezing.

The plaintiff must demonstrate that "the premises possessor had actual or constructive notice of the dangerous condition at issue." *Lowrey v. LMPS & LMPJ, Inc.*, 890 N.W.2d 344, 349 (Mich. 2016).

In *Clark v. Kmart Corp.*, 634 N.W.2d 347 (Mich. 2001), a store invitee slipped and fell on grapes about an hour after they were spilled on the floor. The Court held that this was sufficient time for the store to discover the hazard.

In this case, Buffalo Wild Wings did have actual notice that the sidewalk was slippery. The temperature was hovering around freezing, and it was raining. That combination in December in Michigan obviously produces slippery conditions.

At the very least, the restaurant had constructive notice, that is, they should have known that ice could form on the sidewalks, ramps, and parking lot. They had roughly the same amount of time—30 minutes to an hour—that the court in *Clark* said was sufficient to put the store on notice.

And, more likely, there is a genuine issue of material fact as to precisely what the conditions were. Mr. Trout admits that there is conflicting information about the weather conditions. So a jury should be allowed to sort out the facts and determine precisely what the conditions were.

(4) CAUSATION: There is at least a genuine issue of material fact as to whether the fall caused Mr. Trout's spinal issues, so this case should proceed to trial to let the jury determine the facts.

Defendant Buffalo Wild Wings argues that the fall did not cause Mr. Trout's injuries. While it is true that Mr. Trout has had medical issues with

7

his spine, the condition complained of here is related only to the spinal cord at the C2 level, and two doctors have said on the record that the fall caused that injury. Because Mr. Trout's and Buffalo Wild Wings' doctors disagree, there is a genuine issue of material fact as to whether the fall caused this injury.

The emergency room medical records from Gratiot Community Hospital noted that Mr. Trout's chief complaint was hand numbness and not back pain. And they needed an MRI to rule out cervical spinal cord injuries, so they sent him to St. Mary's for an MRI examination. The MRI report noted a "cord contusion from recent injury." (Exhibit C.) That recent injury was a result of the fall.

While the report indicated that prior MRI films of Mr. Trout should be reviewed to determine whether the contusion existed contemporaneous with his surgical procedures in April 2018, Mr. Trout's prior medical records and examinations were completely devoid of any reference to a lesion, contusion, or syrinx on his cervical spine.

Furthermore, a neurosurgeon, Dr. Field, opined a month after the accident that, in light of the recent onset of paresthesia in Mr. Trout's hands and myelopathy, that the fall caused the syrinx, and that there is a correlation between the paresthesia and the fall. (Exhibit E.) Dr. Field will be available to present trial testimony substantiating the above opinion.

So there is a genuine issue of material fact regarding causation.

Sometimes, a one-sentence paragraph can be persuasive because it demands so much attention.

At the very least, the fall aggravated dormant injuries. As indicated in his deposition, Mr. Trout, unfortunately, continuously suffers from paresthesia in his hands. His treating physicians have advised him that other than seeking a warmer climate, nothing further can be done medically to improve his condition. In fact, Mr. Trout's physicians have advised him that to resolve his condition, they would have to invade the spinal cord to relieve pressure. The risks of invading the spinal cord are obviously great, and as a result, Mr. Trout could be paralyzed from the neck down. (Deposition of Troy Trout, 85–86, Exhibit A.)

Mr. Trout's day-to-day activities have been dramatically affected by the fall. Since the fall, he continuously experiences numbness and tingling, which radiate into his hands. Furthermore, he has a lack of sensation in the hands. He cannot feel cuts or injuries to his hand unless a laceration is quite deep. Mr. Trout recalled that, on several occasions, he would cut his hand and observe his hand bleeding, but he was not even aware that he had cut himself. Mr. Trout also lacks fine motor skills since the accident and routinely drops items from his hands. He experiences difficulty dressing himself, especially with routine activities such as buttoning shirt collars and sleeves.

While Mr. Trout has attempted to work with hand tools in the building trades industry, he is unable to lift heavy items and fears that his condition may worsen to the point that he will no longer be able to generate an income.

RELIEF REQUESTED

For these reasons, Mr. Trout respectfully requests this Honorable Court to deny Defendant's Motion for Summary Disposition and award to him costs, attorney fees, and any other relief this Court deems equitable.

Respectfully submitted,

HASAN & ABDUL PLLC

Everette P. Hasan

By: Everette P. Hasan, III P97842402
Attorneys for Plaintiff
273 S. Main St.
P.O. Drawer 9928
Grayling, MI 49738 (989) 555-5232
ehas@hasanabdul.com

December 4, 2022

Date and Signature Block. Because the motion is often considered a document that is separate from the brief, you need a date and signature block. Include the information you see here.

9

2.8 Appellate-Court Brief

The preceding two briefs were filed in a state trial court. You can compare those to a federal appellate-court brief here in 2.8. You will notice more similarities than differences.

Here are the document specifications:

Purpose: Persuade an appellate court that the lower court erred.

Mood: Persuasive.

Structure: AREAC (**A**rgument > **R**ule > Caselaw **E**xample > **A**pplication > **C**onclusion. 4.6(A); 5.3)

Audience: Primarily, the court hearing the matter. Secondarily, the court's staff and opposing counsel.

Length: Very case-specific, though most court rules limit briefs to around 20 or 25 pages.

Final format: PDF, hard copy, or both.

Conveyance: Saved in the firm's electronic filing system, filed with the court, and served on opposing counsel.

Caption the Document. Section 14.2 explains how to properly caption a brief. Always go off of an actual caption from the court you're litigating in (i.e., **deconstruct a sample document**, Ch. 3). Make sure your caption looks like the sample document. You can see that this appellate brief has a somewhat different look compared to trial-court briefs.

United States Court of Appeals
for the Sixth Circuit

DETROIT WATER TEAM JOINT VENTURE,
a Michigan Joint Venture,
Plaintiff-Appellee

v.

AGRICULTURAL INSURANCE COMPANY,
an Ohio Corporation,
Defendant-Appellee

and

AMERICAN NATIONAL FIRE INSURANCE COMPANY,
an Ohio Corporation,
Defendant-Appellant.

Title the Document. See section 13.5.

Defendant-Appellant American National
Fire Insurance Company's Brief on Appeal

Table of Contents

Check your court's local court rules for what's required in a brief. But also check local practice by getting your hands on sample briefs filed in that court. In the Sixth Circuit, for example, a table of contents is almost always included.

The same goes for the Table of Authorities: check local court rules and local practice.

Table of Authorities

Cases

iii

Statement Requesting Oral Argument

This appeal presents substantial questions regarding the interpretation of standard, widespread insurance contract language. Given the importance of the rights and obligations at stake, and the number of citizens impacted, Appellant respectfully submits that this Court's decisionmaking process would be aided by oral argument.

This court's local court rule requires this statement. Always check local court rules!

Jurisdiction

The district court had subject-matter jurisdiction under 28 U.S.C. § 1331. This is an appeal from the district court's final judgment entered on October 31, 2022. R.40, J. Appellants timely filed their notice of appeal on November 15, 2022. R.41, Notice of Appeal. This Court has jurisdiction under 28 U.S.C. § 1291.

This court's local court rule requires a statement about jurisdiction. Deconstruct it to figure out its parts. Ch. 3.

Statement of Question Presented

American National's insurance policy excludes liability coverage for claims concerning damage to "that particular part of real property on which" Detroit Water Team "or any . . . subcontractors . . . are performing operations." Detroit Water Team's demolition subcontractor's job included demolishing a reservoir wall that also formed one side of an abutting "manhole" structure. Was the manhole within "that particular part of real property" on which the subcontractor performed operations, thus excluding coverage?

Frame the Issue. The issue is framed here in Garner's deep-issue structure, which uses separate sentences and follows a syllogistic structure of law, fact, and then question. 6.6(D) and 6.7.

By reverse engineering (Ch. 3) briefs from this appellate court, you'll realize that they include a Statement of the Case. As you can see, set the context for the case, introduce the parties, and tell the procedural history of the case.

Statement of the Case

This appeal concerns an insurance-coverage dispute. Plaintiff Detroit Water Team Joint Venture was hired to demolish an old water plant and to build a new one in its place. During the job, Detroit Water's demolition subcontractor demolished a reservoir wall, and a "manhole" structure attached to that wall came down with it. Detroit Water paid $240,000 to restore damaged electrical feeds that had passed through the destroyed manhole. Then Detroit Water sought liability coverage for that amount under a commercial-general-liability (CGL) policy issued by American National. American National denied coverage based on a number of policy exclusions and provisions.

Detroit Water sued American National, alleging that American National wrongfully denied coverage. The parties filed cross motions for summary judgment. The district court held that American National owed coverage to Detroit Water and entered a $240,000 judgment against American National. American National now appeals that decision.

Tell a Story. Start with context. Then tell the story chronologically, emphasizing the legally relevant facts and giving context for them along the way. 12.2. Because this is a persuasive document, shape favorable and unfavorable facts by changing their airtime and placement. 12.4. But always maintain an air of objectivity.
Use headings to emphasize significant plot points. 12.2(D)(4).

Statement of Facts

A. The Detroit Water-Plant Project

Detroit Water Team Joint Venture (Detroit Water) was formed by a number of corporations and joint ventures spanning three states. (R.34, Stipulation, at ¶¶ 1–5.) Its purpose was to contract with the City of Detroit Water & Sewage Department to demolish an old water-treatment plant and to design, construct, manage, and maintain a new water-treatment plant in its place. (*Id.*) Detroit Water's proposal was accepted by the City of Detroit, and it entered into a design-and-build contract with the City. (*Id.* at ¶ 6.)

Cite sources in the Facts. Section 17.7 explains how to create citations to the factual record. It's conventional to put citations to the record in parentheses because it signals these are not primary sources of law.

Detroit Water hired a demolition subcontractor, Adamo Demolition Company, to demolish parts of the old water plant. (*Id.* at ¶ 7.) Adamo's job included substantial demolition of an existing underground reservoir serving the old water plant. (*Id.*) Adamo was to remove the reservoir's concrete roof, supporting columns, and parts of the reservoir's concrete wall. (*Id.*)

1

Detroit Water purchased a CGL insurance policy from American National Fire Insurance Company for the water-plant project. (*Id.* at ¶ 8.) This policy also named Adamo as an additional insured. (*Id.* at ¶ 12.)

B. The July 2, 2020, Loss

Headings in the Facts can help tell the story persuasively. 12.2(D)(4).

Detroit Water divided the project into different phases. During Phase I, it planned to demolish existing facilities that were not essential for operating the old water plant; it also planned to build some new facilities. (*Id.* at ¶ 22.) The Phase I demolition work included Adamo demolishing the reservoir. (*Id.* at ¶ 23.)

By July 2, 2020, Adamo was demolishing a portion of the reservoir's east wall near Manhole 3094. (*Id.* at ¶ 36.) Manhole 3094 was an access formed by abutting a semi-circular masonry structure against the outside of the reservoir's concrete wall. (*Id.* at ¶ 38.) Thus, the reservoir's concrete wall formed one side of Manhole 3094. (*Id.*) On July 2, 2020, and before then, Manhole 3094 was covered with soil. (*Id.*)

Manhole 3094 allowed workers to gain access to the electrical feeds and control wires that passed through it. (*Id.* at ¶ 37.) Within Manhole 3094 were live electrical feeds, control wires, and air lines that provided electrical power to electrical equipment inside the old water plant's low-lift pump station (and other buildings). (*Id.* at ¶ 39.) Outside Manhole 3094, the electrical feeds, control wires, and air lines were encased by "duct banks." (*Id.*)

Adamo's demolition of the reservoir's wall brought down the portion of the reservoir wall that formed one side of Manhole 3094. (*Id.* at ¶ 40.) When that wall came down, so did the rest of Manhole 3094, which collapsed in its entirety. (*Id.*) Moreover, some of the electrical feeds, control wires, and air lines located inside Manhole 3094 were severed. (*Id.*)

Tell a Story. Ch. 12. The writer is using several paragraph breaks on this page to help the reader, and this also creates more topic sentences to highlight important information. 12.2(D)(2).

Detroit Water's internal memorandums raise questions about whether Adamo intentionally demolished Manhole 3094 in its entirety while tearing down the reservoir's east wall. A July 2, 2020, memo to the Detroit Water file, drafted by Irving Schuraytz, reflects that Mr. Schuraytz "was informed by an electrical worker that the manhole contained abandoned communications cable that was no longer in service." (R.38, Exhibit 4 of

Tell a Story. When citing the factual record, you may wonder whether the period should go within or outside the closing parenthesis. Either way is acceptable; just be consistent. Contrast to the citations in the Facts sections of the briefs in 2.6 and 2.7.

2

American National's MSJ, at 1.) Mr. Schuraytz also wrote that "Larry Dixon had previously stated the steam manhole could be demolished because it was against the reservoir wall." (*Id.*)

Another memorandum, drafted by Eneise Breaux, corroborated this. It stated, "Irving brought up the subject of the manhole along the east wall and he was told that everything along that wall has been disconnected." (R.38, Exhibit 5 of American National MSJ.)

After Manhole 3094 was destroyed, Detroit Water quickly designed and constructed a new, temporary power supply for the old water plant. (R.34, Stipulation at ¶ 43.) It installed new above-ground conduit, new electrical feeds, new control wires, and new air lines from "upstream" Manhole 3093 to the low-lift pump station. (*Id.*) These repairs were temporary; none of it would be incorporated into the final design of the new water plant. (*Id.*)

C. *Detroit Water's Claim for Liability Coverage*

Detroit Water notified American National (and its builder's risk insurer) of the July 2 loss. (R.34, Stipulation at ¶ 44.) American National denied the claim based on the policy provisions that it continues to rely on in this lawsuit. (*Id.* at ¶ 45; *see also* R.1, Complaint attachments.)

D. *Procedural History*

Detroit Water sued American National, as well as its builder's risk insurer, Agricultural Insurance Company, after its claims were denied. (R.1, Complaint.) Defendant Agricultural Insurance Company removed the case to the United States District Court for the Eastern District of Michigan based on diversity jurisdiction.

The parties engaged in discovery concerning the events surrounding the July 2, 2020, loss (as well as the May 1, 2020, loss that is no longer at issue), but the district court eventually entered an order suspending discovery on nondispositive issues, anticipating dispositive motions on the coverage issue. (*See* R.32, Order.) The parties later stipulated to certain facts and submitted the stipulation to the district court. (R.34, Stipulation).

3

Note that the headings are formatted differently to show their hierarchy. 12.2(D)(4). Consider the formatting rules in 5.4(G).

1. The Parties' Cross Motions for Summary Judgment

As anticipated, the parties then filed cross motions for summary judgment. American National argued that Exclusions 2.j.(5) barred coverage. This exclusion essentially bars coverage for claims concerning property damage caused by the insured or its subcontractor to the particular part of real property on which it was performing operations. American National asserted that Manhole 3094 was included within the particular part of the real property on which Detroit Water's demolition subcontractor was performing operations—especially considering that the east reservoir wall that Adamo was demolishing formed one side of the manhole structure.

2. The District Court's Decision

The Honorable Robert H. Cleland of the United States District Court for the Eastern District of Michigan heard oral arguments on the cross motions; he then issued a written opinion granting Detroit Water's motion for summary judgment against American National and denying American National's motion for summary judgment. (*See* R.93, Hearing TR; see also R.68, 10/31/22 Opinion.)

Judge Cleland rejected American National's argument that business risk exclusions 2.j.(5) precluded coverage for damage to Manhole 3094. He concluded that "despite the unity in structure between the Reservoir and Manhole," the "only evidence" was that the demolition subcontractor did not intend to damage the wiring or conduits within the manhole, and that this was "precisely the type of injury for which third-party liability insurance is procured." (*Id.* at 24.) Judge Cleland noted that to the extent his conclusion was "contrary to that" of the United States District Court for the Western District of Michigan in *Oscar W. Larson Company v. United Capital Insurance Company*, 845 F. Supp. 451 (W.D. Mich. 1993), he "disagree[d] with that holding." (R.68, 10/31/22 Opinion at 24 n5.)

American National now appeals the district court's judgment.

Summary of Argument

American National did not owe liability coverage to Detroit Water for a potential claim concerning the collapse of Manhole 3094 or for damage

4

Preview the Analysis. Ch. 16. Early on in the document, give away the answer. That helps the reader get oriented to the Argument section and analyze what's to come. Be sure that you don't skimp on summarizing the reasoning because that is especially helpful to orienting the reader on your case.

This is a standalone analysis preview. See 16.4.

to electrical feeds, control wires, or air lines within Manhole 3094. Exclusion 2.j.(5) of the American National policy excluded coverage for claims related to property damage to "that particular part of real property on which you or any contractors or subcontractors . . . are performing operations, if the 'property damage' arises out of those operations." Therefore, coverage is excluded if the manhole structure was within "that particular part of real property" on which the demolition subcontractor was performing operations. It was. It is undisputed that the demolition subcontractor's job encompassed pulling down a concrete wall that formed one side of the manhole structure. The trial court erred in concluding otherwise and should be reversed.

Give a Rule Foundation. Ch. 7. This Rule Foundation is particular to just the standard of review for deciding an appeal. See 7.9 to learn how to create one.

Standard of Review

"This Court reviews a district court's grant of summary judgment de novo." *Davis v. McCourt*, 226 F.3d 506, 511 (6th Cir. 2000). Moreover, the Court "review[s] de novo the district court's interpretation of an insurance contract." *Parameter Driven Software v. Massachusetts Bay Ins. Co.*, 25 F.3d 332, 336 (6th Cir. 1994).

American National argued that exclusion 2.j.(5) precluded coverage in its motion for summary judgment and its brief opposing plaintiff's cross-motion for summary judgment. (See R.38, American National's MSJ and Brief, at 2, 7–14; R.57, American National's Brief Opposing SJ, at 8–9). Therefore, this issue was properly preserved in the district court for appellate review.

AREAC: State the argument in a persuasive point heading. 5.4. This is a global point heading because it states the global argument that encompasses everything to come in the Argument section. 5.4(C).

Argument

Detroit Water is not entitled to coverage because Exclusion 2.j.(5) of the American National Policy excludes coverage for claims concerning damage to "that particular part of real property."

Preview the Analysis. Ch. 16. These next two paragraphs give an *internal* overview of what arguments are to come. 16.5. This gives the answer to the judge and structure for the following analysis. Yes, you already included a preview in the Summary of the Argument. This section is here because there's a long Argument section and the reader may or may not have read the Summary.

The trial court erred in holding that exclusion 2.j.(5) of the American National CGL policy does not apply. Exclusion 2.j.(5) precludes coverage for claims concerning property damage to "that particular part of real property" on which Detroit Water's subcontractors were performing operations if the property damage arose out of those operations.

5

Detroit Water's subcontractor's demolition work included demolishing a concrete wall that formed one side of Manhole 3094, so that manhole structure was within "that particular part of real property" on which Detroit Water's demolition subcontractor was performing operations. Therefore, the trial court erred in refusing to enforce exclusion 2.j.(5) and should be reversed.

You may wonder why there's no global Rule Foundation here. You'll learn in 4.6(E) that you should tie together multiple AREAC packets with an Analysis Preview or a global Rule Foundation. But include a *global* Rule Foundation only when it ties the AREAC packets together. Below, the issues discussed in the separate AREAC packets are not based on the same rules of law, so there's no need to tie them together for the reader.

A. Michigan law controls and dictates that unambiguous exclusions must be enforced as written.

AREAC: **Give a Rule Foundation**. Ch. 7. This entire section A is a Rule Foundation. There are a lot of rules behind the arguments that follow, so the writer chose to put them all in one section. Chunking rules of law can help the reader better understand how everything relates, and it makes learning the law more manageable.

The district court applied Michigan law in deciding the parties' cross motions for summary disposition, and the parties have not disputed the applicability of Michigan law in this diversity case. (*See, e.g.*, R. 68, Opinion at 14, 16, 26, 27, 30).

Michigan has long recognized that clear insurance policies should be enforced as written—including policy exclusions. Where an insurance contract is clear, "a court will enforce its terms and will not rewrite it." *Auto Club v. Lozanis*, 546 N.W.2d 648, 651 (Mich. Ct. App. 1996). And where an insurance-contract term is not ambiguous, "the trial court must enforce it as written." *Royce v. Citizens Insurance*, 557 N.W.2d 144, 147 (Mich. Ct. App. 1996).

Exclusions, like other terms in an insurance contract, must be enforced as written. *Allstate v. Freeman*, 443 N.W.2d 734 (Mich. 1986). It is entirely proper for an insurance company to limit the risks it assumes and to fix its premiums accordingly. *Scanlon v. Western Fire*, 144 N.W.2d 677 (Mich. Ct. App. 1966). "Clear and specific exclusions must be given effect." *Pacific Insurance v. Michigan Mutual*, 549 N.W.2d 872, 875 (Mich. 1996).

Coverage under a policy "is lost if any exclusion applies to an insured's particular claim.... It is impossible to hold an insurance company liable for a risk it did not assume." *McGuirk v. Meridian Mutual*, 559 N.W.2d 93, 96 (Mich. Ct. App. 1996). Clear exclusions "may have the effect of frustrating the abstract coverage wishes and desires of policyholders," but that "cannot be viewed as frustrating their reasonable expectations" of coverage. *Id.* at 98, n. 1.

6

Determining the "reasonable expectations" of the insured depends on "reading the contract language." *Powers v. DAIIE*, 398 N.W.2d 411, 424 (Mich. 1986). And the "insured is held to a knowledge of the conditions of his policy" as he would with any other contract or agreement. *House v. Billman*, 66 N.W.2d 213, 216 (Mich. 1954).

Although ambiguities in an insurance contract are interpreted against the insurer that drafted it, courts are not quick to find ambiguities. "If a policy, though inartfully worded or clumsily arranged, fairly admits of but one interpretation, it may not be said to be ambiguous or fatally unclear." *Raaska v. Farm Bureau Mutual*, 314 N.W.2d 440, 441 (Mich. 1982). A policy may initially appear confusing, but that does not mean that it is ambiguous. *Id.* at 441.

AREAC: State the argument in a persuasive point heading. 5.4. In persuasive documents like briefs, persuasive point headings play a crucial role in clearly stating the argument.

B. Exclusion 2.j.(5) precludes coverage for claims concerning damage to that "particular part of real property" because the manhole and reservoir wall are the same and cannot be artificially dissected into separate parts to find coverage.

Exclusion 2.j.(5) of the American National CGL policy precludes coverage for damage to the particular part of real property on which Detroit Water's subcontractors were performing operations if the damage arose out of those operations:

AREAC: This is a secondary Rule Foundation that pertains only to this subissue. 7.5.

2. Exclusions

This insurance does not apply to:

* * *

j. Damage to Property

* * *

(5) that particular part of real property on which you or any contractors or subcontractors working directly or indirectly on your behalf are performing operations, if the "property damage" arises out of those operations; ...

(R.34, CGL Policy, Exhibit A to Stipulation, at 4.)

Michigan's appellate courts have not yet considered the scope of Exclusion 2.j.(5). But at least one federal district court applying Michigan law has, and that court recognized that an insured cannot plausibly deny that it has performed operations on a particular part of real property where it has "dug into, drilled, moved or disturbed" the property during its construction work. *Oscar W. Larson Co. v. United Capital Ins. Co.*, 845 F. Supp. 451 (W.D. Mich. 1993). In *Larson*, a supermarket hired a contractor to install underground field-distribution systems. The supermarket intended to create an environmentally secure gasoline-delivery system, but after the contractor finished the job, the supermarket discovered that gasoline was leaking into the soil and ground water. It alleged that the contractor performed its work incorrectly, causing the leaks. The contractor's liability insurer denied coverage based, in part, on Exclusion 2.j.(5), and the contractor sued its insurer, seeking coverage.

AREAC: Give examples of the element or rule by explaining caselaw. Note the strong topic sentence to begin this full Case Illustration. Ch. 9. A good topic sentence advances the thought by stating new information. After the topic sentence, give the citation, facts, holding, and reasoning.

Applying Michigan law, the United States District Court for the Western District of Michigan held that Exclusion 2.j.(5) did include the contractor's work on the pipe and the surrounding soil. *Id.* at 456. In adopting a broad interpretation of the exclusion's language, "that particular part of real property," the court reasoned that the property and piping was part of a system, and the coverage excluded operations where the contractor "dug into, drilled, moved, or disturbed in the construction of the system." *Id.* at 455.

When applied in the present case, the *Larson* analysis compels a finding that Exclusion 2.j.(5) applies, precluding coverage for damage to pieces of Manhole 3094 that were undeniably "dug into," "moved" or "disturbed" during Detroit Water's subcontractor's demolition work. It is undisputed that Manhole 3094 was destroyed when the subcontractor demolished the reservoir and manhole's common wall. Even if the reservoir and manhole's wall were not adjacent—which they were—they were still part of the same system that was "dug into, ... moved, or disturbed." *Id.* That satisfies the *Larson* "moved or disturbed" test.

AREAC: Chapter 10 explains how to do legal reasoning. And 10.3 in particular shows how to organize it.

Notice how on this page and the next every topic sentence states an actual argument. Nowhere in the Rule Application does the writer merely state fact or merely state law. They always apply the law. 10.8.

This paragraph is also a great example of reasoning by analogy. 10.6.

Federal and state courts throughout the country have taken the same view as *Larson*, resisting insureds' attempts to avoid Exclusion 2.j.(5) by artificially dissecting "that particular part of real property." For instance, in *Vinsant Electrical Contractors v. Aetna Casualty and Surety Co.*, 530 S.W.2d 76 (Tenn. 1975), the insured was hired to install two circuit breakers in a

8

AREAC: Give examples of the element or rule by explaining caselaw. Ch. 9. This argument section is a good example of the integrated style where the writer logically organizes it to progress through arguments while both explaining the law and applying it.

shopping-mall switchboard. One of the insured's workmen dropped a wrench that came into contact with two "buss" bars. *Id.* at 76. This produced a short that caused the entire switchboard to explode. The insured sought liability coverage, arguing that its work only encompassed the installation of two circuit breakers and that it was not performing operations on the entire switchboard.

The Tennessee Supreme Court rejected the insured's attempt to construe exclusion 2.j.(5) to apply only to the precise and isolated spot on which its work was being done:

See 17.8(E) for the proper way to format a block quotation.

> [T]he switchboard, in its entirety, or as a unit, is "that particular part" of the property "upon which operations are being performed." We cannot so construe this provision as to limit the exclusion to the precise and isolated spot on which work was being done. Such a construction would lead to illogical and absurd results and would completely nullify the intent of the endorsement. An exclusion so limited could well result in being, in practical effect, no exclusion at all. Such would abort the whole purpose of the exclusion. It was designed to liberalize but not liquidate the exclusion.

Id. at 78.

Likewise, in *William Crawford Inc. v. Travelers Insurance Co.*, 838 F. Supp. 157 (S.D. N.Y. 1993), the court rejected the insured's attempt to limit "that particular part of real property" on which it was "performing operations" to certain rooms in a spacious, 7,000 square-foot apartment so that it would be covered for claims concerning property damage to other parts of the apartment.

The insured in *Crawford* was a general contractor that took on a three-year job to renovate the entire luxury apartment. It ran into problems while plastering the apartment's living room and library because those rooms were not adequately humidified, but its steam humidifier could only reach the apartment's foyer. So the insured used electric fans to blow the steam from the foyer into the other rooms in the apartment. One of the fans caused a fire that damaged the entrance area—and also caused smoke damage throughout the apartment.

The court held that the exclusion's language broadly applied to include not only the foyer where the fire was but the entire apartment. *Id.* at 159. The court came to this conclusion by observing that courts in other jurisdictions do not, when applying the exclusion language, isolate the damage narrowly to just where work is being performed. *Id.* Rather, the court seemed to find that the exclusion language where "operations are being performed" should be more broadly interpreted. *Id.*

In a number of other cases, insureds unsuccessfully tried to avoid exclusion 2.j.(5) where they had not intended to affect certain parts of real property in the course of their work but nevertheless damaged it while working nearby. For example, in *Utility Maintenance Contractors Inc. v. West American Ins. Co.*, 866 P.2d 1093 (Kan. Ct. App. 1994), the insured was hired to clear a blocked sewer line. The insured determined that tree roots had obstructed a particular portion of the sewer pipe about 115 feet from the manhole access point, but that the rest of the pipe was in good condition and without any blockages.

After the insured inserted a water-jet root cutter into the sewer line and removed the obstruction, a video camera revealed that a bolt had fallen off the root cutter during the procedure and damaged about 160 feet of good pipe. The city demanded that the insured immediately repair and replace the damaged sewer line, and the insured sought liability coverage.

Once again, the court rejected the insured's attempt to isolate "that particular part of real property" on which it was performing operations to the precise location of the intended repair, instead concluding "that the sewer pipe and the clog point should be viewed as a whole." *Id.* at 1097. Therefore, the court held that Exclusion 2.j.(5) precluded coverage for damage to the entire 115 feet of sewer between the manhole access and the clog site. *Id.* The court noted that even damage to the sewer line beyond the clog site "may be excluded by section 2.j.(5)" depending on whether the facts elicited on remand showed that it was the usual and necessary practice to use the cutter beyond the initial clog point. *Id.* at 1098.

These cases reflect a national view that courts should construe Exclusion 2.j.(5)'s "that particular part of real property" term broadly according to its plain meaning. When identifying the part of the real

AR**E**AC: After explaining a lot of caselaw, it can be very helpful to the reader to synthesize the best parts. This clarifies what the reader should focus on. This paragraph is an example of a "synthesis paragraph." 9.9(B)(3).

property an insured was working on when the loss occurred, courts must not artificially dissect or partition that property to expand a liability insurer's contractual coverage obligation.

AREA**C**: Apply the Law. Ch. 10.

In the present case, the demolition of the concrete reservoir falls within Exclusion 2.j.(5). The reservoir wall formed one side of Manhole 3094, so it is "that particular part of real property" in a literal sense. As recognized in *all* cases cited above, such an artificial dissection of "that particular part of real property" is at odds with the plain language of exclusion 2.j.(5). Because the wall and the manhole shared the same wall of concrete, the same elements, it would be "absurd" to say that they are separate entities. *See Vinsant*, 530 S.W.2d at 78.

Just as two circuit breaks cannot be separated from an electrical panel, a foyer cannot be dissected from an apartment, and a clogged portion of a pipe cannot be separated from the entire pipe, two construction elements that share the same wall cannot be separated from each other.

Even if the reservoir wall and the manhole were adjacent, they would be part of the same system. The demolition subcontractor was performing operations on Manhole 3094 when it tore down the reservoir wall that formed one of Manhole 3094's sides and caused the remaining portions of Manhole 3094 to collapse. Such cause-and-effect conduct shows that Manhole 3094 cannot be dissected in piecemeal fashion to find coverage for claims concerning damage to some parts of it, but not other parts. Manhole 3094, and the entire reservoir wall for that matter, "should be viewed as a whole." *Utility Maintenance*, 866 P.2d at 1097.

AREA**C**: The writer ties up the analysis by restating the conclusion. This is an *internal* conclusion because it's part of an AREAC packet and separate from the document conclusion below. 11.2.

For these reasons, the trial court's decision should be reversed, with instructions that summary judgment be granted on American National's behalf. Alternatively, summary judgment in Detroit Water's favor was inappropriate given lingering factual questions concerning whether its subcontractor intended to demolish Manhole 3094, in its entirety, while performing its demolition work. If the trier-of-fact determines that the demolition subcontractor intended to take down the entire manhole structure, then it was "performing operations" on *all* portions of Manhole 3094, and that coverage is therefore barred.

11

Relief Requested

Defendant-Appellant American National Fire Insurance Company asks the Court to reverse the district court's grant of summary judgment in plaintiff's favor, and to order the district court to instead grant summary judgment on American National's behalf. In the alternative, American National asks the Court to remand the case for a trial on the disputed factual questions.

January 17, 2023

By: ____________________
Your Name
Attorney for Appellant American National Fire Insurance Company
8475 Grant Ave.
Detroit, Michigan
(317) 555-9038
lawyers@insurance.com

Conclude and Recommend. For briefs, simply write the relief requested here. You may state in a phrase the overall conclusion, but do not rehash any reasoning. Keep it simple and to the point. 11.4.

Checklist for Appellate-Court Brief

Caption Your Document

Did you:

___ include the court name at the top, the parties on the left, and the case number and judge on the right? (Or make it look like a typical caption in your jurisdiction.) 14.2(B).

___ use consistent typography, especially with the parties, so there are consistent line spaces between the parts? 14.2(B)(2).

___ punctuate the parties correctly? 14.2(B)(2).

Title Your Document

Did you:

___ write a title directly below the caption? 13.5.

___ follow the accepted formatting convention for your court? 13.5.

Use Document Headings

In looking at the entire document as a whole, did you:

___ include the appropriate whole-document headings? Ch. 3; 15.2.

___ bold and center each heading or otherwise set it off as a heading? 15.2.

___ use headings in the Argument section *where necessary* to separate different issues? 5.4.

Table of Contents

Did you:

___ include all the brief's major headings and every persuasive point heading in the Argument section?

___ use your word processor's automated features to create the dot leader and right-aligned page numbers?

___ check that the page numbers perfectly line up vertically? (Note: the only way to do this is to use your word processor's automated features.)

Table of Authorities

Did you:

___ include every legal authority in your brief?

___ organize the authority by constitutional provisions, statutes, caselaw, and secondary authority? Include only the categories you need.

___ use your word processor's automated features to create the dot leader and right-aligned page numbers?

___ use *passim* instead of page numbers when the source is used on more than five pages?

___ check that the page numbers perfectly line up vertically? (Note: the only way to do this is to use your word processor's automated features.)

Request for Oral Argument

Did you:

___ deconstruct the parts of a Request for Oral Argument and include those parts in your document? Ch. 3.

___ explain persuasively why an oral argument is justified?

Statement of Jurisdiction

Did you:

___ deconstruct the parts of a Statement of Jurisdiction for your court? Ch. 3.
___ make a clear statement explaining why the court has jurisdiction to hear the matter?
___ cite legal authority?

Frame the Issue (Question Presented)

Did you:

___ follow either the single-sentence or deep-issue format? 6.6.
___ enumerate the issue statement if you have more than one? (You'll mirror the same enumeration in the Summary of the Argument and in the global point headings in the Argument section.) 4.7(D); 5.3(A)(1).
___ include just the right amount of information for each part, neither framing the issue too narrowly or too broadly? 6.6(B)–(D).
___ in the facts portion, ensure that they are grammatically parallel? 6.6(B)(4).
___ in the facts portion, tell a brief, chronological story including only significantly relevant facts? 6.6(B)(4).
___ make the symmetry between the law clause and the question clause clear (i.e., if you stated a rule for negligence, then the question is likewise about negligence)?
___ ensure that the entire sentence is readable and hangs together?
___ end the sentence with a question mark?

Statement of the Case

Did you:

___ deconstruct the parts of a Statement of the Case for your court? Ch. 3.
___ begin with the type of case?
___ introduce the parties early in the statement?
___ tell the brief factual story?
___ briefly summarize the case's litigation history?
___ conclude with a statement of who is appealing?

Tell a Story (Facts)

In your Facts section, did you:

___ include legally significant, background, and emotional facts? 12.2(A).
___ include even unfavorable facts? 12.2(A)(1).
___ begin with contextual information that introduces the parties and the broad issue? 12.2(B).
___ prefer to organize the facts chronologically? 12.2(C)(1).
___ avoid organizing the facts according to which document you got them from? 12.2(C)(1).
___ where appropriate, organize the facts by each character's perception (i.e., where characters disagree on the facts)? 12.2(C)(3).
___ consider using headings for longer, more complex factual statements? 12.2(D)(4).
___ use lots of paragraphs, averaging three to five per page? 12.2(D)(2).

___ use names, not role designations like *plaintiff* or *customer*? 12.2(D)(3).

___ make your story persuasive? 12.4.

Preview the Analysis (Summary of Arguments)

Did you:

___ overall follow the four-part syllogism (conclusion, core rule, reasoning, and conclusion)? 16.4(A); 16.4(C)(3).

___ conclude by stating how the court erred? 16.4(C)(3).

___ if you have more than one Question Presented, enumerate the paragraphs in the Summary of Arguments so they mirror the enumeration in the Questions Presented?

Standard of Review

Did you:

___ state the correct standard of review? 7.9.

___ cite binding authority for the standard? 7.9.

Use Document Headings (Persuasive Point Headings)

Beginning with this section of the checklist, the skills pertain to writing the Argument section. Throughout the Argument section, did you:

___ clearly state each argument in a persuasive point heading? 5.3; 5.4.

___ properly format each heading as a (1) bolded sentence (2) that is single-spaced (3) with sentence capitalization and (4) ends with a period? 5.4(E).

___ ensure that each point heading is an argument with (1) an assertion and (2) a reason? 5.4(D).

___ ensure that the entire sentence is readable and hangs together?

___ enumerate your headings? 5.4(G).

___ avoid enumerating just one heading at a level (i.e., you can't have a 1. if you don't have a 2.)? 5.4(G).

___ format headings at different levels to give visual clues of the arguments' hierarchy? 5.4(G).

Preview the Analysis (Internal Style)

After the Global Point Heading but before the Global Rule Foundation, did you:

___ consider adding an internal analysis preview? 16.5. This is especially helpful when you have more than one AREAC packet; it can help tie them together. 4.6(E).

Give a Rule Foundation

When teaching the court the controlling legal rules, did you:

___ if writing multiple subissues, include one global Rule Foundation and, for each subissue, a secondary Rule Foundation? 4.6(E); 7.5.

___ synthesize the relevant rules, whether from codified law, caselaw, or both, *before* illustrating them with caselaw? 7.1–7.6(D).

___ teach the reader the rules of law in a logical, step-by-step sequence, and didn't rush it? For example, you started by teaching the broadest rule and ended with the narrowest rule. You taught general rules before teaching exceptions to those rules. 7.1–7.6.

___ if appropriate, refine the issue by focusing the reader on just the elements that are at issue? 7.3.

___ prefer paraphrasing when possible? 7.6(E).

___ include a citation to binding legal authority for each rule? Ch. 17.

Explain Codified Law

When explaining codified law, whether in the Rule Foundation or elsewhere, did you:

___ place codified law before caselaw? 8.2(A).

___ help the reader make sense of codified law by explaining its elements? 8.2(B)–(C).

___ include the essential elements and important contextual information? 8.2(C).

___ where applicable, cohesively synthesize several statutory provisions? 8.2(E).

___ prefer paraphrasing? 8.2(D).

___ quote unique language that cannot be paraphrased? 8.2(D).

___ cite a source for each rule? 17.2–17.3; 17.6.

Explain Caselaw

___ Did you include two or three Case Illustrations or one directly on-point Case Illustration? 9.3.

___ Does each Case Illustration have a topic sentence, a citation, the case's facts, the court's holding, and the court's reasoning? 9.4.

Case Illustration > *Topic Sentence*

In the topic sentence of your Case Illustration, did you:

___ transition from the preceding paragraph by showing how the case fits into the big picture? 9.4(A)(1).

___ avoid starting with a source of law? Instead, cite the source after the topic sentence. 9.4(B).

___ state a new point that you have not yet stated in the Rule Foundation? 9.4(A)(2).

___ give a substantive point rather than merely announcing the topic you're going to address? 9.4(A)(3).

___ where appropriate, create an implicit rule from the case where it may not be immediately clear from the specifics of the case how it could apply to the client's matter? 9.4(A)(3)(b).

___ avoid cramming too much information into the topic sentence? Although your topic sentence is a helpful transition/preview for your reader, it can include only so much information.

Case Illustration > ***Citation***

Immediately after the topic sentence, did you:

___ cite a case for the source of the topic sentence, whether it be explicit or implicit? 9.4(B); 17.4.

___ follow ALWD or Bluebook rules for formatting the citation? Ch. 17.

___ put the citation in a separate citation sentence? 9.4(B).

Case Illustration > ***Case Facts***

When explaining the facts of the precedent case, did you:

___ capture the story to teach your reader what happened in the case you're writing about? 9.4(C).

___ give contextual information that sets the stage for the story? 9.4(C).

___ include the legally significant facts (i.e., the ones used in the court's reasoning)? 9.4(C)(1).

___ avoid unnecessary information like names, dates, party arguments, and lower-court procedure unless they directly relate to your issue? 9.4(C)(2).

___ if writing about a civil case, use informative status words to identify the parties and other "characters" in the story (like *tenant* and *landlord* or *buyer* and *seller*), rather than using their actual names or party designations like *plaintiff* or *defendant*? 9.4(C)(3).

___ if writing about a criminal case, use *the defendant* to refer to the person charged with the crime, which is informative to readers? But for other people, you've tried to come up with informative status words, such as *witness, victim, accuser, arresting officer, police officer, companion, prosecutor,* etc. 9.4(C)(3).

Case Illustration > ***Court's Holding***

When writing about the court's holding in a Case Illustration, did you:

___ give the court's actual decision rather than state a pure rule of law or give only the ultimate procedural outcome like *affirmed* or *reversed*? 9.4(D).

___ state the global holding and any secondary holdings on your issue? 9.4(D).

___ ensure that the holding addresses the narrow issue you're writing about? 9.4(D).

Case Illustration > ***Court's Reasoning***

When summarizing the court's reasoning in a Case Illustration, did you:

___ give *details* about why the court decided the case the way it did? If the court decided multiple *relevant* subissues, you've quickly explained the court's reasoning for each of those subissues, and you've done that in a logical sequence, with signposts to help your reader follow along. 9.4(E).

___ avoid restating the rules the court applied? Rather, put the rules either in the Rule Foundation or in the Case Illustration's topic sentence. 9.4(E).

Case Synthesis

If you've given more than one Case Illustration for a single issue, did you:

___ create coherence among the cases by using the trophy, rubber-band, or paragraph-synthesis method? 9.9(B).

___ apply the checklist in 9.11 for *synthesizing* caselaw?

Apply Law

When applying the law to our client's facts, did you:

- ___ start a new paragraph and use an appropriate transition? 10.3(A).

  E.g.:

  Here, …

  In our case, …

  In the present case, …

  In Ms. Hanni's case, …

- ___ after the transition, write an informative topic sentence announcing your global conclusion you want the court to agree with? 10.3(B).
- ___ after the global conclusion, clearly state an argument? 10.3(C).
- ___ after clearly stating an argument, prove the argument with rule-based and analogical reasoning? 10.3(D); 10.5; 10.6.
- ___ repeat an Argument-and-Proof combo for each argument? 10.3(E).
- ___ begin every paragraph after the first one with a clear topic sentence that states a legal argument and doesn't merely rehash law or facts? 10.8(F).
- ___ pass the two-question test in 10.4(B) to ensure you're actually applying law? See also 10.8(C).
- ___ weave in counterarguments where appropriate? 10.3(D)(3).
- ___ analogize to caselaw in meaningful, strategic places where it helps support a specific point? 10.7(C).
- ___ analogize to caselaw in meaningful ways by using one or a variety of the nine techniques explained in 10.6(A)?
- ___ avoid false comparisons? ("Like the *Jones* case, Mary Smith did not …."—*Jones* is a case, but Mary is a human being.) 10.7(E).
- ___ avoid organizing your analysis by case? 10.8(D).
- ___ signal closure of your analysis? ("Thus, …" "Therefore, …" "So …"). 10.3(F); 11.2.

Conclude and Recommend (Conclusion)

In the Conclusion, did you:

- ___ state the global conclusion? 11.4.
- ___ state the relief you seek from the court? 11.4.
- ___ avoid rehashing any of the reasoning? If so, delete it. 11.4.

Quoting

Throughout the brief, did you:

- ___ insert quotation marks around verbatim language if you lifted exact language from another source? Four or more consecutive substantive words from a source constitute a phrase that requires quoting. 18.5(C); 7.6(E).
- ___ properly format a block quotation? If you've written a block quotation (quotation of 50 words or more), which you should do only sparingly, you've followed conventional rules. 17.8(E).

___ avoid using quotation marks for paraphrased information? If you have paraphrased the court's (or other source's) language, you do not need to insert quotation marks, but you still need to cite the source after the sentence to show your reader where you got the idea from. 7.6(E).

___ cite a source after every quotation? 17.2; 7.6(E).

Use Standard Document Format and Pagination

In setting up the whole document, did you:

___ double-space the text but not the caption, signature blocks, or point headings?

___ use 1" margins on all sides?

___ use a professional font (e.g., Calibri, Times New Roman, Arial, or their ilk)? 18.4(C).

___ include page numbers (no page number on the cover page; Roman numerals beginning with the Table of Contents; Arabic numerals beginning with the Statement of Facts)? 18.4(A)(2).

Revise and Edit

Use Enticing Typography

Throughout the document, did you:

___ ensure that the document's typography (the layout of information, white space) is consistent with professional standards? 18.4.

___ ensure that each *heading* in the same level throughout the document has consistent spacing before and after the heading? Usually put more space before each heading than after it. 18.4(D).

___ use the same amount of space after and before each *paragraph*? 18.4(E).

___ consistently space first-line indents? (Note: You may choose to use a modern block style without indents; in that case, add more line space between paragraphs to set off each paragraph.) 18.4(F).

___ consistently use one or two spaces after a period? 18.4(H).

___ consistently use curved quotation marks and apostrophes (as opposed to straight ones you get when pasting from the internet)? 18.4(I).

Use Guru Grammar

Before submitting the final document, did you:

___ edit the final draft for punctuation and grammar? 18.5.

___ use quotation marks (" ") whenever you lifted exact, verbatim language from a case or statute (with a post-sentence citation)? 18.5(C).

___ avoid quoting/paraphrasing from—or citing to—a case's synopsis or headnotes (which are not part of the court's actual opinion but rather are supplied by the publisher's staff)?

Ensure Rad Readability

Throughout the document, did you:

___ remember that you are a teacher on the page? (Whether writing a short memo, a brief to an appellate court, or a law-school essay answer, great lawyers and law students are always teachers, striving to make the complex as clear and simple as possible. That's very hard to do, but it's always the goal.) 18.6.

___ create new paragraphs to avoid intimidating walls of dense, unbroken text? 18.4(E), (F). The goal is three to five paragraphs per page.

___ write in a confident and direct style while avoiding legalese or unnecessarily inflated language? (In other words, you avoided the lawyer tics and plodding, stilted prose that plague so many of the cases you've read in your casebooks.) 18.6.

___ create a well-organized, cohesive message?

Ensure Sightly Citations

When explaining the law, did you:

___ cite every rule of law the first time you stated it? 17.2.

___ use a full citation the first time you cited a source? 17.3.

___ cite after every sentence in a Case Illustration (except for perhaps the facts) and include a pinpoint page number? 17.2.

___ use *Id.* whenever possible, but only after giving the full citation? 17.3.

___ include "at" and a page number for each *Id.* citation? 17.3; 17.4(A)(2).

___ use a short citation when appropriate? 17.3.

___ include the right content, punctuate it correctly, and get the spacing right for each citation? 17.4–17.6.

Final Edits

Before submitting the document, did you:

___ save it as a PDF?

___ print the document after saving it as a PDF and proofread it one more time, even though you were sick of it? (This step is important because sometimes the format changes in the conversion from a word-processing document to a PDF.)

Chapter Three

Deconstruct Sample Documents

3.1 The Skill

You won't learn in law school how to write every document that you'll have to create in the practice of law. Instead, you need to learn the skill of deconstructing a document to identify its components and then reconstructing it for your current client.

When you are in the madman and architect stages of writing—those initial stages, you need to have in mind what the final document should look like. If you don't already know, you'll call on this skill of deconstructing and reconstructing to create the right kind of document for your client.

To recreate any type of legal document, or even a part of a document, (1) find a sample, (2) deconstruct it, and (3) reconstruct it.

3.2 Find a Sample Document

Especially when you're a new attorney and your boss asks you to write a memo or motion or brief or interrogatories or—you get the picture—any document, the first thing out of your mouth should be, "Do you have a sample I could follow?" They'll then likely direct you to another case on the firm's file-sharing drive with a sample document in it. Or the firm may even have a database of templates.

If that doesn't work, you could Google for a sample document. Adding *pdf* to the search ensures that you get an actual document instead of discussion of a document.

Westlaw, Lexis, and Bloomberg Law also have brief and form databases with thousands of sample documents.

Or your local continuing-legal-education group will have plenty of sample forms for you.

3.3 Deconstruct the Sample

To deconstruct something is to reverse engineer it—figure out how it was put together. This requires breaking the document down into its components. You will develop your own process of deconstructing documents, but, for now, here's an approach to try.

A. Create an Outline of the Entire Document

Creating an outline of the entire document ensures that you read the entire document and understand all the parts and how the parts relate to each other; that will prevent you from changing one section and unintentionally affecting a related section. So make an outline of the entire document to see the big picture.

Making the outline is especially straightforward when the document has helpful headings, but sometimes the headings are absent or there are actually several components under a heading.

So start the outline by incorporating the headings into it from the sample document. Then use the skills you're learning about in law school and this book to identify the parts under each heading. For example, if you're asked to write an appellate brief for a court you've never litigated in, you'll deconstruct the Argument section and find that there's an Analysis Preview, point headings, Rule Foundations, Case Illustrations, and so on—all the things you're learning about in your research-and-writing classes.

B. Deconstruct the Components Within Each Section

In doing the step above, you identified broad parts of the document. Now is the time to increase the magnification to just the sentence or maybe paragraph level. Identify what's happening in each paragraph and add that to your outline.

The annotations to the sample documents in Chapter 2 are basically doing that for you. Use that as a guide.

C. Research the Law to Learn About the Parts

Sometimes a document has required sections. For instance, local court rules for many courts across the country detail what information needs to be in a brief. Or regulations require certain clauses in a contract. So part of the deconstruction process is to research the law—or the rules—behind what goes in a document. For a brief, you'd research local court rules. For a contract, you'd find a treatise with forms that explain each section.

D. Patterns Reveal the Details

As you deconstruct a document, you need to figure out more than just that there are certain broad parts. Anyone can look at a memo, for example, and determine that it has a Question Presented, Brief Answer, Facts, Discussion, and Conclusion section. But what goes in each section?

Comparing and contrasting several documents will allow you to find patterns that reveal the details. When analyzing how a certain jurisdiction writes a question presented, you might realize that most attorneys use the *whether* format. This is true of briefs filed before the U.S. Supreme Court. It's a largely disfavored practice, but that's the convention in that court. A pattern revealed that detail to you.

3.4 Reconstruct the Document

Once you have the sample document and you understand its parts, you then need to begin reconstructing it for your client. Most attorneys will either copy and paste the document to create a new one or use the "Save As" or "Make a Copy" feature in their word processor.

Then go through the document—very carefully—and make it apply completely to your client.

But you must take the time to review every word of the reconstructed document. Why? Well, many attorneys—instead of recreating a document from scratch—will copy and paste a document from one file and use it for a new client. Or they'll use "Save As" to create a new document. Then they'll go through it and update the information for the new client.

The problem? Attorney-writers are usually in a hurry, so not all of the information gets updated. Several court staff often report receiving documents and forms with the wrong file number, law that doesn't apply, arguments that seem to go to another case, and even names, parties, and characters that aren't even related to the current case.

It's okay to use former documents like this, but you must have a process in place to ensure that the entire document applies correctly to the new client's matter. If you don't, you'll waste precious time and lose money, and worse—you'll lose credibility.

3.5 Examples of Deconstructing Documents

Example #1

You work in a litigation firm, and your task is to write a motion and brief. The motion asks the court to order a federal prosecutor to disclose the identity of a confidential informant. Have you ever written one of those before? Heck no. Can you? Of course! So you find a sample after your boss led you to one. And you start figuring out the parts.

As you're deconstructing the brief, you notice that one page is titled Controlling Authority, and the only other thing on the page is a citation to a constitutional amendment and a citation to a seminal case that interprets it. This is especially bizarre because the brief already had an Index of Authorities that listed all the law referenced in the brief.

You've never seen any brief like that before. Your legal-writing professor certainly never taught you how to write such a section in a brief. And none of the foundational legal-writing skills outlined in this book seem to come to mind. No worries, you employ your *research* skills and check out the local court rules, and you realize that they require such a page—but, darn it, the rules don't detail what should go in it.

You got this. You look at several sample briefs, and you realize that the *pattern* is to simply state the main area of law. That's the purpose: give the judge one page they can glance at to determine what area the brief addresses. So if it's a search-and-seizure case, you'd simply include a citation to the U.S. Constitution's Fourth Amendment and maybe one seminal U.S. Supreme Court case that addresses it, but only if it's a well-known case.

You then reconstruct that section by determining what primary area of law your case comes from, and you write a citation for it.

You just figured it out, and you didn't have to bug anyone.

Example #2

Your boss asks you to write a promissory note for a loan your client is making. You have never written a promissory note. So you find several samples, you deconstruct them, and you then reconstruct them for your client.

In the process, you realize that there's a section called "integration," and it seems that the sample promissory notes have different information. What should you do?

If you have an expert at the firm with time to teach you, ask them. If not, find a treatise that explains each provision of a promissory note. Between the expert advice and the samples, you'll be able to figure out what goes into that provision.

PART TWO

IREAC Skills

In Part 2, you'll learn about the primary building block of any legal analytical document: IREAC.

Chapter 4, Use IREAC to Structure Analysis, will introduce you to IREAC as the structure of analysis.

Chapters 5, Spot Broad Issues and Arguments, and 6, Frame the Issue, will teach you skills related to the I of **I**REAC, finding and stating the issue or an argument.

Chapters 7, Give a Rule Foundation, and 8, Explain Codified Law, will teach you about the R of I**R**EAC, how to explain the governing rules.

Chapter 9, Explain Caselaw, does all the heavy lifting to teach you about caselaw examples, the E of IR**E**AC.

Chapter 10, Apply Law, perhaps the most important, dives into legal reasoning, the A of IRE**A**C.

And brief Chapter 11, Conclude and Recommend, covers how to tie off an IREAC packet with a conclusion, the final C of IREA**C**.

Chapter Four

IREAC: Use IREAC to Structure Analysis

4.1 Analyze Issues and Their Subissues

Each letter in the acronym IREAC represents parts of the structure of legal analysis. But before learning about that, you need to understand what attorneys analyze in the IREAC structure. So, then, before you can fully appreciate IREAC, you need to understand the relationship between issues and subissues.

An issue is a *broad* question about whether a certain cause of action or rule of law is satisfied by the client's facts. And it's usually the question your boss or client asks, something like this:

- When our clients celebrate the opening of their bar, can they invite minor family members to the bar?
- Would hiring Mr. Spivey violate his noncompete agreement with his former employer?
- Is Officer Fakhoury immune from tort liability when he left a drunk woman chained in a jail cell who was later found dead?

So issues are questions of broad law: Will this violate liquor-establishment laws? Was this a breach of a noncompete employment agreement? Is a police officer immune from tort liability?

Every issue sits on rules of law—such as liquor laws, contract law, or governmental immunity—and, drilling down a layer, these rules are composed of elements, components of the broad rule. Each element can give rise to a subissue, directly linking subissues to the overarching issue. The resolution of a subissue, therefore, directly bears on the outcome of the broader issue.

Issue: cause of action, broad rule

The subissue controls the outcome of the issue

Subissue: one element of the cause of action or broad rule

You will often get the broad, primary issue from your boss or the person asking you the legal question. And then you'll figure out the subissues as you research the law and identify the elements of law underlying the broad issue.

A straightforward example of issue and subissue will make this clearer. Every state has a law that any person under 21 years old may not consume alcohol. Your client who owns a bar asks if he can serve alcohol to his children in the bar for a special occasion. So the issue and subissue would look like this:

Issue: Can a bar owner serve alcohol to his children in the bar?
The statute: (1) A person may not (2) serve (3) alcohol to a person (4) under the age of 21.

The subissues control the outcome of the issue

Subissue: Are any of the children under 21 years old?

While researching the broad rule, you'd identify the elements of the rule. In this case, there are four different elements that go into proving the rule. But three of the elements are very easily satisfied: The bar owner is a "person"; the bar owner wants to "serve alcohol"; and the children are "persons." Those elements are not "at issue," as we'd say. But we do need to know whether the children are minors, so that would be the subissue that the broad issue turns on.

Now let's up the ante a bit. What if there are two subissues that go into resolving an issue? Imagine that your client is about to open a bar, and they want to invite families to attend a celebratory opening. You helped your client with all the business-entity, property, construction, and licensing issues. It's finally time to celebrate the opening of the bar!

You receive an invitation to the opening, and you notice that your family is invited. And this makes you think about the legality of inviting, at least potentially, minors into a bar where alcohol will be served. You have minor children, and you can only imagine that other invitees also have minor children. Can they attend the bar's opening party—even if they don't drink alcohol?

That's the broad issue: May minors simply enter a bar that sells alcohol even if they don't drink the intoxicating beverage?

As any good attorney would, you research this issue and draft an email to your client with your findings. You will begin the email with the broad *issue*: May children of the invitees bring their minor children to the bar's opening party? But now you need to state the actual issue, the *sub*issue or *sub*issues that the primary issue turns on. For that, you need to know the elements of law.

Your research finds a statute directly on point: "A child under 17 years of age shall not be permitted to remain in a [bar] ... unless the minor is accompanied by parent or guardian." Now, the statutory law is not broken down into enumerated elements; you, as the attorney need to do that.

Section 8.2(B) goes into detail about parsing statutes into elements, but, for our purposes, something like this will do: (1) A child, (2) under 17 years old may not enter a bar (3) unless accompanied by a parent or guardian.

Analyzing those three elements will determine the outcome of the broad issue, whether the children may enter the bar. You've probably astutely identified that two of the three elements are at issue; these will become the subissues—the ones you actually analyze in the document.

The first subissue is whether any children 16 years old or younger will attend the bar opening, element number (2) from above. And the second subissue is (3), whether those minor children will be accompanied by a parent or guardian.

Graphically, the relationship between the issue and subissues would look like this:

Issue: When our clients celebrate the opening of their bar, can they invite minor family members of the staff?
(1) A child (2) under 17 years old may not enter a bar (3) unless accompanied by a parent or guardian.

Subissue 1: Are any of the children 16 years old or younger?

The subissues control the outcome of the issue

Subissue 2: Will a parent or guardian accompany the children at all times?

In your email or memo to the client, you need to address each of those subissues to answer the broader issue of whether he may let minors into the bar to celebrate the bar's opening.

But what format should you use to write up your analysis? Should you use the five-paragraph essay you learned about in elementary school or high school? Nope. As an attorney, you'll discuss each subissue in IREAC structure.

4.2 IREAC Is the Building Block of Analysis

You just learned that issues are decided by analyzing subissues. As an attorney, you'll analyze subissues in the IREAC structure. It is the building block of any legal analytical document like an opinion letter, memo, or court brief.

Without further ado, IREAC stands for Issue, Rule, Examples, Application, and Conclusion.

The mnemonic IREAC, by the way, is an evolution of the well-known IRAC structure, familiar to most law students. If you already know IRAC, you can use it as a foundation to advance to this evolved iteration. The only difference is that IREAC adds the E as a reminder to include caselaw *examples* of the rules of law. The E, in other words, supports the R.

Here are the parts.

I — Issue

Begin any legal analysis by stating the issue. A legal issue is a question that arises from the facts of a case and requires the application of law to resolve. And, by the way, even though we really mean "subissue" because we analyze just one element at a time, attorneys often use the general term "issue." So just know that we really mean "subissue" whenever we're talking about IREAC.

Now, back to the I of IREAC. Reading an issue statement at the beginning of the analysis allows the reader to focus on just one part of the law at a time.

Here's one straightforward example of stating the issue:

> Under the civil battery law, did Sarah *intend* to contact Jed when she was stretching in a law-school class, accidentally hit his coffee cup and spilled hot coffee on Jed?

File those facts away because we'll keep building this IREAC packet for this one subissue of "intent" under a civil battery lawsuit.

You'll learn about identifying the issue in more detail in Chapter 5, Spot Broad Issues and Arguments, and Chapter 6, Frame the Issue. For now, though, we're focusing on just the basic structure of IREAC.

R — Rule

After you clearly state the issue, explain the rules that govern or control the outcome of that issue. These so-called black-letter rules come from constitutions, statutes, ordinances, regulations, or even caselaw. This part of your document will be just rules of law. As an example, let's continue with the "intent" issue framed above. Here's how you'd state the rules for that issue:

> Intent in civil battery means that the defendant either (1) desired to cause a harmful or offensive contact or (2) knew with substantial certainty that such contact would result from their actions. The focus is on whether the defendant intended the contact, not necessarily whether they intended to cause harm.

Two chapters in this book go into great detail about stating the rules, and you'll get to them soon enough. If you want a sneak peek, check out Chapter 7, Give a Rule Foundation, and Chapter 8, Explain Codified Law.

E — Examples from Caselaw

Most law schools call this "explanation," but "examples" is probably a better description of what happens in the third part of legal analysis. This is where you give examples of past court cases applying the same law to facts that are similar to your client's. Why would you do this? Well, when the reader first reads the rules, they have an abstract idea of them, but things become really concrete when they read the examples of how the rules are applied to different factual scenarios. So, then, rules applied to stories and a court's judgment of them help the reader understand the rules of law.

Continuing the civil-battery example from above, note how adding a case example immediately after stating the rules illustrates the intent element:

> In *Smith v. Jones*, during a party, John Jones playfully swung his arm while telling a story, accidentally hitting Sarah Smith, causing her injury. Smith sued for civil battery. The court ruled that while Jones didn't intend to hit Smith specifically, he knowingly swung his arm in a crowded space, making contact with someone substantially certain. This was enough to establish intent for civil battery.

Do you see how a story brings the abstract element to life? That's the power of the E in IREAC.

These caselaw examples are called "Case Illustrations." Chapter 9 is a deep-dive into how to write them.

A — Application

Up to this point in your analysis, the client has taken a back seat because you needed time to explain the issue, rules, and any relevant caselaw examples, the I, R, and E of IREAC. With all that laid as a foundation, it's now time to fulfill the culminating function of legal analysis: apply the law to the facts to explain whether the facts satisfy what the law demands. This will finally resolve the subissue and play a contributing role in determining the outcome of the broad issue.

Now let's continue the battery case from above and apply the rules and caselaw example to our client's facts. Because this is where the facts become most relevant, remember that we represent Sarah, and Jed claims that Sarah committed a battery when she stretched during class and knocked over his coffee cup, spilling hot coffee on him. Here's an example of what applying the law of "intent" might look like:

> In this case, a court is likely to find that Sarah did not intend to contact Jed. Sarah was reflexively stretching, so it wasn't something that she desired or had much control over. Plus, she was unaware that Jed was in the vicinity because the lecture hall was large and had plenty of open seats. So, unlike the intentional waving of the arm in *Smith v. Jones* in a crowded room, here, Sarah did not intend to make contact with the cup of coffee that then burned Jed.

Mastering legal reasoning is worth the hard work and sacrifice. This is where you earn all the points on law-school exams and make the big bucks in practice. So you won't be surprised to learn that Application gets the biggest chapter in this book, Chapter 10, Apply Law.

C — Conclusion

End your IREAC analysis by stating the conclusion. This is the final bow on your analysis and ties it all together, like this:

> Therefore, Sarah did not intend to contact Jed.

Yes, it's often that simple.

Here's the entire IREAC packet in one place:

> IREAC: Under the civil battery law, did Sarah *intend* to contact Jed when she was stretching in a law-school class, accidentally hit his coffee cup, and spilled the coffee on Jed?
>
> IREAC: Intent in civil battery means that the defendant either (1) desired to cause a harmful or offensive contact or (2) knew with substantial certainty that such contact would result from their actions. The focus is on whether the defendant intended the contact, not necessarily whether they intended to cause harm.
>
> IREAC: In *Smith v. Jones*, during a party, John Jones playfully swung his arm while telling a story, accidentally hitting Sarah Smith, causing her injury. Smith sued for civil battery. The court ruled that while Jones didn't intend to hit Smith specifically, he knowingly swung his arm in a crowded space, making contact with someone substantially certain. This was enough to establish intent for civil battery.
>
> IREAC: In this case, a court is likely to find that Sarah did not intend to contact Jed. Sarah was reflexively stretching, so it wasn't something that she desired or had much

control over. Plus, she was unaware that Jed was in the vicinity because the lecture hall was large and had plenty of open seats. So, unlike the intentional waving of the arm in *Smith v. Jones* in a crowded room, here, Sarah did not intend to make contact with the cup of coffee that then burned Jed.

IREAC: Therefore, Sarah did not intend to contact Jed.

(No, on a law-school exam or in a professional document, you would not include the "IREAC" notations; they're just there so you can identify the parts.)

All in all, using the IREAC format helps ensure that legal writing is organized, logical, and persuasive. Whether you're writing an essay in school, an opinion letter to a client, a memo to a boss, or a brief to a court, you'll use IREAC to structure each subissue. Goodbye forever, five-paragraph essay.

4.3 IREAC Is Logical and Methodical

You may be wondering why law schools are so in love with mnemonics like IREAC, IRAC, CRAC, CREAC, or AREAC. It's because law schools and the attorneys they produce have no choice if they want to follow ancient traditions of logical thinking. Logical thinking happens in the form of a syllogism.

A syllogism is a thinking structure where from the relation of two propositions to each other, we infer, a conclusion.

This syllogistic structure is time-tested. It's been around at least from the time of Aristotle, more than 2,300 years ago. Aristotle taught his students a syllogism very similar to this:

All people are mortal.
Socrates is a person.
Therefore, Socrates is mortal.

He labeled each part the Major Premise, Minor Premise, and Conclusion, like this:

Major Premise: All people are mortal.
Minor Premise: Socrates is a person.
Conclusion: Therefore, Socrates is mortal.

In terms of pure logic, we would say that the relationship between the proposition of the Major Premise and the proposition of the Minor Premise compels a certain Conclusion. And that conclusion is true, correct, and right because the Major Premise and the Minor Premise are true, and their relationship compels a true Conclusion.

We can even use this structure to think about daily interactions. In an all-too-common workplace travesty, imagine that Jerry got caught eating Sally's food from the work refrigerator. We can put that scenario in a syllogistic frame to allow us to think about the situation and see it logically:

Major Premise: Rules of social etiquette dictate that employees should eat only what they've brought to work unless they get permission from the food's owner.
Minor Premise: Jerry ate Sally's food without her permission.
Conclusion: Therefore, Jerry violated social etiquette.

All people think like this all day long; now you're just getting into the details of it. Attorneys also use this logical structure in their professor duties. For attorneys, the Major Premise is the rule of law; the Minor Premise are the client's facts; and the Conclusion is the, well, uh, the conclusion.

Here is a perfect legal syllogism:

Major Premise (Rule):	A person under 21 years old may not drink alcohol.
Minor Premise (Facts):	Tom is a 17-year-old person.
Conclusion:	Therefore, Tom may not drink alcohol.

That's a perfect syllogism because there are no gaps in the law or facts, and the relationship between the rule about being 21 years old and the fact that Tom is 17 years old compels a logical conclusion.

Okay, but you may be thinking, "Hey, IREAC has five parts, but there's only three in a syllogism." That's true. IREAC adds to the picture an issue statement and caselaw examples. An issue statement simply focuses on and shows the significance of the subissue to be discussed. And caselaw examples are really part of the Major Premise, the rule of law.

The only other difference is that IREAC does not have an explicit spot for facts; there's no F in IREAC, in other words. That's because the A in IREAC, Application, is the operation of applying the law, the Major Premise, to the client's facts. We call it Application to focus on the reasoning aspect of it, but reasoning by necessity involves the facts, the Minor Premise.

Here's what the syllogism from above looks like translated into IREAC format:

Major Premise (Rule):	Issue:	Can Tom, a 17-year-old minor, drink alcohol?
	Rule:	A person under 21 years old may not drink alcohol.
	Example:	[This rule is so clear that no caselaw examples are necessary.]
Minor Premise (Facts):	Application:	The prohibition on minors' drinking alcohol applies to people aged 20 and younger. Tom fits into that category because he is 17 years old.
Conclusion:	Conclusion:	Therefore, Tom cannot legally drink alcohol.

There you have it: the syllogistic structure is the magic of IREAC. In the rest of the chapter, you'll see several different ways to use IREAC and organize your analysis no matter what the document or the landscape of the law.

4.4 Use IREAC to Mind Gaps in Analysis

Organizing the issue, rule, caselaw, application, and conclusion in the IREAC structure allows you to check your logic to ensure that your conclusions are credible and well-reasoned. This is what Professor Chris Trudeau calls "minding the gaps"; thanks to him for that clever pun and for the examples below.

In particular, we need to find and fill gaps

- in the law,
- in the facts, and
- in the application of the law to the facts.

A. Find and Fill Gaps in the Law

Before you read the paragraph after this syllogism, try to spot the gap in the law, which is the R part of IREAC:

I: Did Tom assume the risk of playing tackle football? Tom, a high-school student, blew his knee out after he was side tackled by someone from the opposing team. He was in his senior year and lost college scholarship offers as a result. He wants to sue the opposing player who injured him.

R: A person who plays a dangerous sport assumes the risk of injury. (From a statute.)

E: No caselaw examples identified yet.

A: Tom played tackle football.

C: Therefore, Tom assumed the risk by playing tackle football.

This logically does not work because there is a legal gap: we must define *dangerous sport* according to the law (not according to our own opinions on whether football is dangerous).

How do we fill this legal gap? We fill gaps in the law by defining vague terms with definitions from statutes or caselaw, or we fill the gaps with stories from past cases.

1. Look at definitions in statutes.

Continuing the example above, the attorney who wrote that analysis spotted the gap in the law and did more research. They found a statutory definition of *dangerous sport*, and they also discovered the legislature's intent behind the law. So we'll add that to the Rule below in bold emphasis. You can then see that the application of law to fact is now more complete as well. Is the logic now sound, or do you see another gap in the law?

I: Did Tom assume the risk of playing tackle football? Tom, a high-school student, blew his knee out after he was side tackled by someone from the opposing team. He was in his senior year and lost college scholarship offers as a result. He wants to sue the opposing player who injured him.

R: A person who plays a dangerous sport assumes the risk of injury. **A dangerous sport means that the sport poses a substantial risk of significant injury. The legislature enacted this law to prevent players from recovering for injuries in sports that traditionally have caused life-threatening injuries that cannot be fully eliminated by wearing**

equipment. (You found this definition in the statute, but there were no cases interpreting this definition, so you looked to the legislative intent behind the statute.)

E: No caselaw examples identified yet.

A: Tom played tackle football, which involves a substantial risk of significant injury because ________________________________. (Use the definition and the legislative intent to create arguments on why football does or does not impose a substantial risk of significant injury.)

C: Therefore, football is a dangerous sport, so Tom assumed the risk of injury by playing tackle football.

The gap in law is filled!

2. Look to precedent.

You may also fill a gap in law with precedent, which just means past cases that judges have ruled on.

American jurisprudence is based in part on precedent, meaning that judges follow past cases that have the same law and similar facts as the case before them. We are going to change the hypothetical from above and now imagine that you find a case directly on point: it holds that tackle football is a dangerous sport. So your syllogism would look a lot less gappy. Find the case in the Rule section:

I: Did Tom assume the risk of playing tackle football? Tom, a high-school student, blew his knee out after he was side tackled by someone from the opposing team. He was in his senior year and lost college scholarship offers as a result. He wants to sue the opposing player who injured him.

R: A person who plays a dangerous sport assumes the risk of injury.

E: **Tackle football is a dangerous sport.** ***Doe v. Benson.***

A: Tom played tackle football, which is a dangerous sport according to caselaw. (Set forth in your Application.)

C: Therefore, Tom assumed the risk of injury by playing tackle football.

This works. There are no logical gaps in the law.

But what if there is no case focusing on just tackle football? Then look for an analog, something similar to tackle football. What sports can you think of that are similar to tackle football?

You research caselaw and find a case stating that hockey is a dangerous sport. You can fill the gap in the law by explaining in the Rule position a case about hockey, which is indeed factually similar to tackle football. Then, in the Application position, you would apply the law to the facts like this:

I: Did Tom assume the risk of playing tackle football? Tom, a high-school student, blew his knee out after he was side tackled by someone from the opposing team. He was in his senior year and lost college scholarship offers as a result. He wants to sue the opposing player who injured him.

R: A person who plays a dangerous sport assumes the risk of injury.

E: Hockey is a dangerous sport because there is contact on nearly every play and the goal is to use this contact to prevent players from scoring. *Jansen v. Ahmad.*

A: Tom played football, which is a dangerous sport because ______. **(Use the reasoning of the hockey case to help you explain why football may or may not be a dangerous sport.) Moreover, football may be even more dangerous than hockey because ______. (Include any logical extensions from the hockey case).**

C: Therefore, Tom assumed the risk of injury by playing tackle football.

Gap filled! In fact, all the gaps are filled. Well done.

B. Find and Fill Gaps in the Facts

The Minor Premise of a legal syllogism is the client's facts, the messy story the client dumps in your lap when they come to you. Okay, that is a bit cynical. Clients tell all kinds of stories, some about current problems but many about future happiness.

As an attorney researches the law and, by so doing, begins to apply that law to the client's story, they realize that they need more information. Thus, oftentimes, an attorney will email or call the client to gain more detail about a situation, a detail that was not important until the attorney knew the specifics of the law.

Look at this syllogism. Read each part, and then identify where the gap in facts is:

I: Is Megan qualified and eligible for a promotion? Megan had good performance reviews and won numerous employee-of-the-month awards.

R: To get promoted, an employee must be qualified.

E: An employee who has had good performance reviews and has won multiple employee-of-the-month awards in the past two years is a qualified employee. *Adams v. Burns.*

A: Megan had good performance reviews and won numerous employee-of-the-month awards.

C: Therefore, Megan was qualified and is eligible for promotion.

That ostensibly may appear like we have enough information, but we really do not. This one is sneaky. The law, at least according to one case from the State Supreme Court, has a lookback period of two years. Thus, we need more facts about the timing of Megan's reviews and awards before we can do proper analysis. Time to call the client.

There's really not much else to say here. In law school, the facts are provided to you on exams and in your research-and-writing classes. In the actual practice of law, you will gather facts from a variety of sources. You will learn more about that in the rest of your law-school career.

C. Find and Fill Gaps in the Application of Law to Facts

An all-too-common problem in the law is omitting or going really thin on the application of law to facts. This book's author used to work in a courthouse reading thousands of briefs that, allegedly, were trying to convince the court to agree with them. Most of them, though, had very little in the way of analysis. Most simply stated the law, threw in a few facts, and came to a conclusion. They omitted the *WHY*.

You want to matter as an attorney. To really matter, you need to logically, soundly, thoroughly apply the law to the facts.

The IREAC analysis below—which is based on false imprisonment—would, at most, earn a C on a law-school essay. Focus on the Application section and figure out what the gap is.

I: Was Daphne detained by coercion, an element required to prove false imprisonment? Daphne took her poodle to Derryl's house so Derryl could watch the poodle while Daphne was on vacation. They agreed on a price before the vacation. After the vacation, Daphne went to get her poodle from Derryl. She explained to him that she would pay him in a week after she got paid. Derryl demanded the payment immediately and would not return her poodle until she paid. Daphne waited at Derryl's house for several hours until Derryl finally relented and let her leave with her poodle; it's that forced waiting that might amount to false imprisonment.

R: Personal coercion may amount to false imprisonment. If a store employee detains a valuable item of a customer, then the customer has been personally coerced. Taking bed sheets worth $250 is taking a customer's valuable item. (From the *Clarke* case.)

A: Derryl took Daphne's poodle away from her. We can assume that Daphne probably loved or at least liked per poodle.

C: Therefore, Daphne has been personally coerced, which amounts to false imprisonment.

The analysis gap is found in the poodle's value. Is it a thing of value enough to be detained by coercion? The writer has just assumed the reader will understand that a poodle is valuable. Yes, we may make permissible inferences about dog ownership and whether an owner likes their animal. But, above, the writer failed to connect the dots in the application between the law and the facts in any meaningful way. That is, they failed to use the facts to explain why Daphne's poodle is a valuable item.

Compare the Application section above to this one:

A: Here, Daphne was coerced to stay at Derryl's house. Holding the poodle hostage was personally coercing Daphne to stay near her poodle. A poodle is an item of value both financially and emotionally. Any purebred animal like a poodle cost at least several hundred dollars. And any dog owner will obviously have an emotional connection to the canine friend; that is why people own animals. Some dog owners would even argue that a dog is invaluable. At least one celebrity even cloned their dog so they could continue to enjoy at least some characteristics of their former beloved dog. Further, combining the actual economic value with the emotional value of a poodle would definitely add up to more than the $250 bed sheets from *Clarke*. People can replace bed sheets, but they cannot replace the unique personality of their dear canine friend.

This thorough reasoning fills all the gaps in analysis. The writer used a combination of rule-based reasoning and analogical reasoning to explain how the facts satisfy the "coercion by confinement" element of false imprisonment. All of Chapter 10, Apply Law, is devoted to learning how to do that type of reasoning.

4.5 Use One IREAC Packet Per Subissue

You're now ready to see the IREAC structure in its native context like an opinion letter, memo, or brief. You can check out the IREAC structure in simple form in the first three sample documents in Chapter 2, the Opinion Letter (2.2), eMemo (2.3), and Short Office Memo (2.4). You can go there now and look for the IREAC structure; the annotations in the margin will point out the IREAC parts.

(As a bit of a warning, for the rest of the chapter, expect to be flipping back and forth between the examples in Chapter 2 and this chapter.)

Because this is likely your first introduction to IREAC, let's analyze one of those sample documents together, the Short Office Memo in 2.4. In that memo, the broad issue was whether the Academy of Motion Pictures falsely imprisoned Michaels, which is based on actual events. For more details about the case, you can read the facts section of that memo.

Here's the broad rule that controls the issue of false imprisonment:

> In California, the tort of false imprisonment "consists of 'the nonconsensual, intentional confinement of a person without lawful privilege for an appreciable length of time, however short.'" *Fermino v. Fedco*, 872 P.2d 559, 567 (Cal. 4th 1994) (citation omitted).

All the elements are satisfied on the facts except for whether Michaels was confined. Because he was not physically confined, the only subissue is whether he was confined some other means, like duress.

This chart shows the relationship between the issue and subissue. Because just one element is at issue, the outcome of that element determines the outcome of the broader issue: whether Michaels was falsely imprisoned.

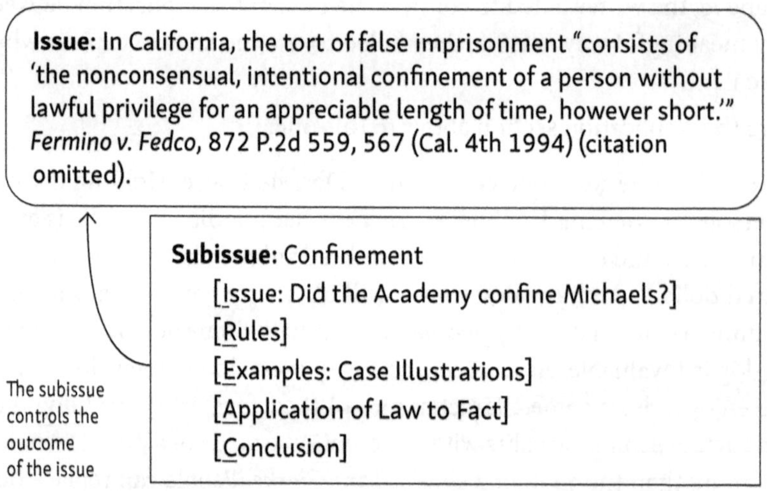

So that's the basic structure of the issue and subissue. Now let's turn this into an outline for the Short Office Memo in section 2.4. Look for the IREAC parts in the I – R – E – A – C order:

Overview

[The Issue and Conclusion are stated here.]

Controlling Rules

[The Rules are stated here.]

Relevant Caselaw

[The caselaw Examples illustrate the rules.]

Application

[The Application of rules and caselaw to the facts happens here.]

Conclusion

[The Conclusion is stated here.]

You likely observed a couple of things while reading that outline. First, the headings don't usually line up with Issue, Rule, Examples, Application, and Conclusion. The constituent parts of legal analysis may go by other names and under different headings, but the analysis is always made up of those five parts in that order. Alternatively, you may write the IREAC parts without headings of any kind, especially in situations where the analysis is brief like on a law-school exam or in an opinion letter or email memo.

Second, you may have noticed that the writer stated a conclusion in the first section right after stating the issue. As you'll see in 4.6(D), the C of IREAC, the conclusion, must always be stated at the end of each IREAC packet, but it often gets slipped in right after the Issue and at the beginning of the Application. Conclude early and often! That keeps the reader focused.

4.6 Adapt IREAC to Fit Your Needs

As the creator of your analytical document, yes, you generally need to use the IREAC structure, but you may and should adapt it to fit the particular document and the landscape of the law. In the rest of the chapter, you'll see examples of typical adaptations.

A. For Persuasive Analysis, Use AREAC

It's a weak move when trying to persuade someone that your position is correct to begin with an objective statement of the *issue*: "The issue is whether Sarah intended to contact Jed" is fine for an objective analysis, but it's not persuasive. Instead, when you need to persuade like in a court brief or a demand latter, you'd write it as an argument: "Sarah did not intend to contact Jed because her actions were reflexive."

In terms of document structure, when writing persuasively, start your IREAC packet with a strong *argument*; in other words, swap the I out for an A. Thus, use AREAC for persuasive documents: **A**rgument > **R**ule > Caselaw **E**xamples > **A**pplication > **C**onclusion. Only the first part changes; everything else remains the same.

AREAC, by the way, is pronounced like a pirate would say it: aRRR – ee – ack. Emphasis on the "RRR."

For examples of AREAC in the sample documents, check out the Argument sections of the briefs in sections 2.6, 2.7, and 2.8. The margin annotations take you through the AREAC parts.

And sections 5.3 and 5.4 in the next chapter go into great detail about creating those arguments and packaging them in persuasive point headings.

B. Omit the R of IREAC If There Are No Rules

Sometimes, a subissue may not have specific controlling rules. For those subissues, you'd skip the R of IREAC and launch right into caselaw examples, the E of IREAC.

You'll find one example of this in subargument C of the sample Trial-Court Brief on page 66. Note that the argument is really a counterargument focusing on the inapplicability of a case, so the analysis didn't need a rule statement—the writer went directly to caselaw.

You'll see another example on page 84. Argument (4) of that Trial-Court Brief (Nonmoving Party) relies on a teeny-tiny court rule, so the R is nearly nonexistent. Most of the section is simply an analysis of the facts.

C. Omit the E of IREAC If There Are No Caselaw Examples

Not every subissue you analyze will need a caselaw example. Some issues are so straightforward that just black-letter rules of law can take care of them. And, conversely, when cases are needed to illustrate a vague rule, you may not be able to find any. That's just the way it goes sometimes.

Either way, you'd simply omit the E of IREAC. And you may want to alert your reader as to why you're doing so. Something like this is all you need: "Because this is an issue of first impression, there are no cases on point; therefore, we'll analyze this using the basic rules of statutory interpretation."

As one example, the Opinion Letter in 2.2 was so straightforward that the attorney didn't need to include any caselaw examples.

D. Conclude Early and Often

While you'll always end with the conclusion, the C of IREAC, you may choose to slip in extra conclusions before then. Why? Because readers like to know where the analysis is heading from the very beginning. Surprise endings are great for novels and true-crime podcasts but not so much for legal analysis.

Often, legal writers put the conclusion

- immediately after the Issue statement,
- at the beginning of the Application, and
- where it always belongs, at the very end of the IREAC analysis packet.

As one example, you'll see in the Opinion Letter in section 2.2 that the writer put the conclusion in the very first paragraph right after the Issue statement; they put it at the beginning of the Application section; and they put it where it always belongs, at the end of the IREAC packet in the final paragraph. So the conclusion is stated three times.

That's actually pretty typical to state the conclusion that often.

E. Use Multiple IREAC Packets for Multiple Subissues, But Tie Them Together

So far, you've learned about analysis structures where just one element is at issue, but sometimes more than one element is at issue. Thus, you'll have a broad issue and then several subissues, one for each element at issue. Simply use one IREAC packet for each subissue.

But you must tie the packets together so the reader can see how each IREAC packet is related. Do this with an introductory sentence or paragraph that explains how the IREAC packets are connected. For informal analysis like a law-school exam, a sentence is good enough (see example immediately below in 4.7). But for more formal documents, tie the IREAC packets together with

- a global point heading (5.4(C)),
- an Analysis Preview (Ch. 16),
- a global Rule Foundation (7.5), or
- any combination of these three.

How you tie the IREAC packets together is less important than actually doing it.

The examples throughout 4.7 below will demonstrate cohesively connecting multiple IREAC packets.

4.7 Study Examples of IREAC in Action

A. Law-School Essay

Here's the sample law-school essay from section 2.1. It's annotated so you can see how the writer properly used IREAC to address each subissue:

This first-sentence roadmap/global point "ties" the multiple IREAC packets together.

You'll note that the E of IREAC, caselaw examples, is missing because the professor on this closed-book exam did not require the students to remember caselaw.

To be successful in a claim for intentional infliction of emotional distress (IIED), Craig will need to satisfy four elements. [IREAC] First, he must show that Professor Zet's conduct was intentional or reckless. [IREAC] As with any intentional tort, **the defendant's conduct must have been done with actual intent or substantial certainty to cause harm.** [IREAC] Here, Craig was Zet's student at the Drama School Academy. Zet was especially critical of Craig's work. He mocked and ridiculed him, leading to further ridicule by classmates. [IREAC] This constitutes intentional conduct by Prof. Zet.

Note that the writer correctly uses the IREAC structure when addressing each subissue.

[IREAC] The second element to be proven is that the conduct was extreme and outrageous. [IREAC] **Courts often articulate this by saying it is conduct that exceeds all bounds usually tolerated by decent society. For a person in an authority position to so abuse his power is a classic example of extreme and outrageous conduct.** [IREAC] Indeed, a thematic issue in these cases is a power imbalance between the defendant and the victim, [IREAC] so Prof. Zet's conduct was extreme and outrageous.

Using signposts like "third" in this paragraph and "fourth" in the next one improves the overall cohesion of the writing because they relate back to the roadmap about "four elements" in the first paragraph.

[IREAC] The third element of the claim is a causal connection between the wrongful conduct and the emotional distress. [IREAC] **Causation is satisfied when the injury occurs after the outrageous conduct and would not have happened otherwise.** [IREAC] Since Zet's mistreatment, Craig is suffering myriad physical and psychological symptoms. Zet continued to harass Craig even after Craig informed him of the impact. There is no indication that Craig had any preexisting condition. He began seeing a psychologist only because of the abuse. [IREAC] Causation seems present.

[IREAC] Finally, the emotional distress must be severe. [IREAC] **Although physical manifestation of emotional harm is not required**, as indicated, [IREAC] Craig has various symptoms. [IREAC] **The case law is exacting on this element,** [IREAC] but Craig would seem to satisfy it. [IREAC] Overall, the IIED claim is strong.

(As noted before, you would not include the [IREAC] notations or the bold and underline emphasis in your actual document.)

B. Objective Memo with Multiple Subissues

Okay, that's how you'd use IREAC on a law-school essay with multiple subissues. What about when you're in practice, and you need to write objective analysis in a memo that has subissues: what would that look like? Well, you won't be surprised to learn that you still follow IREAC!

As an example, let's use a property cause of action called "adverse possession," something you'll learn about in your Property course. A client explains that he's been mowing the strip of lawn behind his house for 18 years; he knew the strip of lawn belonged to the County Drain Commission, but they weren't maintaining it, and it would be unsightly without his excellent mowing prowess. Now he wants to add an addition to his house, and the extra 10'-by-50' strip of land he's been mowing would allow for a bigger and better addition.

These facts trigger you to think about a claim to the property based on adverse possession. There are several elements to such a claim, but only three are at issue. (Section 5.2 in the next chapter takes you through this problem to figure out what's at issue, the I of IREAC; in this section, we're still focused on the overall structure of IREAC and writing multiple IREAC packets.)

Here is the rule with the three elements at issue: A person adversely takes over land not previously owned by them when the possession of the land is hostile, exclusive, and continuous. So resolving the broad issue of adverse possession requires analyzing those three subissues.

We'll use one IREAC packet for each of the three subissues. The outline would look like this:

Issue: Did our client adversely possess the strip of land he's been mowing? To gain ownership through adverse possession, the possession must be actual, open and hostile, exclusive, and continuous for a certain period. The hostile, exclusive, and continuous elements are at issue.

Subissue 1:
[Issue: Was our client's possession hostile?]
[Rules]
[Examples: Case Illustrations]
[Application of Law to Fact]
[Conclusion]

Subissue 2:
[Issue: Was our client's possession exclusive?]
[Rules]
[Examples: Case Illustrations]
[Application of Law to Fact]
[Conclusion]

Subissue 3:
[Issue: Was our client's possession continuous?]
[Rules]
[Examples: Case Illustrations]
[Application of Law to Fact]
[Conclusion]

The subissues control the outcome of the issue

Okay, but how would this look in an office memo? Below is an outline of that. Note how Subissue 1 about *hostile* is addressed below in subsection A, and Subissue 2 is in B, and so on.

As explained in 4.6(E) above, legal writers tie several IREAC packets together with a global point heading, an Analysis Preview, a global Rule Foundation, or a combination of them.

In objective memos, a simple descriptive heading introduces the issue, so you don't need to explicitly state it as you might on a law-school exam.

Discussion

[Global Point Heading: Our client probably did adversely possess the County Drain Commission's land.]

[Global Rule Foundation: List the controlling rules here. See Chapter 7.]

A. [Issue:] **Hostile**

[Rules: The Rules about just the *hostile* element are explained here. See Chapter 7.]

[Examples: The rules are fleshed out here with Case Illustrations. See Chapter 9.]

[Application: The Application of rules and cases happens here. See Chapter 10.]

[Conclusion: State the conclusion. See Chapter 11.]

B. [Issue:] **Exclusive**

[Rules: The Rules for just the *exclusive* element are explained here.]

[Examples: The rules are fleshed out here with Case Illustrations.]

[Application: The Application of rules and cases happens here.]

[Conclusion: State the conclusion.]

C. [Issue:] **Continuous**

[Rules: The rules for just the *continuous* element are explained here.]

[Examples: The rules are fleshed out here with Case Illustrations.]

[Application: The Application of rules and cases happens here.]

[Conclusion: State the conclusion.]

The structure above for the Discussion section in a full office memo could just as easily be the Argument section of a brief. Swap out the heading *Discussion* for *Argument* and replace the one-word headings with persuasive point headings and, bam!, you've got a brief. So the same analysis structure is used regardless of whether you're writing an objective or persuasive document.

C. Persuasive Brief with Multiple IREAC Packets

Speaking of briefs, here's another example of how to organize one issue with several subissues but in a brief. Imagine that you represent someone who signed an agreement to not compete with their employer after leaving the company. So the broad issue is whether your client would violate the noncompete agreement by going to work for a new company. You research the law and find the elements for a valid noncompete agreement:

> Under the State Antitrust Reform Act, a covenant not to compete is valid if it "protects an employer's reasonable competitive business interests and ... is reasonable as to its duration, geographical area, and the type of employment or line of business."

After researching the law, you determine that the "competitive business interest," "geographical area," and "duration" are at issue and need to be analyzed. So you'd organize those three subissues like you see in the outline below. Notice, as you learned in 4.6(A), that with persuasive writing, you'd turn the "Issue" part of IREAC into a bold and confident *argument*, so we actually use AREAC for persuasive arguments. You'll see each argument in persuasive point headings A, B, and C:

Argument

[Global persuasive point heading] **This case should be dismissed because Plaintiff's noncompete agreement is unenforceable.**

[Analysis Preview]

[Global Rule Foundation] Under the State Antitrust Reform Act, a covenant not to compete is valid if it "protects an employer's reasonable competitive business interests and ... is reasonable as to its duration, geographical area, and the type of employment or line of business."

These three paragraphs, global persuasive point heading, Analysis Preview, and global Rule Foundation each play a different function, but they all tie the multiple AREAC packets below together. They create a cohesive reading experience.

A. [AREAC] **United, Inc.'s public processes are not competitive business interests.**

[AREAC: Rule Foundation]

[AREAC: Case Illustrations]

[AREAC: Application]

[AREAC: Conclusion]

See how this first argument is about competitive business interest? The next is about geographic limit? And the third is about duration? The global Rule Foundation above explains how they all relate to each other. It ties the AREAC packets together.

B. [AREAC] **United, Inc.'s geographic limitation of 100 miles is unreasonable because that would destroy any chance of working in the niche market of bio-medical-anthropological engineering.**

[AREAC: Rule Foundation]

[AREAC: Case Illustrations]

[AREAC: Application]

[AREAC: Conclusion]

Use AREAC instead of IREAC packets for each argument in a persuasive document like a letter or court brief. What's the difference? Begin with an argument rather than an objective statement of the issue.

C. [AREAC] **United, Inc.'s duration on employment of 3 years is unreasonable in light of current customary practice.**

[AREAC: Rule Foundation]

[AREAC: Case Illustrations]

[AREAC: Application]

[AREAC: Conclusion]

The example above comes from a court brief, but you could easily adapt that structure to an objective memo. The principles universally apply, meaning that you can transfer what you're learning here to any kind of legal analytical document.

D. Two Issues, Several Subissues

Sometimes, you'll be asked to analyze related but different broad issues in one document. You might be asked, for example, to analyze whether a criminal defendant's right to confront their witnesses was violated and determine whether there was a reasonable search and seizure. These two issues relate to the same client with the same facts, but different bodies of law underly them (6th Amendment and 4th Amendment). You need to physically separate them in your document.

Or what if you represent a person who caused an auto accident. The injured driver of the other car, Mr. Minkle, wants to recover (1) for pain and suffering and (2) the insurance deductible they had to pay to get their car fixed. You research the law and determine that different rules govern those two broad issues. This chart captures how you would organize these two separate issues:

Issue 1: May Minkle recover in tort for an auto accident that caused him hearing loss? To recover, Minkle must prove that he suffered a serious impairment of body function, which has three elements: (1) objectively manifested impairment, (2) of an important body function, (3) that affects his general ability to lead his normal life.

Subissue 1:

[Issue: Is the hearing loss objectively manifested?]
[Rules]
[Examples of Caselaw]
[Application of Law to Fact]
[Conclusion]

Subissue 2:

[Issue: Is hearing an important body function?]
[Rules]
[Examples of Caselaw]
[Application of Law to Fact]
[Conclusion]

Subissue 3:

[Issue: Does the hearing-loss affect Minkle's general ability to lead his life?]
[Rules]
[Examples of Caselaw]
[Application of Law to Fact]
[Conclusion]

Issue 2: May Minkle recover in tort the deductible he had to pay his insurance company to get his car fixed? Minkle may sue the driver who caused the accident and recover up to $3,000 to cover his deductible if he wasn't 50% or more at fault.

Subissue:

[Issue: Was Minkle less than 50% at fault?]
[Rules]
[Examples of Caselaw]
[Application of Law to Fact]
[Conclusion]

Your first issue about recovering pain and suffering has three subissues, and your second issue about recovering the deductible has just one subissue. Here's one way you might outline this in the Discussion section of a Full Office Memo:

Discussion

I. **Global Point Heading for Serious Impairment**

[Analysis Preview]

[Global Rule Foundation]

> You'll note that Issue 1 here has an Analysis Preview and a Global Rule Foundation, yet Issue 2 does not. The writer includes a Global Rule Foundation because it ties the multiple subissues together; it creates cohesion. Below in Issue 2, there's just one subissue, so there's no need to tie anything together there.

A. [IREAC] **Objectively Manifested**

> With objective analysis, the heading is usually just the name of the element and nothing more. That takes the place of stating the issue in a complete sentence. 6.5(C).

[IREAC: Rule Foundation]

[IREAC: Case Illustrations]

[IREAC: Application]

[IREAC: Conclusion]

B. [IREAC] **Important Body Function**

[IREAC: Rule Foundation]

[IREAC: Case Illustrations]

[IREAC: Application]

[IREAC: Conclusion]

> Not every subissue will have its own rules, so, if that's the case, simply leave that part out and go right to caselaw examples. Likewise, not every subissue will have caselaw examples, so you'd omit that part of the IREAC packet. Bottom line: Adapt each IREAC packet to the landscape of the law.

C. [IREAC] **General Ability to Lead His Normal Life**

[IREAC: Rule Foundation]

[IREAC: Case Illustrations]

[IREAC: Application]

[IREAC: Conclusion]

II. **Global Point Heading for the Deductible**

> This broad issue about the deductible is decided by just one subissue, so only one IREAC packet is needed. Thus, as explained above, there's no need to tie anything together with an Analysis Preview or a global Rule Foundation.

[IREAC: Rule Foundation]

[IREAC: Case Illustrations]

[IREAC: Application]

[IREAC: Conclusion]

E. Factor Analysis

Whereas an element is something that must be proven, a factor is merely a point that the writer weighs or balances to determine whether an element has been satisfied. These factors may already be established, or perhaps you as the writer have culled factors from caselaw. See 9.4(A)(3)(b); 9.9(B)(3).

Use IREAC or AREAC packets for factor analysis just like you would for analyzing elements of law. Here's what factor analysis would look like in the Argument section of brief, but this could just as easily be objective analysis in an intraoffice memo:

Argument

[Global Point Heading]

[Analysis Preview]

[Global Rule Foundation: Lay out (1) the global rule to be proven and (2) flexible factors to be balanced. Roadmap by stating which factors apply; then address them below]

A. [AREAC: **Persuasive point heading for first argument based on one or more factors]**

[AREAC: Rule Foundation that explains the factor or factors underlying this argument]

[AREAC: Case Illustrations that flesh out with caselaw stories the factor or factors underlying this argument]

[AREAC: Application of factor or factors to prove or disprove the global rule]

[AREAC: Instead of stating an absolute conclusion, you'd state that the factor "weighs" in favor of or against the global rule.]

B. [AREAC: **Persuasive point heading for second argument based on one or more factors]**

[AREAC: Rule Foundation that explains the factor or factors underlying this argument]

[AREAC: Case Illustrations that flesh out with caselaw stories the factor or factors underlying this argument]

[AREAC: Application of factor or factors to prove or disprove the global rule]

[AREAC: Instead of stating an absolute conclusion, you'd state that the factor "weighs" in favor of or against the global rule.]

C. [AREAC: **Persuasive point heading for third argument based on one or more factors]**

[AREAC: Rule Foundation that explains the factor or factors underlying this argument]

[AREAC: Case Illustrations that flesh out with caselaw stories the factor or factors underlying this argument]

[AREAC: Application of factor or factors to prove or disprove the global rule]

[AREAC: Instead of stating an absolute conclusion, you'd state that the factor "weighs" in favor of or against the global rule.]

4.8 Checklist for Organizing Analysis with IREAC Packets

To organize your analysis, did you:

___ use IREAC to analyze each subissue?

___ when using multiple IREAC packets, tie them together with a point heading (5.4(C)), Analysis Preview (16.5), global Rule Foundation (7.5), or a combination of them?

___ use AREAC for persuasive documents like a brief?

___ adapt IREAC to fit your needs and the landscape of the law?

Chapter Five

IREAC: Spot Broad Issues and Arguments

5.1 Spot the I of IREAC or the A of AREAC

This chapter will help you figure out the I of IREAC, which is the issue for objective or persuasive analysis, or the A of AREAC, which is an argument in a persuasive document. An issue and argument are really the same thing; the only difference is that an argument converts the issue from a question to a statement. Put another way, the subject of the issue and argument is the same thing; they're just packaged slightly differently.

Once you know the broad issues and arguments, you can then organize the analysis in your document. This skill is not about organizing the entire document from caption to overview to statement of facts all the way to the end; you learned that skill in Chapter 3, Deconstruct Sample Documents. Rather, this chapter applies to organizing just pure legal analysis. In concrete terms, identifying issues and arguments will help you organize an entire opinion letter, an entire email memo, just the Discussion section of a full office memo, or just the Argument section of a brief—you know, where we do legal analysis.

5.2 Determine What Law Is at Issue

An issue is created where law intersects with facts and where it's not immediately clear if the facts satisfy what the law demands. Thus, an issue requires a bit of law, a bit of fact, and a bit of mystery.

When the issues in a client's case aren't immediately clear, attorneys use a mix of skills or factors to determine what's at issue:

- Understand the client's facts
- Intersect the facts with the law at four levels
- Identify vague parts of the law
- View the case from opposing counsel's perspective

Subsections (A) through (D) will show how these guidelines lead to identifying what's at issue. After reading this section, you should practice this skill of determining what's at issue by applying these guidelines to the document you're creating at school or for your job; that's where you really learn.

A. Understand the Client's Facts

Because an issue requires both law and facts, you obviously need to thoroughly understand your client's situation. This usually happens during the initial intake interview with the clients, but you'll often have follow-up questions for your clients and requests for documents related to the client's case.

For purposes of learning to spot the issue, assume that your client, Jackson, is a wedding photographer. She was hired to record a wedding, and the bride asked that she also include drone footage of all events. At the indoor wedding reception, Jackson was video recording the revelry on the dance floor by flying her drone over the dancers. The drone hit a lighting fixture on the ceiling, spun out of control, and hit the bride. It knocked her out cold. And because the drone's rotor blades weren't guarded, it caused a 2-inch laceration on the bride's face. Needless to say, the bride was humiliated; the wedding celebrations were immediately cancelled, and the bride was rushed to the hospital. She's been in weekly therapy ever since.

After the incident, the bride sued the photographer, our client.

Okay, we now have the basic facts. The next step is to intersect them with law to determine the issues, which you'll do in section (B) below. (We'll call this the "wrecked wedding" situation as we continue it through all four ways of determining what's at issue.)

B. Intersect the Facts with the Law at Four Levels

After initially meeting with your client (or reading about the facts on a law-school assignment), your next step to identifying what law is at issue is to ... well ... research the law! When you research the law, you need to drill down at least through four layers: cause of action, element, definition, and caselaw reasoning. The cause of action is the broad issue. The elements are the parts of the rule underlying the broad issue. Then the definitions are the rules that define the elements. And, finally, caselaw provides court reasoning about how elements and their definitions apply to real-life situations.

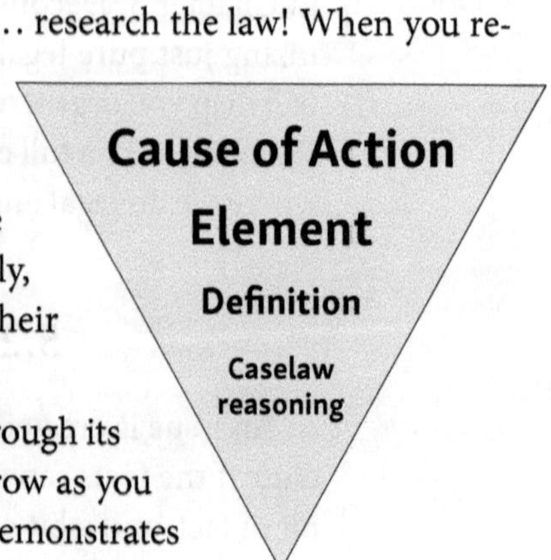

So the law gets more and more detailed as you drill down through its layers. Accordingly, the issue similarly goes from broad to narrow as you identify all four layers of the law. The inverted-triangle graphic demonstrates how the issue narrows the more you drill down through the layers of law.

Continuing our "wrecked wedding" problem from above, you can identify as broad causes of action at least Intentional Infliction of Emotional Distress (IIED) and Negligence. You came to these broad causes of action because of your training in law school. Once you've identified the broad cause of action, it's time to find the elements underlying it. We'll focus on just IIED here and leave Negligence for another day.

Drilling down one layer from the cause of action, you then research IIED and discover its elements: (1) Extreme and outrageous conduct; (2) intent or recklessness; (3) causation; (4) severe emotional distress.

You go down one more layer and discover the elements' definitions. As you read through the definitions, apply each one to the client's facts parked in your brain. While reading the definitions below, note where your brain flashes a question mark for "maybe this element is satisfied" and where it flashes a check mark for "definitely satisfied":

(1) Extreme and outrageous conduct: The defendant's conduct must be so extreme and outrageous that it exceeds all bounds of decency tolerated in a civilized society.

(2) Intent or recklessness: The defendant must act with the intent to cause severe emotional distress or with reckless disregard for the likelihood that the conduct will cause such distress.

(3) Causation: The defendant's conduct must be the actual and proximate cause of the plaintiff's emotional distress.

(4) Severe emotional distress: The plaintiff must suffer severe emotional distress as a result of the defendant's conduct. This distress must be more than transient or trivial; it must be significant.

Based on the client's facts, the "extreme and outrageous" element might be at issue. Being assaulted and maimed on one of the most important days of life is pretty horrible, but does it go beyond all bounds of decency? So this one is a "maybe" for an issue. We'll keep thinking about it.

As to the second element, there was definitely no intent, but, objectively speaking, Jackson the photographer, was reckless to fly a drone with so many obstacles. So this one is feeling like it's satisfied, but we're not totally sure.

The third element is absolutely satisfied because the drone is what caused the injury. This seems pretty clear cut, so as the defendant, we'll have to concede this element.

Now for the final element about severe emotional distress. Based on all the facts about the wedding celebrations being cancelled, the maiming of the face, and the therapy, this element is likely satisfied. On a law-school exam, that much focus on those kinds of facts means that the professor doesn't want that to be an issue. In real life, though, we're pretty sure that's not an issue, but we're not positive about it.

So we just applied the third layer of the law, definitions of elements. After that, we concluded that element one is a "maybe," element two is a "probably not," element three is a "definitely not," and element four is a "probably not."

Now let's go to the fourth layer of law, caselaw facts and the court's reasoning about them. There are two aspects of caselaw that will help you determine what's at issue in your case. First, apply the court's reasoning to your client's facts. Second, compare and contrast facts in precedent to your client's facts; if your client's facts are similar to the facts in precedent, then you can predict a similar outcome.

For this final layer of law, imagine that you further research the law and find several cases that are factually similar examples of what does and does not satisfy each of these elements. After all that hard work, it becomes clear that the "extreme and outrageous" element is at issue in our situation because it's unclear what the outcome may be. The other three elements are clearly satisfied.

C. Identify Vague Parts of the Law

So far, you've been using common sense to determine what's at issue based solely on the intersection of the client's facts with elements of law, their definitions, and caselaw applying them. One additional factor is to simply focus on the type of element: is it vague or is it specific? Vaguer elements and definitions of law are usually at issue. Any element of law that has the word "reasonable" in it is going to be at issue, as one example.

In our "wrecked wedding" scenario, see if you can't identify some vague words in the law stated above. Do that before reading the next paragraph.

Words like "extreme," "outrageous," "reckless," and "severe" are all pretty vague because we don't have a standard, universal way of interpreting those terms. So that reinforces our thoughts from above about which elements might be at issue.

D. View the Case from Opposing Counsel's Perspective

One final guideline for determining what's at issue is to step into the shoes of opposing counsel. What would a *reasonable* attorney representing the opposing party say about whether the elements are met? In this case, we actually represent the defendant, the wedding photographer. The plaintiff's attorney opposite us will likely argue that all four elements are not at issue and that their client is entitled to recover damages. Yes, but that's because plaintiff's attorneys will always say that, but what would they really think based on all the other factors, (A) through (D) above? They would probably admit that this may not be "extreme and outrageous" enough; after all, the bride signed off on having the photographer use the drone. So is it really intolerable in our society to have a drone malfunction and injure someone when they asked for the drone to be there in the first place? It's questionable.

Thus, both sides would agree that the first element of "extreme and outrageous" is really where the battle will be fought. Yes, we might as the defendants try to argue that the other vague elements are "at issue," too, but the real battle is with the first element.

That's exactly what we'd write in an objective memo that stays inside the law firm. In the Rule Foundation—the I of IREAC, we'd lay out all the elements, but we'd immediately explain that "causation" isn't at issue given the facts and the law. We'd then use one IREAC packet for each of the other three elements. We'd spend most of our time with the element likely to be most at issue, the first one. And we'd have short IREAC packets addressing the other two elements that are also likely at issue.

In the Discussion section of a Full Office Memo (example in 2.5), or perhaps even as a Short Memo (example in 2.4), the outline would look like this:

A court is likely to find that Jackson is not liable for IIED.

[Global Rule Foundation: This ties all the IREAC packets together by giving the big picture of the law; it also dispenses with any elements that are not at issue, like causation.]

IREAC: **A. Extreme and Outrageous**

IREAC: Secondary Rule Foundation

IREAC: Caselaw Examples

IREAC: Application

IREAC: Conclusion

IREAC: **B. Recklessness**

IREAC: Secondary Rule Foundation

IREAC: Caselaw Examples

IREAC: Application

IREAC: Conclusion

IREAC: **C. Severe Emotional Distress**

IREAC: Secondary Rule Foundation

IREAC: Caselaw Examples

IREAC: Application

IREAC: Conclusion

So that's how you determine the issues and subissues. More than anything, as you gain experience in an area of law, you'll gain more confidence figuring out what's at issue.

5.3 Find Broad Arguments in Persuasive Analysis

This section will teach you how to find the A of AREAC—arguments—for persuasive documents. In law school, this means that you'll use this section to write the persuasive point headings of your brief assignment. The persuasive point headings—where you write the arguments—are the ones in bold in the Argument section of a brief:

This is the global argument stated in a persuasive point heading. 5.4.

Argument

This Court should dismiss this case because the noncompete clause in the franchise agreement is unreasonable and thus unenforceable.

[Global Rule Foundation ties AREAC packets together.]

Each secondary point heading states the argument for each subargument, which is the A of AREAC. This is similar to a subissue in objective writing. 5.4.

A. [AREAC] **The multistate geographical limitation in this noncompete agreement is unreasonable because it is vastly broader than what is necessary to protect Little Caesars.**

[AREAC Secondary Rule Foundation]
[AREAC Case Examples]
[AREAC Application]
[AREAC Conclusion]

B. [AREAC] **Limiting the Lins' entire line of work is an unreasonable restraint on their employment because they are not relying on any confidential information gained from Little Caesars.**

Each argument packet is laid out in the AREAC format, the A replacing the I of IREAC. 4.6(A).

[AREAC Secondary Rule Foundation]
[AREAC Case Examples]
[AREAC Application]
[AREAC Conclusion]

C. [AREAC] **On whole, the noncompete agreement is unreasonable because it weighs only in favor of Little Caesars while destroying the Lins' ability to engage in their lifelong trade of running a restaurant.**

[AREAC Secondary Rule Foundation]
[AREAC Case Examples]
[AREAC Application]
[AREAC Conclusion]

And, if you'd like to see arguments as persuasive point headings in the context of actual legal documents, check out these sample documents in Chapter 2:

2.6 Trial-Court Brief (Moving Party)—Argument section on page 61
2.7 Trial-Court Brief (Nonmoving Party's Response)—Argument section on page 81
2.8 Appellate-Court Brief—Argument section on page 96

With that out of the way, let's jump into learning about finding arguments for persuasive documents, the A of AREAC.

Your goal with arguments is to find (1) each global argument and (2) its secondary arguments. Each global argument will be stated as a global persuasive point heading, which you'll learn about more in section 5.4, and the subarguments are stated in secondary point headings; subarguments prove the global argument just like subissues prove the issue. Also similar to writing about issues and subissues, each subargument is written as one AREAC packet. And, yes, the AREAC packets could be organized in any way, just like you learned about IREAC packets in Chapter 4.

As you can see from the example above, this section 5.3 is all about finding the global and secondary arguments, and those create your persuasive point headings. For the detailed arguments in the Application part of AREAC, see Chapter 10, Apply Law; there you'll learn how to prove each subargument with rule-based and analogical reasoning.

A. The Process for Landing on Good Arguments

The thinking to determine good arguments generally progresses through six steps. This section 5.3(A) explains the steps, and then the real magic is in subsection 5.3(B) below where you'll see the steps applied to an actual case. Here are the six steps:

First, find the global argument

Second, identify all possible subarguments.

Third, consolidate and prune subarguments to no more than three.

Fourth, organize subarguments in a logical way.

Fifth, edit the global argument and its subarguments.

Sixth, write an AREAC packet for each subargument.

1. First, find the global argument.

You first need to find the global argument, the one you put in the global persuasive point heading immediately below the Argument heading in a brief. And, yes, you may have more than one global point heading in a brief like you learned about in section 4.7(D); here, we'll focus on just one.

The global argument is usually a statement about the broad cause of action and sometimes an element of law.

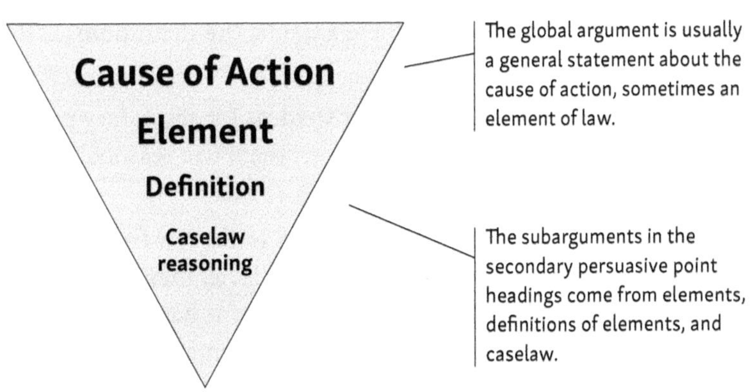

Here are a few sample global arguments. Note that they either focus on the cause of action or an essential element or component of the cause of action:

> **Taco Gong infringed Taco Bell's trademarked bell logo by using a gong in the same color and style.**

or

> **This Court should grant the motion for summary judgment because governmental immunity is a complete defense.**

or

> **Buffalo Wild Wings owed no duty to protect Mr. Trout from an open and obvious danger.**

The first example above is a global argument based on a cause of action, trademark infringement. The second example is a total defense, which is similar to a cause of action in that it's the broadest statement of the law. And the third example is focused on just one element of a negligence cause of action, duty.

How will you know what to focus on? First, your boss will tell you. Second, the broad issues will be outlined in a lawsuit or demand letter—or whatever action triggered your involvement in the case. Or, finally, the global argument will become clear while researching the law.

How can you test that you landed on the right global argument? If it's a linchpin argument. A linchpin argument is one that the entire case hangs on. To determine that, answer this question: If the reader agrees with the global argument, will they be required to give you what you're asking for? In other words, is the thing you're arguing about in the global argument the crux of the matter? If it is, then you know you have found the global argument for that issue.

Once you've landed on the global point you need the reader or court to agree with, write that in the global persuasive point heading.

The example below in section 5.3(B) will bring this all to life.

2. Second, identify all possible subarguments.

At this point, you've identified the broad argument. Now you need to find all rational and reasonable secondary arguments or subarguments that prove the global argument. Eventually, after much thinking, these go in the secondary point headings. You'll find good arguments for your secondary point headings while researching the elements, the definitions of the elements, and caselaw reasoning.

After this step, you may have a pile of a dozen or so ideas for secondary point headings. That's totally normal. You'll consolidate and prune them to get them to a reasonable number in the next step.

To identify subarguments, simply drill down one layer in the law from where the global argument is. If your global argument is at the cause-of-action level, then your subarguments will be based on the elements. And, likewise, if the global argument is based on an element, you'll drill down to the next level and base your subarguments on the element's definition.

Taking the Taco Gong infringement case as an example, because that deals with a cause of action, trademark infringement, the subarguments would be based on its elements: likelihood of confusion, similarity of trademarks, and so on.

And jumping off the Buffalo Wild Wings example, the subarguments below it would focus on one or more aspects of the *definition* of "duty." Because "duty" is an element as opposed to a cause of action, you'd drill down a layer to how duty is *defined*.

Which elements you actually include depends on whether and to what extent the facts support an argument. That takes us to the next step.

3. Third, consolidate and prune subarguments to no more than three.

In the second step, identify all possible subarguments, you'll likely compile a dozen or more possible arguments. That's too many. The goal is to have no more than three subarguments for each global argument.

Why three? First of all, it takes cognitive load into account. The human brain processes information more easily when it's presented in smaller, manageable chunks. Three arguments hit a sweet spot—it's enough to show thorough reasoning, but not so many that it overwhelms the reader or loses focus. Second, persuasiveness. Rhetoricians since ancient times (e.g., Aristotle's "rule of three") have found that listing three examples or points often comes across as more complete and persuasive. Finally, retention. Readers, including judges and clerks, are more likely to remember and retain key points if there are three. Research in cognitive psychology shows that people often recall things in groups of three more effectively than longer lists.

So how do you pare down ten or so arguments to three? Start by consolidating arguments that are closely related; to do this, join subarguments with similar concepts in one argument. That might get you down to five, six, or seven arguments. Then prune away the *less* persuasive arguments and keep the three *most* persuasive arguments. Determine the most persuasive arguments by getting a feel for which ones "have legs" to walk on their own based on the client's facts.

4. Fourth, organize subarguments in a logical way.

Once you've determined your global argument and your subarguments, figure out which order to put them in. Follow these guidelines, from most to least important:

- Always start with the strongest argument.
- Put substantive, law-based arguments before policy arguments.
- Without violating the guidelines above, put arguments in the same order as they appear in the law (e.g., if elements are listed as (1), (2), and (3) in caselaw, then follow that order in your document).

If you have multiple subarguments, tie them together by putting an internal Analysis Preview (16.5), a global Rule Foundation (Ch. 7), or both after the global argument and before the subarguments. (See the explanation in section 4.6(E) along with the examples throughout Chapter 4.)

5. Fifth, edit the global argument and its subarguments.

Section 5.4 below explains how to write up persuasive point headings so your reader immediately understands them. So this step is really just a reminder to follow the tips in that section.

6. Sixth, write an AREAC packet for each subargument.

Yeah, there's no way we can even begin to explain this here. Chapter 4 explains the overall organization of IREAC and AREAC. And then there are several chapters throughout the textbook that explain how to complete each part of AREAC, which you can easily spot in the table of contents.

B. An Example of Landing on Good Arguments

In this subsection, you'll see the six steps above for finding good arguments applied to a real case.

Landing on good arguments requires a lot of thinking, so lock in for a few moments to see all the glorious detail of finding the best arguments. After seeing the process modeled here, you should then try it with the document you're writing.

The facts we'll use for the example come from an actual case about a really interesting restauranteur. In this case, Little Caesars sued Creative Restaurants, Inc. for violating a franchise agreement. We all know Little Caesars and their affordable edibles. The Lin family created Creative Restaurants to run a restaurant, a Little Caesars franchise.

Little Caesars and the Lins entered into a franchise agreement allowing the Lins to open a Little Caesars franchise. The agreement included a noncompete clause that took effect upon termination of the agreement. These are the most critical facts about the noncompete clause you'll need to determine the global argument and its secondary arguments:

- This clause restricts the Lins from engaging in businesses that sell "pizza, pasta, sandwiches, chicken wings, and/or related products."
- The restriction lasts for one year.
- The restriction covers parts of New Jersey, Connecticut, Pennsylvania, all of New York City, and other parts of New York State. Notably, there are no other Little Caesars restaurants in Bay Ridge, Brooklyn, where the Lins' restaurant is located.

The Lins made substantial investments in the franchise and did not seek legal counsel to review the franchise agreement.

For various reasons, Little Caesars terminated the franchise agreement, and that started the clock ticking on the one-year limitation on running a business that might compete with Little Caesars. The rub is that the Lins needed a way to make a living, and running a fast-food restaurant was all they knew. With no other options, the Lins started their own pizza place.

The Lins hired you after Little Caesars sued them for breaching the franchise agreement. After a bit of discovery, you want to write a motion that asks the court to immediately dismiss the lawsuit. In the accompanying brief, you need to argue why the noncompete agreement shouldn't prohibit the Lins from running a new pizza restaurant in the same area.

We'll apply the six-step process explained above in 5.3(A) to find (1) the global argument and (2) its subarguments. That will allow us to write the global persuasive point heading and the secondary persuasive point headings.

We have to begin researching the law to find our arguments. For our issue, we're going to get the law from *Certified Restoration Dry Cleaning Network, L.L.C. v. Tenke Corp.*, 511 F.3d 535 (6th Cir. 2007). You may look it up by Googling the entire title or by putting just this into Lexis's or Westlaw's search bar: 511 F.3d 535.

All the arguments we need for the Argument section of our brief will come from these four case excerpts, which appear consecutively in the *Certified Restoration* case. As we go through the six steps, we'll refer to these excerpts:

Excerpt #1:

The Michigan Antitrust Reform Act generally prohibits any "contract ... between 2 or more persons in **restraint of... trade**." However, the statute explicitly authorizes agreements not to compete as long as they are *reasonable*. Section 4(a)(1) of the Act provides:

> An employer may obtain from an employee an agreement or covenant which protects an employer's *reasonable* **competitive business interests** and expressly prohibits an **employee from engaging in employment or a line of business** after termination of the employment if the agreement or covenant is *reasonable* as to its **duration, geographical area**, and the **type of employment or line of business**. To the extent any such agreement or covenant is found to be *unreasonable* in any respect, a court may limit the agreement to render it *reasonable* in light of the circumstances in which it was made and specifically enforce the agreement as limited.

Mich. Comp. Laws § 445.774a(1). The Michigan courts have clarified that this statute "represents a codification of the common-law rule that 'the enforceability of noncompetition agreements depends on their *reasonableness*.'"

Excerpt #2:

With respect to duration, Michigan courts have not provided any bright line rules. Rather, they "have upheld non-compete agreements covering time periods of **six months to three years**." *Whirlpool*, 457 F. Supp. 2d at 813. See *Coates*, 276 Mich. App. 498, 741 N.W.2d 539 (one year); *Rooyakker & Sitz PLLC v. Plante & Moran PLLC*, 276 Mich. App. 146, 742 N.W.2d 409 (2007) (two years); *St. Clair Med.*, 715 N.W.2d at 917 (one year); *In re Spradlin*, 284 B.R. 830 (E.D. Mich. 2002) (five years).

Excerpt #3:

Michigan courts have similarly not imposed any strict limitation on the permissible **geographic** scope of non-compete agreements. Instead, they have indicated that a "restriction that is not limited in its geographic scope is not necessarily unreasonable." *Capaldi*, 2006 WL 3019799, at *4 (finding that a geographically unlimited six-month restriction on employment with any healthcare information systems consulting business was reasonable when the employer operated in forty-three states and several foreign countries). The guiding principle is that such **geographic limitations "must be tailored so that the scope of the agreement is no greater than reasonably necessary to protect the employer's legitimate business interests."** *Id.* (*quoting Superior Consulting Co., Inc. v. Walling*, 851 F. Supp. 839, 847 (E.D. Mich. 1994)).

Excerpt #4:

The consideration of whether the **type of business** prohibited is reasonable is also generally determined by the competitive business interests that the non-compete covenant is designed to protect. With respect to these interests, the Michigan Court of Appeals has provided some guidance:

> Because a prohibition on all competition is in restraint of trade, an employer's business interest justifying a restrictive covenant must be greater than **merely preventing competition**. To be reasonable in relation to an employer's

> competitive business interest, a restrictive covenant must protect against the employee's gaining some **unfair advantage** in competition with the employer, but not prohibit the employee from using general knowledge or skill.
>
> *St. Clair Med.*, 715 N.W.2d at 919 (internal citations omitted). "Reasonable covenants may protect such legitimate interests as **trade secrets, confidential information,** close contact with the **employer's customers** or **customer lists,** or **cost factors** and **pricing.**" *Kelsey-Hayes Co. v. Maleki*, 765 F. Supp. 402, 407 (E.D. Mich. 1991). However, "[a]n employer may not reasonably prohibit future use of **general knowledge or skill.**"

Okay, let's jump into it.

1. First, find the global argument.

We know that the main issue is whether the noncompete agreement is valid to prohibit the Lins from running a new pizza place. And because we represent the Lins, we want to argue that the noncompete agreement is invalid. So with that focus, let's look for the global argument as we read the law.

To do that, read just Excerpt #1 and look for possible global arguments before coming back here. And, if you need to, reread 5.3(A)(1) for a reminder of what we do in this step. The main point of that section is that the global argument is based on the broadest statement of the law—the cause-of-action level. Okay, go read that before continuing to read.

[Jeopardy music playing while you read Excerpt #1 to look for global arguments.]

Welcome back. There's a lot going on there, but keep in mind that all law can be organized from broad to narrow. The broadest point here is the policy statement in the first sentence that the state generally prohibits restraints of trade, so that could be our global argument:

> **The Court should dismiss this case because the noncompete agreement is an illegal restraint of trade.**

(For context, that could be the global persuasive point heading directly below the Argument heading in our brief.)

That's one possibility, but let's keep reading.

We read in the second sentence of Excerpt #1 that there appears to be an exception to restraints of trade: reasonableness. So that's what we should really focus on. If we focused on the overall policy banning restraint of trade, the plaintiff could say, "Yes, the noncompete is a restraint of trade, and the law allows them if they're reasonable." So the real battle will be over "reasonableness."

A possible global argument based on "reasonableness" could look like this:

> **The Court should dismiss this case because the noncompete clause in the franchise agreement is unreasonable and thus unenforceable.**

But perhaps we're not sure if "reasonableness" is the right thing to focus on. As we keep reading the law, we notice that "reasonableness" is mentioned no less than six times within three paragraphs! That pattern, that repetition corroborates our hunch that we should focus all of our subarguments on reasonableness. (Yes, the emphasis was added to help you see the ubiquity of "reasonableness.")

To be sure that's the right global issue to focus on, let's apply the linchpin test we learned about in Step 1: If a court were to agree that the franchise agreement is unreasonable, would we get what we want? Yes, the court would have to declare that the franchise agreement is unenforceable. Thus, Little Caesars could not prohibit the Lins from running a restaurant in the Bay Bridge area.

This proves that, strategically, "reasonableness" is the only path forward.

Therefore, we can officially declare that we have found our global persuasive point heading:

> **The Court should dismiss this case because the noncompete clause in the franchise agreement is unreasonable and thus unenforceable.**

Now let's determine what subarguments will support our global argument.

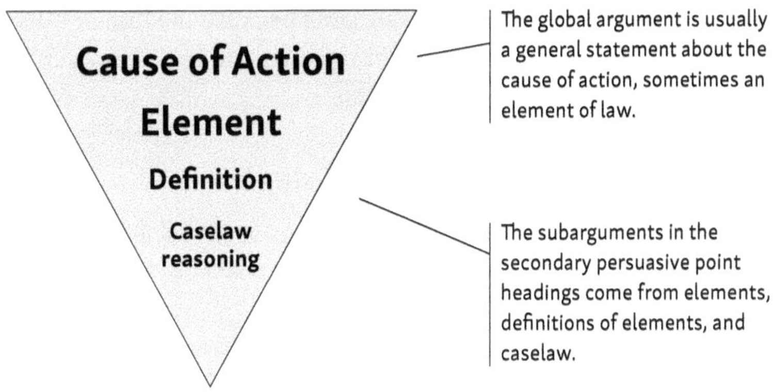

2. *Second, identify all possible subarguments.*

So "reasonableness" is the main rule to prove the enforceability of a noncompete agreement. Now we need to find all possible subarguments to prove that the noncompete agreement in our case was unreasonable.

a. Look for arguments in the *elements*.

To find subarguments for our noncompete-agreement brief, we need to drill down a layer in the layer from "reasonableness." What are the elements of "reasonableness"?

Look again at Excerpt #1, and, before reading on, try to determine some subarguments based on the elements there. These arguments need to address the overall unreasonableness of the non-compete agreement (e.g. "The noncompete agreement is unreasonable because ...." (Or something like that.)

[Jeopardy music playing while you read Excerpt #1 to look for subarguments in the elements.]

From Excerpt #1, did you notice in the second paragraph, the indented block quotation, that the law sets up a balancing test? Courts need to balance an employer's competitive business interests against an employee's right to engage in employment after termination. Those are competing elements. After reading that, we think of a couple of possible subarguments to prove unreasonableness:

> A. **The noncompete agreement is unreasonable because it supports Little Caesars' competitive business interests while eliminating the Lins' ability to make a living.**
>
> B. **The noncompete agreement is unreasonable because it destroys the Lins' ability to engage in their lifelong trade of running a restaurant.**

As they say, not everything will be gold when first brainstorming subarguments! But we've got to start somewhere, and we'll refine them in Step 3.

Okay, let's keep going. Later in that second paragraph in Excerpt #1, after the balancing test, the statute lays out three different facets—or elements—of reasonableness: duration, geographical area, and the type of employment or line of business. Based on that definition of "reasonableness," we add three more possible subarguments to our bucket:

C. **The noncompete agreement is unreasonable because its duration prohibits the Lins from earning an income for an entire year.**

D. **The noncompete agreement is unreasonable because its geographical limitation covers an entire city that does not have a Little Caesars restaurant.**

E. **The noncompete agreement is unreasonable because the line of business—fast-food restaurants—is ubiquitous in the area and has been even when Little Caesars first approved the franchise.**

b. Look for arguments in the *definition of elements.*

Now we have five possible subarguments that support our global argument about reasonableness, but we're not done yet because we need to drill down a level to identify the element's definition. (Think of how the law is organized from cause of action > element > definition of the element > caselaw reasoning.)

Excerpt #2 is where the court begins drilling down to define the "duration" element. Go read it and see if you can think of subarguments that could prove that the franchise agreement is not reasonable.

[Jeopardy music playing while you read Excerpt #2 to look for more subarguments in the element definition for "duration."]

Thanks to the helpful transition phrase that begins Excerpt #2, we know that this paragraph addresses the "duration" factor for reasonableness, but did you feel your heart sink as you read it? Yep. We have a one-year limitation in our noncompete agreement, and this paragraph tells us that anywhere from six months to three years is generally held to be reasonable. So arguing the "duration" factor may not be wise. Subargument C above may be tossed in the wastebasket, but we'll see.

Let's march on in the opinion to keep building our pile of subarguments. Now read Excerpt #3 to land on good arguments based on the definition of the "geographical" element.

[Jeopardy music playing while you read Excerpt #3 to look for subarguments in the "geographical" definition.]

Again thanks to a great transition-topic sentence, we know this paragraph addresses the geographical factor. And that last line about tailoring the scope of the contract presented a rule that gives rise to another possible subargument:

F. **The multistate geographical limitation in this noncompete agreement is unreasonable because it creates an absolute restraint on the Lins' ability to earn a living doing what they've done their entire lives.**

Wait a second! That subargument F just came out; that rule about the limitation being "no greater than reasonably necessary" got me thinking about something else. That's how writing works: a word or phrase will give you an idea for an argument; capture that lightning! But now we need a subargument actually about that "no greater than" rule. Here's a go at that:

G. **The multistate geographical limitation in this noncompete agreement is unreasonable because it is vastly broader than what is necessary to protect former franchisees from competing against the former franchisee's one location.**

That argument just popped out, and while writing it, you may have thought: "Mmmm, am I making this argument too narrow because it focuses on competition against the one location?" I need to check the law to see if that's what this geographical factor is really about. That's the recursive nature of writing and research, research and writing—we go back and forth as we refine our thoughts and arguments.

Finally, read Excerpt #4 to find arguments related to the final and third element: "type of business."

[Jeopardy music playing while you read Excerpt #4 to look for more possible subarguments.]

So this final quotation goes to the last factor where the court is supposed to weigh everything in light of the type of employment or line of work. The line of work here is fast-food service and pizza in particular.

Look at the bolded bits in the final quotation in Excerpt #4. Why do those concepts stand out? They stand out because they give us ideas for possible ways to prove that the noncompete agreement is unreasonable. So let's try our hand at turning those concepts into subarguments:

H. **Given the ubiquity of fast-food restaurants, an absolute limitation in a multistate region on an entire line of work—restaurants serving not just pizza but sandwiches and wings—is an unreasonable restraint on the Lins' ability to make a living.**

Note that as you draft the subarguments, you always need to be mindful of using some direct language of the law. Using "limitation," "line of work," "unreasonable," and "restraint" all echo the law. This reinforces for the reader that your argument is in line with the law.

Now let's try one using the "merely preventing competition" rule:

I. **Little Caesars' multistate restriction is merely preventing competition because it's broader than is necessary to protect its actual competitive business interests.**

And here's one about the "unfair advantage" rule:

J. **The Lins' new restaurant does not benefit from an unfair advantage because they are not relying on any confidential information gained from Little Caesars.**

We can honestly say that the Lins do not have an unfair advantage because they, as franchisees, did not actually learn any confidential information. The ingredients are provided to the franchisees, and all the technology is proprietary and not transferable to any other pizza joint or restaurant.

c. Look for arguments in *caselaw reasoning*.

To avoid belaboring this step of finding all possible arguments, let's just say that you should also read the reasoning in caselaw to see if the courts have given any good nuggets that we could turn into arguments. Sometimes they give factors, whether in a neat and tidy list or randomly. Sometimes they give a snappy little phrase that really sums up a great point. Whatever it is, courts' reasoning can be full of great ideas for arguments. We'll forgo that analysis here because you get the point, and we already have so many good arguments from just the elements and their definitions.

3. *Third, consolidate and prune subarguments to no more than three.*

Let's inventory where we're at. As you can see, Step 2, identify all possible arguments, happens while researching the law, and you're going to generate a lot of subarguments based on rules, definitions, and caselaw reasoning.

We ended up with a total of ten subarguments, A through J, to prove the one global argument about the noncompete agreement being unreasonable. Step 3 will help us consolidate and prune these to no more than three subarguments.

For this step, it's helpful to put all the possible subarguments in one place, so here they are:

A. **The noncompete agreement is unreasonable because it supports Little Caesars' competitive business interests while eliminating the Lins' ability to make a living.**

B. **The noncompete agreement is unreasonable because it destroys the Lins' ability to engage in their lifelong trade of running a restaurant.**

C. **The noncompete agreement is unreasonable because its duration prohibits the Lins from earning an income for an entire year.**

D. **The noncompete agreement is unreasonable because its geographical limitation covers an entire city that does not have a Little Caesars restaurant.**

E. **The noncompete agreement is unreasonable because the line of business—fast-food restaurants—is ubiquitous in the area and has been even when Little Caesars first approved the franchise.**

F. **The multistate geographical limitation in this noncompete agreement is unreasonable because it creates an absolute restraint on the Lins' ability to earn a living doing what they've done their entire lives.**

G. **The multistate geographical limitation in this noncompete agreement is unreasonable because it is vastly broader than what is necessary to protect former franchisees from competing against the former franchisee's one location.**

H. **Given the ubiquity of fast-food restaurants, an absolute limitation in a multi-state region on an entire line of work—restaurants serving not just pizza but sandwiches and wings—is an unreasonable restraint on the Lins' ability to make a living.**

I. **Little Caesars' multistate restriction is merely preventing competition because it's broader than is necessary to protect its actual competitive business interests.**

J. **The Lins' new restaurant does not benefit from an unfair advantage because they are not relying on any confidential information gained from Little Caesars.**

Now let's roll up our sleeves and get to work. We'll first consolidate as many as possible, and then we'll prune what's left over to end up with no more than three subarguments to prove reasonableness.

Consolidating the subarguments will be a breeze because we know that the law looks at three facets of reasonableness. The lesson here is that you need to let the law guide you as you determine what to focus on. Those three facets are duration, geography, and line of work. Subargument C goes to duration; D, F, and G go to geography; and E, H, I, and J go to line of work.

But there's also the underlying policy, which is that the law doesn't support absolute restraints on trade. Subarguments A and B address that.

And, yes, there is some overlap in these subarguments, but we're looking primarily at which rate of reasonableness they address.

Now that we've organized the subarguments according to how the law is organized, let's consolidate as many as possible. There's only one duration subargument, so there isn't anything to do there. But what about the geographical element? We need to consolidate and prune these three subarguments that go to geographical limitation:

D. **The noncompete agreement is unreasonable because its geographical limitation covers an entire city that does not have a Little Caesars restaurant.**

F. **The multistate geographical limitation in this noncompete agreement is unreasonable because it creates an absolute restraint on the Lins' ability to earn a living doing what they've done their entire lives.**

G. **The multistate geographical limitation in this noncompete agreement is unreasonable because it is vastly broader than what is necessary to protect former franchisees from competing against the former franchisee's one location.**

We can consolidate these geographical subarguments into this one:

> **The multistate geographical limitation in this noncompete agreement is unreasonable because it is vastly broader than what is necessary to protect former franchisees from competing when there is no other Little Caesars restaurant in the entire city.**

This point heading is focused on the geographical limitation, but it also uses some of the policy to support it, so it presents a double-whammy argument.

To create the consolidated subargument, we needed to drop these concepts: "absolute restraint of trade" and "right to earn a living." That's okay. We can argue those in the Application section under this subargument.

Whereas we started with ten possible subarguments, this consolidation brings us down to eight total.

Now let's look at the "line of work" element of reasonableness. These subarguments all relate to that:

E. **The noncompete agreement is unreasonable because the line of business—fast-food restaurants—is ubiquitous in the area and has been even when Little Caesars first approved the franchise.**

H. **Given the ubiquity of fast-food restaurants, an absolute limitation in a multistate region on an entire line of work—restaurants serving not just pizza but sandwiches and wings—is an unreasonable restraint on the Lins' ability to make a living.**

I. **Little Caesars' multistate restriction is merely preventing competition because it's broader than is necessary to protect its actual competitive business interests.**

J. **The Lins' new restaurant does not benefit from an unfair advantage because they are not relying on any confidential information gained from Little Caesars.**

We'll consolidate these into one subargument for line of work. When consolidating, yes, we need to focus on elements of law, their definitions, and underlying policy, but, to really consolidate, we need to prioritize the strongest concepts and keep those in the subargument. Subargument H actually covers most of the most compelling concepts, so we'll go with that with a few minor tweaks:

> **An absolute limitation in a multistate region on an entire line of work is an unreasonable restraint on the Lins' employment because they are not relying on any confidential information gained from Little Caesars.**

Again, any concepts found in the other subarguments that we had to cut out will go below in the Application section. Here, we're focusing on the broad concepts in the persuasive point headings.

Let's take tally of where we're at. Before this consolidation, we were at eight total subarguments. This brings us down to five.

The only other possible consolidation are the subarguments A and B that relate to the overarching policy behind the noncompete law. We can consolidate those into one policy subargument:

> **The noncompete agreement is unreasonable because it destroys the Lins' ability to engage in their lifelong trade of running a restaurant even though the Lins do not compete with Little Caesars.**

Drum roll, please!!! That brings us to these four subargument point headings:

> **The noncompete agreement is unreasonable because it destroys the Lins' ability to engage in their lifelong trade of running a restaurant even though the Lins do not compete with Little Caesars.**
>
> **The noncompete agreement is unreasonable because its duration prohibits the Lins from earning an income for an entire year.**
>
> **The multistate geographical limitation in this noncompete agreement is unreasonable because it is vastly broader than what is necessary to protect former franchisees from competing when there is no other Little Caesars restaurant in the entire city.**
>
> **An absolute limitation in a multistate region on an entire line of work is an unreasonable restraint on the Lins' employment because they are not relying on any confidential information gained from Little Caesars.**

The final step is to winnow down the arguments to the best three and no more. Because the "duration" factor isn't very strong for us, strategically, we're better off buying credibility with the reader, a court, by conceding that point. So we won't have a subargument addressing that factor. Thus, at this point, we're moving forward with just these three subarguments to prove that the noncompete is unreasonable:

> **The noncompete agreement is unreasonable because it destroys the Lins' ability to engage in their lifelong trade of running a restaurant even though the Lins do not compete with Little Caesars.**
>
> **The multistate geographical limitation in this noncompete agreement is unreasonable because it is vastly broader than what is necessary to protect former franchisees from competing when there is no other Little Caesars restaurant in the entire city.**
>
> **An absolute limitation in a multistate region on an entire line of work is an unreasonable restraint on the Lins' employment because they are not relying on any confidential information gained from Little Caesars.**

4. Fourth, organize subarguments in a logical way.

Applying the factors for organizing the arguments explained in 5.3(A)(4), we'll start by moving the policy argument to the last spot because arguments based on elements are always stronger than policy ones.

And because the statute lists geographical limitation before "line of work," we'll follow that order—unless we feel that the "line of work" argument is stronger. So the organization of the law should be reflected in the organization of our subarguments.

And, of course, we'll put the global argument at the top, because that gives context for all that follow.

So this is our first draft for organizing the subarguments:

> **This Court should dismiss this case because the noncompete clause in the franchise agreement is unreasonable and thus unenforceable.**
>
> A. **The multistate geographical limitation in this noncompete agreement is unreasonable because it is vastly broader than what is necessary to protect former franchisees from competing when there is no other Little Caesars restaurant in the entire city.**
>
> B. **An absolute limitation in a multistate region on an entire line of work is an unreasonable restraint on the Lins' employment because they are not relying on any confidential information gained from Little Caesars.**
>
> C. **The noncompete agreement is unreasonable because it destroys the Lins' ability to engage in their lifelong trade of running a restaurant even though the Lins do not compete with Little Caesars.**

5. Fifth, edit the global argument and its subarguments.

When it comes to editing argument point headings, we never want to go over 35 words. That's a good benchmark for when the length of the sentence trips up the reader. Second, make sure the argument is obvious from the first reading. Third, make sure the arguments are obviously distinct. And, finally, follow all the tips in section 5.4 about writing persuasive point headings.

Here, subarguments A and B are quite long at 37 and 34 words, respectively, so we'll want to simplify them a bit. We'll also make sure each argument is obvious. And did you notice how similar B and C are? Arguments that are too similar lose their punch, so we really need to differentiate those two arguments.

After editing the arguments according to those notes, here's our second draft:

The Court should dismiss this case because the noncompete clause in the franchise agreement is unreasonable and thus unenforceable.

A. **The multistate geographical limitation in this noncompete agreement is unreasonable because it is vastly broader than what is necessary to protect Little Caesars.**

B. **Limiting the Lins' entire line of work is an unreasonable restraint on their employment because they are not relying on any confidential information gained from Little Caesars.**

C. **On whole, the noncompete agreement is unreasonable because it weighs only in favor of Little Caesars while destroying the Lins' ability to engage in their lifelong trade of running a restaurant.**

Subargument A went from 37 words to 23. The original was simply trying to do too much. A reader can really take away just one or two concepts per sentence anyway. A simple sentence has a much higher chance of being comprehended. Subargument B underwent a similar trimming. Any concepts we have to prune away will show up in the Application section within the respective AREAC packet.

And now subarguments B and C are distinct arguments. B focuses on "line of work" and "confidential information" while C is more of a policy argument focusing on weighing competing interests. Perhaps in a further edit that subargument might even begin with "As a policy matter."

6. Sixth, write an AREAC packet for each subargument.

Really, truly most of the hard thinking has been done at this point because you have the primary arguments—the A of each AREAC packet. Now you need to flesh out each argument by completing one AREAC packet for each subargument. And then add in a couple of writing devices to tie the AREAC packets together. So an outline of your analysis would look like this:

Argument

This global persuasive point heading is based on the broadest layer of law.

The Court should dismiss this case because the noncompete clause in the franchise agreement is unreasonable and thus unenforceable.

These parts tie the AREAC sections below together. 4.6(E).

[Analysis Preview]

[Global Rule Foundation]

Each secondary argument proves the global argument; these are based on elements, element definitions, and caselaw reasoning.

A. [AREAC] **The multistate geographical limitation in this noncompete agreement is unreasonable because it is vastly broader than what is necessary to protect Little Caesars.**

[AREAC: Rule Foundation]

[AREAC: Case Examples]

The detailed arguments in the Application section prove the secondary argument. See Ch. 10, Apply Law.

[AREAC: Application]

[AREAC: Internal Conclusion]

B. [AREAC] **Limiting the Lins' entire line of work is an unreasonable restraint on their employment because they are not relying on any confidential information gained from Little Caesars.**

[AREAC: Rule Foundation]

[AREAC: Case Examples]

[AREAC: Application]

[AREAC: Internal Conclusion]

C. [AREAC] **On whole, the noncompete agreement is unreasonable because it weighs only in favor of Little Caesars while destroying the Lins' ability to engage in their lifelong trade of running a restaurant.**

[AREAC: Rule Foundation]

[AREAC: Case Examples]

[AREAC: Application]

[AREAC: Internal Conclusion]

The other chapters in the book explain how to complete the other parts of AREAC.

5.4 Write Arguments in Persuasive Point Headings

A. Persuasive Point Headings

Attorneys as a convention write arguments and subarguments in a formal heading called a "persuasive point heading." As you'll see below, it's a hybrid between a sentence and a heading.

These headings in persuasive documents like a court brief do more than merely announce what topic is addressed in that subsection. Rather, they play a crucial role in communicating arguments. They clearly state an argument that proves why the court should grant what you desire in the litigation (i.e., dismiss the case, grant a motion to suppress evidence, etc.).

Judges expect persuasive point headings in the Argument section, and they rely on them for clear statements of each argument. If you do not have them or have ineffective ones, you will frustrate your reader.

In fact, point headings are so important that they also go in the brief's table of contents, if it's a convention within your court to include one. (You can see an example on page 89.) Time-starved and weary-eyed judges often read the table of contents first to get a quick understanding of the case—the big picture. Knowing that, ask yourself:

> If the judge read *only* my point headings, could they get a fairly good idea of *why my client should win*?

That's the importance of well-written persuasive point headings.

B. Observe Persuasive Point Headings in Their Natural Habitat

To gain a bit of context, check out the persuasive point headings in the three sample briefs in Chapter 2. These are not the whole-document headings like Introduction, Statement of Facts, or Argument; rather, these headings are found only in the Argument section.

In the Trial-Court Brief (Moving Party), you'll see a global point heading on page 61, and then each of the three arguments are captured in persuasive point headings on pages 62, 64, and 66.

In the Trial-Court Brief (Nonmoving Party), the attorney responds to the above brief with four counterarguments. You'll find those arguments captured in persuasive point headings on pages 81, 83, and 84.

And, finally, in the Appellate-Court Brief, you can see how all the persuasive point headings go into the Table of Contents on page 89 for a quick snapshot and first impression of the entire case.

Then there's a global point heading on page 96, followed by two secondary point headings on pages 97 and 98.

Looking at those sample persuasive headings will help you understand the explanations below.

C. Write a Global Point Heading and Secondary Point Headings

Directly beneath the Argument heading in a brief, you should clearly state the broad argument that captures the entire thrust of the brief. This means that it will focus on a broader rule of law like the Confrontation Clause's right to confront a witness, negligence, or copyright infringement. Then put the supporting arguments in the secondary point under the global heading. You learned about determining the global point headings in 5.3(A)(1) and 5.3(B)(1) and the secondary headings in remaining parts of those 5.3(A) and 5.3(B).

Now it's time to finally dive into what actually goes into a persuasive point heading, whether global or secondary.

D. Include an Assertion and a Reason in Each Persuasive Point Heading

The judge reading your brief wants to know *what* you want and *why* you want it. That's what must go in each persuasive point heading. State the *what* as an assertion or a conclusion. And then state the *why* as a reason. So each point heading, to be helpful to your reader, needs an assertion (what you want) and a reason (why you should get it). Thus, the formula for a point heading looks something like this:

[Assertion] because [reason].

Here's an example:

The nature of the copyrighted-work factor favors Wymann	because	the Clarizac ads are original works and are accorded a high degree of protection.

And here's how it would look in a brief:

A. The nature of the copyrighted-work factor favors Wymann because the Clarizac ads are original works and are accorded a high degree of protection.

[Rule Foundation]

[Examples of caselaw]

[Application]

[Conclusion]

See what a beautifully clear statement of the argument that is? If you were a judge, you would be so grateful for a clear and readable argument.

Observe also that including an assertion and a reason forces you to make the persuasive point heading specific to your client. Simply stating a rule of law will not persuade the judge to agree with your client's position. As an example, compare these two point headings, and decide which one is more persuasive:

Example 1:

> **If the nature of the copyrighted work is original, then it is more protected.**

Example 2:

> **The "nature of the copyrighted work" factor favors Wymann because the Clarizac ads are original works and are accorded a high degree of protection.**

The first point heading is a mere statement of the law and is not persuasive because it does not relate to any one party. Instead, make your point headings persuasive by making them fact-specific to your client's situation.

You may be wondering what types of assertions or conclusions you should be making. There are three general categories: (1) What you want from the court, (2) a conclusion about an element of law, and (3) factors of a multipart balancing test. Yours might include any of these.

First, your assertion might simply be what you want from the court:

> **This case should be dismissed because …**

or

> **Mike Lindell's statements should be suppressed because …**

or

> **The confidential informant's identity must be disclosed because …**

Second, your assertion might simply be a conclusion on an element of law you want the court to reach:

> **The "nature of the copyrighted work" factor favors Wymann because …**

or

> **A hot-dog stand midway down a ski slope is not an obvious and necessary danger because …**

or

> **Defendant's right to confront his accuser was violated when …**

or

> **The trial court erred when …**

Finally, your point headings might focus on a few of several factors as part of a balancing test:

> **There was an ongoing emergency, and thus the statements were not testimonial, because of the type of dispute and the weapon used.**

or

> **Of the twelve best-interest factors, eight weigh in Ms. Mitchell's favor.**

So think about (1) what you want from the court, (2) the elements at issue, and (3) any factors a court might weigh when applying a rule of law. Those are the assertions or conclusions you'll write in the secondary point headings.

Now, as to the other half of the persuasive point heading—the reason—you will figure that out while you're researching the law and writing your application of law, the reasoning. All of that thinking will help you see what you need to focus on. It will clarify the main thrust of the brief and the detailed arguments that support what you want from the court.

While you're researching and writing the reasoning, be sure to capture that lightning in a bottle because it often strikes only once. Have a document going where you write down the specific arguments you need the court to agree to.

When you're done researching the law and writing the arguments, you're going to have a pile of several arguments—each one a potential persuasive point heading. Organize all of those arguments around one global point heading and then three or four subordinate point headings. Again, this is what you learned about under Steps 2 and 3 in 5.3(A) and 5.3(B).

Now, let's apply everything you've learned about persuasive point headings so far. Read the three sets of point headings below, and decide which set of arguments would be the most persuasive to a judge:

<u>Example 1</u>

Three-part test for compensable work.

A. Benefit to the employer.

...

B. Controlled or required by employer.

...

C. Integral to principal activity.

...

<u>Example 2</u>

Jashawn Brown's after-hours training does not meet the three-part test for compensable overtime work.

A. Brown's training did not benefit the employer.

...

B. Brown's training was not controlled or required by the employer

...

C. Brown's training was not integral to his principal activity.

...

<u>Example 3</u>

Jashawn Brown's after-hours training does not meet the three-part test for compensable overtime work.

A. Brown's training did not benefit the employer because the dog never became a part of the canine unit.

...

B. Brown's training was not controlled or required by the employer: the employer merely knew about it.

...

C. Brown's training was not integral to his principal activity because he had little occasion to use a dog on road patrol.

...

Example 3 is the best because each point heading states an argument (assertion + reason) that is specific to the client's case. Example 1 merely has descriptive headings; they miss a great opportunity to argue on behalf of the client. Yes, Example 2 is a bit better than Example 1, but it largely has assertions with no reasoning. Example 3 is the most persuasive because each point heading is an argument specific to the case.

Those are the basics for what goes into a persuasive point heading.

E. Format Your Persuasive Point Headings According to Conventions

There are very specific conventions for formatting point headings. Follow these rules to make your point headings pop and "look right." Each persuasive point heading must

- be single-spaced;
- be written as one sentence;
- begin with a capital letter;
- end with a period;
- use sentence capitalization (capitalize only the first letter of the first word in the sentence and proper nouns; nothing else gets capitalized);
- be stated in no more than 35 words;
- be in bold emphasis; and
- be left justified.

From that list, hopefully you're picking up that a persuasive point heading is a marriage of a typical descriptive heading and a sentence.

You will find in practice that a handful of attorneys write their point headings in all-caps. AVOID DOING IT BECAUSE IT SCREAMS OFF THE PAGE AND IT'S MORE DIFFICULT TO READ. And you'll find a few more attorneys who apply typical heading capitalization to the persuasive point heading. You should avoid this as well because that capitalization style also makes longer sentences more difficult to read. Compare these two:

> **Buffalo Wild Wings Did Not Have a Duty to Warn About or Remedy the Alleged Black Ice Because the Black Ice Was an Open-And-Obvious Danger.**

versus

> **Buffalo Wild Wings did not have a duty to warn about or remedy the alleged black ice because the black ice was an open-and-obvious danger.**

Most find sentence capitalization easier to read.

F. Point Headings Are Part of a Cohesive Network

Above, you learned that each point heading must be an argument that makes sense on its own; from one reading, the court should understand what you want (the assertion or conclusion) and why you should get it (the reason). Now you need to broaden your focus and look at the entire Argument section: all the persuasive point headings within that one section should create a meaningful outline of your argument. The judge-reader should be able to understand the structure of all your arguments by reading just the point headings.

The cohesion usually comes because the Rule Foundation (Ch. 7) at the beginning of the argument section lays out the analytical framework for the Argument section of the brief. Then the point headings focus on the main parts of the rules laid out in the Rule Foundation. So the Rule Foundation is a type of map, and then the point headings and the analysis below them are the individual destinations.

Below is a portion of the argument section from the Trial-Court Brief on page 68. Use it to understand how a writer shows how the point headings are all connected. Under the Controlling Rules section, which is just a Rule Foundation, the writer lays out the analytical framework, and then all the point headings connect back to it—creating a cohesive document ecosystem.

The global **Persuasive Point Heading** captures the broad point of the brief. Note the assertion and reason.

Argument

This case must be dismissed because Buffalo Wild Wings did not owe a duty under the open-and-obvious body of law and the accident did not cause Mr. Trout's pre-existing injuries.

...

This paragraph is the **Rule Foundation.** This is the map for the rest of the Argument section. The words in bold emphasis, which you wouldn't do in an actual document, are the elements at issue. You'll see them pop up again in the secondary persuasive point headings.

2. Controlling Rules

"To establish a prima facie case of negligence, a plaintiff must prove (1) that the defendant owed a **duty** to the plaintiff, (2) that the defendant breached the duty, (3) that the defendant's breach of the duty **caused** the plaintiff's injuries, and (4) that the plaintiff suffered damages." *Case v. Consumer Powers Co.*, 615 N.W.2d 17, 20 (Mich. 2000). As will be explained below, Mr. Trout cannot satisfy the duty and causation elements to establish a prima facie case of negligence, and, hence, there is no genuine issue of material fact, and this case should be dismissed as a matter of law.

3. Buffalo Wild Wings did not have a duty to warn about or remedy the alleged black ice because the black ice was an open-and-obvious danger.

...

Persuasive point headings 3, 4, and 5 address the duty element. Repeating that word, *duty*, is essential to cohesively connecting all the headings.

4. Buffalo Wild Wings did not owe a duty to Mr. Trout because the black ice does not include special aspects that give rise to a high likelihood or severity of harm.

...

5. Buffalo Wild Wings did not owe a duty to Mr. Trout because they did not have notice of the alleged dangerous condition or even sufficient time to be notified.

...

This final **persuasive point heading** takes care of the second element at issue, causation. See the connection to the **Rule Foundation** above?

6. This case must be dismissed because the fall did not cause Mr. Trout's preexisting injuries.

...

In sum, use a Rule Foundation to map the big picture; then, in the persuasive point headings, repeat the words of the elements from the Rule Foundation to show how everything is connected.

G. Enumerate and Format Point Headings to Show the Hierarchy of Arguments

The hierarchy of arguments can immediately help your reader see that arguments at the same level prove a parent argument, a broader point. It's a way to keep everything sorted so the reader knows which subarguments go with which global arguments.

Show the hierarchy of arguments by enumerating and using typography.

Typical enumeration looks like this:

Roman numeral > Capital letter > Arabic numeral

I. Heading

A. Subheading

1. Sub-subheading

2. Sub-subheading

B. Subheading

II. Heading

Or you could do something a bit more modern, which avoids Roman numerals, like this:

Capital letter > Arabic numeral > Lowercase letter

A. Heading

1. Subheading

a. Sub-subheading

b. Sub-subheading

2. Subheading

B. Heading

There's no magic to these enumeration schemes. The main thing is to alternate between numerals and letters. For numerals, it's conventional to alternate between Roman and Arabic. And for letters, alternate between uppercase and lowercase. You can create your own scheme as long as it clearly communicates the relationship between the arguments.

But maybe we should back up a bit: When do you actually need to enumerate a heading? Enumerate a heading only if you have two or more headings at the same level. This means that if you have just one global point heading, it won't be enumerated, but the secondary point headings would be enumerated, assuming you have more than two. In the example above, note how each heading is enumerated because there are two or more headings at each level. Same with the example below. You can also study the enumeration patterns in the sample briefs in Chapter 2 for more examples.

In addition to enumeration, use typography. *Typography* is the layout of text on the page. Use indents and character emphasis to show the different levels of arguments. In the example below, setting the enumeration aside, the typography alone shows the hierarchy of the headings. Subheadings a and b obviously prove the secondary argument in 2. And the arguments in 1, 2, 2a, and 2b all prove the global argument in A.

A. Main issues, such as individual grounds for relief or trial court errors, are often introduced by point headings preceded by Roman numerals, Arabic numerals, or capital letters.

1. Subissues are indented and preceded by either a number or a letter, opposite of the enumeration in the parent level above. Italicizing the second level further distinguishes this argument.

2. *Because this second argument uses the same indentation and numbering scheme, it's clear that arguments 1 and 2 both work to prove the main argument in A.*

    a. You may also further divide subheadings, when necessary, by using the opposite numeration as above. Above we used Arabic numerals, so we need to use a letter here. Because we already used a capital letter, we'll use a lowercase letter for this level.

    b. This argument clearly works at the same level as argument a above; both arguments a and b prove the argument in 2.

B. Because enumerated argument headings require at least two, there will always be a B to an A or a II to a I. In other words, you'd never have just an A all by itself.

H. Less-Effective Examples of "Persuasive" Point Headings

Now let's apply everything you learned about persuasive point headings in sections (A) through (G) above by identifying how less-effective point headings could be more persuasive.

The following examples are all less effective, but you can learn a lot by comparing bad and good examples. For these examples, you need to know that the main thrust of the arguments is that Nick Noyer invoked his right to counsel during a custodial interrogation by police officers. His invocation of the right to counsel must be unequivocal and unambiguous to be enforceable.

In the examples below, the global point heading is the same. Focus on the secondary persuasive point headings. Take all the points you learned above about effective point headings, and apply them to these examples. You may want to steal a glance at the Checklist for Persuasive Point Headings in section (J) below.

Without further ado, observe what needs to change to make these point headings more persuasive:

<u>Less-Effective Example 1:</u>

Nick Noyer's statement must be suppressed because he unambiguously invoked his right to counsel.

1. **Nick Noyer's first ambiguous statement.**

    ...

2. **Nick Noyer's second ambiguous statement.**

    ...

3. **Nick Noyer's last ambiguous statement.**

    ...

4. **Nick Noyer's statement after the fact cannot be used to establish or disestablish a request for counsel during a custodial interrogation.**

    ...

The first three point headings are merely descriptive, which means that they don't make an argument. They don't even make an objective statement of whether Noyer did or did not invoke his right to counsel. Each point heading must have an assertion (conclusion or statement) and a reason that supports that assertion.

And I'm not sure what the final argument #4 means.

Okay, see what you think about these arguments:

Less-Effective Example 2:

> **Nick Noyer's statement must be suppressed because he unambiguously invoked his right to counsel.**
>
> 1. **Following a request for counsel, a reasonable officer would have acknowledged that the suspect made a clear and unambiguous invocation of an attorney requesting.**
>
>   . . .
>
> 2. **The officer persisted in wearing down the client's resistance to talk without an attorney various times to make him confess, where every resistance represented an unambiguous invocation for an attorney.**
>
>   . . .

These persuasive point headings have more substance to them, so we're heading in the right direction. Point heading #1 above has an assertion (that a reasonable officer would have known it was an invocation), but it lacks a reason. It doesn't answer *why* a reasonable officer would have thought it was clear.

And the argument in #2 doesn't make sense. It seems that the argument is less focused on a clear invocation of the right to counsel and more about overcoming the defendant's will. The argument isn't clear.

Let's see if we're getting any better.

Less-Effective Example 3:

> **Nick Noyer's statement must be suppressed because he unambiguously invoked his right to counsel.**
>
> I. **Under *Abela*, by stating Professor Flores's name, Noyer unambiguously and unequivocally exercised his "Right to Counsel" under *Miranda*.**
>
> . . .
>
> II. **When the officer continued the interrogation and changed topics to keep Noyer talking, the officer engaged in conduct the procedural safeguards derived from *Miranda* sought to eliminate.**
>
> . . .
>
> III. **The fact Noyer signed a waiver and continued to answer the officer's questions after invoking his right to counsel did not negate his demand to call Professor Flores.**
>
> . . .

It's possible to be too specific, which makes it so the reader cannot really comprehend what the argument is. All three of the point headings above suffer from *over*-specificity. The reader should understand the argument by reading the one-sentence point heading. In I above, the reader will not understand the significance of "Professor Flores's name." In heading II, it's not clear what the procedural safeguards are; explicitly stating them would give some context for the very specific information given.

What about these?

Less-Effective Example 4:

Nick Noyer's statement must be suppressed because he unambiguously invoked his right to counsel.

1. **A reasonable officer would contend that Mr. Noyer invoked his right to counsel and by practicing good police work, should've clarified his request and terminated interrogation until a counsel was present.**

   ...

2. **Mr. Noyer clearly and unambiguously invoked his right to counsel, which should've terminated the interrogation until a counsel was present; therefore, it was the fruit of the poisonous tree.**

   ...

The first one has odd framing. Why would an officer ever be "contending" that a defendant did indeed invoke their right to counsel? As attorneys, we must write to avoid unnecessary distractions of thought.

The second point heading above does not include a reason, and it suffers from improper grammar. The grammar violation is a diva because it hogs the spotlight, leaving the substance in the dark.

For this next set, look at just the formatting:

Less-Effective Example 5:

Nick Noyer's statement must be suppressed because he unambiguously invoked his right to counsel.

a. **Defendant Noyer Made Statements Which Expressed His Desire to Speak with an Attorney**

   ...

b. **Defendant Noyer's Request for an Attorney was Clear and Unambiguous**

   ...

Did you notice it? It should stick out like a sore thumb. These point headings are formatted like a descriptive heading with title capitalization where each significant word (not prepositions, articles, or conjunctions) are capitalized. Instead, this should be capitalized as a regular sentence.

Less-Effective Example 6:

NICK NOYER'S STATEMENT MUST BE SUPPRESSED BECAUSE HE UNAMBIGUOUSLY INVOKED HIS RIGHT TO COUNSEL.

A. **THE INTERROGATING OFFICER MUST USE THE REASONABLE OFFICER IN THE CIRCUMSTANCES STANDARD WHEN DECIDING WHETHER A REQUEST FOR COUNSEL IS CLEAR AND UNAMBIGUOUS.**

   ...

> **B. THERE IS NO EXACT FORMULA FOR THE ONLY WAY AN ACCUSED CAN ASK FOR AN ATTORNEY IN ORDER FOR IT TO BE CLEAR AND UNAMBIGUOUS.**
>
> . . .
>
> **C. THE INTERROGATING OFFICERS DO NOT HAVE TO BELIEVE THAT THE ATTORNEY WHO IS BEING REQUESTED BY THE ACCUSED IS ACTUALLY AN ATTORNEY FOR THERE TO BE A PROPER INVOCATION OF THE ACCUSED FIFTH AMENDMENT RIGHTS.**
>
> . . .

How did you experience the all-caps above? A minority of attorneys do use all caps to write their persuasive point headings. Many studies have shown that text in all caps is more challenging to read. The content alone of legal analysis can be challenging to understand, so the last thing we need is to unnecessarily increase the difficulty of understanding by using all caps. Do not use all caps.

Formatting aside, all three of the point headings above are mere statements of the law, so they cannot persuade a judge to agree with your client's position. Make each point heading specific to your client, and include an assertion and a reason.

I. Examples of Effective Persuasive Point Headings

Now that you have seen what not to do, here's an example of what to do:

> **Nick Noyer's statement must be suppressed because he unambiguously invoked his right to counsel.**
>
> **I. Noyer's multiple mentions of "Professor Flores" along with his credentials as an attorney was a request for counsel.**
>
> . . .
>
> **II. Given the context of Noyer's request, a reasonable interrogating officer would have taken Mr. Noyer's statements as a request for counsel.**
>
> . . .

The first argument above has an assertion and a reason, and it clearly states the argument. The assertion is that multiple mentions of "Professor Flores" was a request for counsel. The reason is that Noyer also stated that he was an attorney.

The second heading above also has an assertion and a reason, though it is a bit thinner. That's okay because your goal is to convey the gist of the argument. A judge would gather from this point heading that looking holistically at the context leads to the conclusion that Noyer requested counsel.

Here's another example of effective persuasive point headings. This comes from a brief filed in the Michigan Court of Appeals, which is an appellate court. That explains why some of the point headings are focusing on how the lower court erred. Here it is:

> **I. The circuit court's errors in allowing alternative service and service by publication resulted in Post being required to defend against a time-barred claim and thus affected his substantial rights.**
>
> . . .

II. Post did not waive his challenge to service of process because he raised it in his first motion to the circuit court.

…

III. The circuit court abused its discretion by entering Hills's order allowing ineffective service by publication.

…

A. The circuit court erred when it allowed alternate service because two attempts at service do not show service cannot reasonably be made.

…

B. The circuit court's order failed to comply with the requirements of MCR 2.106.

…

The example above comes from an actual brief filed in court, and it's very well written. Many attorneys let the pressing of time be an excuse to not write well. That only puts their clients at a disadvantage. Take the time to do the job right for each client.

J. Checklist for Persuasive Point Headings

Structure

When looking overall at the Argument section, did you:

- ___ consider using one global persuasive point heading to capture the main thrust of the entire brief?
- ___ use one secondary persuasive point heading for each argument?
- ___ organize the headings from broad points to more narrow points (i.e., the global point heading is the broadest and the subordinate ones are more specific)?
- ___ coherently connect all point headings by using a Rule Foundation section that maps out how they relate?
- ___ coherently connect all point headings by using the language of the law from the Rule Foundation to telegraph how each point heading relates to the bigger picture?
- ___ when looking at all the arguments in one place, as they often are in the brief's table of contents, create a coherent set of arguments?

Substance

For each persuasive point heading, did you:

- ___ include an assertion or conclusion that clearly states what you want from the court or what conclusion you want it to agree to?
- ___ include a reason that explains why the court should agree with the assertion or conclusion?
- ___ specifically relate the argument to the client's facts rather than merely state a rule of law?
- ___ state the entire argument in fewer than 35 words?

Format

When formatting each persuasive point heading, did you:

- ___ apply bold emphasis to the entire heading?
- ___ use sentence-case capitalization?
- ___ single-space the heading?
- ___ end the heading with a period?
- ___ enumerate the point headings when you have more than one point per level?
- ___ use typography to visually show the hierarchy of the point headings (i.e., use indentation and different bold or italics emphasis)?

Chapter Six

IREAC: Frame the Issue

6.1 Role of the Issue Statement

It's rumored that Einstein said that everything should be made as simple as possible, but not simpler. Doing that requires great skill, care, and time. Only the greatest attorneys do that, and it's an absolute joy to read their work. Framing a client's issue is all about making the case as simple as possible.

Simply framing the issue—the I of IREAC—is all about decluttering and seeing through the information fog to what must be decided to resolve the client's issue. Any given case will have thousands of words of facts, maybe millions, and dozens or hundreds of words of law. But your job as the issue framer is to figure out which of those words really matter—which of the words of fact and law frame the issue.

Why is framing the issue important? It's important because all parties need to be on the same page: your client, other parties involved in the dispute, the mediator, the judge, and on and on.

What's the goal with framing the issue? Every reader should know the document's primary issue within 90 seconds of picking it up. Bryan Garner famously said this about court briefs, but it applies to all analytical documents like opinion letters, email memos, and full office memos.

So the goal is to pass the 90-second test.

As a quick example of framing the issue and helping the reader see the issue under 90 seconds, take the landmark 2015 case from the United States Supreme Court: *Obergefell v. Hodges*, 576 U.S. 644 (2015). There were over 350 documents filed before the Supreme Court for that case alone. Those filings amounted to thousands of pages of story, fact, analysis, and policy discussion. But what did those millions of words really boil down to? This simple issue:

> whether the Fourteenth Amendment requires a State to license a marriage between two people of the same sex.

That's how the Court framed the issue in its opinion. Crafting clear, simple issue statements like that is what this chapter is all about. Reading the chapter and applying it to your writing will prepare you to write any type of issue statement in any kind of legal document.

6.2 Spotting the Issue

A client comes into your office and relays a story to you. Maybe the story is that they own a business and need to fire an employee. Or perhaps someone just received a cancer diagnosis and wants to get their affairs in order. Whatever the client or whatever type of law you practice, the whole process begins with a client telling a story. Those are the facts.

Then, as an attorney, your job is to figure out which law the client must follow to achieve their goals.

If the law clearly applies to the client's facts, we'd say that there is "no issue." You won't need to write a document to analyze the issue.

If, however, it's unclear how the law applies to the client's facts, you'll need to analyze that in a memo or brief. The starting point in the document is to clearly state what the issue is, that is, where the law intersects with the facts and the result isn't clear. You need more analysis to predict a clear result.

Researching the law, by the way, will often make the issue clearer. You will see in caselaw, for example, what usually gets litigated for a certain area of law. You can bet your bottom dollar that those same issues will occur in your case.

You can read more about spotting the issue in 5.2.

6.3 Two Types of Legal Issues

Legal issues come in two varieties. A legal issue may simply ask what the law is. There's no discussion of facts with this one. You'll have this kind when the current state of the law is unclear. And the other type, which you'll usually be working with, asks how the law applies to your client's fact. The former is a question of law, and the latter is a question of application.

A. Question of Law

A question of law is the rarer type of question because most the time the law is clear and published, so you're able to find it. But sometimes we have issues of first impression. The question above from *Obergefell*, by the way, is a pure legal question, which you often see with issues of first impression.

Below are two more examples of pure questions of law. Notice how they do not include any of your client's facts:

> Does the Michigan No-Fault Act permit treble damages for grossly negligent conduct that causes a serious impairment of an important body function?
>
> You asked me to research whether Michigan's No Fault Act recognizes a traumatic brain injury as a "serious impairment of an important body function."

In these two examples, the person who gave the assignment obviously already knows about the No-Fault Act and the main rule at issue (i.e., serious impairment), but they are a little fuzzy on an esoteric area of the law. Thus, they gave you the assignment to clarify if the statute specifically allows recovery for a certain type of injury. These questions simply ask about the state of the law.

B. Question of Application of Law to Fact

The vast majority of issue statements you write will be questions of how the law applies to the facts, so your task will be to find that exact moment that the element of law at issue intersects with your client's legally relevant facts.

Note in the three examples that follow how the writer intersects the law with the facts:

> Was an automobile driver grossly negligent when he ignored eight "Bridge Out" signs and smashed through three barricades before crashing into a river?

Where do the law and facts intersect? Where gross negligence, a rule of law, meets a person who took the chances of Dukes-of-Hazarding it over a river, the facts.

Likewise, in this next example, there are bits of the significantly relevant law and bits of the significantly relevant facts intersecting to frame the issue:

> Is a covenant not to compete reasonable in time and territory, as required to make it valid under Michigan law, when it prohibits a former employee from working in a similar business in that same state for three years, and when the employer conducts business in just one city in that state?

6.4 Two Conventions for Writing an Issue Statement

Issue statements may be informal or formal. If you're writing an informal analytical document like an opinion letter or an email memo, you'll write the issue as a simple sentence, either posed as a statement or a question. If, however, you're writing a more formal document like an office memo or a court brief, there are more strict—formal—conventions for how to write them up.

Below, you'll learn how to write both an informal issue statement and a formal one.

6.5 Informal Issue Statement

A. Observing Informal Issue Statements in the Wild

It always helps to start with a bit of context, so before you read the details about informal issues, you should observe them in their wild habitat.

In informal documents, the issue statement will be in the first paragraph. You can see that by looking at the Opinion Letter on page 11, the eMemo on page 19, or the Short Office Memo on page 28. Look for the annotation "Frame the Issue." Those are examples of what this section 6.5 is all about.

B. Informal Issue Statement for a Whole Document

In informal analytical documents like email memos, opinion letters, and short memos, the issue statement is often just restating what your boss or client asked you, like this:

> You asked me to research whether losing a spleen amounts to a serious impairment of an important body function, which would allow our client to recover noneconomic damages.

The sample issue statement above is asking for a straight application of law to fact. The law is known. The facts are known. So the only question is whether the facts satisfy the law. This is the most typical type of issue, a question of application. Note how simply it's stated without extraneous information.

Here's another informal issue statement that asks for a simple application of law to fact:

> When we spoke, you reported that one of your former employees printed out and took LucyCo's password-protected customer list when he left the company. You asked for my opinion on whether that customer list is a trade secret.

But observe how this next informal issue statement is looking for something a bit different:

> In Michigan, what is the appropriate cause of action for appearance discrimination?

The informal issue statement above is simply asking a procedural question about what law we should even be looking at for a certain cause of action. Because it's a simple question of law, it's stated in one tight sentence.

Here's one last example.

> This memo explains under what circumstances a judge is required to order the losing party to pay attorney fees.

That's another example of a question of pure law. And it demonstrates that the issue could be framed as a statement as opposed to a question.

In summary, follow these rules for writing an informal issue statement:

- As the I of IREAC, state it in the beginning of the document.
- It's usually just one sentence, sometimes two.
- It may be stated as a question or a statement.
- It's usually the question your boss asked.
- It usually asks about a broad cause of action, which you'll narrow in the analysis.

C. Sometimes, an Issue Statement Is Just a Heading

In objective documents with multiple subissues, the "issue" will be just a descriptive heading. If you look at the Discussion section of the Full Office Memo on page 43, you'll see an example. There, the I of IREAC for each subissue is simply a heading. That heading announces the issue to be discussed in that section. The writer doesn't need to explicitly state, "The issue in this section is whether ...." In that sample office memo, subsection A's heading simply reads Adverse Employment Actions. From that, the reader knows what the issue is in that section. Likewise, subsection B is just Causation. Those simple descriptive headings are "stating" the issue.

Now, this isn't the case for persuasive documents like court briefs and demand letters where every heading in the analysis section must be persuasive, so your headings will be complete sentences in persuasive documents. (That's what 5.4 is all about.) But for objective documents, a simple heading is often enough to signal subissues.

(See 15.3(D) for more information about formatting such headings.)

6.6 Formal Issue Statement

A formal issue statement goes deeper than a simple informal issue statement. That makes sense because the analytical documents that require a formal issue go into great detail about the issue, so framing of the issue is more complex.

To gain context for what's to come in this section, check out some formal issue statements in the sample documents in Chapter 2. The Full Office Memo's issue statement is on page 41, and the Appellate-Court Brief's issue is on page 91.

A. Two Types of Formal Issue Statements

In formal legal writing, there are two popular conventions for structuring a formal issue statement: the one-sentence format and the deep-issue format. It's like Beta versus VHS, Taylor Swift versus Beyonce, DoorDash versus Grubhub. You get it.

Really, though, this is serious business. When asked to write a formal document like a full office memo or a brief, you must follow one of these two conventions. Your firm will tell you which one to use.

B. One-Sentence Issue Statements

The one-sentence issue statement is the tried-and-true convention. It has been used for centuries in the practice of law.

The one-sentence issue statement has three parts: the law, the question, and the facts. We call it the Under-Does-When format because those words conventionally introduce the law, the question, and the facts. *Under* introduces the law. *Does* begins the question. And *when* starts off the facts.

The order can change, but it always includes those parts. For instance, you may write it as Under (state the law), Does (ask the question), When (tell the story). Or you may write it as Does (ask the question), Under (state the law), When (tell the story).

Here's a more detailed formula for stating the law first, Under-Does-When:

> **Under** [identify the common-law theory or state the statute's popular name], **which** [requires (or other appropriate word) followed by the rule of law], [is, can, **does**, was (or other appropriate word) state the core question] **when** [list the essential, legally relevant facts]?

Of course you wouldn't bold those words in your actual document. I've done it here just to point out the structure.

Note that attorneys often add a *which* clause to give a bit more detail about the law. So the *under* clause gives the general context (i.e., the cause of action or name of the statutory scheme), and the *which* clause gives the actual rule or element at issue.

Here's a fleshed-out example of the Under-Does-When format:

> **Under** Michigan's No-Fault Act, **which** requires auto-accident victims to prove a serious impairment of body function to recover noneconomic tort damages, **can** John Dover recover damages for pain and suffering **when** he sustained a broken collar bone and whiplash in an auto accident, missed two weeks of work, required pain medication for eight months, but did not need surgery or a cast?

Here's another example of the Under-Does-When model:

> **Under** Michigan's common law, **does** Snow Schuss owe Carl Phillips a duty of care, **which** is required to prove negligence, **when** Jenny Gordon, a patron of Snow Schuss, landed on top of him after she skied off a snow-covered ridge while he was watching his son participate in a charity toboggan race?

In the issue statement immediately above, you can see that the writer still followed the basic order of Under-Does-When, but they put the *which* clause after the question. Doing so avoided repeating "duty of care." As long as the issue statement is clear, you can choose where to put the *which* clause.

Now, here's a formula for a one-sentence formal issue statement that puts the questions first, what we call Does-Under-When:

> [Is, Can, **Does**, Was (or other appropriate interrogative) followed by the core question] **under** [identify the common-law theory or state the statute's popular name], **which** [requires (or other appropriate word) followed by the pertinent rule of law], **when** [list the essential, legally relevant facts]?

Here are the two examples above reorganized into Does-Under-When format:

> **Can** John Dover recover damages for pain and suffering **under** Michigan's No-Fault Act, **which** requires auto-accident victims to prove a serious impairment of body function to recover noneconomic tort damages, **when** he sustained a broken collar bone and whiplash in an auto accident, missed two weeks of work, required pain medication for eight months, but did not need surgery or a cast?

And here's the second example:

> **Does** Snow Schuss owe Carl Phillips a duty of care, **which** is required to prove negligence **under** Michigan's common law, **when** Jenny Gordon, a patron of Snow Schuss, landed on top of him after she skied off a snow-covered ridge while he was watching his son participate in a charity toboggan race?

You'll find immediately below another example of a one-sentence question you'd find in a formal analytical document. But what went into writing such a good statement? Many choices! Below the issue statement, we'll analyze the many choices you have to make as a writer for each of the parts, the Under (the law), the Which (the elements), the Does (the question), and the When (the facts).

Here's the final issue statement:

> Under the parental liability statute, which requires proving that a minor maliciously or willfully injured a person, are parents liable for the actions of their child in shooting other students and teachers at his school, when the child was 17 years old and living at home, and when the parents knew that the child had some violent ideas, but the parents did not know that the child planned the attack?

(By the way, if you want to look at the statute at issue here, put this into Google, Westlaw, or Lexis: MCL 600.2913.)

Now let's go through each part and the decisions the writer had to make to land on just the right kind and amount of information.

1. Under

Under establishes the rule context by referring to applicable law (the underlying rule). The rule should be neither too specific nor too general. Here are different rule statements you might write:

- Under Mich. Comp. Laws Ann. § 600.2913, ...

  Problem? Too specific. Putting the citation in the issue statement will not mean much to the reader the moment they are reading the issue because most attorneys do not know all the statutes by chapter and section number. So don't put citations in the issue statement.

- Under a Michigan statute, ...

  Problem? Too general. Instead, give either the name of the statutory act or, if it does not have one, create a descriptive name for the statute.

- Under Michigan law, ...

  Problem? Too general. If the common law is involved, writing "Under Michigan common law" would be more helpful to your reader.

- Under the parental liability statute, ...

  Just right. This is specific and descriptive. Even if the reader is not familiar with the statute, the description alone will inform the reader about the law.

2. Which

Yes, the *which* clause is really part of the *does* clause, but it deserves its own section because it plays an important role. With any client issue, disputes with other parties will come down to a word or phrase. So, for example, cases will turn on phrases like "serious impairment," "assured clear distance," or "intent." That's what goes in the *which* clause.

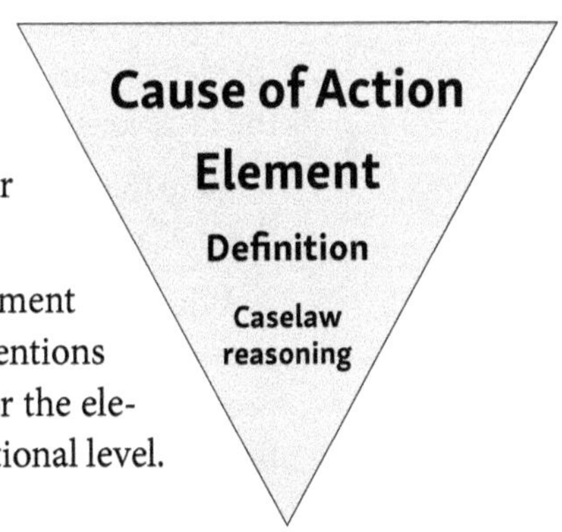

The law exists in at least four layers: the cause of action, the elements, element definitions, and caselaw reasoning. (See Chapter 5.) The *under* clause usually mentions the area of law. And the *which* clause is where you slip in the cause of action or the elements. We almost never have space to get down to frame the issue at the definitional level.

With that being said, check out these *which* clauses:

- ... which allows a government entity to recover up to $2,500 from parents if their minor child maliciously or willfully destroys physical property or injures another person ...

Problem? This includes extraneous parts of the rule. The amount recoverable is not an element anyone needs to prove; rather, it's the consequence of proving the elements. Include just the part of the rule that is at issue, meaning the opposing party would disagree with you on that element.

- … which requires proving that a minor maliciously or willfully injured a person …

  Just right.

3. Does

Does introduces the legal question. It might be "can" or "will," but it's a question. Again, it should be neither too broad nor too narrow. Here are some choices you might make when writing:

- … will a father be held liable for his son's actions in killing eight students and one teacher … .

  Problem? Too narrow. See how it specifies *father*? What about any parent? And *eight* is too specific. What if it were ten or eleven?

- … is a party liable for the conduct of a child who harms others … .

  Problem? Too broad. *Party* is too vague, even though a parent would be a party to this litigation. *Harms others* does describe what happened, but it is too broad. Give the reader a bit more of a frame through which to see the issue.

- … are parents liable for the actions of their child in shooting other students and teachers at his school. …

  Just right. Goldilocks would be happy with this one.

4. When

When introduces the legally relevant facts. Begin with context for the story: An employee claimed her boss … ; a skier lost control on a ski run … ; John was driving his car while. …

Then include the key facts that frame the issue. The key facts are ones that directly relate to the rule at issue. You can identify the key facts by observing which facts you mainly rely on in the document's arguments (i.e., the Application or analysis sections).

State the facts objectively. Do not present the facts as conclusions of law. Check this by looking for elements of law intermingled with the facts. If you've done that, strip out the law and keep just the facts for the *when* clause.

State the factual story in 20 or 30 words. If the key facts are too long, summarize or categorize them. Certainly do not include the entire statement of facts—just the key facts.

When you need to state several facts in an issue statement, it makes sense to put them in list format. You may enumerate the list or not. But what's nonnegotiable is that you write the list with proper grammar, meaning, among others, that the facts are grammatically parallel. It's just more beautiful like that, and it'll make more sense to your reader.

A list that is grammatically parallel is where each list item (1) begins with the same part of speech (i.e., adverb or adjective) and (2) reads with the lead-in stem.

Here's a parallel list where the words are all adverbs:

> The jury weighed the evidence carefully, skillfully, and wisely.

And here's a list of facts where all the listed words are verbs:

> The perpetrators drove to Minnesota, changed cars, and dropped the box on the side of the road outside St. Paul.

In the examples above, each list item begins with the same part of speech. And each list item independently reads with the lead-in. What does that mean? Well, take a look at the last example above where the lead-in to the list is *The perpetrators*. So each list item needs to independently make sense after *The perpetrators*. Let's test that.

> The perpetrators drove
>
> The perpetrators ... changed
>
> The perpetrators ... dropped

Yes, each verb makes sense after *The perpetrators*, so this is a grammatically parallel list.

To summarize, when stating the facts, give the gist of the story, include only the most legally significant facts, don't make legal conclusions, and make sure any list of facts is grammatically parallel and reads with the lead-in.

Now let's apply this to the parental-liability issue statement we've been working on.

Here are some versions of the facts that you might write.

- ... when the child was 17 years old at the time of the occurrence, and the parents knew that the child had played violent video games, had written violent stories, and had joined a group at school that always wore black clothing and was interested in violence, but when the parents did not know that the child had acquired automatic weapons or that the child and one of his friends had planned an attack at their school?

  Problem? Too many facts. Include enough facts (1) to give a gist of the story and (2) identify the most legally relevant facts.

- ... when the child maliciously and willfully killed ... ?

  Problem? Included conclusions of law. The statutory elements require that the plaintiff prove malice or willfulness. The writer can't answer the question while framing the question.

- ... when the parents knew that the 17-year-old child had played violent video games, violent stories were involved, and the child joined a group at school that always wore black clothing, but when the parents did not know that the child had acquired automatic weapons or that the child had planned an attack at their school?

  Problem? The facts are not stated in grammatically parallel terms, so the readability is lower than what it could be.

- ... when the child was 17 years old and living at home, and when the parents knew that the child had some violent ideas, but the parents did not know that the child planned the attack?

  Just right.

Now let's put all the pieces together in a great issue statement:

> Under the parental liability statute, which requires proving that a minor maliciously or willfully injured a person, are parents liable for the actions of their child

in shooting other students and teachers at his school, when the child was 17 years old and living at home, and when the parents knew that the child had some violent ideas, but the parents did not know that the child planned the attack?

C. Checklist for Formal One-Sentence Issue Statements

We'll finish this section about formal one-sentence issue statements by reviewing what makes good ones.

Structure

- Be sure to end the issue statement with a question mark because it is a direct question.
- Ensure that the entire sentence is readable.
- Follow Under-Does-When or Does-Under-When.
- Do not cite authority in the issue statement.

Law (i.e., the Under section)

- Give context by including either "Michigan common law," the popular name of the statute, or, if there is no popular name, a description of the statutory scheme (e.g., No Fault Act, parental liability statute, assault-by-maiming statute, motor vehicle code).
- Include a "which" clause and lay out the specific elements that are at issue.

Question (the "does" section)

- Properly focus the question on the element or phrase of the law that is actually at issue.

Facts (the "when" section)

- Tell a very brief story that gives a gist of what happened.
- Include the primary facts you use in the argument sections to prove the rule was or was not satisfied.
- Do not explain the facts as legal conclusions (e.g., Not this: "There was an ongoing emergency when the officer heard Lindell exclaim that Igor stabbed him." But this: "When the officer approached Lindell, he heard him say that Igor stabbed him.").
- State the list of facts so they are grammatically parallel.

D. Deep-Issue Statement

1. *The Parts of a Formal Issue Statement in the Deep-Issue Style*

Fed up with one-sentence issue statements that were cumbersome to read, the consummate legal writer Bryan Garner wrote an article in 1995 encouraging attorneys to use separate sentences to write an issue statement. Bryan A. Garner, *The Deep Issue: A New Approach to Framing Legal Questions*, 5 Scribes J. Legal Writing 1, 6–7 (1994–1995). Today, it's called the "deep-issue method."

The adherents to this method grow every day, but it still does not enjoy majority status. Most attorneys still frame the issue using the one-sentence method. But many believe that this is a superior structure for framing issues, so it's worth learning. Chances are you'll work for someone who requires it, and, if not, you could be the agent for change in that institution.

As Mr. Garner explains, there are three parts to a deep-issue statement: (1) the element/rule, (2) facts, and (3) a narrow question. Look familiar? These are the exact same parts that comprise a one-sentence issue statement. The main difference is that this method uses separate sentences to convey the information.

Here's what the formula for a deep issue statement looks like:

> [**Law**: Identify the common-law theory or state the statute's popular name]. [**Facts**: State the relevant facts]. [**Question**: Ask the specific question]?

Here's an example:

> Michigan's statute of limitations requires clients alleging legal malpractice to sue within two years after their lawyer discontinues serving them. After a fee dispute, Perry Jarvis moved to withdraw as Jane Ithikari's attorney, and the court granted his motion in June 1998. Ms. Ithikari sued Mr. Jarvis for malpractice in July 2000. Was Ms. Ithikari's suit timely?

Why is this structure so beautiful to read? It follows the millennia-old structure of a syllogism, the one you learned about in Chapter 4:

Major Premise:	All humans are mortal.
Minor Premise:	Socrates is human.
Conclusion:	Therefore, Socrates is mortal.

The legal version of this plays out in a deep issue statement:

Major Premise (Law):	Limitation period is two years for medical malpractice.
Minor Premise (Facts):	Ms. Ithikari is suing for medical malpractice two years and one month after he withdrew.
Question:	Was Ms. Ithikari's suit timely?

The deep issue statement is logical and should feel natural to read.

In writing the three parts—law, facts, question, follow the guidelines you learned above when writing the facts, law, and question of a one-sentence issue statement. In addition to those rules, follow these four rules that are unique to the deep-issue style. The issue statement must

- consist of separate sentences;
- include the law, facts, and question in that order;
- contain no more than 75 words; and
- be simple enough that a stranger, preferably even a nonlawyer, can read and understand it.

You can see these rules in action in the following five examples.

2. Deep-Issue Examples

Deep-Issue Example #1:

> The Immigration Act makes it a crime to bring an undocumented alien to the U.S. Meanwhile, the Maritime Act makes it a crime for the master of a vessel to fail to rescue persons aboard a vessel in distress. Does a master commit a crime under the Immigra-

tion Act when he rescues illegal aliens aboard a ship in distress and brings them to the U.S.? [65 words]

Deep-Issue Example #2:

The Internal Revenue Service requires all persons who receive more than $10,000 in cash in a trade or business to report the payment and provide the name of the payor. Paul Smith, an attorney, receives $14,000 in cash from a client and reports the payment but omits the client's name in the belief that disclosure would violate the attorney-client privilege. Is there an attorney-client-privilege exception to the IRS disclosure requirements? [73 words]

Deep-Issue Example #3:

The California Political Reform Act prohibits a public official from participating in a decision in which he or she has a material financial interest. Georgette Frye, Mayor of Monrovia, California, owns two office buildings in downtown Monrovia. Is Frye prohibited from voting on a Council resolution to provide a new sewer system for downtown Monrovia? [55 words]

Deep-Issue Example #4:

Johnson was convicted of aggravated robbery in 1988 at the age of 16. Five years later, the Kansas Legislature enacted the Sentencing Guidelines Act, requiring that prior juvenile convictions be used to enhance the sentence of an adult convicted of a crime. After Johnson was convicted of criminal damage to property in 1994, the court used his 1988 conviction to enhance the sentence. Does this procedure violate the U.S. Constitution's ex post facto clause? [74 words]

Deep-Issue Example #5:

In Missouri, a party to a contract cannot tortiously interfere with its own contract. Dr. Borstead claims that St. Anthony's Hospital tortiously interfered with a lease between himself and St. Anthony's Properties, Inc., the hospital's wholly owned subsidiary. Can St. Anthony's Hospital tortiously interfere with the lease of its wholly owned subsidiary? [54 words]

3. *Checklist for Deep-Issue Statement*

We'll finish this section about formal deep-issue statements by reviewing what makes good ones.

General Comments

- The entire issue statement must be under 75 words.
- Make sure the entire statement cohesively flows.
- Include the law, facts, and question in that order.
- Use separate sentences for the law, facts, and question.
- The law statement and the question need to be at the same level of law (e.g., both at cause-of-action level or both at element level).
- Do not cite authority in the issue statement.

Law

- Give context for the rule (e.g., "Under the Condominium Act, ..." or "The Michigan penal code requires ...").

- State the rule, but succinctly.
- If possible, include the actual element or phrase of law the issue turns on.
- Do not cite in any issue statement.

Facts

- Give enough background information so the reader gets the gist of the story.
- Include the most legally significant facts (i.e., the core facts relied on in the arguments).
- The facts must be grammatically parallel.
- Do not make legal conclusions when stating the facts.

Question

- Ask the question so it's clear how it relates to the law statement in the first sentence.
- Because the final sentence is a direct question, it must end with a question mark.

6.7 Persuasive Issue Statement

So far in this chapter about issue statements, you've learned how to write an informal and a formal issue statement. You now know how to write them in the one-sentence Under-Does-When format and the deep-issue multi-sentence style.

Now it's time to put a twist on that. But just a slight one. When writing a persuasive document like a brief, your goal is to frame the issue so that it reads with an air of objectivity but subtly leans toward your client's position. Subtly persuade your reader in the issue statement by being mindful of the issue statement's structure, rule statement, and fact choices.

A. Persuasive Structure

Use the syllogistic structure of the deep-issue method explained above in 6.6(D).

A syllogistic format is the most persuasive structure we write in. It's just so darn logical. This means that you should favor the deep-issue style because it uses separate sentences in exactly the syllogistic order of law first, then facts, then the question.

And, during those revisions, make sure the entire issue statement hangs together, that it flows seamlessly from one sentence to the next. That means writing in transitions and linking one sentence to the next.

B. Persuasive Rule Statement

Frame the rules so they favor your client's position. If, for instance, for your client to win, you need the court to find that something is not valid, then you should state the rule like this: "A will is invalid when ..." as opposed to "A will is valid when ...." Make it easy for the judge to see what it takes for your client to win. If the judge has to find the opposite of what the rule states, then that creates a bit more psychological work for the judge to agree with you.

C. Persuasive Fact Choices

More than anything, you need to maintain an air of objectivity when telling the story. Even though you're advocating for your client, you want to be and appear as a reasonable, fair, and truthful advocate, who you actually are. You do that by including both facts that help your client and facts that go against your client. The trick is to emphasize the good facts and deemphasize the bad facts.

Under no circumstances should you use cheap tricks of persuasion when writing the facts. Avoid hyperbole and intensifiers like *clearly*, *obviously*, and *egregiously*.

Maintain high ethos with the court by writing in a professional, nonadversarial tone.

And it should go without saying that you should avoid legalese. Speak plainly using modern language.

D. Example of a Persuasive Issue Statement

Without knowing anything about the case, which is how a judge would read an issue statement, read this and look for the techniques of persuasion above:

> Michigan's Uniform Trade Secrets Act defines "trade secret" as information that outsiders cannot "readily ascertain[ ] by proper means." LuLu Corp's customer list contains business names, addresses, and phone numbers that the public can find in trade publications, in phone directories, and on websites. Is the customer list a trade secret?

What did you notice? What about this persuaded you? Or maybe it's so subtle that you did not consciously register it. Sneaky.

In terms of the structure, it's in a syllogism: Law, Facts, Question. That alone gives an air of correctness. It just feels logical and true. And the entire paragraph reads well.

The rule is also stated in a persuasive way. Note that the writer is framing the law part of the issue using "readily ascertain." And then the facts have the word "public" in it (i.e., "that the public can find."). Those two bits of law and fact play off of each other: things that are readily ascertainable are also things the public can find. So this rings true. The reader will want to agree with it.

Overall, the structure, rule, and facts are all chosen in a way to make this subtly persuasive while still maintaining an air of objectivity.

Let's look at two more examples. Both examples come from a civil case where a patient was allegedly injured by a paramedic's gross negligence. One of the examples below was written by the patient's attorney, and the other one was written by the paramedic's attorney. So we have a real battle of the briefs. Identify (1) which issue statement was written by whom (the patient or the paramedic) and (2) what makes each one persuasive for its party.

Here's the first issue statement:

> Under the Emergency Medical Services Act, paramedics are liable if they commit gross negligence, meaning conduct "so reckless as to demonstrate a substantial lack of concern for whether an injury results." Paramedic Eldrick Woods admits that he deviated from standard protocol and "basic best practices" by failing to clear Mary Smith's airway or administer oxygen while transporting her to the hospital. Is Woods immune from liability for Ms. Smith's death?

And here's the second issue statement:

> Michigan paramedics are immune from tort liability unless their conduct is willful or "so reckless as to demonstrate a substantial lack of concern for whether an injury results." While performing emergency CPR on a heart-attack victim en

route to the hospital, paramedic Eldrick Woods unknowingly left some vomit in the patient's air passage but heard no wheezing indicating a blockage. Did Woods willfully harm the patient or show a substantial disregard for her welfare?

The dead give away is in the first sentence and how the rule is framed. In the first statement, it says "paramedics are liable," and the second statement says that "paramedics are immune." Based on that, we can tell that the patient's attorney wrote the first one, and the paramedic's attorney wrote the second one. And that is the first way these statements are persuasive: the law is framed in a way that supports the conclusion the authoring party wants.

The choice of facts also makes these persuasive for the respective parties. The patient's statement really focuses on failure to follow best practices while the paramedic's statement points to negligence (e.g., "unknowingly left some vomit in the patient's air passage") but certainly not *gross* negligence.

E. Less-Effective Persuasive Issue Statements

The three example below are less-effective ways of framing the issue. They are each from actual briefs filed in Michigan courts. Identify what could be improved about the following issue statements:

> In determining as a matter of law the adequacy of an attorney's actions to "win" a motion for summary disposition, under the principles established in *Simko v. Blake*, 332 N.W.2d 842 (Mich. 1995), did the Court of Appeals err by failing to apply the same law that was applied by the Court of Appeals to determine the legal adequacy of the actions taken to oppose the motion for summary disposition in the underlying case?

Honestly, I'm not sure I understand what the issue is after reading this. So the structure could definitely improve. And the rule governing the issue isn't that clear, either. Normally, we don't cite authority, but the citation here is critical to the question, apparently, so they get a pass on that.

Check out the second bad example, and pay attention to how you're perceiving it:

> WHETHER MCL 768.20a CONTROLS WHEN A DEFENDANT WISHES TO PURSUE AN INSANITY DEFENSE IN THE STATE OF MICHIGAN AND IF A DEFENDANT IS AFFORDED HIS CONSTITUTIONAL RIGHT TO PRESENT A DEFENSE WHERE HE IS REQUIRED TO COMPLY WITH THAT STATUTORY FRAMEWORK?

The structure really struggles here. A *whether* clause is dependent on an independent clause, so this is an incomplete sentence. Now, you do see some attorneys write in this *whether* style, but it is overall falling out of favor. Also, never use all caps to write any paragraph because it is more difficult to read. Finally, it appears that there are two questions in this one paragraph. Ask just one question per issue statement.

And here's the final bad example:

> <u>DID THE MACOMB COUNTY PROSECUTOR'S OFFICE VIOLATE DEFENDANT JAMES CARNEY'S CONSTITUTIONAL RIGHTS WHEN IN OCTOBER OF 2006 ASSISTANT PROSECUTING ATTORNEY JANICE ISSUED A NOLLE PROSEQUI OF THE CRIMINAL CHARGES AGAINST HIM DURING THE SELECTION OF HIS JURY IN MACOMB COUNTY</u>

CIRCUIT COURT OVER DEFENSE COUNSEL'S OBJECTIONS AND DID NOT REFILE THE CASE UNTIL 22 MONTHS LATER IN AUGUST OF 2008?

Definitely don't use all caps, and for heaven's sake, don't use all caps and underlining. The structure of this question is good, but we do not know what the controlling rule is. Without knowing the rule, the issue cannot be framed. Also, we need to always write directly and concisely; avoid mildly relevant information and include only the most significantly relevant stuff.

Chapter Seven

IREAC: Give a Rule Foundation

7.1 Cohesively Synthesizing Rules Is Key

If every legal matter could be resolved by one tight sentence of law, you wouldn't need to read this chapter and learn the skill of synthesizing rules of law. But, unfortunately, the law for one legal matter often requires piecing together rules from several different sources. In a way, it's like gathering ingredients in a grocery store before bringing them all together to make a tasty treat. You might need to go to the baking aisle for cardamom and flour and then to the dairy aisle for whipping cream. Then you might need to grab some raspberries and lemons before checking out and heading home. Once in your kitchen, you then bring all the ingredients together to make a tasty cake.

Likewise, the law is sometimes disparately organized like the items in a grocery store. The rules governing your client's case—like the scattered ingredients in a store—may come from several different sources, like a statute, perhaps a regulation, and maybe a few cases.

So we often need to synthesize the rules of law from several different sources. That's what this chapter is all about.

7.2 Include Elements and Guiding Rules in a Rule Foundation

A Rule Foundation is the collection of rules that govern your client's issue. Those rules will be (1) elements of law and (2) guidance rules or guidelines to help courts and attorneys apply the elements to the facts.

Here is a sample Rule Foundation from an objective memo that gives the rules for deciding whether a contract to not compete with a former employer is valid. Because the case arose in Michigan but was litigated in federal court, the attorney wrote the memo relying on both state and federal law.

IREAC: This objective memo states the issue as a conclusion in the global point heading.

IREAC: This is the **Rule Foundation**. The first three sentences contain the **elements** for determining whether the contract is valid.

This final "fact specific" rule is a **guiding rule**, not an element of law. It merely guides how to apply the elements above to the facts.

Discussion

The former employer's noncompete agreement is unenforceable because the geographic and time limitations are unreasonable.

The Michigan Antitrust Reform Act generally prohibits any "contract ... between 2 or more persons in **restraint of ... trade**." Mich. Comp. Laws § 445.772 (2002). "However, the statute explicitly authorizes agreements not to compete as long as they are reasonable." *Certified Restoration Dry Cleaning v. Tenke Corp.*, 511 F.3d 535, 546 (6th Cir. 2007). In evaluating a non-competition clause for reasonableness, Michigan courts generally examine the clause's duration, geographic scope, and the type of employment prohibited. *Id.* at 546. Deciding an agreement's reasonableness is "inherently fact specific." *Id.* at 547 (citation omitted).

[The Case Illustrations and Application would go after the Rule Foundation.]

You may wonder how a writer figured out what should go in this Rule Foundation. That all begins when you're researching the law. You will find a collection of rules in secondary authority, like treatises, encyclopedias, or law-review articles, and you'll also find the controlling rules in caselaw. Those are good sources to draw from.

As you read those sources and you come across the rules, first decide which rules are the elements—the required parts of the law. All of those need to go in your document. In the example above, the first three sentences of the Rule Foundation contain the elements: the prohibition on restraint of trade; the reasonableness rule; and the elements of duration, geography, and type of employment. If a court were to decide your client's issue, they must apply all that law.

Ok. So now you know that the elements must go in the Rule Foundation.

But there are also guiding rules that guide *how* the elements should be applied to the facts. You are not required to put those rules into your document, but you should if they help the reader understand how to apply the rule or they give your client an advantage. Guiding rules about whether a certain element is a high or low bar to prove are especially helpful. In the example above, the guiding rule about "inherently fact specific" analysis isn't an element a party needs to prove; rather, it's a clue or guidance on how to go about applying the law. Whether to include rules like that are up to the writer's discretion.

But where does a reader find the rules? In the memo portion above, the Rule Foundation's writer took the rules from the *Certified Restoration* case below. The rules in bold emphasis ended up in the Rule Foundation. As you read through the case, see if you can spot the elements versus the guiding rules. You can peek at the annotations if you find that helpful.

Certified Restoration Dry Cleaning Network, L.L.C. v. Tenke Corp.

511 F.3d 535
(6th Cir. 2007)

[Facts and first issue omitted.]

b. Reasonableness of the Non-Compete Covenant

In addition to erroneously finding the non-compete clause ambiguous, the district court improperly concluded that there was insufficient evidence to determine whether Plaintiff would likely succeed in convincing the court that the non-compete clause was reasonable and therefore enforceable.

The Michigan Antitrust Reform Act generally prohibits any "contract ... between 2 or more persons in restraint of ... trade." Mich. Comp. Laws § 445.772 (2002). **However, the statute explicitly authorizes agreements not to compete as long as they are reasonable.** *Coates*, 274 Mich. App. 498, 2007 WL 2452721, at *4; *Bristol Window & Door, Inc. v. Hoogenstyn*, 250 Mich. App. 478, 650 N.W.2d 670, 678 (Mich. Ct. App. 2002). Section 4(a)(1) of the Act provides:

> An employer may obtain from an employee an agreement or covenant which protects an employer's reasonable competitive business interests and expressly prohibits an employee from engaging in employment or a line of business after termination of the employment *if the agreement or covenant is* ***reasonable as to its duration, geographical area, and the type of employment or line of business***. To the extent any such agreement or covenant is found to be unreasonable in any respect, a court may limit the agreement to render it reasonable in light of the circumstances in which it was made and specifically enforce the agreement as limited.

Mich. Comp. Laws § 445.774a(1) (emphasis added). The Michigan courts have clarified that "§ 4(a)(1) represents a codification of the common-law rule that 'the enforceability of non-competition agreements depends on their reasonableness.'" *St. Clair Med.*, 715 N.W.2d at 918 (quoting *Bristol Window & Door*, 650 N.W.2d at 679). Although § 4(a)(1) only refers to non-competition agreements between employers and employees, Michigan courts have "reject[ed] the suggestion that with its enactment of [§ 4(a)(1)] the Legislature intended by implication to prohibit all noncompetition agreements entered into outside the employer-employee context." *Bristol Window & Door*, 650 N.W.2d at 680. Rather, they have concluded that "[a]greements not to compete are permissible under Michigan law as long as they are reasonable." *Coates*, 276 Mich. App. 498, 2007 WL 2452721, at *4.

In evaluating a non-competition clause for reasonableness, Michigan courts generally examine the clause's duration, geographic scope, and the type of employment prohibited. *See* Mich. Comp. Laws § 445.774a(1). They also consider the reasonableness of the competitive business interests justifying the clause. *See, e.g.*, *St. Clair Med.*, 715 N.W.2d at 919; *Whirlpool Corp. v. Burns*, 457 F. Supp. 2d 806, 812 (W.D. Mich. 2006) ("The reasonableness of a covenant not to compete is not analyzed in the abstract, but in the context of the employer's particular business interest and the function and knowledge of the particular employee."). **This reasonableness inquiry**

The two rules in this paragraph about restraint of trade and reasonableness are stated as mandatory **elements** of law. That's why the memo's writer included them in the Rule Foundation.

Statutes almost always provide **elements** of law rather than secondary guidelines. Plus, the court goes into much more detail about duration, geography, and employment type below in the opinion; that contextual clue tells us that these are important **elements**.

The first statement in this paragraph gives the history of the statute: it comes from common law. That's not an element to prove, so it's a **guiding** rule.

The second half of this paragraph goes to the scope of the rule. Because our issue is in the employer-employee relationship, we can ignore this rule.

The court repeats these **elements** from above. Same with the second sentence in this paragraph.

The "fact specific" rule is **secondary** to the elements, but the writer strategically decided to include it in the Rule Foundation because their client *narrative* is strong.

is "inherently fact specific." *Capaldi v. Liftaid Transport, L.L.C.*, No. 267981, 2006 Mich. App. LEXIS 3199, 2006 WL 3019799, at *5 (Mich. Ct. App. Oct. 24, 2006) (unpublished); *Northern Mich. Title Co. v. Bartlett*, No. 248751, 2005 Mich. App. LEXIS 733, 2005 WL 599867, at *3 (Mich. Ct. App. Mar. 15, 2005) (unpublished). However, "[t]he reasonableness of a noncompete provision is a question of law where relevant facts are undisputed." *Coates*, 276 Mich. App. 498, 2007 WL 2452721, at *4.

The final rule in this paragraph about the issue being a question of law is redundant of a procedural rule for summary-judgment motions. Besides, it doesn't go to the elements, so it may be omitted from the Rule Foundation.

So there you have it. In the Rule Foundation, include the elements. And include any guiding rules or guidelines that directly apply to the goals of your analysis.

7.3 Refine the *Issue* as the Rule Foundation Progresses

As you go from broad to narrow rules, keep focusing your reader on which parts of the law are actually at issue. In other words, keep refining the issue.

Law students often wonder whether they must always begin their Rule Foundation by reciting all the elements of a claim. You have some discretion on how broad (or how "deep") to start. There is no black-and-white rule. But if the legal question you're writing about relates directly to an element of the claim, then it is fair game to begin with all the elements. The elements can help your reader understand context.

If you start your Rule Foundation with the elements, remember to narrow your focus immediately—usually in the next sentence—to the single element or elements at issue. There's no time to dawdle or stray.

For instance, if you're discussing whether a plaintiff can satisfy the falsity element of a defamation claim, you might state the elements in the first sentence of your foundation. But in the second sentence, you'd immediately narrow to the falsity element—never to mention the other elements again. Here's an example:

> A plaintiff suing for defamation must prove (1) a **false** and defamatory statement concerning the plaintiff, (2) an unprivileged publication to a third party, (3) fault amounting at least to negligence, and (4) either actionability of the statement irrespective of special harm (defamation per se) or the existence of special harm (defamation *per quod*). [citation]. As the first element reflects, a plaintiff's claim will fail if he or she cannot establish that the defendant's statement was **false**. [citation].
>
> To be **false**, a statement must be one of "actual fact," meaning a statement whose truthfulness can be objectively verified. [citation]. Statements of opinion that are necessarily subjective cannot satisfy this requirement. [citation].

And it can be very helpful to explicitly state which elements are and are not at issue. In the Rule Foundation for the eMemo in 2.3, this is how the writer explicitly narrowed the issue for the reader:

> Under Mich. Comp. Laws Ann. § 257.625 (West 2023), a person "shall not operate a vehicle upon a highway ... if the person is operating while intoxicated." **For our**

> **case, the main issue will be whether Mr. Vivek was "operating" the vehicle.** The Motor Vehicle Code defines "operating" as "[b]eing in actual physical control of a vehicle." MCLA § 257.35a.

Readers love clarity like that.

7.4 Put the Rule Foundation Near the Beginning

As the R in IREAC, you must put the rules near the beginning of any analysis. More than anything, remember that a Rule Foundation is the ... well ... *foundation* that the rest of the analysis is built on. Therefore, the Rule Foundation must go at or near the beginning of the analysis portion of your document. And you may even have more than one.

A. A Rule Foundation in Informal Analysis

In informal or smaller-scale documents like opinion letters and eMemos, the Rule Foundation will be in the first or second paragraph. Check this out in the sample Opinion Letter on page 11 of this book. You can also see a sample Rule Foundation on page 19 in the Controlling Law section of an eMemo.

Again, the Rule Foundation is the starting point for the analysis, so it goes early in the document.

B. A Rule Foundation in Formal Analysis

In more formal documents like a full office memo or a court brief, the Rule Foundation begins the main section of analysis. For a full office memo, that is the Discussion section. And the main analysis section in a brief is called the Argument section. Look at the Discussion section of the Full Office Memo on page 43. The annotation there points you to the second paragraph; that's where the Rule Foundation begins, and it goes all the way until the heading for the first element at issue.

You can find the same thing in the sample Trial-Court Brief on page 61.

7.5 Sometimes, Include Global and Secondary Rule Foundations

If you have just one issue in your analysis section, then you'll have just one Rule Foundation. This was the case in the Appellate Brief on page 97. Section A, the entirety of it, is a single Rule Foundation for the entire Argument section. In IREAC terms, there's just one R for the one IREAC packet.

But if you have two or more subissues, you'll have two or more IREAC packets. In those situations, you'll have one global Rule Foundation that acts as a preamble before all the IREAC packets; and then each IREAC packet will have its own synthesis of rules, what we call a secondary Rule Foundation. So if you have two subissues, you'll have two IREAC packets, and each packet will have its own Rule Foundation. Each IREAC packet's Rule Foundation is specific only to the analysis in that one subissue. Those rules don't apply to the other IREAC packets.

As you learned in 4.6(E), you need to tie multiple IREAC packets together with a global Rule Foundation that goes before any of the IREAC packets begin.

In the sample Full Office Memo in Chapter 2, you can see a global Rule foundation on page 43. (Note the annotations in the margin there.) And then, for each subissue on pages 44 and 47, you'll see specific Rule Foundations that pertain to their respective sections. The global Rule Foundation on page 43 applies to the entire analysis while the secondary ones apply just to that one element at issue.

And you can see the same technique in the Trial-Court Brief in section 2.6. On page 61, you'll see a global Rule Foundation. And then on pages 62, 64, and 66 you'll see individual arguments, and each individual argument has its own Rule Foundation for rules that pertain to just the one argument.

Below is an outline of the Argument section for that Trial-Court Brief beginning on page 61. Because this is a persuasive document, we use AREAC instead of IREAC, the only difference being that we start with an argument rather than by objectively stating the issue:

Tie together multiple AREAC packets. Here, the writer does that with the global point heading and the global Rule Foundation. 4.6(E).

Argument

[I. Global Persuasive Point Heading for Duty]

[Global Rule Foundation for Duty]

[AREAC: **A. Persuasive Point Heading for Open and Obvious]**

[AREAC: Secondary Rule Foundation for Open and Obvious]

[AREAC: Case Illustrations]

[AREAC: Application of Law to Fact]

[AREAC: Conclusion]

[AREAC: **B. Persuasive Point Heading for Special Aspects]**

[AREAC: Secondary Rule Foundation for Special Aspects]

[AREAC: Case Illustrations]

[AREAC: Application of Law to Fact]

[AREAC: Conclusion]

[AREAC: **C. Persuasive Point Heading for *Slaughter* Counterargument]**

[AREAC: Secondary Rule Foundation for *Slaughter* Counterargument]

[AREAC: Case Illustrations]

[AREAC: Application of Law to Fact]

[AREAC: Conclusion]

[AREAC: **II. Global Persuasive Point Heading for Notice]**

[AREAC: Global Rule Foundation for Lack of Notice]

[AREAC: Case Illustrations]

[AREAC: Application of Law to Fact]

[AREAC: Conclusion]

7.6 Make the Rule Foundation Readable

A. Organize the Rules from Broad to Narrow

Context is everything when learning something new. We need to know how everything connects. As a teacher in every legal analytical document you write, you need to give context to the rules. That context happens when you start with the broadest rules and work your way to the narrower rules. This warrants a bit more explanation, but that's really all it is.

When teaching the rules of law in your Rule Foundation, start broad to give your reader some context—and then quickly narrow to the specific rules that control the outcome. You don't want to belabor anything, but it pays to take this step by step. Remember, you are always the teacher when you write about the law. Don't presume expertise on your reader's part. Walk your reader from rule to rule.

So the first sentence in your foundation will capture the broadest concept. Then, each sentence grows progressively narrower in focus. The final sentence of your foundation will, if you construct your discussion well, transition seamlessly into the next part of the discussion, perhaps an analysis of a specific case.

Here's an example without the citations to help you concentrate on the substance. Remember to take it step by step, starting broad and narrowing quickly:

> Michigan has adopted the Uniform Trade Secrets Act. [citation]. The Act is designed to ensure that businesses can realize the value of their ingenuity without unfair interference. [citation]. It achieves this goal, in part, by allowing businesses to sue those who have misappropriated trade secrets. [citation]. But a business cannot prove a claim for the misappropriation of a trade secret until it first proves that there was a trade secret to begin with. [citation].
>
> The Act defines "trade secret" as "information," including a "compilation, drawing, or schematic." [citation]. The definition also requires proof that the purported trade secret is information that outsiders "cannot readily ascertain through proper means." [citation].

There. Now your reader knows the governing legal rules. Note the foundation's broad start. It began by stating simply that Michigan has adopted the uniform act. Then, the writer added a sentence giving the reader a flavor for the statute's purpose. That helped orient the reader. And sometimes stating a statute's general purpose can help readers better understand the specific statutory rules that follow. So those first two sentences were very broad. But then things quickly narrowed. And each sentence got narrower in scope, until the foundation ended.

Because of the broad-to-narrow approach, you might think of this shape while writing your foundation:

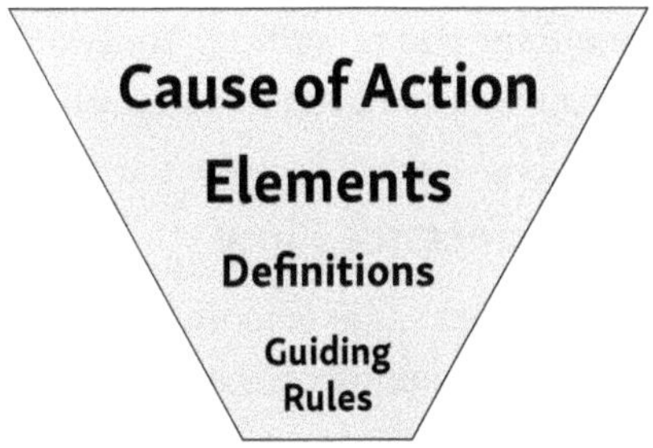

B. Logically Sequence the Rules

It's crucial that you teach the rules in a logical sequence. For instance, teach a general rule before introducing its exception. State a term of art before defining it.

Here's an excerpt of a United States Court of Appeals decision. See how the court lays its foundation of legal rules. Again, the citations are omitted so that you can concentrate on the substance:

> Under the Fourth Amendment, a search warrant may only issue "upon probable cause." [citation]. Probable cause exists when "there is a fair probability that contraband or evidence of a crime will be found in a particular place." [citation]. This "practical, common-sense decision" must be made based on "all the circumstances set forth in the affidavit" provided by the officers seeking a warrant. [citation]. The magistrate's finding of probable cause "'should be paid great deference by reviewing courts.'" [citation].

Did you notice the sequence of ideas? When beginning to lay its foundation of legal rules, the court started with the broadest point: the Fourth Amendment's rule requiring probable cause for a search warrant. Then the court defined "probable cause." Then it explained how magistrates decide whether an affidavit satisfies this definition, and, finally, how reviewing courts should review the magistrate's decision. In short, it's a logical, step-by-step sequence of ideas, starting broad and quickly narrowing.

C. Use Paragraph Breaks for a Long Rule Foundation

The Rule Foundation part of a legal analysis is not called the foundation *paragraph* for a reason: the length of your foundation depends on the complexity of the legal issue you're writing about. So it may be one sentence or two sentences. And it may be three paragraphs. You'd never want a writer to think that he or she must teach all the pertinent legal rules in a single paragraph. That's an artificial limitation.

There may be times when a single paragraph is enough space to lay out the controlling legal rules effectively. If so, use a single paragraph. But you shouldn't think of that as a goal or a default.

Plus, if writers believe that the Rule Foundation must be a single paragraph, they may try to accomplish this by writing a long, run-on paragraph. You don't want to fall into that trap. You'll want to keep your paragraph length manageable for readers—usually no more than four or five sentences. A long block of solid text, with no indents to give your reader momentary mental rests, is intimidating. You want your writing to look inviting to readers, not intimidating.

This approach isn't advocating for long Rule Foundations. You're not writing a treatise, after all. And the goal of every legal writer is to produce the shortest *complete* document possible. You want to strike the appropriate balance between brevity and thorough rule teaching. It's not easy, but you'll develop a savvy for how much is too much and how much is too little. The length will also depend on the nature of the document you're writing. You won't spend as much time teaching rules in an email to your boss as you will in a brief to an appellate court.

D. Obsess Over Sentence-to-Sentence Flow

The worst thing you could do for your reader is to dump a bunch of disconnected rules of law on their eyeballs. Instead, help the reader out by connecting each sentence. Connect the sentences by (1) repeating some old information before new information and (2) using pronouns like *this* and *that*. These two methods for connecting are in bold below:

> Under the Fourth Amendment, a search warrant may only issue "upon **probable cause.**" [citation]. **Probable cause** exists when "there is a fair probability that contraband or evidence of a crime will be found in a particular place." [citation]. **This** "practical, common-sense **decision**" must be made based on "all the circumstances set forth in the affidavit" provided by the officers seeking a warrant. [citation]. The magistrate's **finding** of **probable cause** "'should be paid great deference by reviewing courts.'" [citation].

Your reader will love you for it.

8.2(E) has several more examples of how to improve flow sentence to sentence.

E. Use a Combination of Paraphrasing and Quoting

Nobody likes to read a series of quotations, and nobody certainly is overjoyed reading a block quotation. A lack of eagerness means that reading comprehension will suffer, so why would you write something knowing that the reader probably isn't going to fully appreciate or understand it.

Instead, use a combination of paraphrasing and quoting to make the rules enjoyable to read. Follow these rules when writing your Rule Foundations:

(1) Prefer to paraphrase.
(2) Quote essential words of phrases that cannot be paraphrased.
(3) Most legal writers do a mix of heavy paraphrasing and light quoting.
(4) Avoid writing dense walls of text.

You'll notice in all the examples in this chapter on Rule Foundations that the writers follow these rules for the most part. Use them as examples when writing your own Rule Foundations.

7.7 Cite a Binding Source After Every Rule

A. Every Rule Must Have a Binding Source

Cite a source after every sentence in which you state a rule of law for the first time. And that citation must be to binding authority. If there is no binding authority for that rule, then you need to explain to the reader why you're citing persuasive authority for a rule of law. This usually happens when any area of law is underdeveloped, and so a lower court itself in a published opinion will open the door to relying on rules from persuasive caselaw. But you'd need to explain that in the document you're writing.

B. Include a Pinpoint Page Number for Quotations

And be sure to include pinpoint page citations for quotations. You'll find the pinpoint page number in the following example in bold:

> The "made whole" doctrine applies when an insurer has not yet made claim payments. *Intervest Construction of Jax, Inc. v. General Fidelity Insurance Co.*, 133 So. 3d 494, **504** (Fla. 2014).

That makes it so your reader doesn't have to hunt all over the opinion for your quotation.

By the way, if you don't know how to find the pinpoint page number in caselaw, see 17.5, Find the Right Page Number in Cases Online.

C. Put the Citation *After* the Rule

Do not lead by stating the source and then stating the rule. Readers first and foremost want to know the rules of law, not the sources. So give them what they want first.

> **This is wrong:** The Florida Supreme Court in *Intervest Construction of Jax, Inc. v. General Fidelity Insurance Co.*, 133 So. 3d 494, 504 (Fla. 2014), stated that the "made whole" doctrine applies when an insurer has not yet made claim payments.
>
> **This is much better:** The "made whole" doctrine applies when an insurer has not yet made claim payments. *Intervest Construction of Jax, Inc. v. General Fidelity Insurance Co.*, 133 So. 3d 494, 504 (Fla. 2014).

In the "better" example above, the emphasis is on the rule, not the source. Readers are reading your analysis to learn the substantive rules, not the source of them. They can quickly pick up the source by skimming the citation. The rule is the important part.

Here's one more example:

> **This is wrong:** As the court in *Williams v. Trans World Airlines*, 509 F.2d 942, 948 (2d Cir. 1975), stated, "The test of whether or not the airline properly exercised its power... rests upon the facts and circumstances of the case as known to the airline at the time it formed its opinion ...."
>
> **This is much better:** "The test of whether or not the airline properly exercised its power... rests upon the facts and circumstances of the case as known to the airline at the time it formed its opinion ...." *Williams v. Trans World Airlines*, 509 F.2d 942, 948 (2d Cir. 1975).

Now, if *Williams* on its own was somehow significant and there was a question about what the law is, then perhaps beginning with the source would be helpful to your reader. But that is a rare circumstance.

You'll see more examples of the correct way to cite in the *Certified Restoration* case in section 7.2 above; notice how the court explained the rules by first stating the rule, and then citing a source for each rule after the rule. You should do the same.

7.8 Sometimes, Make Rule Foundations Persuasive

When you need to persuade your reader, like in a letter or brief, do so by subtly shaping the rules in the Rule Foundation.

For most types of legal writing, you should state the rules objectively. Lay them out in a way that does not favor one side or the other.

But in persuasive documents, like some letters and all court briefs, you should state the rules in a way that subtly favors your client's position. Always be honest about the rules, yet you may frame any rule accurately and make it bend toward your client.

Here are the techniques to make an objective statement of the rule more favorable to your client's theory of the case:

a. **Create a favorable context.**
b. **State favorable rules as *broadly* as possible** (use words like "always" or "whenever").

c. **If you must include unfavorable rules, state them as *narrowly* as possible** (use words like "only if"). Also weaken their impact by placing them in a dependent clause preceded by "Although."

d. **Emphasize favorable rules and deemphasize unfavorable rules:**

   i. Burden of proof (which party has the burden to succeed on a motion for summary judgment?)

   ii. Airtime (spend more time describing ideas that favor your client's theory of the case)

   iii. Position of emphasis (statements at the beginning and end of paragraphs generally are given more attention)

   iv. Sentence construction (use passive voice or nominalizations to deemphasize unfavorable rule; put unfavorable rule in a dependent clause of a sentence)

   v. Sentence length (a short sentence can be used for emphasis; short sentences at the end of a paragraph can be particularly emphatic)

e. **Select words carefully** (are there any synonyms that might make the rule sound more favorable, or make your opponent's actions seem less so?)

To see these techniques in action, below you'll find three statements of the same rules. The first one immediately below are the rules stated objectively, perhaps as a court would state them. And then, below that, you'll find the same rules stated by first the plaintiff and then the defendant. The rules concern the display of a religious message on public land. In these cases, the plaintiff is usually claiming that the government cannot display a religious message on public demand because it violates the United States Constitution.

Here's an objectively stated Rule Foundation:

> In determining the constitutionality of a religious display, the court considers whether the display has any secular purpose; whether its principal or primary effect advances or inhibits religion; and, finally, whether the display fosters "an excessive government entanglement with religion." [citation]. Courts generally defer to the government's assertion that a religious display has a secular purpose. [citation].

Now see how a plaintiff pours on the magic of subtly reshaping the rules so they keep their original meaning, but they lean towards a plaintiff's position:

> A religious display on public land is unconstitutional **whenever** it (1) lacks a secular purpose, (2) has the primary effect of advancing or inhibiting religion, or (3) fosters excessive government entanglement with religion. [citation]. If the display fails any one of these three prongs, then it violates the Establishment Clause and **must be found** unconstitutional. [citation]. Although courts try to defer to the avowed secular purpose claimed by the government, it is insufficient for the government to simply assert that a display has a secular purpose. [citation]. The court must distinguish a "sham secular purpose from a sincere one." [citation].

Opening line creates **favorable context** for the plaintiff: "unconstitutional." And then "whenever" implies a **broad**, easy-to-satisfy rule.

The "fails any one" language also creates **broad**, easy-to-satisfy rule. Lots of **airtime** given to finding the display unconstitutional.

Sentence construction de-emphasizes court deference by putting that part of the rule in a dependent clause in the middle of the paragraph.

The Rule Foundation ends with a **favorable** guiding rule.

In summary, this is how the plaintiff shaped the rules to subtly, persuasively favor their client's position:

- Started with favorable context.
- Gave lots of airtime to find a display unconstitutional.
- Used broad language to invite agreement.
- Used sentence construction to de-emphasize a rule.
- Ended with a favorable statement.

Now contrast how the plaintiff wrote the rules above to how the government, the defendant, would write it. To win, the defendant needs to argue that it's supporting the display is constitutional:

Opening line creates **favorable context** for the defendant: It implies that it has wiggle room to decide these matters.

Airtime to favorable rule statements: "permitted." Uses **narrow language** like "unless" to show that the plaintiff has an uphill battle. Giving airtime to plaintiff's burden of proof **emphasizes** the presumption in the defendant's favor.

A new paragraph is a **place of emphasis** for a **favorable rule**.

> The neutrality guaranteed by the Establishment Clause dictates neither the obliteration of all religious displays nor the total separation of church and state. [citation]. Religious displays on public property **are thus permitted** unless the plaintiff can **prove** that the government lacked a legitimate secular purpose in presenting the display, the display has the primary effect of advancing or inhibiting religion, or that the display fosters an excessive entanglement with religion. [citation].
>
> Courts are obliged to give deference to the government's avowed secular purpose and can invalidate a display based on secular purpose **only** when there was no question that the action was motivated wholly by religious considerations. [citation]. Thus, even when the benefits to religion are substantial, a legitimate secular purpose can override a concurrent religious purpose. [citation].

Using "only" here is **narrow language** that makes it seem like the plaintiff's path to victory is improbable.

The Rule Foundation ends with a **favorable** guiding rule.

How did the government transform the rule to support its position?

- Started by creating favorable context. The first sentence supports the government's conclusion.
- Gave more airtime to words that make it sound like religious displays are "permitted" more often than not.
- Used narrow language for the plaintiff's path to victory.
- Emphasized that the other party has the burden of proof.
- Emphasized favorable deferential rule—by including it *and* by beginning a new paragraph with it.
- Ended with a favorable statement.

So after you create a Rule Foundation in a persuasive document, take a few moments to shape it so it slants toward your client's interests.

7.9 For Briefs, Add a Procedural Rule Foundation

A. Standard of Review

So far, this chapter has been about a Rule Foundation that is the foundation of an argument; it's the R of IREAC and AREAC. But briefs have a unique paragraph separate from the typical Rule Foundation that explains the rules that are specific to the type of motion being brought. In trial-court briefs, this is generally called the Standard of Review, and it gets its own section right before the Argument section; see one in context on page 67. And in an appellate brief, the section is called a Standard of Review; check one out on page 108.

Here's an example of an Standard of Review in a defendant's brief where Little Caesars sued a franchisee for breach of contract. The defendant is asking the court to dismiss the case. You'll see that these rules are unrelated to the substantive issues of breach of contract; rather, they relate to the procedure of how the court should decide the motion. And, finally, note how the plaintiff's attorney slightly, subtly shaped the rules to favor their client, the franchisee.

> **Standard of Review**
>
> Summary judgment is appropriate when there is no genuine issue as to any material fact and the moving party is entitled to judgment as a matter of law. Fed. R. Civ. P. 56(c). The central inquiry is "whether the evidence presents a sufficient disagreement to require submission to a jury or whether it is so one-sided that one party must prevail as a matter of law." *Anderson v. Liberty Lobby, Inc.*, 477 U.S. 242, 251–52 (1986).
>
> The movant has an initial burden of showing "the absence of a genuine issue of material fact." *Celotex Corp. v. Catrett*, 477 U.S. 317, 323 (1986). Once the movant meets this burden, the non-movant must come forward with specific facts showing that there is a genuine issue for trial. *Matsushita Electric Industrial Co., Ltd. v. Zenith Radio Corp.*, 475 U.S. 574, 587 (1986). To demonstrate a genuine issue, the non-movant must present sufficient evidence upon which a jury could reasonably find for the non-movant; a "scintilla of evidence" is insufficient. *Anderson*, 477 U.S. at 252.
>
> The court must believe the non-movant's evidence and draw "all justifiable inferences" in the non-movant's favor. *Id.* at 255. The inquiry is whether the evidence presented is such that a jury applying the relevant evidentiary standard could "reasonably find for either the plaintiff or the defendant." *Id.*

B. Creating the Standard of Review

How did the attorney who wrote the standard immediately above get that into the brief?

First off, the reality is that most firms have templates of documents they regularly use, including briefs with procedural standards of review. But you nonetheless need to know how to create one and keep it updated.

To create the procedural standard section in your brief, follow these steps:

- Find the standard in a binding case.
- Make sure the standard is specific to the issues in your brief.
- Copy the standard and paste it in your document.
- Make the standard "your own" to avoid clunky block quotations and plagiarism.

First, find the standard in a binding case. Almost always, you'll find the standard in a case that you're already using in the Argument section of the brief. Searching within the document or on the computer screen for "standard" will generally lead you right to it.

You can also do a search in Westlaw or Lexis for it. Try this search formula:

> "standard of review" /s [state the court rule you're relying on]

So something like this:

> "standard of review" /s "motion for summary judgment" OR "standard of review" /s "12(b)(6)"

Second, make sure the standard is specific to the issues you discuss in the brief. In the sample Standard of Review immediately above in section (A), the issue was ruling on a motion for summary judgment. And in the example below, the standard was specific to a lower-court ruling on subject matter jurisdiction.

Third, once you find the correct standard in caselaw, copy and paste it into your document. Be sure to paste it without formatting to avoid any weird formatting leaching into your document. Yes, you'll have to re-italicize any case titles, but that little inconvenience is worth not having grayed-out text, random HTML code, and different fonts in your document.

At this point, the pasted collection of rules will be a large block quotation (17.8(E)). And, yes, you could simply keep the monolith of text and cite to the case you got that block quotation from, but readers usually fly through block quotations or entirely skip over them, so you should take the time to do the final step.

Finally, make the pasted Standard of Review "your own" by using a mix of paraphrasing and quoting.

To make the Standard your own, prefer paraphrasing, but quote when necessary. As for the citations, cite the case you actually got the standard from. Because that case undoubtedly cited to other cases, add the *(citation omitted)* or, more modernly, the *(cleaned up)* parenthetical after the citation. You can see these rules applied in the example below on the right.

The writer on the right paraphrased most of the rules and quoted only when necessary. And the writer also improved the sentence-to-sentence flow. Another technique is to cut down on the number of citations to increase readability.

Here's how the standard would look if you didn't make it your own:

> "[S]ubject matter jurisdiction issues present questions of law that we review de novo, even when [they are] raised for the first time on appeal." *Dupree v. Owens*, 92 F.4th 999, 1004 (11th Cir. 2024) (quotations omitted). Subject matter jurisdiction can never be waived and "courts have an independent obligation to determine whether subject matter jurisdiction exists, even in the absence of a challenge from any party." *Id.* (quotations omitted).

Hensley v. Hartford Cas. Ins. Co., 113 F.4th 1327, 1332 (11th Cir. 2024).

Compare the block quotation on the left to this more readable version:

> A court reviews subject-matter jurisdiction issues de novo. *Hensley v. Hartford Cas. Ins. Co.*, 113 F.4th 1327, 1332 (11th Cir. 2024) (citation omitted). The court's jurisdiction cannot be waived, regardless of whether a party raises the issue. *Id.* In fact, "courts have an independent obligation to determine whether subject matter jurisdiction exists ...." *Id.*

Chapter Eight

IREAC: Explain Codified Law

8.1 Codified Law

You have or will soon learn that codified law—statutes, regulations, court rules, and constitutions—is the apex species of the law kingdom. A law passed by a publicly elected legislature carries more weight than any other type of law—except for constitutions, the god of the legal kingdom.

What this practically means for you is that you will begin your analysis of a legal problem with codified law. And this usually occurs in a global or secondary Rule Foundation section of an IREAC analysis packet. (You can learn about Rule Foundations in Chapter 7, if you haven't already.)

If at any point while reading this chapter you want to see codified law explained in the wild, you can see it in the sample documents in Chapter 2 on these pages:

Opinion Letter — page 11

eMemo — page 19

Full Office Memo — page 43 (just a bit)

Trial-Court Brief (Moving Party) — page 67, Standard of Review; the rest of the brief applies the common law

Appellate-Court Brief — page 91, Jurisdiction; the rest of the brief applies the common law

After observing codified law in those documents, you'll be ready to learn the details of how to seamlessly convey codified law to your reader.

8.2 Five Things to Know About Explaining Codified Law

We're going to focus on writing about statutes, just one type of codified law. But once you learn how to explain one type of codified law, you can then transfer those skills to write about any other type like court rules, regulations, or constitutions.

Here are the five things you need to know:

(1) Where statutes go in a document

(2) How to analyze a statute

(3) How much of a statute to include

(4) How much of a statute to quote versus paraphrase

(5) How to synthesize several statutory provisions

A. Where Statutes Go in a Document

Statutes always go near the beginning of smaller documents like opinion letters, eMemos, and short office memos. For longer documents like a full office memo or a brief to a court, the statutes go at the beginning of the analysis section in what's called a Rule Foundation. You'll find it at the beginning of the "Discussion" in a full office memo and "Argument" in a brief. In our sample Full Office Memo in Chapter 2, you can see the codified law explained on page 43 of this text.

The bottom line is that they go near the beginning of explaining the law because codified law trumps caselaw; when codified law is applicable, it controls the outcome. Yes, hopefully there is caselaw to illustrate the codified law, but, in the explanation of the law, that would come after the codified law.

So start with statutes and then transition to caselaw to illustrate the caselaw.

B. How to Analyze a Statute

1. *Follow three steps to analyze a statute.*

Analyzing a statute happens when you're researching the law. You have to analyze a statute to know what to focus on in your research and then, eventually, when writing up your analysis.

When you're researching the law and you determine that a statute controls your client's situation, follow these three steps:

Step 1: Break statute into elements.

Step 2: Determine which elements are at issue given the facts.

Step 3: Focus on those elements, not only in your research, but also in your document.

These three steps are beautifully illustrated in a 2009 opinion from the U.S. Supreme Court. That case involved the Gun Control Act. You've heard of that act if you've heard that a felon can't possess a firearm. But that act also prohibits people convicted of some misdemeanors from carrying a firearm. With that setup, you should be able to see how the court applied the three steps above to explain the controlling statutes. As you read this passage from the Court, try to identify the three steps of analyzing a statute:

United States v. Hayes

555 U.S. 415 (2009)
(Justice Ginsburg writing for the Court)

Section 922(g)(9) makes it "unlawful for any person ... who has been convicted in any court of a misdemeanor crime of domestic violence ... [to] possess in or affecting commerce, any firearm or ammunition." Section 921(a)(33)(A) defines "misdemeanor crime of domestic violence" as follows:

> [T]he term "misdemeanor crime of domestic violence" means an offense that—
>
> (i) is a misdemeanor under Federal, State, or Tribal law; and
>
> (ii) has, as an element, the use or attempted use of physical force, or the threatened use of a deadly weapon, committed by a current or former spouse, parent, or guardian of the victim, by a person with whom the victim shares a child in common, by a person who is cohabitating with or has cohabitated with the victim as a spouse, parent, or guardian, or by a person similarly situated to a spouse, parent, or guardian of the victim (footnotes omitted).

This definition, all agree, imposes two requirements: **First**, a "misdemeanor crime of domestic violence" must have, "as an element, the use or attempted use of physical force, or the threatened use of a deadly weapon." **Second**, it must be "committed by" a person who has a specified domestic relationship with the victim. **The question here** is whether the language of § 921(a)(33)(A) calls for a further limitation: Must the statute describing the predicate offense include, as a discrete element, the existence of a domestic relationship between offender and victim? In line with the large majority of the Courts of Appeals, **we conclude** that § 921(a)(33)(A) does not require a predicate-offense statute of that specificity. Instead, in a § 922(g)(9) prosecution, it suffices for the Government to charge and prove a prior conviction that was, in fact, for "an offense ... committed by" the defendant against a spouse or other domestic victim.

Step 1: Break statute into elements: The "First" and "Second" sentences are doing that.

Step 2: Determine which elements are at issue. The Court does that beginning with "The question here."

Step 3: Focus on the element at issue. That begins here and continues throughout the document.

This example above of explaining a statute is exactly what you should do in a memo or brief. This clear way of explaining and analyzing a statute should be used whenever explaining a statute.

Did you find the steps? All three steps occurred in the last paragraph after the Court paraphrased and quoted the relevant portions of the Gun Control Act. For Step 1, the Court identified two elements in the statutory section at issue. Then, beginning with "The question here," the Court does Step 2 by stating what part of the statute is at issue. And Step 3 occurs at the end of the paragraph when the Court gives the answer—and in the rest of the opinion, which is omitted—when the Court focuses on just that question of whether a domestic relationship is also required.

Again, the thinking required to analyze a statute like this occurs when researching the law. Once you have at least Step 1 (identify the elements) and Step 2 (identify what's at issue) figured out, you can then write it up in your document.

2. *Practice doing the three steps.*

You saw above how the U.S. Supreme Court analyzed a statute; now it's your turn to practice. We'll use another U.S. Supreme Court opinion to do that. Be sure to pay attention to this section because we're going to rely on this case again below.

The case is *United States v. Eurodif*, 555 U.S. 305 (2009). In that case, a French consortium of uranium enrichers started selling uranium-enriching services far below market value. The U.S. Commerce Department alleged in an official declaration that this was to put the sole American enricher out of business, which would make America completely reliant on foreign manufacturers for uranium fuel to power nuclear power plants. The main question was whether the United States could apply antidumping import duties on uranium rods enriched in France.

Just giving very basic information, here is what a uranium enricher does:

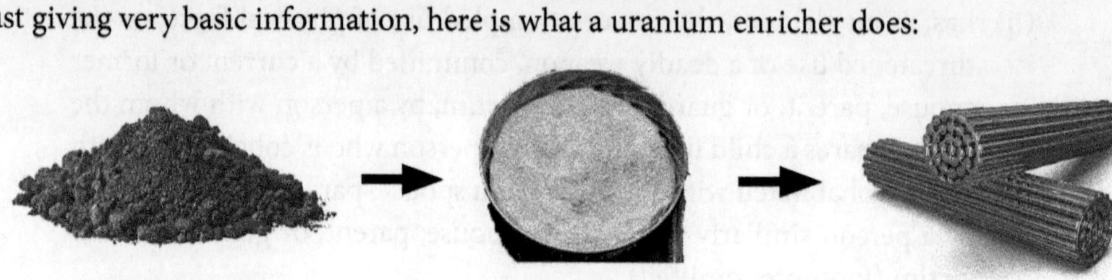

An enricher takes uranium ore ... **converts it to yellowcake ...** **and then to uranium fuel rods.**

You now know the facts of the case. As a researcher, you'd go out and find 19 U.S.C. § 1673, which is a federal statute part of the Tariff Act of 1963. That act prohibits foreign merchandise from being sold below fair market value in a way that injures U.S. manufacturing.

Let's run through the three steps of analyzing a statute:

Step 1: Identify the Elements

In the relevant statutory provision below, identify what elements the U.S. Commerce Department would have to prove before it can apply an antidumping duty to bring the French uranium processing up to fair market value. To identify the elements, insert slashes between the elements, underline them, or use a highlighter—whatever suits you.

Here's the statute:

If—

(1) the administering authority determines that a class or kind of foreign merchandise is being, or is likely to be, sold in the United States at less than its fair value, and

(2) the Commission determines that—

(A) an industry in the United States—

(i) is materially injured, or

(ii) is threatened with material injury, or

(B) he establishment of an industry in the United States is materially retarded, by reason of imports of that merchandise or by reason of sales (or the likelihood of sales) of that merchandise for importation,

then there shall be imposed upon such merchandise an antidumping duty ....

(By the way, we added the bold and underline emphasis just to help understand how the statute is set up.)

Below, you'll find the same text but with lines between the elements:

> **If** –
>
> (1)|the administering authority|determines|that a class or kind of foreign|merchandise|is being, or is likely to be, sold|in the United States|at less than its fair value,| and
>
> (2)|the Commission|determines that|–
>
> (A)|an industry|in the United States|–
>
> (i)|is materially injured,| or
>
> (ii) is|threatened with|material injury,|or
>
> (B) the|establishment of an industry|in the United States|is materially retarded,| by reason of imports of that merchandise|or by reason of sales (or the likelihood of sales) of that merchandise for importation,|
>
> **then** there shall be imposed upon such merchandise an antidumping duty ....

Step 2: Identify the Elements at Issue

Any case—even important ones before the U.S. Supreme Court—usually boils down to the interpretation of a word or phrase. In legal vernacular, we say that that word or phrase is at issue. After identifying all the elements, you next need to determine which of the elements is at issue. An element is at issue when there's a question as to whether the facts satisfy the element. (See 5.2.) One practical way to think about this is to ask, "Would an attorney representing the opposing party disagree with us on any of these elements?" Apply this to the elements you identified above and determine which element is actually at issue given our facts.

The next paragraph analyzes what's at issue. Before you read it, first determine which elements you think are at issue. To do this, you may need to read the facts again, and then intersect those facts with your list of elements from the statute above.

Okay, here's the analysis to determine what's at issue: The "administering authority" is the U.S. Commerce Department, so there's no question there. That authority needs to "determine," which the Department did when it wrote an official declaration. The authority must determine "that a class or kind of foreign merchandise is being" sold below market value. The enriching of uranium ore is happening in France, which is a foreign country. But is it "merchandise"? Is Eurodif selling enrichment services or are they selling merchandise (i.e., uranium fuel rods)? From just looking at the statute and our facts, we can't determine the answer to this question; therefore, one issue is whether enriching uranium and selling fuel rods is "merchandise" under the Tariff Act.

As to the other elements, we know that the uranium rods are being sold in the United States, and the Department said that they are sold below fair market prices. And the Department also determined that sustained dumping of underpriced uranium will cause the only American enricher to go out of business, which is a material injury.

Thus, of all the many elements in this anti-dumping statutory provision, the only one really at issue is whether enriching uranium and selling fuel rods is "merchandise."

Step 3: Focus on that Element at Issue

In the rest of the *Eurodif* opinion, the Court focused on that issue. It's a really fascinating read. In the end, the Court determined that the processing of uranium ore into yellowcake and then into fuel rods was indeed "merchandise." You should read the opinion to see how the Court got to this conclusion. As a little teaser, the Court compared enriching uranium to taking shirts to a dry cleaner. To find the opinion, Google or put this, without the final period, into Westlaw or Lexis: 555 U.S. 305.

That does it for analyzing a statute.

C. How Much of a Statute to Include

For the reader to understand the analysis, you need to include **all the essential elements** that comprise the statutory clause and any other sections that give **vital context.**

As an example, recall the *Eurodif* opinion above. When the Court analyzed that issue, it quoted the entire statutory provision provided above. That's the entire statutory provision except for the final sentence. The final sentence gave a rule about leasing merchandise, which was not an essential element and did not give vital context—so the Court omitted it.

That's an example where almost the entire statutory provision was needed because of essential elements and to give context. But more often, the legal writer needs to pull several provisions from many different sections of an act. The case of *303 Creative v. Elenis*, 600 U.S. ___ (2023), is one example of this.

In *303 Creative*, a website designer in Colorado sought an injunction to prohibit Colorado from finding that the designer would violate Colorado's Anti-Discrimination Act by refusing to offer wedding websites to gay couples. The Court, when explaining the statutory law, referenced eight different sections of the act. Together, those sections comprise about 1,000 words of the law. But when the Court wrote about the act, it used just 138 total words. Those words comprised the (1) essential elements and (2) contextual information.

Here are those 138 words:

> [T]he Colorado Anti-Discrimination Act ... defines a "public accommodation" broadly to include almost every public-facing business in the State. Colo. Rev. Stat. § 24-34-601(1) (2022). In what some call its "Accommodation Clause," the law prohibits a public accommodation from denying "the full and equal enjoyment" of its goods and services to any customer based on his race, creed, disability, sexual orientation, or other statutorily enumerated trait. § 24-34-601(2)(a). Either state officials or private citizens may bring actions to enforce the law. §§ 24-34-306, 24-34-602(1). And a variety of penalties can follow. Courts can order fines up to $500 per violation. § 24-34-602(1)(a). The Colorado Commission on Civil Rights can issue cease-and-desist orders, § 24-34-306(9), and require violators to take various other "affirmative action[s]." § 24-34-605; § 24-34-306(9).

What should you take away from the quoted example above? You must include (1) essential elements of a statute and (2) contextual information, but you don't need to quote the entire statute.

Because this is an essential part of legal writing, hopefully you can bear to look at one more example. It really showcases the focus in this subsection of including just the most essential information, but it also demonstrates what you'll learn in the next section about quoting sparingly and paraphrasing as much as possible. In this excerpt, the Michigan Supreme Court is explaining the statutory provisions for bringing a claim of sexual harassment:

> M.C.L. § 37.2201(a) defines an "employer" for purposes of the [Michigan Civil Rights Act (CRA)] as "a person who has 1 or more employees, and includes an agent of that person." As recognized by plaintiff, the language of the statute does not otherwise narrow the scope of who may be considered an employer. Thus, M.C.L. § 37.2202 forbids any employer from engaging in acts of discrimination that are prohibited by the CRA. M.C.L. § 37.2202 does not state that an employer is only forbidden from engaging in such acts against its own employees. Indeed, the CRA appears to clearly envision claims by nonemployees for the failure or refusal to hire or recruit, M.C.L. § 37.2202(1)(a); the improper classification of applicants by a status prohibited under the CRA, M.C.L. § 37.2202(1)(b); and the discrimination against former employees by operation of a benefit plan or system, M.C.L. § 37.2202(1)(c). Accordingly, to limit the availability of relief under the CRA to those suits brought by an employee against his or her employer is not consistent with the statute.

McClements v. Ford Motor Co., 702 N.W.2d 166, 173 (Mich. 2005).

The next section below dives more deeply into when to paraphrase and when to quote from a statute.

D. How Much of a Statute to Quote Versus Paraphrase

The goal is to include all the essential information but to make it enjoyable to read. A tough target to hit, no doubt. Attorneys strive for this goal by following these four rules when deciding whether to paraphrase or quote:

(1) Prefer to paraphrase.

(2) Quote essential words of phrases that cannot be paraphrased.

(3) Most legal writers do a mix of heavy paraphrasing and light quoting.

(4) Avoid writing dense walls of statutory text.

Consider again the block quotation above where the Court explained the Colorado Anti-Discrimination Act. Instead of quoting almost 1,000 words of statutory text, it did a mix of paraphrasing and quoting. That is a good example of what attorneys do most of the time.

Here's one more example to show you that most the time you should be doing a combination of quoting and paraphrasing. In this example, which comes from the U.S. Supreme Court case *United States v. Hansen*, 600 U.S. ___ (2023), Helamen Hansen told foreigners that they could become citizens because he would "adult adopt" them. He took their money and "adopted" them, but, of course, this is not a legal path to citizenship. The question became whether he violated 8 U.S.C. § 1324. Note how the court explained the statute by including all the essential elements but minimally quoted:

> To judge whether a statute is overbroad, we must first determine what it covers. Recall that 8 U.S.C. § 1324(a)(1)(A)(iv) makes it unlawful to "encourag[e] or induc[e] an alien to come to, enter, or reside in the United States, knowing or in reckless disregard of the fact that such coming to, entry, or residence is or will be

in violation of law." The issue is whether Congress used "encourage" and "induce" as terms of art referring to criminal solicitation and facilitation (thus capturing only a narrow band of speech) or instead as those terms are used in everyday conversation (thus encompassing a broader swath). An overbreadth challenge obviously has better odds on the latter view.

E. How to Synthesize Several Statutory Provisions

Often, your client's issue will be controlled by several statutory provisions. The best writers synthesize the statutory sections by showing the reader how they relate to each other. Use four techniques to do this:

(1) Use transition words.
(2) Repeat words from the preceding sentence.
(3) Use roadmaps and signposts to show a statute's structure.
(4) Characterize provisions.

1. Use transition words.

You know about transition words. You use them all the time. Be sure to use them to show how statutory provisions relate one to another.

Here's an example from the U.S. Supreme Court case *Jack Daniel Properties v. VIP Products*, 600 U.S. ___ (2023). The question in this case was whether a dog toy that resembles a trademarked whiskey brand—Jack Daniel's—violates trademark law. In the image below, the dog toy is on the left, and the ubiquitous Jack Daniel's label is on the right.

To decide this question, the Court had to synthesize seven different statutory provisions. Note how they used transition words, which are bold below, to bring everything together:

> [T]he Lanham Act creates a cause of action for the dilution of famous marks, which can succeed without likelihood of confusion. A famous mark is one "widely recognized" by the public as "designati[ng the] source" of the mark owner's goods. § 1125(c)(2)(A). Dilution of such a mark can occur "by tarnishment." § 1125(c)(1). **As the statute describes** the idea, an "association arising from the similarity between" two marks—one of them famous—may "harm[ ] the reputation of the famous mark," and thus make the other mark's owner liable. § 1125(c)(2)(C). **But** there are "[e]xclusions"—categories of activity not "actionable as dilution." § 1125(c)(3). One exclusion protects any "noncommercial use of a mark." § 1125(c)(3)(C). **Another** protects a "fair use" of a mark "in connection with ... parodying, criticizing, or commenting upon the famous mark owner or [its] goods." § 1125(c) (3)(A)(ii). The fair-use exclusion, **though**, comes with a caveat. A defendant cannot get its benefit—even if engaging in parody, criticism, or commentary—when using the similar looking mark "as a designation of source for the [defendant's] own goods." § 1125(c)(3)(A). **In other words**, the exclusion does not apply if the defendant uses the similar mark as a mark.

2. Repeat words from the preceding sentence.

In the same example from above, the Court also simply repeated old information in a sentence to connect it to the preceding sentence. There are three examples of this below, which are denoted by underlining, italics, and bold.

> [T]he Lanham Act creates a cause of action for the dilution of famous marks, which can succeed without likelihood of confusion. A famous mark is one "widely recognized" by the public as "designati[ng the] source" of the mark owner's goods. § 1125(c)(2)(A). Dilution of such a mark can occur "*by tarnishment.*" § 1125(c)(1). As the statute describes *the idea*, an "association arising from the similarity between" two marks—one of them famous—may "harm[ ] the reputation of the famous mark," and thus make the other mark's owner liable. § 1125(c)(2)(C). But there are "**[e]xclusions**"—categories of activity not "actionable as dilution." § 1125(c)(3). One **exclusion** protects any "noncommercial use of a mark." § 1125(c)(3)(C). **Another** protects a "fair use" of a mark "in connection with ... parodying, criticizing, or commenting upon the famous mark owner or [its] goods." § 1125(c) (3)(A)(ii). The fair-use **exclusion**, though, comes with a caveat. A defendant cannot get its benefit—even if engaging in parody, criticism, or commentary—when using the similar looking mark "as a designation of source for the [defendant's] own goods." § 1125(c)(3)(A). In other words, the exclusion does not apply if the defendant uses the similar mark as a mark.

A simple one is to simply repeat *mark* throughout. That connects the entire paragraph. And then the Court uses *the idea* instead of *tarnishment*, but that also connects the provisions. And, finally, as you can see from the bold above, the Court uses and repeats *exclusion* to create cohesion.

3. Use roadmaps, signposts, and enumeration to show a statute's structure.

An example from 8.2(B) demonstrates this well. It's the *United States v. Hayes* opinion where the Court looked at the Gun Control Act. After quoting the essential elements, the Court helped the readers make sense of the statute by roadmapping and then enumerating. You can see this below in bold:

> This definition, all agree, **imposes two requirements**: **First**, a "misdemeanor crime of domestic violence" must have, "as an element, the use or attempted use of physical force, or the threatened use of a deadly weapon." **Second**, it must be "committed by" a person who has a specified domestic relationship with the victim. The question here is whether the language of § 921(a)(33)(A) calls for a further limitation: Must the statute describing the predicate offense include, as a discrete element, the existence of a domestic relationship between offender and victim?
>
> In line with the large majority of the Courts of Appeals, we conclude that § 921(a)(33)(A) does not require a predicate-offense statute of that specificity. Instead, in a § 922(g)(9) prosecution, it suffices for the Government to charge and prove a prior conviction that was, in fact, for "an offense ... committed by" the defendant against a spouse or other domestic victim.

It's a simple technique, but it can make all the difference to your reader.

4. Characterize provisions.

Help the reader understand what they're looking at. If a statutory provision is the principal rule, then call it that. Or if the statute has an exception, exclusion, or caveat, call it that. Or perhaps there's a penalty. Or maybe a statute makes an accommodation. Don't just paraphrase or quote the statutory language, but also characterize provisions to help your reader understand how each section relates to the others.

If you go through the quoted decisions above in this section, you'll see examples of such characterizations.

8.3 Checklist for Explaining Codified Law

When explaining codified law in your document, did you:

___ analyze the statute by breaking it down to its elements?

___ put the relevant, on-point codified law before caselaw, unless you had a good reason not to?

___ include the (1) essential elements and (2) vital context, but nothing more?

___ prefer to paraphrase codified law?

___ quote the essential parts that can't be paraphrased?

___ do a mix of paraphrasing and quoting?

___ avoid creating a dense block quotation of codified law?

___ if writing about several codified-law provisions, synthesize them with excellent sentence-to-sentence flow?

Chapter Nine

IREAC: Explain Caselaw

9.1 Attorneys Are Storytellers

Attorneys are storytellers because some stories are law, and attorneys need to tell them to resolve a client's issue. Storytelling actually begins with the client when they entrust their story to the attorney. The attorney then takes that story and compares it with past stories to resolve the client's issue. These past stories are called "caselaw," "opinions," "cases," "decisions," or "precedent." They all mean the same thing.

These past stories are law—as much as statutes or regulations are law.

They're law because the American legal system says they are. America's common-law system is based on stare decisis. Under the doctrine of stare decisis, a court hearing a case that involves the same law and similar facts as a precedent case must come to the same conclusion. This creates predictability and consistency in the judicial system. All but French-born Louisiana follow the common-law doctrine of stare decisis.

How do the courts know about these past cases? Attorneys find them through research and communicate them to the court.

This chapter will empower you to clearly and logically tell the stories in past cases. Then, in Chapter 10, Apply Law, you'll learn how to relate those past cases to your client's current case.

9.2 The Role a Case Plays in Your Document

Overall, caselaw plays two roles in your document. First, you may use a case for just pure rules of law detached from the story in that case. Second, you may use a case for just the story and what the court said about that story. Depending on the law you're applying and your client's facts, you may use a case in either of these ways, one of these ways, or none of them.

This chapter is all about the second way of using a case for the story and what the court thought about it. In Chapter 7, Give a Rule Foundation, you learned about the first way and how caselaw sometimes provides just black-letter rules of law.

So what role does a case's *story* play in your analysis?

The case's role is to illustrate the rules of law that you would have just explained in the Rule Foundation, the R of IREAC. To illustrate the rules means to flesh them out with stories, and that brings the rules to life. And this brings us to placement because the case stories always go after the Rule Foundation in the E of IREAC. And, finally, the case's story is applied in the Application section where you explain whether the case is similar to or different from your client's case.

A brief example will give context to how caselaw stories are used in analysis. In the example below, observe the placement, illustrative power, and application of caselaw:

Mr. Levesque,

IREAC: State the **issue** first. Ch. 6.

You asked me to research the elements for operating a vehicle while intoxicated and whether our client violated them.

IREAC: This paragraph is a **Rule Foundation**. Ch. 7.

Under the Motor Vehicle Code, "A person, whether licensed or not, shall not operate a vehicle upon a highway ... within this state if the person is operating while intoxicated." Mich. Comp. Laws Ann. § 257.625 (West 2024) (emphasis added). For our case, the main issue will be whether our client was operating the vehicle. The Code defines *operating* as "[b]eing in actual physical control of a vehicle." MCL § 257.35a.

IREAC: **Explain Caselaw, the point of this chapter**. Ch. 9. See how the Case Illustration brings the element *operating* more to life? It also provides a rule and reason we need to apply to our client's facts.

And the Michigan Supreme Court put a finer point on this definition by defining *operating* in terms of the danger of colliding with another vehicle. *People v. Wood*, 538 N.W.2d 351, 353 (Mich. 1995). In *Wood*, a driver was passed out in a vehicle at a fast-food drive-thru. The vehicle's transmission was engaged in Drive, but the driver's foot was on the brake.

IREAC: We often split a Case Illustration to make it easier to read. Put the holding and reasoning in a separate paragraph.

The Court held that the driver was operating the vehicle because the risk of collision with another vehicle was high: all he had to do was remove his foot from the brake, and the vehicle would be in motion and possibly cause a collision.

IREAC: **Apply the law**. Ch. 10. Note how the attorney uses the case precedent throughout this Application to analyze whether the client was operating the vehicle.

In our case, our client was probably not operating his vehicle; thus, he did not violate § 257.625. He certainly was not in "actual physical control of the vehicle" because he was unconscious. But the Michigan Supreme Court seemed to lower the standard for *operating* in *Wood*. Still, the risk our client's vehicle posed was very low compared to the risk the driver in *Wood* posed. The main difference is that our client's vehicle was in Park the entire time he was sleeping behind the wheel. Whereas in *Wood* the driver only had to remove his foot from the brake to create a collision, our unconscious driver would have to (1) put his foot on the brake and depress it, (2) shift the transmission into Drive, and (3) remove his foot from the brake. So many concerted actions are impossible for someone who is unconscious.

Therefore, our client did not pose a risk of collision, which means he was not operating a vehicle.

IREAC: **Conclude**. Ch. 11. End each IREAC packet with a conclusion.

Best,

Associate Attorney

Okay, let's compare notes. First, the placement. The Case Illustration is placed right after the black-letter rules of law; this makes sense because a Case Illustration's purpose is to illustrate the rules at issue. After reading the rules, whether from codified law, caselaw, or both, your reader will begin to wonder how these rules play out in real life and whether any past cases have applied them. The black-letter rules begin to make sense when the reader sees how courts have applied those rules to real-life situations.

Second, the illustration. The Case Illustration brought the statutory element *operating* to life by giving the reader a real-life example of the bounds of *operating*. Who knew that a verb like *operating* could actually include passive activity like sleeping? The reader now has the rule *and* a factual example of the rule.

Finally, the application. The Case Illustration plays a critical part of reasoning, the rule application that happened in the paragraph after the Case Illustration. In that paragraph, the writer-attorney applied the court's reasoning from *Wood* and compared and contrasted the facts from *Wood*. See 10.6(A). By doing this, the writer can predict how a court is likely to rule on the client's current issue.

9.3 How Many Cases Do I Need?

Choose enough cases to illustrate vague elements of law with a spectrum of cases. This usually means finding between two and four cases per element at issue. And, yes, you may reuse cases within one document (see 9.8 and 9.9).

The number of cases you need can be illustrated by an everyday example. Have you ever read a dictionary definition of a word that left you still wondering about its meaning? It wasn't until you saw the word used in *multiple* sentences that you finally gain a full understanding of what the word means. *Heuristic* might be one such word. Merriam-Webster defines it this way: "involving or serving as an aid to learning, discovery, or problem-solving by experimental and especially trial-and-error methods." *Heuristic*, Merriam-Webster.com.

What? But then you ask a well-informed friend for examples. The friend might tell you that for the noun form, a heuristic could be an outline for a law-school class, a chart you make to understand The Mailbox Rule, or a diagram of a complicated case. That clears things up quite a bit. So *heuristic* is just a fancy word for anything we use to help us learn something.

Well, the same applies in the law. An element will be at issue, so you need to find cases—which will serve as examples of the element—that help the reader (and yourself) understand it. Just like "outline," "charts," and "diagrams" are three examples of a heuristic, a gun, brass knuckles, and a baseball bat—examples from three separate cases—are three examples of a "dangerous weapon." After reading three cases, the reader will understand what the element looks like in real life.

In a best-case scenario, you'll illustrate each element at issue with a spectrum of cases from examples where the element has been met to examples where the element has not been met.

To create sound and convincing analysis, we must include sufficient authority to accurately represent the body of caselaw on our issue. When choosing these representative cases, we have as our goal to create a spectrum of the relevant factual scenarios on which the courts have passed judgment. Then we can set our client's facts against this backdrop of cases in the Application (or argument) section of the document. Putting our client's facts on a spectrum will make it easier for the reader to see what a judge would likely do with our case.

If, for example, our client is charged with drunk driving while intoxicated on a riding lawn-mower, we'd research the law to determine what has qualified as a vehicle in past caselaw, past stories. We'd include enough cases in our analysis, the E of IREAC, to flesh out what is and what is not a vehicle. The chart below represents different cases you'd include for such an analysis.

Is a motor vehicle			Is *not* a motor vehicle
Bulldozer is a vehicle because it is self-propelled and may transport things on a public road.	**Snowmobile is a vehicle because it's not propelled by human power.**	**Go-cart is a vehicle because it's motor-driven, even if not on public roads.**	**Land yacht is not a vehicle because the wind powers it, and it's usually used only on beaches and dunes.**

So, if the cases are available, include enough in your analysis to create a spectrum from where the element is met to where the element is not met.

9.4 The Case Illustration

Whenever you write about a case in your document, we call it a "Case Illustration." When you're going to rely on that case in a significant way, you need to do a full Case Illustration, which is where you include these five parts in this order:

(1) topic sentence,

(2) citation,

(3) facts,

(4) holding, and

(5) reasoning.

These five parts comprise the fundamental building blocks to describe a case to anyone in the context of legal analysis. Observe these five parts by reading the Case Illustration below along with the annotations to it.

> Confinement can also occur by unreasonable duress where a defendant exercises undue influence over a vulnerable plaintiff. *Wilson v. Houston Funeral Home*, 50 Cal. Rptr. 2d 169, 174 (Cal. App. 4th 1996). In *Wilson*, a funeral home director had a widow driven to a local bank instead of to the burial of her late husband. Even though the plaintiff and director arranged for payment at a later time, the funeral director demanded immediate payment in the bank, shouting, "Ain't nobody going nowhere until I get paid." *Id.* at 174.
>
> The court held that the funeral director confined the plaintiff by unreasonable duress. *Id.* It reasoned that the shouted statement could be interpreted as a threat not to conduct the burial service until he was paid. *Id.* And the plaintiff could not simply walk away and abandon her husband's remains under these circumstances. *Id.*

(1) The **topic sentence** states the most important point from the case as it relates to your client's issue.

(2) Give the **citation** immediately after the topic sentence so the reader knows the source and can evaluate its weight.

(3) State the story, the **facts**. This is the story, and it gives context to what comes next: the holding and then reasoning. You will use the case's facts later in the Application when you compare or contrast them to your client's situation.

(4) This is the **holding**, the court's judgment on the issue. Any case may have several holdings; convey, though, only the one that is relevant to your narrow issue.

(5) Note the **reasoning**. Explain how the court justified its holding. This is essential law, and you'll apply it to your client's case in the Application.

Creating a helpful Case Illustration—one that accurately teaches the reader about the case—takes a lot of practice. The sections below address each of the parts to help you on your journey to writing about cases in a way that makes your reader happy. If at any point you need context to understand anything, you can find it by looking at the five sample case illustrations below in section 9.5 and by looking at the Case Illustrations in the sample documents in Chapter 2 starting with the eMemo.

A. Topic Sentence

Clarity is everything in legal writing. If you do not clearly explain what a case stands for, you will frustrate your reader—largely because they'll have to look up the case themselves. Clearly explaining a case begins in the very first sentence, the topic sentence. Achieve this helpful clarity in the topic sentence by doing these three things:

(1) **Transition** in a topic sentence from the preceding paragraph to the new case.

(2) State something **new** in the topic sentence.

(3) Make a **substantive point** in the topic sentence.

1. *Transition in the topic sentence.*

A good transition simply helps the reader see the relationship between what's already been stated in the document and the new thing in the current paragraph. This cohesiveness increases reader comprehension. For each of these sample topic sentences, imagine that either the Rule Foundation or another case came right before it. The bolded words are repeated from those earlier sections:

> A **risk is foreseeable** if the tortfeasor had knowledge that the injury was likely to occur. *Samson v. Saginaw Professional Building, Inc.*, 224 N.W.2d 843 (Mich. 1975). In *Samson*, an office ....
>
> An attorney's promise to provide legal services **in return for a person's promise to vote** for a judicial candidate is illegal. *Trushin v. State*, 425 So. 2d 1126 (Fla. 1983). In *Trushin*, an attorney ....
>
> An **explicit credible threat** must state intent to actually harm and not merely to frighten the victim. *People v. Czemerynski*, 786 P.2d 1100 (Colo. 1990). In *Czemerynski*, the defendant ....
>
> A **public building's dangerous or defective condition** is determined by the intended use or purpose it is to serve. *Scameheorn v. Bucks*, 421 N.W.2d 918 (Mich. Ct. App. 1988). In *Scameheorn*, a motorcycle operator ....

Each of the bolded phrases above are what connects the topic sentence to what has already been discussed in the document. So you can see that simply repeating the element at issue helps to connect or show the relationship between the preceding paragraph and the new paragraph.

Sometimes the writer shows the relationship of a new case by giving contextual clues about how the case relates to other cases. See if you can spot how this next example does that:

> Other jurisdictions also strictly enforce pre-suit notice requirements. For example, in *Jones v. Fred's Tavern, Inc.*, 520 A.2d 121 (N.J. 1999), the court held that there was no good-faith exception to New Jersey's 120-day notice requirement ....

The topic sentence transitions from the previous paragraph by using "other jurisdictions." That phrase helps the reader see where this case fits compared to other cases: the cases before it obviously were from another jurisdiction.

This usually happens by giving a contextual clue to its relationship to the other cases. Spot the contextual clue in this next example:

> Another case in effect narrowed the definition of a dwelling house by adding a requirement that it be capable of being lived in. *People v. Reed*, 163 N.W.2d 704 (Mich. Ct. App. 1968). In *Reed*, the building was in a residential neighborhood but had been unoccupied for over a year. [continue with facts, holding, and reasoning.]

Using "another case" gives context. And pointing out that it "narrowed the definition" helps the reader understand this case's relationship to the preceding paragraph. Finally, the writer repeated just a bit of old information from the preceding paragraph to transition by using "definition of a dwelling house," which was obviously the topic of this part of the document. The bit of repeated information connects the new information in the sentence to the preceding paragraph.

Do you know what makes a really poor transition in a topic sentence? Starting with a citation to a source of law. Never lead with a source when writing a topic sentence. The reader wants the law, not the source, so give the reader what they want. Compare how one topic sentence below quickly delivers the goods to the reader while the other only teases the reader.

Compare this Case Illustration:

> *Barrett v. Mount Brighton, Inc.* addresses what dangers can be considered inherent to the sport of skiing. *Barrett v. Mt. Brighton, Inc.*, 712 N.W.2d 154 (Mich. 2006). In *Barrett*, a skier collided with a snowboard rail. The Court held that the skier accepted that danger because it was inherent to the sport of skiing and the rail was obvious and necessary. *Id.* at 156. [Continues with more reasoning.]

To this one:

> Skiers and snowboarders accept the risk of colliding with permanent fixtures regularly used in snowboarding. *Barrett v. Mt. Brighton, Inc.*, 712 N.W.2d 154 (Mich. 2006). In *Barrett*, a skier collided with a snowboard rail. The Court held that the danger was inherent to the sport of skiing and the rail was obvious and necessary. *Id.* at 156. [Continues with the reasoning.]

In the second example, the writer gets right to the point. There's no suspense in legal writing; readers want the goods, and they want them now! Don't frustrate them by frontloading the topic sentence with less-important information.

So be sure to write coherently by transitioning into the topic sentence and avoid putting a source before substantive information.

2. State something new in the topic sentence.

When explaining the law, in the R and E parts of IREAC, every sentence must say something new. And this certainly applies to writing your Case Illustrations. The biggest temptation for you will be to repeat something in the topic sentence that you already wrote in the Rule Foundation or in another case before the one you're writing. Instead, trust that your reader has at least average short-term memory, and make sure to build on the Rule Foundation in a Case Illustration's topic sentence by stating new information.

The example below is the typical setup where a paragraph of rules lays out the elements and then the Case Illustration illustrates the elements. Read the example below and ask, "Did the topic sentence add something new to the Rule Foundation?"

> A physician owes a duty to use ordinary care and diligence in diagnosing and treating patients. *Rios v. Bigler*, 555 N.W.2d 212, 213 (Mich. 2004). The **physician** must "exercise that reasonable degree of learning, **skill**, and experience ... **ordinarily possessed** by other physicians in the same or similar locations under like circumstances." *Id.* at 214. In other words, the law only requires what is reasonable and ordinary; it does not require physicians to ensure favorable results or guarantee cures. *Broughton v. Riehle*, 502 N.W.2d 1, 2 (Mich. Ct. App. 1997).

This paragraph is a **Rule Foundation**. It gives the controlling black-letter rules for the standard of care used in medical-malpractice cases.

> A physician is only required to exercise **ordinary skill** when treating patients. *Mills v. Berrios*, 523 N.W.2d 112 (Mich. Ct. App. 2006). In *Mills*, a patient sought treatment for ....

This is the **topic sentence** to the first Case Illustration after the Rule Foundation.

No! It didn't! See how the topic sentence for the Case Illustration merely repeated a rule from the Rule Foundation? It repeated the ordinary-skill rule without adding anything to it. The reader will feel that you are wasting their time. Get to the point by always stating something new—build on what comes before the Case Illustration.

Contrast the preceding example to this one and notice how the topic sentence adds something new to the discussion. It begins with the same Rule Foundation as above, but there's a new topic sentence in the Case Illustration after it:

> A physician owes a duty to use ordinary care and diligence in diagnosing and treating patients. *Rios v. Bigler*, 555 N.W.2d 212, 213 (Mich. 2004). The physician must "exercise that reasonable degree of lwearning, skill, and experience... ordinarily possessed by other physicians in the same or similar locations under like circumstances." *Id.* at 214. In other words, the law only requires what is reasonable and ordinary; it does not require physicians to ensure favorable results or guarantee cures. *Broughton v. Riehle*, 502 N.W.2d 1, 2 (Mich. Ct. App. 1997).
>
> A physician is presumed to exercise ordinary skill when they follow published, peer-reviewed best practices. *Mills v. Berrios*, 523 N.W.2d 112 (Mich. Ct. App. 2006). In *Mills*, a patient sought treatment for ....

Do you see how this topic sentence adds something new to the Rule Foundation?

Now we're getting somewhere! Every sentence in the example above states a new point. The topic sentence to the case adds a definition for *ordinary skill.* Happy reader.

3. Give substantive information in the topic sentence.

A topic sentence must state a substantive point. By now, you have noticed that legal writing is quite different than whatever genre of writing you have done before. Here's one of those differences: the topic sentence of a paragraph must do more than merely introduce a point. A legal reader is busy and wants the analysis to get to the point. Do that by writing substantive topic sentences.

It can't merely announce a topic or state that a court "looked" at something or "addressed" a certain rule; that's all too vague. Instead, it should answer this question: What's the most important thing this case added to our understanding of the law as it relates to our issue? If the case added multiple layers of information about an element, then pick the one or two things that you will base your arguments on in the Rule Application section, and focus on that in the topic sentence.

When stating the primary point you want to make about a case, prefer to paraphrase. You will find that you can usually paraphrase the point of a case and convey it more effectively than with a quotation.

A substantive point may be an explicit concept the court said in the case, or it could be a rule that you induced from the case, what we call an implicit rule.

a. Substantive Point—Explicit Variety

Sometimes you will need to simply convey a point a court explicitly made. Here are four examples of that:

> A recent opinion added a third factor of whether the injured person was visiting during normal hours. [citation]. In *Samuelson*, ...
>
> But a later case in effect narrowed the definition of "dwelling house" by adding a requirement that it be capable of being lived in. [citation]. In *Jones* ....
>
> On the other hand, a few states—a minority—require a landowner to give only constructive notice. [citation]. For instance, in *Morgan* ....
>
> A California case involved not just verbal resistance but also physical resistance; yet the store owner was again found to be not liable. [citation]. In *Johnson*, ...

In the examples above, you can see how the attorney-writer is simply reporting what a court explicitly said in a case. When courts are that clear and it directly pertains to your case, you can count your lucky stars! Oftentimes, though, we have to create an implicit rule from a case to see how the case applies to our client's case.

b. Substantive Point—Implicit Variety

Because we usually will not find precedent caselaw that is factually identical to our client's situation, we'll have to fashion a conceptual rule from the specifics of a case. When the facts in precedent aren't similar to our client's facts, we look to see if the same concepts or ideas might be at play behind the specific facts in the precedent. We'll then fashion a conceptual rule—an implicit rule—from the precedent and apply it to our client's case.

Why is it so important to state an implicit takeaway in the topic sentence? It's much more obvious to the reader how that case relates to the client's facts. Stating the specific facts of a precedent case in the topic sentence would lose the reader; they'd wonder, "How does this relate to our case?" But if you state implicit, more general concepts, the reader can more easily see how the precedent relates to the client's facts. Implicit rules cast a broader net than explicit ones.

You will need to read between the lines of the facts and the court's reasoning to pull out a substantive implicit point. This "reading between the lines" is a process of inductive reasoning where we induce a general rule from the specifics of the case.

Before we dive into how this works, here are some examples so you can compare explicit topic sentences to implicit ones:

Explicit Rule in Topic Sentence	Implicit Rule in Topic Sentence
A snowboarder assumes the risk of injury from a snowboard rail that was improperly welded.	Snowboarders do not assume the risk of injury from defective equipment.

If you have a case where a snowboarder was injured on a rail with a bad weld in it, then the explicit rule is great! But what if your case deals with a snowboarder who rode a box in a terrain park and fell through the box because it wasn't sturdy enough? Or what if your client was a snowboarder who crashed after a drone malfunctioned and hit them on the head? If either of those cases were your client's facts, your reader would appreciate seeing a more generally applicable implicit rule in the topic sentence. They can then easily see how "injury from defective equipment" would apply to them.

Compare these two sentences in this next example.

Explicit Rule in Topic Sentence	Implicit Rule in Topic Sentence
Jones held that a fractured arm satisfies the "objectively verifiable" element because a doctor can see a fractured arm with an x-ray.	An impairment is "objectively verifiable" when treating doctors rely on purely objective tests, such as an x-ray or a physical examination, to diagnose it rather than relying on the patient's subjective pain complaints.

If your client had a broken bone, then the explicit rule is excellent. But what if your client's impairment is a bruised spleen, a collapsed lung, or even PTSD? The implicit rule would be much more on point because it's generally applicable and captures the wider category of things—wider than just "x-ray."

Did you see how the writer created the explicit rule? They simply found broader categories that the specific things belong to and used those categories to create an implicit, generally applicable rule. Thus, *fractured arm* became *impairment*, and *x-ray* became *purely objective tests*.

For this final example, imagine that your client is charged with fraud because they stole and re-sold McDonald's Monopoly game pieces. The prosecutor garnered most of the information against your client using a confidential informant who worked at the printing factory where the game pieces were created. You research about disclosing a confidential informant's identity because you want to cross-examine them, and you find a case. Here are two possible topic sentences:

Explicit Rule in Topic Sentence	Implicit Rule in Topic Sentence
A prosecutor had to reveal a confidential informant's identity when they bought drugs from the defendant with the intent to deal them to others.	**A prosecutor must reveal a confidential informant's identity when they actively participate in the crime.**

You get the point by now: If your client is charged with fraud because they stole and re-sold McDonald's game pieces, the explicit rule isn't very helpful because buying and dealing drugs is factually different than stealing and reselling game pieces. But they are conceptually similar, and that's where the implicit rule comes in. You can apply the "actively participate" rule to your fraud case and then compare dealing drugs to dealing game pieces—both situations involve active participation in the underlying crime.

From these examples of implicit rules above, you should have observed that the implicit rule is basically the box that the explicit rule came in. The implicit rule states the category that the specific thing fits in. It's logically consistent to rely on implicit rules because we can treat things of the same category similarly.

You create the implicit rule usually while reading caselaw during the research phase of any writing project. When you read the case, you may realize that the facts are literally different, but they are conceptually similar to your client's case. When that light bulb goes off, you're ready to write the topic sentence for your Case Illustration.

Let's see this in practice.

Imagine that you have a client who slipped and fell on a second-story bridge between two apartment buildings. The bridge was open to the elements, so when it rained, then froze, then snowed, the bridge became more slippery than was immediately apparent to your client. She tried to walk across the bridge but slipped, fell, and sustained severe brain injury. You sue the apartment owners, but they claim that the danger of the ice and snow was "open and obvious without any special aspects," which means that she would have accepted that risk. You research and find this case:

> An Amazon driver was delivering a package to an apartment complex after an ice storm. As they were running up the first flight of stairs, they slipped and fell down the stairs, breaking their ankle. The court held that the icy staircase was an open and obvious danger with no special aspects. The court reasoned that the obvious winter storm should have alerted the driver to the dangerous conditions.

Let's say that you chose to use this case in your analysis to prove that the ice on the bridge was not open and obvious. You would need to capture for your reader what this case teaches about open-and-obvious dangers. What explicit topic sentence would you write for this Case Illustration? Then think about what implicit topic sentence you'd write. Think about that before reading on.

Would you write an explicit one like this?

> An icy staircase may be an open-and-obvious danger lacking special aspects.

Probably not because the reader won't be able to immediately see how it applies to your case about a bridge between apartment buildings. Instead, you'd write a generally applicable implicit rule from the case. Perhaps something like this:

> Icy pathways, such as a staircase, may be an open-and-obvious danger lacking special aspects.

See what the writer did there? It found a category that is common to both *staircase* (the precedent case) and *bridge* (our case). That category is *pathways*, which is a broader term that could include both staircases, sidewalks, and bridges connecting buildings. So when the reader reads it in the Case Illustration's topic sentence, they will be able to quickly determine how that case applies to the client's facts.

In this next example, imagine your client was a victim of emotional abuse at work. Among other causes of action, you sue the employer for intentional infliction of emotional distress. Your client stated in an affidavit that her boss at work over the past two weeks wrote her two cartoons depicting sexual activity. She made it clear to her boss after the first cartoon that it was inappropriate, and she would sue him if he did it again. And then, just a few days later, the boss did it again. So she sued him.

As her attorney, after hearing the story, you researched caselaw and found the following case. You wrote a Case Illustration for it but haven't yet written the topic sentence because you need time to think about what the case stands for. Here's the Case Illustration without the topic sentence and citation:

> Soon after a breakup, a nurse left voicemails on her ex-boyfriend's phone telling him that they'd better get back together, or she'd hurt him where it hurts the most. This took place for three or four weeks. She then started stalking him at his place of work. And, after he begged her to stop, she plunged an axe into his car's windshield. And then about six months later, when her ex-boyfriend started dating someone new, she left lingerie on the new girlfriend's car along with a knife and a threatening note.
>
> The court held that the nurse's conduct amounted to intentional infliction of emotional distress and the "extreme and outrageous" element in particular. Its reasoning was to simply repeat the facts stated above.

How can you clearly convey to the reader what the case stands for? You need a punchy line for the topic sentence that accurately captures what the case teaches us about the extreme-and-outrageous element. This is where inductive reasoning comes in to fashion an implicit topic sentence—that is reasoning from the particular facts to a general rule. Before reading the next paragraph, try the skill of reasoning from the particular facts to the general by thinking of what categories the specific facts fit in. Characterize them, but do so accurately. Basically, finish this sentence: Conduct is likely extreme and outrageous when ....

After you've created a sentence that captures an implicit takeaway of the case, read the next paragraph.

Going from the specific facts described above, we can craft this more general statement about the case that will furnish an implicit topic sentence for the Case Illustration:

> Conduct is likely extreme and outrageous when a person regularly threatens emotional and physical violence that escalates over a long period of time.

Note that the topic sentence transitions and informs the reader that it's going to teach them about "extreme and outrageous," one element of IIED. Now that the reader has focus with the element, the topic sentence uses "regularly" and "long period of time" to capture the essence of the particulars of multiple acts over "three or four weeks" and "six months." And then it uses the phrase "threatens emotional and physical violence" to capture the particular facts of the phone calls, stalking, and destruction of physical property. And then "escalates" is a characterization of verbal abuse that transitions over time into physically destroying property and threatening with deadly weapons like a knife.

Again, we fashion an implicit rule or statement from particular facts. Now a reader can easily see what the case stands for and how it might relate to a variety of factual scenarios. In particular, someone in the firm who reads your Case Illustration of the nurse case will see that your client with the two cartoons probably doesn't have enough to win on IIED.

In this final example of creating an implicit, substantive topic sentence, you'll see the whole process, including how to apply the implicit rule to the client's facts.

For this example, your client is facing a charge of assault with a dangerous weapon because he shot a potato gun at his neighbor. A potato gun is a homemade gun that is constructed out of PVC pipe. It propels a potato at a high speed when the user sparks hairspray or lighter fluid in a chamber. (You can Google it for a better idea.)

You research the law looking for precedent where a court applied the law of assault with a dangerous weapon to potato guns, and you do not find anything. That's not surprising. So you then look for dangerous-weapon cases using homemade devices with the idea that you could analogize conceptually. That research leads you to this case:

> In *Jackson v. Pigs-R-Us, Inc.*, the defendant filled a piano with pig manure, lit it on fire, and flung it at his neighbor with a trebuchet. The court said that anything that can fling an upright grand piano is a dangerous weapon. Its accuracy and capability to maim or kill make it dangerous.

Ok. That's a very specific ruling. But, more importantly, your reader will likely be confused because a trebuchet seems very different than a hand-held potato gun. To help our reader see how it might apply to our potato-gun case, we need to write what the case stands for. Again, we do this by inducing a general principle from the specifics of the case. Here's an implicit rule we might fashion:

> A dangerous weapon includes a homemade instrument that mechanically propels an object that is capable of inflicting a serious injury.

What's the magic? How did we do that? We took the most significant specific aspects of the case and characterized them into categories:

Trebuchet becomes *instrument*
Piano becomes *object* or *projectile*
Maim or *kill* become *serious injury*

Now that we have created an implicit rule, we have a topic sentence for the Case Illustration:

> A **homemade instrument** that mechanically **propels** an **object** that is capable of inflicting a serious **injury** is a dangerous weapon. [Citation.] For example, a trebuchet is a dangerous weapon. In *Jackson*, the defendant filled a piano with pig manure, lit it on fire, and flung it at his neighbor. The court said that anything that can fling an upright grand piano is a dangerous weapon. Its capability to maim or kill make it dangerous.

And, finally, you can see below how the rule is applied to our client's facts about a potato gun. As you read this Application, observe how the writer (1) applies the implicit rule and (2) analogizes to the facts of the case:

> In our case, a court would likely find that a potato gun is a dangerous weapon because it's a **homemade instrument** that **propels an object** with an explosion, and it's capable of causing **death**. Unlike a trebuchet, a potato gun can't hurl large, life-threatening **objects**. But it does **propel** dense, fist-sized **projectiles**—potatoes—at excessive speeds. An impact in a vulnerable spot, such as the temple, could cause **death**. Therefore, a potato gun is a dangerous weapon.

You can see the highlighted terms are where the writer applied the implicit rule from the case.

Okay, that does it for the topic sentence. At the end of the chapter, you'll find a checklist that summarizes all the main points you just learned about.

On to the next part of a Case Illustration.

B. Citation

Because the topic sentence is a substantive rule of law—whether explicitly or implicitly stated—you must give a citation for it. Put the citation in a separate "citation sentence" after the topic sentence. Use the *ALWD Guide to Legal Citation* or *The Bluebook* for the proper format. Chapter 17 in this book summarizes many of the important aspects of citing.

Almost always, the citation should go in a separate citation sentence after the topic sentence, like this:

> Large, stationary manmade structures that are directly related to crucial skiing equipment are considered obvious and necessary. ***Anderson v. Pine Knob Ski Resort, Inc.*, 664 N.W.2d 756, 759 (Mich. 2003).** In *Anderson*, a skier lost their balance during a ski competition run, collided with a timing shack at the bottom of the run, and was injured.
>
> The Court held that the skier accepted the risk of the timing shack. *Id.* at **760.** The Court reasoned that the shack was necessary because it was essential to timing, which is required to determine a race's winner. *Id.* And the Court said that the shack was obvious because of its placement at the end of the run, presumably where everyone looks to determine the winner. *Id.* And, finally, the Court explained that the shack is inherent to the sport because it was similar to the dangerous equipment specifically listed in the statute, characterizing the shack as the "same sort." *Id.*

Putting the citation *after* a sentence of law puts the emphasis on the law and not the source.

Incidentally, note that it's also conventional to give a citation after stating the holding and each sentence of reasoning. That makes it easy for the reader to find it in the case. (And you'd use an *Id.* citation because you already gave the full one after the topic sentence. See 17.4(A)(2). From this Case Illustration, we know that we can find the holding and reasoning on page 760.

C. Facts

After the topic sentence and citation, briefly explain the story in the case. The facts should rarely take more than two or three sentences. Tell the case's story with contextual and legally significant facts, don't distract the reader with unnecessary information, and make it all readable.

1. What Facts to Include

When writing the facts of precedent, briefly tell the case's story chronologically but include primarily contextual facts and legally significant facts. These examples all tell the story:

> In *Anderson*, a skier in a slalom race at a ski resort crashed into the timing shack at the end of the run.
>
> In *Kirksey*, an injured employee, a truck driver, sprained his lower back while securing a load outside a factory loading dock. His insurance provider based the employee's work-loss benefits on recent, sporadic part-time work.
>
> In *Scameheorn*, a motorcycle operator and truck driver avoided a speed bump by driving on a sidewalk. Each vehicle approached from opposite directions, and they collided head on.
>
> In *Stacy*, shortly after an employee announced her pregnancy, her employer decided not to promote her as a securities trader, explaining that "we need someone who would be at work more often."

In each of these examples, the reader can quickly understand the story. They do that in part by giving context, the backdrop, of the story. You need to set the stage for the reader to understand the story. Thus "at a ski resort," "outside a factory loading dock," "on a sidewalk," and "a securities trader" each give context to their respective stories. That will help the reader understand the story quickly.

Finally, and perhaps most importantly, you must include the legally significant facts. To decide which facts are the most legally significant in any given precedent, look at the court's reasoning. Yes, all the facts will be in the first section or two of the opinion, but then the court applies the law to just the most significant facts in the reasoning section. Look there to know which facts to include in your Case Illustration.

In general, you will tend to use fewer facts in the Case Illustration if you are simply going to use the case to apply the court's reasoning to your client's facts. Contrariwise, you will tend to use more facts if you are reasoning by analogy, which is where you compare and contrast the facts of precedent to your client's case.

In the four examples above, they all include the most legally relevant facts.

In the *Anderson* facts above, the specifics about the shack and its placement at the end of the run go directly to whether the shack was an obvious and necessary danger in the sport of skiing.

In *Kirksey*, the facts go directly to whether and how much of an insurance benefit the truck driver was entitled to.

In the *Scameheorn* Case Illustration, the facts about the speed bump are directly related to whether the city had installed a defective speed bump, which, if so, would allow the motorist to recover in tort.

In *Stacy*, what the employer said about not being able to work because of the baby goes directly to sex discrimination.

And, yes, those facts are precisely the ones the writer will analogize to the client's facts in the Rule Application.

2. What Facts Not to Include

Don't include dates or names unless they are significantly relevant to the issue. Compare these two fact statements:

> In *Anderson*, Carl Anderson, in a slalom race at a ski resort on February 18, 2023, crashed into the timing shack at the end of the run.
>
> In *Anderson*, a skier in a slalom race at a ski resort crashed into the timing shack at the end of the run.

The name doesn't teach the reader anything about the law. And the date isn't relevant to whether a timing shack is a danger that the skier accepted. Omit them.

Also, you should not state the issue before the court as a separate sentence. Something like this is unnecessary:

> The issue before the court was whether this amounted to extreme and outrageous conduct under an IIED claim. The court held that the ex-girlfriend's conduct was extreme and outrageous, so the victim's IIED claim was proper.

Why not state the issue? Because you're going to give the holding directly after the facts, and the holding inherently has the issue in it. In the example above, the issue sentence and the holding sentence say the same thing. So stating the issue separately is redundant of the holding. Ditch the issue statement; keep the holding.

And do not include lower-court procedure in the Case Illustration. It has no bearing on the current state of the law, so it doesn't teach the reader anything they need to know. So avoid statements like "The trial-court granted summary judgment."

Finally, do not include what the parties argued. Nobody cares, and it does not teach the reader the law. Simply state the relevant facts.

3. Tips to Improve Readability

When writing the facts, consistently use the past verb tense. Unlike the topic sentence, which is usually written in the present verb tense, write the facts in the past tense because they—ahem—happened in the past.

And improve readability by using informative status words to identify the parties and other "characters" in the story (like *tenant* and *landlord* or *buyer* and *seller*), rather than using their actual names or *appellant/appellee*. These status or character terms teach the reader about the parties much more than just their name or litigation designation like *plaintiff*.

For civil cases, you may use *the plaintiff* or *the defendant* only if you can't come up with a descriptive status word.

If writing about a criminal case, use *the defendant* to refer to the person charged with the crime, which is informative to readers. But for other people, try to come up with informative status words, such as *witness*, *victim*, *accuser*, *arresting officer*, *police officer*, *companion*, *prosecutor*, etc.

Here are the four examples of case-illustration facts from above. The status or character words are in bold. Notice how informative they are compared to just *plaintiff* or *defendant*:

> In *Anderson*, **a skier** in a slalom race at a ski resort crashed into the timing shack at the end of the run.
>
> In *Kirksey*, an **injured employee**, a truck driver, sprained his lower back while securing a load outside a factory loading dock. His **insurance provider** based the employee's work-loss benefits on recent, sporadic part-time work.
>
> In *Scameheorn*, a **motorcycle operator** and **truck driver** avoided a speed bump by driving on a sidewalk. Each vehicle approached from opposite directions, and they collided head on.
>
> In *Stacy*, shortly after an **employee** announced her pregnancy, her **employer** decided not to promote her as a securities trader, explaining that "we need someone who would be at work more often."

D. Holding

The holding is the court's answer to the legal question. If the question is whether a person was falsely imprisoned by unreasonable duress, the court's holding would look like this:

> The court held that Davidson was not falsely imprisoned by unreasonable duress.

The holding is not a rule of law the court applied. Rather, the holding is the conclusion for that particular case. So it will require both a bit of law and a bit of fact. This is *not* a holding:

> A plaintiff is contributorily negligent when he or she is more than 50% at fault.

But this is a holding:

> The plaintiff in this case was contributorily negligent.

This is not a holding:

> The court affirmed the lower-court's holding.

That's not a holding because it doesn't give the court's conclusion on the specific issue. But this is a holding:

> The court held that the skier accepted the shack as a danger inherent in the sport of skiing.

The lower-court procedure is also usually irrelevant to helping the reader understand the element at issue, so omit it. Remember that all cases you're going to write about are appellate cases; what they say is the law, not what the lower trial court said. The reader is interested in what the highest *appellate* court did. So do *not* write things like this:

> The **trial court** held that the prosecutor must disclose the identity of the confidential informant. This appellate court held .... (Skip what the **trial court** did and state only what the highest appellate court said.)

The court reversed the lower-court decision. (This does not teach the reader anything about the rule of law.)

The court granted the motion for summary judgment. (Again, this does not teach the reader anything about the rule of law.)

E. Reasoning

Reasoning explains how the court came to its holding—its conclusion on the result of the law being applied to the facts. The reasoning usually explains whether the facts satisfy what the law demands. Courts reason the same way attorneys do: (1) they apply the plain meaning of the law to the facts and (2) they analogize to past precedent.

Observe in this example how the reasoning explains the court's holding:

> A person can collect increased work-loss benefits if he or she would have earned more if he had not been injured. *Kirksey v. Manitoba Public Insurance Corporation*, 477 N.W.2d 442 (Mich. Ct. App. 1991). In *Kirksey*, the plaintiff, a truck driver, was injured at work. The defendant based his work-loss benefits on recent, sporadic part-time work.
>
> The court held that the driver was entitled to increased work-loss benefits because he proved that he would have earned more if he had not been injured. **The court reasoned that the statute clearly provides that a person is entitled to lost income—what he would have earned if he had not been injured. It does not require the lost income to be based on what the person earned at the time he was injured. Because the driver proved that another employer would have paid him more, he was entitled to increased benefits.**

In a Case Illustration, you need to summarize that, and then you'll apply it in the Application section that follows.

But to really understand how to convey the court's reasoning in a Case Illustration, you need to first see a court's original reasoning and then see how an attorney-writer summarizes it in a Case Illustration. Below is one paragraph from a Michigan Supreme Court case that had to decide if a snow skier running into a timing shack for a ski competition was a "necessary and obvious" danger that is inherent to the sport of skiing. The numbers before each sentence help analyze the reasoning; they are not in the actual opinion. If you'd like to look up the actual opinion, Google this or put it into Westlaw's or Lexis's search bar: 664 N.W.2d 756.

In this paragraph of reasoning from the Court's decision, identify the three points of reasoning as to why a timing shack used in a ski race is an accepted danger:

> [1] There is no disputed issue of fact in this matter that in ski racing, timing, as it determines who is the winner, is necessary. [2] Moreover, there is no dispute that for the timing equipment to function, it is necessary that it be protected from the elements. [3] This protection was afforded by the shack that all also agree was obvious in its placement at the end of the run. [4] We have then a hazard of the same sort as the ski towers and snow-making and grooming machines to which the statute refers us. [5] As with the towers and equipment, this hazard inheres in the sport of skiing. [6] The placement of the timing shack is thus a danger that skiers such as Anderson are held to have accepted as a matter of law.

Anderson v. Pine Knob Ski Resort, Inc., 664 N.W.2d 756, 760 (Mich. 2003).

Let's analyze, shall we? The first point of reasoning is about the *necessary* element—the shack is necessary to protect the timing equipment, and timing is necessary to determine a winner. Sentences [1], [2], and some of [3] explain this point. The second point is about the *obvious* element, and it's found in the second half of sentence [3] when the Court said that its placement was obvious "at the end of the run." The shack's danger would be obvious because everyone can clearly see it at the bottom of the run. And, finally, the Court gave its third point starting in sentence [4] and continuing to the end. That final point explains why a timing shack inheres in the sport of skiing.

Based on this, how would we write the Case Illustration? Something like this:

> **[topic sentence]** Large, stationary structures in prominent places that are directly connected to the mechanics of skiing are obvious and necessary dangers that are inherent to the sport. **[citation]** *Anderson v. Pine Knob Ski Resort, Inc.*, 664 N.W.2d 756, 760 (Mich. 2003). **[facts]** In *Anderson*, a skier lost their balance during a ski competition run, collided with a timing shack at the bottom of the run, and was injured.
>
> **[holding]** The Court held that the skier accepted the risk of the timing shack. **[reasoning]** The Court reasoned that the shack was necessary because it was essential to timing, which is required to determine a race's winner. And the Court said that the shack was obvious because of its placement at the end of the run, presumably where everyone looks to determine the winner. And, finally, the Court explained that the shack is inherent to the sport because it was similar to the dangerous equipment specifically listed in the statute, characterizing the shack as the "same sort."

So be thorough when explaining the court's reasoning. You'll need it when you apply it to your client's facts in the Application. See 10.6(A)(2), Applying the Court's Reasoning.

9.5 Sample Case Illustrations

See all the techniques from section 9.4 in five different sample Case Illustrations.

Example 1:

> A risk is foreseeable if the tortfeasor had knowledge that the injury was likely to occur. *Samson v. Saginaw Professional Building, Inc.*, 224 N.W.2d 843 (Mich. 1975). In *Samson*, an office tenant was stabbed by a mentally unwell person who frequented the clinic that was in the same office building.
>
> The Court held that the injury was foreseeable because the risk was so great. In its reasoning, the Court stated that a reasonable person is expected to anticipate even events that are improbable when that event is great harm or death. It stated that the low probability must be balanced against the "magnitude of the potential harm." *Id.* at 849. Thus, the Court reasoned that, though a rampaging out-of-control person is improbable, the harm the person could inflict would be catastrophic. *Id.* Accordingly, the Court held that the landlord should have anticipated such a risk. *Id.*

Example 2:

> Another case in effect narrowed the definition of a dwelling house by adding a requirement that it be capable of being lived in. *People v. Reed*, 163 N.W.2d 704

(Mich. Ct. App. 1968). In *Reed*, the building was in a residential neighborhood but had been unoccupied for over a year. The interior was in poor condition because of vandalism and neglect, and there was no bathroom. Although the building was not condemned, it had been boarded up by the fire department.

The court held that since the building was not habitable at the time of the fire, it was not a dwelling house. The court based its decision on the common-law view that arson is a crime against people, rather than property. The court reasoned,

> There is general agreement that arson at common law was an offense against the habitation rather than the safety of the property, and was considered a more serious crime than any other unlawful burning because it might result in the destruction of human life as well as property.

Id. at 706. The court then reasoned that since Michigan law prescribes more severe penalties for burning a dwelling house than for burning other structures, a dwelling house must be "a structure that could reasonably be presumed to be a place capable of being dwelt in or lived in ...." *Id.* at 708. Since the house was boarded up and needed substantial renovation, it could not reasonably be presumed to be habitable. *Id.*

Example 3:

An attorney's promise to provide legal services in return for a person's promise to vote for a judicial candidate is illegal. *Trushin v. State*, 425 So. 2d 1126 (Fla. 1983). In *Trushin*, an attorney circulated a letter in an apartment complex. It read, "To every resident ... who comes to my office to pledge their vote to Judge Frederick N. Barrad and Judge Calvin R. Mapp, in the upcoming election, I will prepare a Last Will and Testament without charge." *Id.* at 1127.

The Court found that a will was "a thing of value" and Trushin improperly induced recipients to vote for the judges. *Id.* at 1128. In a straightforward analysis, the court reasoned that the Florida statute, Fla. Stat. Ann. § 104.061, states that no person can promise anything of value to another intending to buy that person's vote or corruptly influence that person in casting his or her vote. *Trushin*, 425 So. 2d at 1128. And that's exactly what happened here. *Id.*

Example 4:

An explicit credible threat must state intent to actually harm and not merely to frighten the victim. *People v. Czemerynski*, 786 P.2d 1100 (Colo. 1990). In *Czemerynski*, the defendant made sexually explicit phone calls and said to a girl, "[I]f you don't help me, I'm around the corner and I know where you live and I am going to get you." *Id.* at 1103. The defendant did not always request sex, but most conversations contained vague threats to "get" the victim. *Id.* The court found that such communications met the harassment statute's credible-threat requirement because the calls were "intended to harass or threaten bodily injury." *Id.* at 1110.

Example 5:

A public building's dangerous or defective condition is determined by the intended use or purpose it is to serve. *Scameheorn v. Bucks*, 421 N.W.2d 918 (Mich. Ct. App. 1988). In *Scameheorn*, a motorcycle operator and truck driver avoided a speed bump by driving on a sidewalk. Each vehicle approached from an opposite direction and collided head on. The plaintiff argued that the speed bumps were defective.

The court held that the speed bumps were not defective because they served the purpose they were created for. The court reasoned that whether a part of a building is dangerous or defective is determined by the use or purpose that part is to serve. The court added that an alleged defect and its relation to an injury is a matter for the fact finder.

9.6 Practice Identifying a Good Case Illustration

Let's take a breather for a moment to inventory what you've learned about explaining caselaw. Below, you'll find a Rule Foundation followed by three versions of the same Case Illustration. Based on what you've already learned, which Case Illustration is most helpful to a reader?

This paragraph is the Rule Foundation.

You asked me to determine whether Ms. Lucas's easement allows her to build a dock on the lake even though she is a backlot owner. Her easement gives her "ingress and egress" rights to the lake. A court looks to the easement language to determine whether it contemplates the riparian right of building and maintaining a dock. *Little v. Kin*, 664 N.W.2d 749 (Mich. 2003). A court cannot look to facts beyond the easement document unless it determines that the language is ambiguous. *Dyball v. Lennox*, 680 N.W.2d 522, 526 (Mich. Ct. App. 2004). Here, we only have to decide whether (A) the easement language is ambiguous and (B), if it is ambiguous, whether the circumstances surrounding the creation of the easement show that the easement creator intended such a use.

A. Is the easement language ambiguous?

This is option 1 of the *Dyball* Case Illustration.

Where the easement's language is plain and unambiguous, a court will interpret it without looking to the circumstances surrounding its creation. *Dyball*, 680 N.W.2d at 526. In *Dyball*, Joyce Sanford obtained on June 28, 1998, an easement with this language: "for the purpose of ingress and egress to and from the premises in which they may have an interest to the water's edge of Lake Fenton." The issue before the court was whether this language unambiguously granted the right to build a dock on the lake. The trial court held that this language was unambiguous and did not grant the right to construct a dock. *Id.* at 524. The Court of Appeals agreed.

OR

This is option 2 of the *Dyball* Case Illustration.

Courts interpret "ingress and egress" narrowly in easement documents to include only access to a lake. *Dyball*, 680 N.W.2d at 526. In *Dyball*, lakefront landowners sought to stop a backlot landowner from using an easement across the lakefront owner's land to maintain a dock on the lake. The backlot owner's easement stated, "for the purpose of ingress and egress to and from the premises in which they may have an interest to the water's edge of Lake Fenton."

The court held that the easement language was unambiguous and did not grant the right to construct a dock. *Id.* at 527. The court implied that the language was unambiguous because there's only one way to read "ingress and egress," and the backlot owner did not provide any proof of ambiguity.

OR

Where the easement's language is plain and unambiguous, a court will interpret it without looking to the circumstances surrounding its creation. *Dyball*, 680 N.W.2d at 526. In *Dyball*, the court held that an easement containing the language "for the purpose of ingress and egress to and from the premises in which they may have an interest to the water's edge of Lake Fenton" was unambiguous language that did not grant the right to construct a dock. *Id.* at 524.

This is option 3 of the *Dyball* Case Illustration.

[Rule Application]

B. What do the surrounding circumstances say about the creator's intent?

...

Explain here which Case Illustration is better and why. When doing that, evaluate it according to the five parts of a Case Illustration described above. You can see the answer in the box below.

Here's the answer: Option 2 is the best, most helpful Case Illustration. It includes all five parts of a full Case Illustration. The topic sentence includes a new substantive rule that doesn't merely repeat a rule from the Rule Foundation. The facts give the gist of the story without including unnecessary detail. The holding is directly on point with the issue at hand, ambiguity. And the reasoning was thorough.

Option 1 isn't as helpful. The topic sentence repeats a rule from the Rule Foundation, so the analysis doesn't move forward, frustrating an impatient reader. The facts include unnecessary details like names and dates. An issue statement is included, which is redundant of the holding. It also includes a procedural holding ("The Court of Appeals agreed.), which doesn't teach the reader anything. There's no reasoning to speak of.

Option 3 likewise isn't helpful. The topic sentence merely repeats a rule the reader already knows about from the Rule Foundation. The facts are missing. The holding is there, but it's buried in a long sentence. And there's no reasoning. Without that reasoning, the writer can't fully apply the case to their client's facts.

9.7 Short Case Illustration

Above, you learned about doing a full Case Illustration: topic sentence, citation, facts, holding, and reasoning. In just about every analytical legal document, you will have at least one full Case Illustration. And often you will support that primary Case Illustration with bolstering ones. Those bolstering ones are often, but not always, so-called "short Case Illustrations." You need bolstering cases because, with just one case, a reader might assume that you cherry picked an anomalous case that just happens to support your position. A full Case Illustration with bolstering ones shows that a pattern of law supports your position, and that creates much more credible and strong analysis.

Learning to adapt documents to fit your situation becomes second nature for attorneys, and this is a perfect example. You learned about the five-part Case Illustration; now you will begin to see how you can use permutations of this structure to fit your specific needs. There is no way we can show you every permutation of organizing and using caselaw in a legal document, but we can show you all the parts and then get you started on learning how to adapt them to the document's unique needs.

To do a short illustration, simply use less than the five parts. That's it. There's a lot of flexibility here, but try these "formulas" first and see how it works:

A. Use a Short Illustration to Bolster a Main Case

You have heard, no doubt, the saying that two witnesses are better than one. Well, the same goes for cases. But often you need just one smaller Case Illustration of a case that supports a main or leading case that you did earlier:

> [Full illustration of a leading case.]
>
> Other cases have come to the same conclusion. For instance, in a case involving baseball, *X v. Y* [citation], the court said, "...." Similarly, in *A v. B* [citation], the court held that the defendant owed no duty to a golfer to protect him from the ordinary risks of golf.

B. Use a Short Illustration to Explain the State of the Law

Instead of just stating a rule from a case, sometimes you may want to include the reasoning behind a rule. The facts of the case are not relevant to your issue, but the rule and the policy behind it are. That's a perfect time to write a short Case Illustration:

> Other jurisdictions also strictly enforce pre-suit notice requirements. For example, in *Jones v. Fred's Tavern, Inc.*, 520 A.2d 121 (N.J. 1999), the Court held that there was no good-faith exception to New Jersey's 120-day notice requirement. The court reasoned that allowing such an exception would undermine the legislature's desire to promote pre-suit settlements.

You could do the same thing and omit the reasoning altogether if it doesn't apply to what you're doing:

> Other jurisdictions also strictly enforce pre-suit notice requirements. For example, in *Jones v. Fred's Tavern, Inc.*, 520 A.2d 121 (N.J. 1999), the Court held that there was no good-faith exception to New Jersey's 120-day notice requirement.

This approach works best when you want to discuss a number of consistent cases in the same paragraph:

> Other jurisdictions also strictly enforce pre-suit notice requirements. For example, in *Jones v. Fred's Tavern, Inc.*, 520 A.2d 121 (N.J. 1999), the Court held that there was no good-faith exception to New Jersey's 120-day notice requirement. Likewise, in *Smith v. Poor Willie's Pub*, 344 P.2d 492 (Wash. Ct. App. 1987), the court held that Washington's 90-day notice requirement could not be excused for "good cause" or because of severe injuries.

Although this next example is long, it's still considered "short" because it has less than the five parts of the full Case Illustration. The writer needed this case only for the law because the factual story was not on point with the client's case:

> Michigan courts have held that irrelevant, stray remarks are inadmissible as direct evidence in establishing discrimination as a motivating factor for termination. *Krohn v. Sedgwick James of Mich.*, 624 N.W.2d 212 (Mich. Ct. App. 2001). In *Krohn*, the court adopted the following four factors from the federal courts to decide whether comments were merely stray remarks or relevant, direct evidence of discrimination:
>
> (1) Were the disputed remarks made by the decisionmaker [sic] or by an agent of the employer uninvolved in the challenged decision?
>
> (2) Were the disputed remarks isolated or part of a pattern of biased comments?
>
> (3) Were the disputed remarks made close in time or remote from the challenged decision?
>
> (4) Were the disputed remarks ambiguous or clearly reflective of discriminatory bias?
>
> *Id.* at 214. The court's reasoning in being so selective in the admission of evidence is that if an irrelevant, ambiguous remark made by someone other than the decision maker is allowed to go to the jury, it could inflame the jury and sway their decision, thus having an unfair prejudicial effect on the defendant.

C. Use a Short Case Illustration to Give Factual Examples

A Case Illustration could even be as short as a parenthetical. This is especially helpful when you want to give several factual examples of a simple element. In the example below, which you may find in context on page 47 of this book in the sample Full Office Memo, the writer illustrated what time periods prove causation and do not prove causation in an employment retaliation lawsuit:

> Courts have found that between three months and five years is insufficient to establish a causal connection while time periods of between two weeks and two months have succeeded. *See, e.g.*, *Aho*, 688 N.W.2d at 110–11 (holding that five years between the discharge and alleged conduct was too remote); *McLemore v. Det. Receiving Hosp.*, 493 N.W.2d 441, 443–44 (Mich. Ct. App. 1992) (holding that approximately two months was sufficient); and *Moore v. Kuka Welding Sys.*, 171 F.3d 1073, 1078–80 (6th Cir. 1999) (holding that two weeks was sufficient).

All the Case Illustrations in the parentheticals above include just the brief on-point facts and a holding; the reasoning was not necessary for purposes of this really quick point. And notice how helpful the topic sentence is at clearly stating the main point of synthesizing all the cases.

9.8 Reusing a Case Within the Same Document

A. All the Different Ways to Use a Case in the Same Document

This entire Chapter 9 has really been about explaining a case's story and what the court said about the story. For just a moment, let's back out and look at using caselaw in the entire document. We need that perspective to set up how you may use the same case multiple times in the same document.

To be clear, you may reuse the same case multiple times within the same document. As you read the various ways to use a case within a document, keep in mind that caselaw offers both (1) black-letter rules of law and (2) facts—or legal stories—to analogize to. Here are all the different ways you could use a case in a document:

- Use a case only for its black-letter rules of law (e.g., in Rule Foundations) and not for its story. See, for example, how the writer used *Fermino* to establish false imprisonment in the Short Office Memo on page 30. That was the only time *Fermino* was used.
- Use a case's story just to illustrate one element (i.e., a Case Illustration with topic sentence, citation, facts, holding, and reasoning) in one IREAC packet. In that same Short Office Memo, the writer used *Parrott*, *Wilson*, and *Schanafelt* for just one issue.
- Use a case *both* as a source of black-letter rules of law and a Case Illustration. In the Full Office Memo on page 47, the writer uses *McLemore* to establish a rule of law. Then, on the next page, it does a full Case Illustration of it.
- Use a case's story for two different elements in two different IREAC packets. See the example below.

B. Reusing a Case in Two Different IREAC Packets

You may use the same case for more than one Case Illustration in a document. The first time you give the Case Illustration, include all five parts: topic sentence, citation, facts, holding, and reasoning. Then apply it to your client's facts for that issue.

Later in the document, when you're discussing a new subissue, a new element, bring up the case again, but focus all the parts on the new subissue. So the topic sentence, facts, holding, and reasoning will be different because you're focusing on a new element of law. And you may omit some of the contextual facts because the reader already read those above when you first referenced the case.

Here's an example of using the same case for two different elements in an objective memo.

Discussion

[Internal Analysis Preview, 16.5]

[Global Rule Foundation, 7.5]

A. Objectively Manifested

[Secondary Rule Foundation]

The topic sentence focuses on the element at issue here.

[Case Illustration] Hearing loss may be an objectively manifested impairment when a doctor performs board-approved medical tests. *Patrick v. Turkelson*, 913 N.W.2d 369, 378 (Mich. Ct. App. 2018). In *Patrick*, a car-accident victim suffered hearing loss and

Because this is the first time explaining this case, the writer gives a few more contextual facts to understand what happened in the case. Then the holding and reasoning focus just on this one element.

tinnitus from deployed airbags. *Id.* at 374. The court held that the symptoms were objectively manifested impairments because they were observed and perceived by an audiologist, an otologist, and Patrick's spouse. *Id.* at 379.

[Rule Application]

B. Important Body Function

[Secondary Rule Foundation]

Hearing loss affects an important body function. *Id.* at 378. In *Patrick*, where a driver lost hearing from airbag deployment, the court held that the driver's impairment did affect an important body function, namely hearing. *Id.* at 379. The court came to this conclusion by observing that the driver, like all people, used hearing every day for essential tasks, but this driver in particular enjoyed using her hearing to attend concerts. Therefore, hearing was an important body function to her.

The same case from above also illustrates another element at issue, important body function. Note that the topic sentence focuses narrowly on just the element at issue in this section. And, for the facts, the writer merely jogs the reader's memory.

Note that the holding and reasoning are tailored to just the element at issue in this section of the memo. Everything focuses on "important body function."

[Rule Application]

9.9 Working With Multiple Cases

A. When to Use Multiple Cases

Sometimes one case will do the trick, like you saw in the email example above on page 220. But, oftentimes, you will need several cases because you will not be able to find one case that squarely, fully, and thoroughly addresses the issue.

The main reasons to use more than just one case are

- to **bolster** a primary case,
- to help your reader understand what facts **satisfy** the law and what facts **do not satisfy** the law (i.e., to create a spectrum of cases),
- to pull from the cases **factors** to weigh in applying an element, and
- to pull out an **implicit rule** from several cases.

B. Synthesize Cases for Fast Comprehension

Attorneys see separate precedent cases as one cohesive mosaic of law. Synthesizing them is an easy way for your reader to quickly see that mosaic. The reader must see not only what the cases teach about the law, but how all the cases relate to each other. This coherence is essential for comprehension.

Here's a more specific reason to synthesize caselaw: Legal rules do not always appear fully formed in a single case or statute because the common law on any given topic often develops over time. So, to get the law right, you have to derive a rule from a *body* or mosaic of law, as well as from a single source.

Here are the three most common ways to synthesize multiple cases:

- Trophy — each case gets a topic sentence
- Rubber Band — use one topic sentence to band multiple cases together
- Synthesis Paragraph — each case gets a topic sentence *and* the writer coheres all the points in a paragraph after the Case Illustrations

1. Trophy Synthesis

In this style of synthesizing Case Illustrations, each case brings something different to the element or rule. Just like every kid in the city soccer league gets a participation trophy, every Case Illustrations gets a topic sentence. Use this only when it's *not* useful to point out what's in common among the cases.

The topic sentences do the work of (1) showing the coherence among the cases (2) while pointing out what each case adds to the body of law.

In this example, the writer illustrates how courts have used parties' past dealings to determine whether a contract is enforceable. There are three on-point cases for the writer's issue. Notice how each Case Illustration begins with a substantive topic sentence, but each one focuses on past dealings and enforceability; in this way, the topic sentences cohere the three cases:

> More recently, the court of appeals relied on the *Jones* **past-dealings** rule to find a contract **enforceable** and reject a commercial buyer's claim of an invalid offer. *Smith v. Johnson*, 555 N.W.2d 987 (Mich. Ct. App. 2011). In *Smith*, the court held that a book seller's offer to ship "the usual number of cases" contained a sufficiently specific quantity term to be enforced. *Id.* at 990. The court reasoned that these offer terms were consistent with the parties' "substantial past dealings and expectations" and thus were not "too vague or inchoate" to be valid. *Id.*
>
> Courts have also considered parties' **past dealings** as a basis to **enforce** offers to purchase commodities. *XHS, Corp. v. QQQ, Inc.*, 515 N.W.2d 987 (Mich. Ct. App. 2010). For instance, in *XHS, Corp.*, the court held that a corn buyer made a valid offer to purchase corn when it said it would "take its old usual amount." *Id.* at 990.
>
> Likewise, a soybean buyer's purchase offer was **enforceable** when it asked for a "standard shipment," which implied reliance on **past dealings**. *MJM, Inc. v. Klancy*, 455 N.W.2d 187, 190 (Mich. Ct. App. 1997).

After reading about those three cases, the reader has a really good picture of what enforceability in this context looks like. The next thing the reader would see would be the Application section where the focus will be on—you guessed it—enforceability of the client's contract using the past-dealings rule.

Here's one more example of using a topic sentence for each Case Illustration to band them all together. In this case, the main issue was whether the client acted in self-defense. The topic sentences are in bold:

> **A defendant who starts a fight cannot claim self-defense unless they reasonably anticipated immediate danger and had no other choice but to use reasonable force.** For instance, in *People v. Stevens*, 858 N.W.2d 98 (Mich. Ct. App. 2014), the defendant surprised an unarmed victim, punched him, and wrestled him to the ground. When the victim got the upper hand, the defendant stabbed him. Later, the defendant claimed that he'd acted in self-defense because while they were wrestling, the victim ended up on top of him, making it hard for the defendant to breathe. In his panic, the defendant took out a knife and stabbed the victim.
>
> The court held that these facts did not justify self-defense. *Id.* at 104. The defendant had no reason to believe that he was in imminent danger because he initiated the attack, and the victim did not have a weapon or use "deadly force against the defendant." *Id.* Likewise, his claimed panic attack did not justify the stabbing. *Id.*

> The stabbing would have been reasonable only if the victim had a weapon or was intentionally choking him. *Id.*
>
> **Similarly, a defendant must try to "safely avoid using deadly force" and can only use enough force to dissipate the threat.** *People v. Riddle*, 649 N.W.2d 30, 46 (Mich. 2002). [facts, holding, and reasoning omitted because they're not similar enough]

With this style, where every case gets its own topic sentence, the key is to both create cohesion by making sure the reader sees how each case relates to each other and state a substantive point about the case. In both of the topic sentences above, they both relate to "force," and they both involve fights or threatening situations.

2. Rubber-Band Synthesis

Here's the basic formula for this style of synthesizing the cases:

(1) State the rule in the topic sentence. [This is the rubber band.]
(2) Give a factual example of that rule with a Case Illustration, but without a topic sentence.
(3) Give another factual example of that rule with a Case Illustration, but without a topic sentence.
(4) And, perhaps, give a third factual example of that rule with a Case Illustration, but without a topic sentence.

That model is assuming three factual examples, but it could be anywhere from two to four factual examples for any given element. Let's look at examples.

Suppose you want to synthesize two cases that agree. Connect the cases by starting with a topic sentence that captures the essence of both cases. You can see that in bold below. And note that for this example, the writer needs only the rule and not the facts or reasoning:

> **The cases agree that the favorable-termination requirement is not satisfied by a joint stipulation to dismiss or by a settlement.** In *Evans v. Alabama Professional Health Consultants, Inc.* [citation], the court said that a joint stipulation of dismissal is like a settlement agreement, "compromising the interests of both parties, but 'in favor' of neither party." [Pinpoint citation.] Because the courts favor settlements, the parties should not be discouraged from settling for fear that one party might still be able to sue for malicious prosecution. Likewise, in *Frye v. Stoneman* [citation], the court said in dictum: "A termination does not satisfy the first element [favorable termination] if it is the result of compromise or settlement of the claim." [Pinpoint citation.]

Suppose the cases disagree—and you just need the rules from the cases, not the facts. Here's an example of that:

> **Although the Michigan cases seem to disagree somewhat on the tests for special injury, they agree that injury to reputation does not qualify.** One Michigan case defined *special injury* in general terms as "some injury which would not necessarily occur in all suits prosecuted for similar causes of action." [citation.] Another case defined *special injury* more narrowly as "the seizure of property or a result equivalent to a seizure of property." [citation.] In both cases, the plaintiffs

were claiming injury to their professional reputation from the earlier suit. And in both cases—although the courts applied the two different tests—the courts held that the plaintiffs' injuries were not a special injury.

Suppose the cases agree—and you want the rule and the facts. It would look like this:

> **The cases seem to agree that reasonable grounds must be judged by an objective standard.** In *Coblyn v. Kennedy's, Inc.* [citation] and in *J. C. Penney Co. v. Cox* [citation] nobody saw the customer take anything and nothing was missing. In both cases, the employee acted on mere suspicion: in *Coblyn*, the employee saw the customer take his own ascot out of his pocket; and in *J. C. Penney*, the employee acted on another customer's "belief' that the plaintiff had stolen something. In both cases, the court held that the employee's subjective belief was not enough. The court in *Coblyn* specifically rejected a subjective test. Likewise, the court in *J. C. Penney* said the detention "must be grounded on some definite information from some person that saw enough to justify the manager's belief that a theft bad been made ...." *J. C. Penney*, 148 So. 2d at 684.

This example above omits the reasoning from the cases. If you needed it, you could probably combine the reasoning too, in a separate paragraph, but now this is starting to get complicated. As an alternative, you might want to pick the better case, do a full illustration, and then do a short illustration of the supporting case.

You can also use the rubber-band method to connect two or more cases just to bolster a primary case. In this example, the first Case Illustration is to the primary case that established the main rule. That single Case Illustration has a topic sentence. Then, to bolster that rule and give a couple of additional examples, the writer synthesized two cases using one topic sentence. Both topic sentences are in bold:

This topic sentence gives the main point of this primary case.

> **The attorney-judgment rule protects trial lawyers from malpractice suits criticizing their informed choices on which witnesses to call at trial.** *Simko v. Blake*, 543 N.W.2d 23 (Mich. 1995). In *Simko*, the client was convicted for possession of cocaine and a firearm, but the conviction was later reversed on appeal. The client sued his trial attorney for malpractice, alleging that he would have avoided the initial guilty verdict if his attorney had called a number of important witnesses.
>
> The Court held that the attorney's decision not to call certain witnesses was protected by the attorney-judgment rule, noting that as long as an attorney "acts with full knowledge of the law and in good faith," a supposed error in that attorney's tactical decision to call or not call certain witnesses cannot establish a breach of duty. *Id.* at 25. The Court reasoned that the client's allegations were "nothing but an assertion that another lawyer might have conducted the trial differently." *Id.* Even if there were an error in judgment and another lawyer would have tried the case differently, the disputed decisions were still tactical in nature, and tactical decisions "do not constitute grounds for a legal malpractice action." *Id.*

This rubber-band topic sentence ties together two Case Illustrations that bolster the primary case above.

> **In two recent unpublished opinions, the Michigan Court of Appeals followed *Simko* in rejecting malpractice claims that second-guessed a trial lawyer's choice of witnesses.** For instance, in *McAdoo v. Satawa*, No. 234628, 2002 WL 31955124, at *2 (Mich. Ct. App. Dec. 17, 2002), the court held that a client's malpractice claim was defective as a matter of law when her affidavit merely criticized her attorney's trial strategy, such as his decision to not call certain witnesses to testify.

> Likewise, in *Diehl v. Abood*, No. 215793, 2000 WL 33534610, at *1 (Mich. Ct. App. Feb. 11, 2000), the court held that a criminal-defense attorney's alleged failure to call a ballistics expert was not actionable, reasoning that "[i]t is a tactical decision whether to call particular witnesses, as long as the attorney acts with full knowledge of the law and in good faith."

Often, the reader will want to see a spectrum of examples from what does to what does not satisfy the law. The example below illustrates how to do that effectively with short Case Illustrations and topic sentences:

> The causation element in a retaliation suit requires the employee to prove that the protected activity was a **"significant factor" in the firing, and that may be established by showing close temporal proximity.** *Rymal v. Baergen*, 686 N.W.2d 241, 264 (Mich. Ct. App. 2004). As a threshold issue to close temporal proximity, the adverse action must have occurred **after** the protected activity. *Id.* at 264.

This paragraph is the Rule Foundation.

> **If the adverse action happened after the protected activity, then most courts will find a functional relationship exists when the time period is less than two months.** For instance, in *Rymal*, the court found that **one week** was "close" and that **one or two months** was attenuated, but still sufficient. *Id.* at 262. Similarly, **two weeks** was sufficient in one United States Circuit Court case. *Moore v. Kuka Welding Sys.*, 171 F.3d 1073, 1078–80 (6th Cir. 1999).

This rubber-band topic sentence creates cohesion and easy comprehension by showing what the cases have in common (causation element is met when less than two weeks between events).

> On the other hand, a Michigan Persons with Disabilities Civil Rights Act case applying the same definition as ELCRA found that **five years** was not closely proximate by relying on persuasive cases of **three months**, **seven months**, and **four years.** *Aho v. Dept. of Corrections*, 688 N.W.2d 104, 110 (Mich. Ct. App. 2004).

The examples above were all taken from memos and briefs written in a law firm. But this final example of rubber-band topic sentences is from a judicial opinion. Even judges synthesize caselaw. In this example, the court fashions an implicit rule from the cases, and it states the rule before giving the sample cases. The implicit topic sentence is in bold:

> Michigan's governmental immunity statute defines "gross negligence" as "conduct so reckless as to demonstrate a substantial lack of concern for whether an injury results." *Id.* Although the Michigan Court of Appeals has refused to rule out the possibility that a failure to act could itself rise to the level of gross negligence, *see Tallman v. Markstrom*, 446 N.W.2d 618, 620 (Mich. Ct. App. 1989), **the majority of cases in which liability has been found involve actions where the risk of harm to a particular individual was clear, and where the defendant obviously made a conscious choice to disregard that harm.** *See, e.g., Kostrzewa v. City of Troy*, 247 F.3d 633, 642–43 (6th Cir. 2001) (holding that claim for gross negligence was stated where officer decided to apply handcuffs that would be too tight and then drove recklessly with the plaintiff in the back seat of the police car, further injuring him); *Soper v. Hoben*, 195 F.3d 845, 851–52 (6th Cir. 1999) (holding that no claim for gross negligence could be stated for failure to have a policy protecting at-risk children and for failing to supervise them properly); *Adams v. Metiva*, 31 F.3d 375, 388 (6th Cir. 1994) (holding that claim for gross negligence was stated where officer sprayed mace in arrestee's face long after he had been blinded and incapacitated); *Johnson v. Wayne County*, 540 N.W.2d 66, 73 (Mich. Ct. App. 1995) (claim for gross negligence stated where deputies incarcerated

> juror in contempt of court in a cell with the alleged murderer on trial, and then shackled them together).

Schreiber v. County of Crawford, 01-10083-BC, 2002 WL 1907974, at *12 (E.D. Mich. Aug. 20, 2002).

3. Synthesis Paragraph

When the cases are a bit more detailed and you need space to lay out what the cases have in common or what they as a group teach about the element at issue, it's best to take a paragraph after the Case Illustrations to synthesize the cases. In that synthesis paragraph, cohesively bring the cases together by (1) showing what the cases have in common or (2) explaining what they collectively bring to the same element or rule of law. What the cases have in common or what each case brings to the same element are often called "factors." A court may explicitly state factors or, more often, an attorney culls them from several cases and states them in a synthesis paragraph.

You can see examples of a synthesis paragraph in the Relevant Caselaw section of the Short Office Memo in section 2.4; in particular, look at page 30. And there's one in the Full Office Memo in 2.5 in the Adverse Employment section; see page 44.

a. Examples of a Synthesis Paragraph

Let's get right to an example.

Your case involves a 14-year-old boy who beat a Jewish man severely with a baseball bat. The parents caught him downloading hate literature, including white-supremacy material, from the Internet. He had never physically harmed another person, although he was caught spraying swastikas on a synagogue.

Suppose the law provides that parents of a minor are civilly responsible for their child's wrongful acts if the parents "know or have reason to know of the child's tortious propensities." As you read the following cases that all apply this rule, look for common threads or what each case brings to the rule about knowledge:

> *Case 1:* Parents held liable for injury deliberately caused by child who was 7 years old at the time of the event, and parents had seen him hurt others but had failed to intervene.
>
> *Case 2:* Parents not held liable for shooting by 17-year-old child who had been involved in vandalism and other property destruction, but there were no previous injuries to persons.
>
> *Case 3:* Parents not held liable for drunken rape by 17-year-old child who had history of substance abuse, but no history of injuring persons or property.

Rather than individually comparing your client's facts to the facts of each of these cases, you could try to derive some common threads or factors from these cases. Those factors will then be the basis of your reasoning.

Before reading the synthesis paragraph below, based on the three cases above, try to sketch out what types of things—what factors—a court will look at to determine whether parents know about their child's tortious propensities.

Okay, here's a sample synthesis paragraph that you would put right after the third Case Illustration:

> Thus, it appears that courts are concerned with the **age** of the child because a younger child may be more under the parents' control than an older one. In addition, the courts consider the child's **previous behavior** and whether that behavior

> would put the parent on notice that the child was likely to commit harm. Finally, the courts consider the **similarity** of the acts committed by the child in the past to the acts involved in this action.

Each of the three cases above looked at age, previous behavior, and repeated similar behavior; thus, that's what goes into the synthesis paragraph.

Now that you have beautifully and clearly synthesized the cases into coherent factors, the reader can easily understand the law. You are now ready to apply the law to the client's facts. The common threads now become the basis of your arguments. In the Application paragraph below, after the client facts, look for the common threads identified above: age, previous behavior, and similar behavior.

> [Application] In our case, although the child was not as close to the **age** of majority as were the children in [cases 2 and 3], he was a teenager and much more likely to be beyond the control of his parents than was the seven-year-old in [case 1].
>
> Furthermore, while the child in our case had demonstrated hateful feelings or attitudes toward minorities in his choice of reading materials, that alone is not likely to result in an inference that the parents should have known of his **dangerous propensities**. Like the children in [cases 2 and 3], he had a **history** of violence toward property, but the courts seem to say that more is needed to hold a parent liable when the child harms another person. Therefore, our case is more **like** those where the courts said that there was no liability, and the parents in our case are not likely to be held liable for their son's act.

At first, you may find it challenging to induce from the specifics in a case common threads, but with practice it will become second nature. In fact, you'll do it naturally while researching caselaw.

b. How to Create a Synthesis Paragraph

As you research caselaw, focus on each case's reasoning, but only the reasoning that applies to your case. Determine whether a group of cases relies on similar concepts in the reasoning sections. That pattern is what you're looking for. Identify that pattern, and then write about it in the synthesis paragraph.

In the above example, the narrow issue was whether the parents had sufficient knowledge. So when researching that issue, you'd focus on the courts' reasoning on the element of knowledge. One trick is to ask yourself what the concept of law "looks like." For instance, ask, "What does sufficient knowledge for parental responsibility look like?" Answering that question involves describing the characteristics the courts touch on in their reasoning. A pattern of common threads or factors the courts discuss in their reasoning will become the synthesis paragraph you write after the Case Illustrations.

Those common threads then become the basis of your arguments in the Application section.

We'll use the example below to go through the process of thinking to create synthesized factors from several cases. That case focuses on one subset of an element of false imprisonment, confinement by duress. The writer uses a network of topic sentences and a synthesis paragraph to cohesively and clearly explain the law for confinement by duress:

> **Confinement by unreasonable duress occurs when one's will is overcome.** *Parrott v. Bank of America*, 217 P.2d 89, 95 (Cal. App. 2d Dist. 1950). In *Parrott*, bank managers accused a teller of stealing a customer's deposit. She became hysterical after the bank manager questioned her for more than two hours and threatened her with an FBI investigation and to publicly humiliate her. As a result, she confessed to stealing the deposit even though she was innocent. The court held that the teller was

Topic sentence pulls an implicit rule from the case. 9.4(A)(3).

confined during the questioning. In support of this conclusion, the court mainly relied on the fact that an innocent person agreeing to sign a confession is evidence of force.

Topic sentence pulls an implicit rule from this case.

The source of the duress may be when a person uses a sacred right as leverage. *Wilson v. Houston Funeral Home*, 50 Cal. Rptr. 2d 169 (Cal. App. 2d Dist. 1996). In *Wilson*, a funeral home director sent a limo to take a family to scheduled burial services. The driver, instead, took the family to a bank where the funeral director demanded full payment even though they previously agreed to payment after the burial services. In the bank, he shouted, "Ain't nobody going nowhere until I get paid." *Id.* at 170. And for 45 minutes he tried to talk the widow into paying him. The court held that the family was confined by unreasonable duress because leaving the bank would have left their deceased loved one to an unknown fate.

Likewise, this topic sentence states an implicit rule. But what do they have in common?

The hallmark of confinement by unreasonable duress is fear. *Schanafelt v. Seaboard Fin. Co.*, 239 P.2d 42, 43 (Cal. App. 2d Dist. 1951). The defendant went to the plaintiff's house to repossess furniture that the plaintiff was unable to pay for. The agent parked his car in the driveway to block the plaintiff's car. He was "abrupt and gruff" in demanding that the plaintiff stay put while a utility truck and a crew came to repossess the furniture. *Id.* at 43. The plaintiff could have left on foot, but she "[f]ear[ed] the consequence of contrary action." *Id.* Plus she was pregnant and was worried about consequences to the unborn child. The plaintiff complained to the agent of being hungry, but he wouldn't let her eat, even though he helped himself to food from the neighbor's house. The whole ordeal lasted a bit over three hours.

The court held that the agent's conduct did amount to confinement because the plaintiff was "effectively prevented" from leaving by the agent's gruff manner, his blocking of the driveway, and the plaintiff's vulnerable status. *Id.*

The synthesis paragraph brings all the cases together and explains what they have in common.

Read together, it appears that courts in California determine that a person is confined by unreasonable duress when the defendant uses **severe fear and intimidation to the point of overcoming one's will.**

Let's analyze the example above to see how the writer created those factors in the synthesis paragraph. A chart will come in handy:

Case	Specific Facts Used in Court's Reasoning		Induced Category	In Common?
Parrott	Innocent person confessed to a crime she did not commit	→	one's will being overcome	Creating severe fear and intimidation to the point of overcoming one's will could amount to confinement by duress.
Wilson	A family cannot bury their loved one until they pay for the funeral services	→	control, manipulation, and leverage of invaluable practice or sacred rite	
Schanafelt	A repo man is "abrupt and gruff" with a pregnant person, demanding that she "stay put"	→	intimidation and fear-inducing behavior	

Going from the specific facts used in the courts' reasoning to a general, but tight, category is the magic of synthesizing cases. In the example above, all three cases had fear, intimidation, and overcoming one's will. The next step in the process of writing the document would be to apply these factors to the client's facts. In doing so, the writer would focus on fear, intimidation, and overcoming one's will.

Here's one final example of creating a synthesis paragraph, and it's, sadly, a true story. In this example, you need to synthesize cases about involuntary manslaughter. Imagine that you're researching and writing about that issue because you represent radio deejays who held a contest to see who could drink the most water without urinating. Someone died in the contest, and the deejays have now been charged with the crime of involuntary manslaughter. One element, and usually the most contested, is whether the defendant had knowledge of the dangerous situation.

As you read the cases summarized below, look for common threads or factors a court would look at to determine whether a defendant had sufficient knowledge. Here are the cases:

> *Albers*: Child started fire in apartment and killed person; before that, many carpet burns in apartment, set bed ablaze, and burnt holes in carpet in hotel; parents "repeatedly" warned; mother tried hiding lighters. Holding: "overwhelming evidence" of "clear danger."
>
> *Sealy*: Father let two-week-old baby die at home; heartbeat and breathing ceased, leading to parent giving mouth-to-mouth resuscitation 10 to 15 times in two days; spit up blood. Holding: should have been "apparent" that failure to help would be "disastrous."
>
> *Moye*: Mother gave birth to child in toilet; mother heard small gurgle; mother called ambulance. Holding: sufficient knowledge. But Court noted "other physical evidence" that isn't in the case.

As you read through these cases, you're probably thinking, "How in the heck are these applicable to a water-drinking contest?" Well, they aren't if you're looking at the actual facts. But conceptually they are very similar. Finding the conceptual pattern among the cases will help you and then your reader see how the cases relate to your client's case.

Before you read the synthesis paragraph below, first try on your own to write down the factors a court would look at to determine whether a defendant had sufficient knowledge of a dangerous situation.

Here's one sample synthesis paragraph:

> It seems, then, that courts will find sufficient knowledge based on a combination of the following factors: (1) the defendant acts to remedy a danger, (2) the defendant observes one obvious or numerous indicative symptoms of potentially serious injury, or (3) the defendant is directly warned. Whatever the situation, the court will look at the totality of the circumstances, requiring fewer external cues where the victim is especially vulnerable or the situation is especially dire.

How did we create these common threads? We induced broader categories from specific facts and concepts the court laid out in their reasoning. This chart attempts to show that process:

<table>
<tr><th>Case</th><th>Specific Facts Used in Court's Reasoning</th><th></th><th>Induced Category</th><th>In Common?</th></tr>
<tr><td>Albers</td><td>Child started many fires before; neighbors warned; mother tried hiding lighters</td><td>→</td><td>Repeated life-threatening behavior; external warnings; acts to remedy</td><td rowspan="3">Courts will find sufficient knowledge when (1) the defendant acts to remedy a danger, (2) the defendant observes one obvious revealing or numerous symptoms of potentially serious injury, or (3) the defendant is directly warned. Fewer external clues are needed when the victim is especially vulnerable or the situation is especially dire.</td></tr>
<tr><td>Sealy</td><td>Two-week-old baby; resuscitation needed often; spitting up blood</td><td>→</td><td>Vulnerable victim; repeated life-threatening behavior; warnings from symptoms; acts to remedy</td></tr>
<tr><td>Moye</td><td>Mother gave birth to child in toilet; mother heard small gurgle; called ambulance</td><td>→</td><td>Vulnerable victim; warning sound; acts to remedy</td></tr>
</table>

Thus the specifics of a mother hiding lighters, a father trying to resuscitate a child, or a mother calling an ambulance become "acts to remedy danger." And spitting up blood, hearing gurgling in the toilet, and knowing about previous arson acts become "numerous indicative symptoms or warnings of potentially serious injury." You get the idea.

Now that you have added a paragraph that synthesizes the caselaw, it's time to apply that law to the facts.

> In our case, the defendants had sufficient knowledge. The deejays observed several **serious symptoms**: the victim said that she was dizzy, her stomach was unusually distended, and she complained that her "head hurts." While these symptoms were not as numerous as in the arson case or the failure-to-provide-medical-care case, few symptoms are required where **death is the possible result**. Likewise, these symptoms may not have been as **obviously revealing** as the blood spit-up in *Sealy*, but they were sufficient to convey knowledge especially in light of the **other warnings**.
>
> Furthermore, like the credible external **warnings** in *Albers*, the deejays were directly **warned** by a nurse that people have died from doing the exact same activity. The nurse even corrected the misinformation about throwing up to prevent death. The nurse's direct warning alone is probably sufficient; but, what's more, the deejays even discussed a recent event where a college student had died. So they knew that **death** was at least a possibility. The knowledge of recent deaths from the same activity coupled with the indicative symptoms is sufficient to alert a reasonable person that care should be taken to avoid a disastrous result.
>
> While the deejays were warned about the possibility of death, they were not warned about the specific **symptoms** that lead up to a person's death. After all, they

> are not doctors. But that doesn't matter: as in *Moye* (infant), *Albers* (children), and *Sealy* (infant), the courts do not hesitate to find sufficient knowledge, especially where the victims are **vulnerable**. The victim in this case was vulnerable because she did not have the same knowledge regarding death that the deejays had. Therefore, the deejays had sufficient knowledge that death was possible.

In the Application example above, the writer (1) applied the implicit rule and factors and (2) analogized to the facts of precedent. Legal reasoning doesn't get any better than that.

c. How *Not* to Synthesize Cases

This is a bad example of a synthesis paragraph after a series of Case Illustrations. Observe why this is not helpful to a reader:

> In summary, the sudden-emergency doctrine establishes a defense to a violation of the assured clear distance statute where the circumstances create an "unsuspected" situation. The *McKinney* court held that the sudden emergency instruction must be given to the jury if there is any evidence of an unsuspected situation. The *Vander Laan* court defined an unsuspected situation as a potential peril within everyday traffic movement, which was not in clear view for any significant period of time and was totally unexpected. The *LaBumbard* court clarified the clear view requirement and held that a situation is unsuspected if the situation was not in clear view until just before the accident. The *Zyskowski* court held that poor lighting could contribute to visibility and establish a situation that is unsuspected.

This is a fine summary of each separate Case Illustration, but it does not go far enough and truly synthesize the cases to arrive at some factors that all cases have in common. Instead, what this leads to is an application of each case to your case—which ends up creating a seesaw effect (e.g., "Our case is like *Vander Laan* because ..., but our case is not like *Vander Laan* because ... On the other hand, our case is like *McKinney* because ...). Instead, identify the common threads like this:

> In summarizing the unsuspected-emergency component of the sudden-emergency defense, circumstances surrounding the accident must be **unexpected**. Furthermore, the potential threat must **not be in view** for any significant period of **time** nor created by the defendant's conduct. If the defendant can present any evidence that the accident did result from an **unsuspected situation**, then they are entitled to the sudden-emergency jury instruction. Courts have regularly given the instruction where a vehicle was unexpectedly in the roadway—regardless of **lights** signaling the potential threat. This is especially true when the lights were not in the defendant's view for any significant length of **time**.

The individuality of the cases is replaced with a holistic view of what the cases have in common.

After that synthesis paragraph, the writer would then apply those factors to the client's facts.

9.10 Organizing Multiple Cases

Consider using a case chart when you have more than one case. It will help you organize your cases and decide which are best. It can also help you see what's in common among the cases so you can write an implicit topic sentence or write a good synthesis paragraph. A case chart looks like this:

Case Name	Facts	Holding	Reasoning	Applicability to My Case
Ramsey	Cadaver dog accidentally sniffed drugs at a gas station.	Court said that the evidence was admissible.	Dog had proven track record of accuracy.	The dog in our case has been in service for ten years and has never been wrong.
Hoffa	Cadaver dog found remains in remote forest. Dog alerted on animal carcasses.	Cadaver dog's findings not admissible.	Dog provided wrong response in two of three cases. Not reliable.	Unlike the unreliable dog in *Hoffa*, our dog has proven correct in over 500 investigations.
Seronotti	Old cadaver dog gave false positive response for cocaine even though person had none. But person did work at pharmacy.	Cadaver dog's findings are admissible to prove governmental gross negligence.	The dog's false positive is relevant to why the government prosecuted the pharmacist.	Doesn't really apply.
In-common factors	How dog found remains less important than reliability. It's all about reliability.			

You could even add a column for topic sentences. Going from chart to memo or brief is much easier than going from case-on-a-computer-screen to memo or brief.

9.11 Checklist for Explaining Caselaw

Each Case Illustration should have a topic sentence, a citation, the case's facts, the court's holding, and the court's reasoning. This checklist summarizes the good practices explained in this chapter.

Case Illustration > ***Topic Sentence***

In the topic sentence of your Case Illustration, did you:

- ___ transition from the preceding paragraph by showing how the case fits into the big picture?
- ___ avoid starting with a source of law? Instead, cite the source after the topic sentence.
- ___ state a new point that you have not yet stated in the explanation-of-law portion of your document?
- ___ give a substantive point rather than merely announcing the topic you're going to address?
- ___ did you give an explicit rule where a reader could easily see how it applies to your case?
- ___ where appropriate, create an implicit rule from the case where it may not be immediately clear from the specifics of the case how it could apply to the client's matter?
- ___ avoid cramming too much information into the topic sentence? Although your topic sentence is a helpful transition/preview for your reader, it can only include so much information.

Case Illustration > ***Citation***

Immediately after the topic sentence, did you:

- ___ cite a case for the source of the topic sentence, whether it be explicit or implicit?
- ___ follow ALWD or Bluebook rules for formatting the citation?
- ___ put the citation in a separate citation sentence?

Case Illustration > ***Case Facts***

When explaining the facts of the precedent case, did you:

- ___ capture the story to teach your reader what happened in the case you're writing about?
- ___ chronologically sequence the facts unless there was a good reason not to?
- ___ give contextual information that sets the stage for the story?
- ___ include the legally significant facts (i.e., the ones used in the court's reasoning)?
- ___ avoid unnecessary information like names, dates, party arguments, and lower-court procedure unless they directly relate to your issue?
- ___ if writing about a civil case, use informative status words to identify the parties and other "characters" in the story (like *tenant* and *landlord* or *buyer* and *seller*), rather than using their actual names or party designations like *plaintiff* or *defendant*?
- ___ if writing about a criminal case, use *the defendant* to refer to the person charged with the crime, which is informative to readers? But for other people, you've tried to come up with informative status words, such as *witness, victim, accuser, arresting officer, police officer, companion, prosecutor,* etc.

Case Illustration > ***Court's Holding***

When writing about the court's holding in a Case Illustration, did you:

- ___ give the court's actual decision rather than state a pure rule of law or give only the ultimate procedural outcome like *affirmed* or *reversed*?
- ___ state the global holding and any secondary holdings on your issue?
- ___ ensure that the holding addresses the narrow issue you're writing about?

Case Illustration > ***Court's Reasoning***

When summarizing the court's reasoning in a Case Illustration, did you:

- ___ give *details* about why the court decided the case the way it did? If the court decided multiple *relevant* subissues, you've quickly explained the court's reasoning for each of those subissues, and you've done that in a logical sequence, with signposts to help your reader follow along.
- ___ avoid restating the rules the court applied? Rather, put the rules either in the Rule Foundation or in the Case Illustration's topic sentence.

Case Synthesis (if you've grouped cases)

If you've given more than one Case Illustration for a single issue, did you:

- ___ create coherence among the cases by using the trophy, rubber-band, or paragraph-synthesis method?
- ___ capture what the illustrated cases—when read together—teach us about how courts apply the rules to facts that are similar to your client's facts?
- ___ if using the trophy method, show that each case addresses the same issue but adds something unique to the element?
- ___ if using the rubber-band method, create a topic sentence that shows what's in common among the two or so cases you're about to illustrate?
- ___ if using the paragraph-synthesis method, capture the factors the cases have in common?
- ___ if using the paragraph-synthesis method, keep the synthesis short: about two sentences?
- ___ for all synthesis methods, avoid merely rehashing rules that you've already taught your reader in the foundation? Instead, you quickly capture (and reinforce) how courts have applied those foundation rules to *facts* like ours. (The synthesis is tomato sauce rather than raw tomatoes.)

Chapter Ten

IREAC: Apply Law

Fragile as reason is and limited as law is as the expression of the institutionalized medium of reason, that's all we have standing between us and the tyranny of mere will and the cruelty of unbridled, unprincipled, undisciplined feeling.

—JUSTICE FELIX FRANKFURTER[1]

10.1 Introduction to Applying Law

Legal reasoning decides presidential elections. It determines rights over your body. Or it does the practical like deciding property boundaries. Through all of its facets, it maintains an ordered society.

So legal reasoning is important, to say the least.

Throughout your time in law school and as an attorney, you'll hear legal reasoning called many different things. First of all, it's the A of IREAC, Application. But it goes

1. *Time*, Sept. 7, 1962, at 16.

by other names, too: "applying law," "argument," "rule application," "legal reasoning," "reasoning," or "analysis." All these terms roughly refer to the same thing: The process of applying law to facts to decide whether the facts satisfy the law.

The Sorting Hat in Harry Potter is a lot like an attorney deciding whether a client's facts fit within a legal rule—whether that rule is satisfied. Just as the hat weighs a student's traits to determine which house best suits them, attorneys analyze the facts of a case to see if they align with the elements of the law. Both processes involve looking closely at characteristics—whether it's the qualities of a student or the details of a case—and making a judgment about where they fit best.

If the facts fit within the meaning of an element or rule of law, we'd say that the facts have "satisfied"—or "met"—the law. That's what this chapter is all about: explaining whether facts satisfy the law.

10.2 A Good Example of Applying Law

If at any point you want to see examples of applying law in actual legal documents, look at the Application sections in the sample legal analytical documents in Chapter 2. Do this when you start to feel lost in the weeds of learning the reasoning techniques in this chapter. Focus on these pages:

Opinion Letter — 11
eMemo — 19
Short Office Memo — 31
Full Office Memo — 46 and 48
Trial-Court Brief (Moving Party) — 63, 65, 66, and 68
Trial-Court Brief (Nonmoving Party) — 82–85
Appellate-Court Brief — 98

And you can also look at the four annotated reasoning examples in section 10.9 later in this chapter.

For now, though, read one example of good reasoning. This will give you context for everything that follows in this chapter. The annotations below preview what you'll learn about in more detail.

Issue: Was Puntab Vivek *driving* his vehicle when he was cited for driving while intoxicated? Law enforcement found Puntab in his vehicle along the side of a road. He was unconscious and inebriated in the driver seat, the engine was running, and the transmission was in Neutral. The car was on flat ground. He was ticketed for *operating* a vehicle while intoxicated.

Below, in the Application, look for where the writer applies the *operate* element.

Rule: A person shall not operate a vehicle upon a highway if the person is *operating* while intoxicated.

Also below, the writer will apply this caselaw definition and example of *operate*.

Example: The Michigan Supreme Court put a finer point on this definition by defining *operating* in terms of the danger of colliding with another vehicle. *People v. Wood*, 538 N.W.2d 351, 353 (Mich. 1995). In *Wood*, a driver was passed out in a vehicle at a fast-food drive-thru. The vehicle's transmission was engaged in Drive, but the driver's foot was on the brake.

Below, the writer will also (1) analogize the client's facts to the facts of *Wood* and (2) apply the court's reasoning to the client's facts.

The Court held that the driver was operating the vehicle, despite not being in actual physical control, because the risk of collision with another vehicle was high: all he had to do was remove his foot from the brake, and the vehicle would be in motion.

Application: In our case, a court is likely to find that Mr. Vivek did not operate the vehicle because he was not in actual physical control of the vehicle and there was no risk of colliding with anything else. If the vehicle had been in Drive, like the defendant's vehicle in *Wood*, then our client would have posed a risk of collision with another person, vehicle, or object. But our client's vehicle's transmission was not engaged, and his foot was not on the brake—ready to be released and start the car moving at any moment. So it did not pose a threat.

This section is what this chapter is all about!

After stating the first argument, the writer proves that argument with rule-based reasoning and analogical reasoning to *Wood*. Those are reasoning techniques you'll learn about in this chapter.

Making the car a risk to others would require two intentional acts that Mr. Vivek was not capable of because he was unconscious. First, he would have had to apply enough pressure on the brake to free the shifter for movement. Second, while holding sufficient pressure on the brake, he would have had to move the shifter into a gear. Then, if those two things had happened, the vehicle could have posed a risk of colliding with someone or something. But that's not what happened in our case. Unlike the threat of harm in *Wood* that was poised to happen at any moment because the vehicle's transmission was engaged, there was no threat of harm in our case.

The reasoning in this paragraph demonstrates more rule-based reasoning and analogical reasoning. Sections 10.5 and 10.6 dive into those details.

Conclusion: Vivek was not driving his vehicle when the police officer found him.

(By the way, the Issue, Rule, Example, Application, and Conclusion (IREAC) labels above are notations to help you see what's going on in each section. Those would not appear in your actual document.)

The Application section above is what this chapter on Applying Law is all about. It's how you'll earn points on your law-school essays, earn high marks in your research-and-writing classes, and impress clients, judges, and employers. It's what it means to think like a lawyer.

10.3 What Goes in the Application

When writing the Application section of any analysis, include these parts in this order:

- Transition
- Global Prediction or Global Argument
  - Argument #1
    - Proof for Argument #1
  - Argument #2
    - Proof for Argument #2
  - Argument #3
    - Proof for Argument #3
- Internal Conclusion

In outline form, it would look like this:

> **[Transition]** In our case, **[Global Prediction]** a court is likely to find that (prediction on element of law) .... **[Argument #1]** (State argument that supports the global prediction). **[Proof for Argument #1]** (State proof using rule-based reasoning, caselaw analogies, and counterarguments).
>
> **[Argument #2]** (State argument that supports the global prediction). **[Proof for Argument #2]** (State proof using rule-based reasoning, caselaw analogies, and counterarguments).
>
> **[Argument #3]** (State argument that supports the global prediction). **[Proof for Argument #3]** (State proof using rule-based reasoning, caselaw analogies, and counterarguments).
>
> **[Internal Conclusion]** For these reasons, (restate the global prediction).

On the next page is an example of what the Application parts look like in an objective document like an opinion letter. The rest of the chapter explains how an attorney came up with the reasoning there. And you'll learn more about the facts of that case later in this chapter, but, briefly, the analysis is about whether our client, Sam, "permanently" took an iPad from their roommate, which, if true, would constitute larceny.

Remember that in a legal analytical document, the Application section comes after the Rule Foundation and the Case Illustrations, so you need to imagine that you just read all of that. The annotations point out the parts to organizing the Application. And then, after the example, you can read about each of the five parts in more detail.

Transition. The **transition** *Here* signals to the reader that explaining the law is done, and it's time to apply it to our case.

Argument #1 is clearly stated.

Proof for Argument #1. The writer uses counterargument to continue proving the time argument.

Global Prediction.

Here, a court is likely to find that Sam's deprivation of Jill's iPad was permanent, so they committed larceny. The time Sam possessed the iPad—more than a month—is in line with permanent deprivation. They kept the iPad continuously for a substantial amount of time: a month. That long possession is worse than the short-term deprivation in *Callison* that a court said was non-permanent because that involved a mother-and-son relationship with implied casual use of items. Here, Sam and Jill are merely college roommates, so there is no implied consent for the use of personal items like an iPad.

Proof for Argument #1. After the argument, the writer proves the argument with rule-based reasoning (i.e., synonyms and factual characterizations) and analogical reasoning to *Callison*.

Yes, Sam did not intend to keep the iPad forever. They borrowed the iPad temporarily so they could work on a short-term project that had a definite end. If the rule about permanently depriving the owner is subjective, then Sam clearly does not satisfy this element because they borrowed the iPad for a specific project in the movie-making course that had an end date established outside of Sam's thinking.

Proof for Argument #1. The writer explains away or neutralizes the counterargument above about time with a new argument about objectivity.

But looking at this objectively, which is what the law requires, it is reasonable to believe that an item that is missing or will be missing for a month is for all intents and purposes lost or stolen. iPads are easily stolen and easily fenced. Even if someone thought they lost an iPad, they would quickly assume that it was stolen if they did not recover it soon because iPads are so valuable and useful to a wide variety of people.

Argument #2 is stated in the first sentence; the argument comes from case-law reasoning. The **Proof for Argument #2** is stated in the last part of the first sentence in the form of analogical reasoning to *Callison*, and the proof continues throughout the paragraph.

What's more, Sam's continuous month-long possession of the iPad was closer to a "definite act of deprivation" like the sale to a pawn shop in *Callison* than it was a temporary deprivation. Hypothetically, Sam's selling of the iPad would be a clear delineation between temporarily depriving and permanently depriving. But, again, because the iPad in our case was taken for such a long time, the essence of the deprivation is nonetheless permanent.

Argument #3 is stated in the first sentence. The **Proof for Argument #3** relies on characterization and inference.

Lastly, we may infer from Sam's character of deception that they may actually intended to keep the iPad for longer if they got away for using it for a month. Sam could have told themselves that they would "borrow" the iPad for a month, but there is nothing to say that the deception would not continue to a permanent deprivation. If Sam was not principled and honest enough to ask the roommate's permission in the first place, there is no telling what will happen in the future.

Therefore, a court is likely to find that Sam permanently deprived Jill of the iPad; thus, Sam is guilty of larceny.

Internal Conclusion (the C of IREAC)

A. Begin with a transition.

Because the Application section comes after explaining the law, you need to snap the reader's attention back to the present with the client's case. This is important because the client isn't discussed in the rules and caselaw examples, in the R and E of IREAC, so you need a transition that signals to the reader that we're done talking about rules and caselaw stories.

Do that with a brief transition, something like these:

Here, …

In our case, …

Applied here, …

In Smith's case, …

In the case at hand, …

In the present case, …

B. State the global prediction or global argument.

After the transition word or phrase, state your overall answer. This is where you put your global prediction for objective analysis, like in opinion letters and memos. Or, if you're writing a persuasive document like a brief, you'd state your global argument here—the conclusion you want the court to agree with.

There should be no intrigue in your writing: spill the beans from the very first sentence. So resist the temptation to "build up" to the answer or "clear your throat" before getting to the answer. There's no suspense in good legal writing.

This first sentence of your Application, the one with the transition and global answer, acts as the topic sentence for not only this one paragraph but the entire Application section.

Here are several examples of topic sentences from different documents:

- Here, a court is likely to find that Sam's deprivation of Jill's iPad was permanent, so they committed larceny.
- In the present case, Smith's fractured arm satisfies the Act's "objectively verifiable" requirement.
- In our case, a court would likely find that the ballet studio's release is not valid.

You can see in the examples above that some predict an outcome; that's appropriate for objective analysis like what you do in memos. For persuasive documents like a court brief, the topic sentence of the Application would ask "this Court" to agree to a conclusion.

After the reader clearly understands the global prediction or argument, they want to know *why* you think that is the correct resolution of how the law applies to the facts. That's where arguments and proof come in.

C. Write Argument #1 after the global answer.

Immediately after the overall, global answer is clear, state the first reason why. Don't necessarily try to start *proving* the argument in that sentence. Rather, simply state the first reason. Here are a few examples of what an argument statement looks like:

- The time Sam possessed the iPad is in line with permanent deprivation.
- Smith's treating physician did not have to rely on subjective pain complaints to diagnose the injury.
- First, as to the scope of parties responsible, the release of liability is missing narrowing language like "solely."

Take at least a full sentence to simply state your argument. Resist the temptation to too quickly jump into an analogy. If you jump into an analogy too quickly, it muddies the waters, and the reader cannot see clearly what the argument is. So just state the argument.

D. Prove Argument #1 after stating it.

By stating the argument, you gave the reader a reason for why your prediction or argument is correct. But now you need to *prove* it. Prove the argument with rule-based reasoning, analogical reasoning, and counterarguments.

1. Rule-Based Reasoning

Section 10.5 below explains the details of rule-based reasoning. For now, in the simplest terms, this is where you use common sense to explain how the facts do or do not satisfy what the law requires. You take the plain meaning of the law and apply it to the facts. Here are a few examples, continuing them from above:

- They kept the iPad continuously for a substantial amount of time: a month.
- The physician relied on an MRI, an objective instrument for determining injuries.
- The release's scope is overly broad because it doesn't make it clear that the reader alone bears the risk of injury. Simply saying "I assume" doesn't necessarily negate the fact that the ballet madame could also be on the hook.

These are obviously brief examples; sometimes that's enough. But rule-based reasoning may take several paragraphs.

2. Analogical Reasoning

Rule-based or common-sense reasoning is essential for helping the reader understand the argument's proof, but that alone isn't enough to convince the reader that your argument is correct. Analogizing to past caselaw—precedent—puts all the reader's worries to rest because that's where you show that your conclusions and arguments are in line with past court judgments. Therefore, all is well in the world.

Besides, every reader knows that the writer, an attorney, has built-in biases favoring the client. Reasoning by analogy inoculates those biases and legitimizes the reasoning.

Section 10.6 below explains all you need to know about making analogies. For now, though, check out these analogies to caselaw that support the rule-based reasoning from the examples above:

- That long possession of another's belonging is worse than the short-term deprivation in *Callison* that a court said was non-permanent because that involved a mother-and-son relationship with implied casual use of items. Here, Sam and Jill are merely college roommates with no familial relationship, so there is no implied consent for the use of personal items like an iPad.
- Like the treater in *Jones*, Smith's physician relied not only on the MRI but could also see and feel the fracture and thus did not need to rely on Smith's subjective pain complaints to diagnose the injury.
- Stated another way, just like it was unclear who bore the burden of risk in *Xu*, it's likewise unclear who of the many involved parties would bear the risk of injury. The release clause does use broad language—*all*—, which would please the *Dombrowski* court, but in reference to *risks*, not in reference to the parties released from liability or the parties responsible for the injury.

3. Counterarguments

Office memos, whether emails or memos, are always objective. Your job is to predict the outcome: whether our client will win, whether we can prosecute a defendant, whether our client can get a tax setoff for paying foreign duties, etc. With predictive writing, your job is to objectively analyze the facts in light of the law. This means that you discuss *both* the good and the bad, and don't shy away from the ugly.

The same largely applies to writing persuasive documents like court briefs and demand letters. After you fully explain your winning position, you then address any counterarguments: "Opposing counsel may argue that ...; however, ..."

But never force a counterargument because you think it's part of the formula for an Application section. Address weaknesses in your argument only if there truly are weaknesses.

You can see an example of a counterargument in the second and third paragraphs in the Application that begins this section 10.3. That's counter-analysis.

E. Repeat an Argument-and-Proof combo for each argument.

Stating an argument and proving it are the dynamic duo of reasoning. For each additional argument, repeat that duo. Once you finished explaining Argument #1 and the Proof for Argument #1, you'd then start a new paragraph and state Argument #2 in the topic sentence. Then spend the rest of that paragraph proving Argument #2 with rule-based reasoning and analogical reasoning. And, yes, of course, if you need more than a paragraph to prove an argument, go for it.

Similarly, you'd start a new paragraph and then state and then prove Argument #3. You get the point.

Generally speaking, we should have two or three arguments in the Application section. Anything less looks weak, and anything more creates cognitive overload and dilutes the overall persuasiveness of your reasoning.

F. State an internal conclusion.

Don't leave the reader hanging by either trailing off or abruptly ending with a point of reasoning. Instead, state your global conclusion again, either in a sentence at the end of the last paragraph or in a short, one-sentence concluding paragraph. This is your "mini conclusion," which brings a nice sense of closure to your analysis. (Yes, this is the C of an IREAC packet.)

10.4 Argument Proofs

A. Two Great Proofs

For the rest of Chapter 10, we're going to focus on just the process of *proving* arguments—the pure application of law to fact. This is the heart and soul of the A of IREAC.

In essence, an attorney proves arguments in these two ways:

> "My client's facts fit within the meaning of the law."

and

> "Past courts would also say that my client's facts fit within the meaning of the law."

These two summations capture the two great modes of proving an argument: deductive and inductive reasoning. Deductive reasoning, the first statement above, is where we deduce a conclusion from the relationship between the law and the client's facts. The syllogistic structure you learned about in Chapter 4 is a visualization of deductive reasoning. Attorneys call this rule-based reasoning because they take the plain meaning of the rule of law and explain whether the facts fit within that meaning. Put in modern terms, does the Sorting Hat put the facts in the house of the law or not?

The second way to prove arguments is through inductive reasoning, which is where attorneys compare and contrast precedent—caselaw. This is usually called "analogical reasoning" or "reasoning by analogy."

You'll learn about rule-based reasoning in section 10.5 and analogical reasoning in 10.6.

B. The Test: How to Know If You Have a Legal Argument

You're going to write the Application, the reasoning, for an assignment in school or at work and then promptly wonder, "How do I know if this is any good?"

A good legal argument doesn't simply report what happened; it doesn't just repeat the facts, in other words. Instead, it uses the facts to make a case for *why* a certain legal rule applies, why the court should take a certain action, or why a specific outcome is justified.

You may not be surprised to know that answering the great *why* happens by way of deductive and inductive reasoning, which you were just introduced to. Using common sense to connect the facts (rule-based reasoning) and making explicit connections between facts and caselaw (analogical reasoning) will help ensure your statements are argumentative rather than merely factual.

Here are two questions you can ask yourself about the sentences in your Application section to determine whether you have a legal argument:

1. *Is this statement* analyzing *the facts rather than merely repeating them?*

Merely repeating fact is not helpful because it doesn't move the analysis forward; it keeps the analysis at the day the client walked in the firm's door. Instead, move the analysis forward by interpreting, analyzing, and characterizing the facts.

Bad Example (just stating fact):

> The defendant drove above the speed limit in a school zone.

This is merely a factual statement without any interpretation or analysis.

Good Example (legal argument):

> By driving above the speed limit in a school zone, the defendant acted recklessly, disregarding the known risk of harm to children nearby. Thus, this conduct meets the standard for gross negligence under [applicable law].

This example interprets the fact and connects it to a legal standard (gross negligence), suggesting that the fact supports a legal conclusion. You may not see it now, but after reading 10.5 below, you'll recognize several types of rule-based reasoning here.

2. *Is this statement connected to the law?*

Bad Example (just stating fact):

> The contract states that payments are due on the first of each month.

This simply states a fact about the contract without relating it to the issue at hand.

Good Example (legal argument):

> Because the contract unambiguously requires payments by the first of each month, the defendant's late payment breaches this explicit term, like the late performance in *Jones*, entitling the plaintiff to seek damages for non-performance under [relevant contract law provision].

This example applies the contractual term (payment date) to the defendant's actions and then connects that to a legal outcome (breach), which is rule-based reasoning. And it also connects the law to the facts using analogical reasoning.

Use these two tests on every sentence of reasoning until you get the hang of it.

10.5 Rule-Based Reasoning as Proof

More than anything, use common sense to explain whether your client's facts fit within the plain meaning of the law. On the law side, we need to make sure we understand what each element means. We do this by defining the element and identifying its synonyms and antonyms. This allows us to better understand the meaning of each element; we're then better equipped with vocabulary to explain whether the client's facts satisfy the meaning of the law.

When we repeat the element's language in our reasoning, we show a connection between the law and facts. And when we use synonyms of the element, we not only show a connection between the law and facts, but we show how the facts belong within the meaning of the element. And the opposite is true for antonyms: if our client's facts amount to an antonym of an element of law, then we would say that the element is not satisfied.

That's about understanding the plain meaning of the law. As for the facts, we're trying to figure out if the facts fit within the meaning of the element. To do this, we need to analyze and bring insight to them. That insight shows that they do or do not fit within the plain meaning of the element. Attorney-reasoners bring insight to the facts by characterizing them, inferring conclusions from them, identifying implications of them, and quantifying them.

Luckily, most of this happens naturally because of our innate ability to reason.

Here is a quick summary in chart form of the basic ways to perform rule-based reasoning. Against the backdrop of our life experience,

for the law, we	and for the facts, we
• **repeat** the element's words,	• **characterize** client's facts,
• use **synonyms** of the element, and	• **infer** from client's facts,
• use **antonyms** of the element,	• **imply** effects from client's facts, and
	• **quantify** client's facts.

Those techniques summarize what it means to use common sense to explain whether the facts satisfy the law.

In the rest of this section, we will apply each of these seven rule-based reasoning techniques using the scenario below, what we might call the "iPad larceny" case. Here's our mission:

Client:	Sam
Document:	eMemo
Reasoning Mode:	Objective analysis (warts and all)
Audience:	Sam (client) and boss
Employment:	Law firm specializing in criminal defense
Strategy:	Use the seven rule-based reasoning techniques from above to brainstorm as many proofs as possible to analyze whether Jill is guilty of larceny.

We'll keep things nice and tidy with the IREAC structure. The goal is to build the Application section because that's where we analyze whether the facts satisfy the law. We'll add to this structure as we work through the seven modes of rule-based reasoning. Okay, here we go. Begin by reading the facts and the rule.

I: Did Sam Smith commit a larceny? Sam needed a second iPad to complete their short documentary for a college class. Because they did not have the funds to purchase a second iPad, Sam took their roommate's iPad without telling her. Sam reasoned that they were just borrowing it because the class would end one month from when they took the iPad. Jill, the roommate, searched high and low for the iPad but eventually ended up buying a new one after two weeks.

R: Larceny is the taking and carrying away of personal property from the possession of the owner with the intent to *permanently* deprive the owner of it.

E: ?

A: ?

C: ?

As you know, we focus on one element at a time. Given the intersection of the law of larceny and these facts, only the *permanently* element is at issue. There's no question that Sam took the iPad and that Jill possessed it as the owner. And Sam also intended to deprive Jill of the iPad. But what's not clear is whether Sam intended to *permanently* deprive Jill, so that's what we'll focus on.

We'll use rule-based reasoning to determine our global prediction, arguments, and argument proof. We'll start by understanding the plain meaning of *permanently* and apply it to our facts—you know, rule-based reasoning.

A. Repeat the Element's Words

Repeating the actual language of the element is really about communicating to your reader that you are now connecting the element to the facts, so it would look like this:

> **A: Sam's deprivation of the iPad was not permanent.**

We're working on an objective memo, by the way, so we may actually conclude that Sam did *permanently* take the iPad. But, for now, we'll go with predicting that it wasn't permanent. The point here is to use—literally repeat—the language of the element.

The technique of repeating the element's language is really that simple, but if you did not do that your reader would not be sure which bit of the law, which element, you were applying at the moment. So be sure to periodically repeat the element at issue.

B. Use Synonyms of the Element's Words

To identify synonyms, you may want to reference a thesaurus or dictionary, but be sure to begin with your own thoughts. The idea here is that because synonyms are so closely related in meaning that satisfying a synonym of the element is the same as satisfying the actual element. Here's a bubble map of *permanent* showing some synonyms:

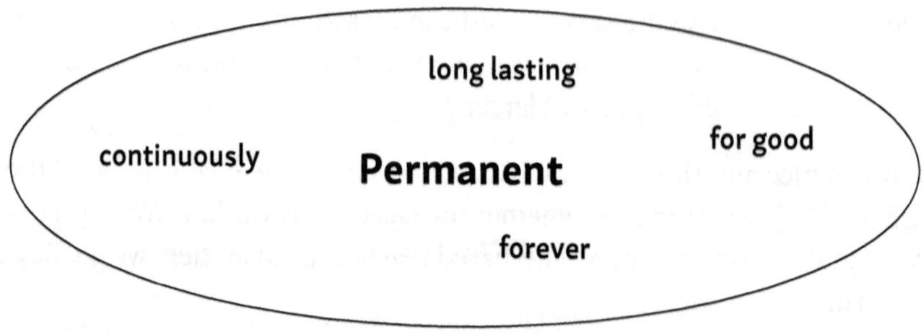

Note how the synonyms are within the meaning of *permanent*. Thus, if certain facts amount to a synonym of *permanent*, then they would also satisfy *permanent*.

Now we can use these synonymous words to think of reasoning statements:

> A: Sam's deprivation of the iPad was not permanent. **Sam continuously kept Jill's iPad for at least two weeks, but Sam did not intend to keep the iPad forever.**

Okay, but, again, this seems pretty simple, right? So you may be wondering if expert legal reasoners do this. They really do. In fact, you can see how Justice Antonin Scalia, one of the best legal reasoners of all time, uses synonyms—and all the rule-based techniques—in Reasoning Example #1 in section 10.9.

C. Use Antonyms of the Element's Words

Now think of antonyms of *permanent*. That will give us even more vocabulary to reason with. Start with what your brain is telling you, but you may also want to consult a thesaurus, which usually offers antonyms in addition to synonyms. Because antonyms are opposites, they do not fit within the element's meaning or category. The idea is that if facts amount to an antonym of the element, then the element is not satisfied. And, contrariwise, if the facts do not amount to the antonym, they may satisfy the element; it wouldn't be absolute proof, but it would be a bolstering reason.

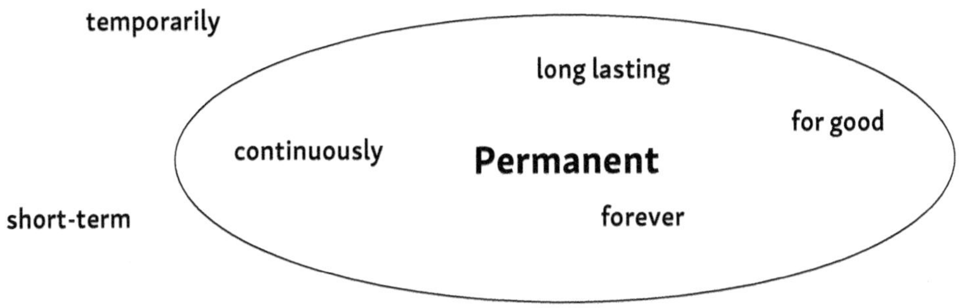

Here is an updated Application with the antonyms thrown in:

> A: Sam's deprivation of the iPad was not permanent. Sam continuously kept Jill's iPad for at least two weeks, but Sam did not intend to keep the iPad forever. **Sam borrowed the iPad temporarily so they could work on a short-term project that had a definite end.**

D. Characterize Client's Facts

Now that we've analyzed the plain meaning of the law, we turn our attention to the facts and how they align with that plain meaning. Our goal is to scrutinize the facts closely, assessing whether they fit within the framework of the law as it's defined. One way to scrutinize the facts is to characterize them. The way those facts are characterized can ultimately determine the outcome of the case.

Think of the courtroom scenes in *Legally Blonde*. When Elle Woods takes on Brooke Windham's case, she reframes the key fact that Brooke didn't want to shower after her workout. While the prosecution presents this as suspicious, Elle re-characterizes it, arguing that it aligns with Brooke's obsession with fitness and preserving her perfect appearance. By interpreting that fact differently, Elle shifts the narrative in her client's favor. This shows—in fictional movies and real life—how a lawyer's skill in characterizing facts can change the direction of a case.

How would you characterize Sam's using the iPad? Make sure that the characterization is about the permanent nature of the possession—the element of law at issue. Here are some possible thoughts:

Hopefully, you thought of even more ways to characterize the facts. You probably noticed that characterizing facts requires looking between the lines and creating a narrative around the facts. Here's the updated Application with characterizations built in:

> **A:** Sam's deprivation of the iPad was not permanent. Sam continuously kept Jill's iPad for at least two weeks, but Sam did not intend to keep the iPad forever. Sam borrowed the iPad temporarily so they could work on a short-term project that had a definite end. **If the rule about permanently depriving the owner is subjective, then Sam clearly does not satisfy this element because they borrowed the iPad for a specific project that had an end date established outside of Sam's thinking (i.e., the movie-making course's due date). But looking at this objectively, it is reasonable to believe that an item that is missing or will be missing for a month is for all intents and purposes lost or stolen. Any person knows that iPads are easily stolen and easily fenced. Even if someone thought they lost an iPad, they would know that it would be stolen if they did not recover it soon because iPads are so valuable and useful to a wide variety of people.**

You can see that the writer got carried away! You will find that as you write, more and more ideas will come to you. They are not all gold, but that is what the pruning process of revising and editing is for. This is just a first draft.

And perhaps you noticed that the analysis is tending toward concluding that the iPad was permanently deprived. As we think through things as attorneys, we often change our minds about whether facts satisfy an element. That's the hallmark of objective analysis. Let's see where this process takes us.

E. Infer from Client's Facts

If you have been inside sleeping all day and you see a wet umbrella by the front door, you may infer that it has been raining. That's called a permissible inference. We use our common sense and life experience to draw conclusions from certain facts.

Put your life experience to the test with this one: On February 14, you observe a couple in a fancy restaurant. One person is angry, and the other person looks sheepish, almost apologetic. What's a permissible inference? We can safely assume that the angry party is disappointed, and the sheepish party did the disappointing.

From there, we can only speculate—and that creates impermissible inferences. Perhaps the angry party was hoping for a marriage proposal, or maybe they were disappointed because the sheepish-looking partner forgot a gift on Valentine's Day. These speculative inferences are what we call in the law "impermissible inferences." Make sure any inferences you draw while reasoning are logically sound.

Turning back to our larceny case, what can we infer from the facts related to the *permanently deprive* element? Have a look at the new thoughts in bold:

> **A:** Sam's deprivation of the iPad was not permanent. Sam continuously kept Jill's iPad for at least two weeks, but Sam did not intend to keep the iPad forever. Sam borrowed the iPad temporarily so they could work on a short-term project that had a definite end. If the rule about permanently depriving the owner is subjective, then Sam clearly does not satisfy this element because they bor-

> rowed the iPad for a specific project that had an end date established outside of Sam's thinking (i.e., the movie-making course's due date). But looking at this objectively, it is reasonable to believe that an item that is missing or will be missing for a month is for all intents and purposes lost or stolen. Any person knows that iPads are easily stolen and easily fenced. Even if someone thought they lost an iPad, they would know that it would be stolen if they did not recover it soon because iPads are so valuable and useful to a wide variety of people.
>
> **Sam's character trait of being comfortable with deception might mean that they did permanently deprive Jill of her iPad. We may infer from Sam's character that they are capable of deception; not telling the roommate shows this. But we do not know if this is a pattern. We may also infer that Sam could have told themselves that they would "borrow" the iPad for a month, but there is nothing to say that the deception would not continue to make the deprivation permanent. If Sam was not principled and honest enough to ask the roommate's permission in the first place, there is no telling what will happen in the future.**

Note that with every reasoning technique, be sure to connect your thinking to the element at issue. Here, the element is *permanent* deprivation, and you can see in the first bolded sentence above the writer connects the inference to that element. And then they do it later on in the paragraph. Repeating the element as you reason helps the reader connect the dots between element and the facts.

And remember not to focus on making the first draft perfect; that part of the brain only inhibits creativity! We'll do the editing later.

F. Imply Effects from Client's Facts

Reasoning by implying is to point out any cause-and-effect scenario in the facts that points to the element at issue.

Cause-and-effect relationships are central to reasoning by implication. For a rule to be satisfied, the cause, the effect, or both must align with the rule itself. In daily life, we often infer by weighing the consequences of our actions. Take, for example, a raffle at an event. What is the implication (or effect) of raffling the grand prize last (the cause)? Imagine you're eager to win the grand prize, but there are several smaller prizes being raffled first, and there's only one pot of tickets, with each person holding a single ticket.

Now, you're asked for advice on when the grand prize should be raffled—at the beginning or the end. What would you suggest? What would be best for you? What would be best for everyone? If the grand prize is drawn last, one implication is that your ticket might be pulled for one of the earlier prizes, eliminating your chance at the grand prize. Understanding this, you might recommend raffling the grand prize first to preserve your chance of winning it. However, from the organizers' perspective, they would likely prefer to raffle the grand prize last, as it builds suspense and serves as the climactic moment of the event.

That's an everyday example of reasoning by thinking about implications. In the larceny example, we already did some cause-and-effect reasoning as we were thinking through the other reasoning techniques. See if you can spot them in our running Application section before looking at the chart below it:

A: Sam's deprivation of the iPad was not permanent. Sam continuously kept Jill's iPad for at least two weeks, but Sam did not intend to keep the iPad forever. Sam borrowed the iPad temporarily so they could work on a short-term project that had a definite end. If the rule about permanently depriving the owner is subjective, then Sam clearly does not satisfy this element because they borrowed the iPad for a specific project that had an end date established outside of Sam's thinking (i.e., the movie-making course's due date). But looking at this objectively, it is reasonable to believe that an item that is missing or will be missing for a month is for all intents and purposes lost or stolen. Any person knows that iPads are easily stolen and easily fenced. Even if someone thought they lost an iPad, they would know that it would be stolen if they did not recover it soon because iPads are so valuable and useful to a wide variety of people. *Soon* for an item such as an iPad, assuming it is used to take class notes in Jill's college courses and for entertainment, means within hours or a day. If Jill does not find the iPad within hours or a day, the permanence of its loss will be keenly felt.

Sam's character trait of being comfortable with deception might mean that they did permanently deprive Jill of her iPad. We may infer from Sam's character that they are capable of deception; not telling the roommate shows this. But we do not know if this is a pattern. We may also infer that Sam could have told themselves that they would "borrow" the iPad for a month, but there is nothing to say that the deception would not continue to make the deprivation permanent. If Sam was not principled and honest enough to ask the roommate's permission in the first place, there is no telling what will happen in the future.

Here are a few instances of using implications to prove whether the facts amount to permanent deprivation:

Cause		Effect
Sam had a project due in 30 days	→	Sam will return the iPad in 30 days
Jill cannot find iPad	→	Assume it was lost or stolen
Sam deceived once	→	Sam will likely deceive again

G. Quantify Client's Facts

A headline on a national news website years ago stated that 1% of Citi Bank credit-card users' information was hacked and leaked on the dark web. No biggie, right? The same day, though, a headline on a different news website about the same story that said 250,000 of Citi Bank's card users had their information hacked. Which headline had more of an impact on you? 1% or 250,000? They are both correct numbers, but they offer different perspectives on the data.

That difference of impact is the power of quantifying. Numbers can put facts into perspective in a way that words sometimes cannot.

But attorneys quantify, not just by using statistics and numbers, but also whenever they measure any aspect of facts. In fact, in our larceny example focusing on permanent deprivation of an iPad, we already used some quantifying when we characterized the facts, but perhaps we can do a bit more:

A: Sam's deprivation of the iPad was not permanent. Sam continuously kept Jill's iPad for at least **two weeks**, but Sam did not intend to keep the iPad **forever**. Sam borrowed the iPad **temporarily** so they could work on a short-term project that had a definite end. If the rule about permanently depriving the owner is subjective, then Sam clearly does not satisfy this element because they borrowed the iPad for a specific project that had an end date established outside of Sam's thinking (i.e., the movie-making course's due date). But looking at this objectively, it is reasonable to believe that an item that is missing or will be missing for **a month** is for all intents and purposes lost or stolen. Any person knows that iPads are easily stolen and easily fenced. Even if someone thought they lost an iPad, they would know that it would be stolen if they did not recover it ***soon*** because iPads are so valuable and useful to a wide variety of people. ***Soon*** **for an item such as an iPad, assuming it is used to take class notes in Jill's college courses and for entertainment, means within hours or a day. If Jill does not find the iPad within hours or a day, the permanence of its loss will be keenly felt.**

H. Concluding Notes About Rule-Based Reasoning

In subsections (A) through (G) above, we used seven techniques of rule-based reasoning, common sense, really, to brainstorm arguments. While the draft shown would be excellent for a law school exam—it's certainly an A-level response—it's only a starting point for a professional document like an email, opinion letter, office memo, or court brief: it needs editing and polishing, the point of Chapter 18.

You might be wondering, "How can I manage all this thinking during an exam?" In a law school setting, this is the kind of analysis you should be doing well before the final exam. Practice it during class, when reviewing your notes, and as you create your outline. Apply it when writing practice essays. Then, during the exam, the skill will be second nature.

For legal documents like memos or briefs, this type of reasoning happens both as you research the law and while you draft the analysis section. With time and practice, these thinking skills will become second nature—you'll apply them almost automatically.

But we're only halfway through reasoning; we also prove arguments by comparing past caselaw. We'll continue the iPad larceny case in the next section before finally wrapping it up in 10.6(B).

10.6 Analogical Reasoning as Proof

Analogical reasoning is when an attorney proves their argument is correct by showing that it aligns with past caselaw. Essentially, the attorney is telling the reader that the client's issue has basically been addressed in an earlier case, and because that earlier case and the client's current case are factually similar, they should share the same outcome.

So how does this relate with rule-based reasoning? In your document's Application section, your reader will primarily understand the main thrust of your argument by reading your common-sense rule-based reasoning, what you just learned about in section 10.5. If your rule-based reasoning is credible, the reader will lean toward agreeing with your conclusions. However, because attorneys are inherently biased, a reader won't fully trust the analysis. You need to remove your own judgment from the reasoning and instead point to how a third party—a court of law—proves that your argument is sound.

If you want to see analogical reasoning in its native environment, check out these documents in Chapter 2:

- Short Office Memo — 2.4, Application section
- Full Office Memo — 2.5, Discussion section
- Trial-Court Brief (Moving Party) — 2.6, Argument section
- Appellate-Court Brief — 2.8, Argument section

Generally speaking, attorneys analogize to caselaw in at least nine different ways. Subsection A below will show you each of those. One Application section would never include all of them, so see the nine techniques as a buffet of options. Once you've fully researched the law and it's time to start writing, use the nine techniques to brainstorm arguments, and then choose just the best ones to actually go in your document.

We'll continue the iPad larceny case in subsection A below to give you examples of the nine analogy techniques. We'll brainstorm nine different analogy arguments and then, finally, in subsection B, we'll put the finishing touches on the iPad-larceny Application section by putting just the best arguments into the Application section. All the reasoning we've done in this chapter for that case will be done, and you can see the final product!

But because this mode of reasoning requires precedent, a past case, we're going to assume that we researched the law and found a factually similar case called *State v. Callison*. Let's add caselaw to that scenario to demonstrate what analogy-by-comparing-facts looks like. We'll add the *Callison* case under the E of IREAC.

Okay, before we jump into the nine ways to analogize, read the Case Illustration of *Callison*:

> **E:** Giving ownership rights in the stolen property to a third party is a permanent deprivation. For example, in *State v. Callison*, the defendant borrowed his mother's laptop without asking, but, a few days later, took it to a pawn shop and sold it for cash.
>
> The court held that this permanent deprivation amounted to larceny. The court reasoned that it was not larceny until the defendant pawned the computer because they were in a close family relationship, which implies use of household items, and the defendant was using it for just three days. But, objectively, the deprivation became permanent upon the sale, and that is when the crime of larceny became complete.

A. All Possible Techniques to Reason by Analogy

Here are the nine possible ways to analogize to precedent (along with their nicknames):

- Compare Facts ("Apples to Apples")
- Apply the Court's Reasoning ("Apply the Why")
- Apply Implicit Rule from a Case ("The Big Takeaway")
- Extend the Court's Reasoning ("Extensions")
- Synthesize and Apply Multiple Cases ("Witnesses")
- Contrast Facts with a Prior Case ("Apples to Oranges")

- Contrast a Narrow Holding ("Scope")
- Point to Factual Gaps in a Prior Case ("Swiss Cheese")
- Apply Policy Behind the Rule ("The Policy")

In any Application section, you'll reason using one of these or a combination of them.

1. Compare Facts ("Apples to Apples")

This is the most traditional technique of reasoning by analogy, and it's the only one you'll likely do in every Application. Simply show how the significantly relevant facts of a certain past case are similar to facts in your case. Because the reader would have just read a Case Illustration for the case you're now analogizing to, all you need is to state a few on-point facts to jog the reader's memory and make an explicit factual comparison to your client's case. It's a true comparison of apples to apples.

Here's how this technique could be used to brainstorm an argument for our iPad-larceny case:

> **The thinking:** In both our iPad-larceny case and *Callison*, the defendants borrowed property without permission. In *Callison*, the defendant sold the laptop; here, Sam kept the iPad for an extended time.
>
> **The write-up:** Like the defendant's unauthorized borrowing became larceny in *Callison* when he sold the laptop, here, Sam's prolonged, unauthorized use of Jill's iPad, which led to her buying a replacement, could also be viewed as a form of permanent deprivation. [Then further explain.]

Stepping away from our iPad-larceny case for just a moment, here's another example of analogizing to caselaw by briefly alluding to a few of the most important facts:

> Like the mother in *Albers* **was warned numerous times by family and friends,** the deejays here were warned numerous times, but by a registered nurse, another deejay, and many serious symptoms of sickness.

See that brief memory jog: "was warned numerous times by family and friends"? Those brief, on-point facts are all the writer needs to prove the similarity between the precedent, *Albers*, and the client's case. And, then, of course, the analogy directly compares apples to apples, the warnings in *Albers* to the warnings in the case at hand.

Like with all of these nine techniques, you can see more examples throughout the Chapter 2 sample documents.

2. Apply the Court's Reasoning ("Apply the Why")

The second way to apply caselaw is to apply the court's reasoning—the "why" of the holding—from caselaw to your client's case. There is no stronger way to signal that caselaw supports your position than to explain how your conclusion about the law's application to your client's facts aligns with a court's conclusion and reasoning.

Recall that a court should explain why they concluded the way they did on each issue. That explanation in their opinion is called reasoning. Take that reasoning and apply it to your facts. If the case's outcome is the outcome your client desires, then you want to show how the court's reasoning aligns with your client's facts. And, obviously, if the case's outcome is opposite of what you are seeking, then show how the court's reasoning does not apply to your client's facts.

If applying the court's reasoning were a formula, it would look something like this:

> **A:** [Transition] In our case, [Global Prediction/Argument] Tom played football, which is a dangerous sport. [Argument #1] It's a dangerous sport because [Proof of Argument #1: rule-based reasoning]. What's more [Proof of Argument #1: analogical reasoning (**use the reasoning of caselaw precedent to help you explain why football may or may not be a dangerous sport.**)] [Continue explaining.]

Here's how this technique could be used to brainstorm an argument for our iPad-larceny case:

> **The thinking:** The *Callison* opinion's reasoning focused on the relationship between the parties and the expectation of using household items, distinguishing between temporary and permanent deprivation.
>
> **The write-up:** Although Sam and Jill are not family, their roommate relationship may create sharing expectations similar to the mother-and-son relationship in *Callison*. However, Sam's failure to inform Jill about taking her iPad raises concerns about whether their actions constitute a temporary borrowing or a potential deprivation of Jill's property, akin to larceny.

You can see more examples of this technique in particular in Reasoning Example #4 at the end of this chapter on page 296.

3. Apply Implicit Rule from a Case ("The Big Takeaway")

A powerful technique of reasoning is to directly apply to your client's facts an implicit rule that you pulled from a case. This is something you state in the topic sentence of a Case Illustration. See 9.4(A). The symmetry of reading about it in a Case Illustration and then seeing the same implicit rule applied moments later in the Application underscores that your reasoning is logical and correct.

Here's how this technique could be used to brainstorm an argument for our iPad-larceny case:

> **The thinking:** The court in *Callison* determined that permanent deprivation without question occurs when the defendant transfers ownership to a third party. (This was in the topic sentence of the *State v. Callison* Case Illustration.))
>
> **The write-up:** Even though Sam only initially borrowed Jill's iPad with the intent to return it, unlike selling the stolen item to a third party like in *Callison*, the failure to inform her and the prolonged use could lead to a similar conclusion. If Jill had deemed her iPad lost and made arrangements to replace it, Sam's action could be construed as creating a permanent deprivation of Jill's property.

4. Extend the Court's Reasoning ("Extensions")

This technique is where you take the reasoning from a case, and you logically extend it to other scenarios. As one example, if a case holds that hockey is a dangerous sport because it involves contact, you might extend that and say that football—the sport at issue in your client's case—"is even more dangerous." That "more" is the logical extension part. Then you'd explain why it's even more dangerous. So you extended the reasoning about hockey to football and showed why the court's reasoning was even more true in your case.

Here's how this technique could be used to brainstorm an argument for our iPad-larceny case:

The thinking: The *Callison* court focused on the fact that permanent deprivation occurred when the defendant sold the laptop, emphasizing that larceny requires an act that shows intent to permanently deprive the owner of their property. This reasoning could expand to include situations where the property is not sold *or* returned in a timely manner, causing an effective loss equivalent to selling it.

The write-up: In Sam's case, although they did not sell Jill's iPad, their failure to return it after two weeks, coupled with Jill's need to purchase a new one, created an effective loss of property similar to a permanent deprivation like the selling of property to a third party in *Callison*.

5. Synthesize and Apply Multiple Cases ("Witnesses")

You learned in Chapter 9, Explain Caselaw, that you generally should have two or three cases—different "witnesses"—supporting any conclusion. And it's best to synthesize those cases to show the reader what they have in common. See 9.9(B). A really strong analogy comes by comparing all the cases at one time to your client's case to show how a bundle of cases—not just one at a time—supports your conclusions.

Here's how this technique could be used to brainstorm an argument for our iPad-larceny case, which requires us to imagine that we added a second case:

Cases: *State v. Callison* (2020); *State v. Roe* (2019)

The thinking: Taken together, both cases emphasize the importance of consent and the implications of taking property without permission. (From the synthesis paragraph. 9.9(B)(3).)

The write-up: Sam's needing the iPad to finish their school course, the sale of stolen property in *Callison*, and the posting on Facebook Marketplace in *Roe* all show intent to deprive for a substantial period of time, if not permanently.

Because this is a common reasoning technique, but one that could easily become clunky, a second example is in order:

In Ms. Lucas's case, the court will probably conclude that the easement language is ambiguous because it's unclear whether she may build a dock. The language of the easement does not explicitly grant "riparian rights" like in *Trivan*, nor does it limit the right to only "ingress and egress" like in *Dyball*. The language for both of those grants is finite and clear; they don't include any open-ended words or phrases. In contrast, our easement language, "right of ingress and egress for all normal uses," includes both finite and clear language ("ingress and egress") and open-ended language ("for all normal uses"). So whether the scope of the easement includes the right to build a dock is unclear.

6. Contrast Facts with a Prior Case ("Apples to Oranges")

When caselaw disagrees with the outcome you desire, you need to contrast it, show how a different result is warranted in your case because the facts are different.

Here's how this technique could be used to brainstorm an argument for our iPad-larceny case:

The thinking: The defendant in *Callison* sold the laptop immediately, while Sam kept the iPad for two weeks before Jill replaced it.

The write-up: In contrast to the son's intent in *Callison*, where the son's intent to permanently take the laptop from his mother was clear upon selling the laptop, Sam's intent to borrow the iPad suggests a temporary use. However, the longer Sam retains the iPad without informing Jill could create a situation where his actions mirror larceny, especially if Jill believed the iPad was lost.

Using signposts like "unlike," "however," and "in contrast," help the reader see that you're distinguishing the case.

7. Contrast a Narrow Holding ("Scope")

Pointing out the narrowness of a holding in precedent is a way to distinguish your case. You're basically saying that the scope of the holding isn't wide enough to include your client's situation, so the case is distinguishable.

Here's how this technique could be used to brainstorm an argument for our iPad-larceny case:

The thinking: The court's ruling in *Callison* focused on the permanence of deprivation upon sale, not just borrowing.

The write-up: While *Callison* clarifies that larceny is complete upon permanent deprivation, it does not explicitly address situations where the victim suffers damages (like purchasing a replacement) after a prolonged borrowing. In Sam's case, Jill did suffer damages. [Continue on to explain significance.]

8. Point to Factual Gaps in a Prior Case ("Swiss Cheese")

Unlike the "Apples to Oranges" reasoning technique, which focuses on contrasting facts, this one points to the absence of facts in the precedent's case.

Here's how this technique could be used to brainstorm an argument for our iPad-larceny case:

The thinking: The *Callison* court did not address scenarios where the borrower has ambiguous intentions about returning the property. In our case, it's unclear whether Sam actually meant to return the iPad.

The write-up: The court in *Callison* did not explore cases where the intent to return was unclear or ambiguous. In Sam's situation, while he may have believed he was borrowing the iPad temporarily, Jill's eventual need to purchase a replacement highlights the risk of permanent deprivation, which could support a finding of wrongful taking similar to larceny.

9. Apply Policy Behind the Rule ("The Policy")

Policy arguments are generally weaker, but if you have a close case, this could help to move the needle off of 50%.

Here's how this technique could be used to brainstorm an argument for our iPad-larceny case:

The thinking: As the court in *Callison* explained, the policy behind prohibiting larceny is to deter theft and protect property rights.

The write-up: The underlying policy in *Callison* aims to uphold property rights and foster trust. In Sam's case, his decision to take Jill's iPad without informing her undermines this policy, as it erodes trust between roommates. If Sam's actions are deemed wrongful, it reinforces the importance of respecting property rights in all relationships, not just familial ones.

B. Putting Analogies in the iPad Larceny Memo

This is the culmination of our iPad larceny memo! We started compiling arguments in section 10.5 when we brainstormed rule-based arguments, and we added to them in 10.6(A) above. Now, through all the thinking we just did about analogical arguments, we're ready to pick the best ones and weave them into our analysis. The bolded lines below are the new arguments. Observe how the analogies support the rule-based reasoning and bring credibility to the arguments overall:

> A: A court is likely to find that Sam's deprivation of the iPad was permanent; therefore, they are guilty of larceny. Sam continuously kept Jill's iPad for at least two weeks, and they intended to keep it for another two weeks for a total of a month. **A few days was considered nonpermanent in *Callison*, but that involved a mother-and-son relationship. Here, we have just college roommates, so there would be no implied use of household items.**
>
> Yes, Sam did not intend to keep the iPad forever. They borrowed the iPad temporarily so they could work on a short-term project that had a definite end. If the rule about permanently depriving the owner is subjective, then Sam clearly does not satisfy this element because they borrowed the iPad for a specific project that had an end date established outside of Sam's thinking (i.e., the movie-making course's due date).
>
> But looking at this objectively, which is what the law requires, it is reasonable to believe that an item that is missing or will be missing for a month is for all intents and purposes lost or stolen—**regardless of whether they are in a close family relationship as the *Callison* court pointed out**. Any person knows that iPads are easily stolen and easily fenced. Even if someone thought they lost an iPad, they would know that it would be stolen if they did not recover it *soon* because iPads are so valuable and useful to a wide variety of people. *Soon* for an item such as an iPad, assuming it is used to take class notes in Jill's college courses and for entertainment, means within hours or a day. If Jill does not find the iPad within hours or a day, the permanence of its loss will be keenly felt.
>
> In our case, **we do not have a definite act of deprivation like the sale to a pawn shop in *Callison***. That would be a clear delineation between temporarily depriving and permanently depriving. But, again, because the iPad in our case was taken for such a long time, the **effective loss** of the deprivation is permanent. Day to day, any owner would say that the iPad's loss is permanent.
>
> We may infer from Sam's character of deception that they may actually intended to keep the iPad for longer if they got away for using it for a month. Sam could have told themselves that they would "borrow" the iPad for a month, but there is nothing to say that the deception would not continue to a permanent deprivation. If Sam was not principled and honest enough to ask the roommate's permission in the first place, there is no telling what will happen in the future.
>
> Therefore, a court is likely to find that Sam permanently deprived Jill of the iPad; thus, Sam is guilty of larceny.

10.7 Making Analogies Immediately Impactful

Here are seven tips to make your analogies crystal clear.

A. If possible, make the primary analogy in one sentence.

In the Application section, which comes after the Case Illustrations, there's no need to first take a sentence and re-explain what the caselaw is about. Why? Remember that the reader would have just read the Case Illustration just moments ago. So don't lapse into repeating your illustration of a case. In other words, don't retell all the facts of that case or repeat the details of the court's holding and reasoning. Yes, you want meaningful links back to the cases, but trust that your reader paid attention when reading the Case Illustration and still remembers it. Keep your case references quick. Here's a good example of that:

> The defendant's conduct was extreme and outrageous. **The extreme and outrageous conduct in *Haverbush* lasted over two years while, in our case, the conduct was one unwitting incident.** True, the time period over which the conduct occurred isn't a dispositive factor. In fact, **the gravity of the one incident in our case is equal to or greater than the sum of incidents in *Haverbush*.** So the defendant's one act of exposing him to violent criminals is likely extreme and outrageous conduct.

And here's one more example to really drive this home; note how the primary analogy occurs in just one sentence; to do this, the writer must assume that the reader can remember the full Case Illustration:

> In the present case, Smith's fractured arm satisfies the "objectively verifiable" element of the statute's serious-impairment threshold. **Like the plaintiff's treating physician in Jones, Dr. Jackson saw Smith's fracture in two different radiological studies: traditional x-rays and an MRI.** Because he could see the fracture on film, he did not need to rely on Smith's pain complaints to diagnose the injury.
>
> **And just as the doctors in Jones supported their diagnosis by feeling the plaintiff's broken clavicle on palpation, Dr. Jackson based his diagnosis, in large part, on feeling "all the classic signs of a fracture" when he touched Smith's arm.** (Jackson Dep. at 23). So again, Dr. Jackson did not need to rely on Smith's subjective complaints to verify the injury. His diagnosis was based on objective medical tests and his physical exam of Smith. Thus, under *Jones*, the court will conclude that Smith's fracture was objectively verifiable, satisfying that element of the statutory definition.

B. Use a signpost to signal a comparison or a contrast.

Oftentimes, attorney-writers use *like* or *unlike* to signal that precedent may be favorably compared to the client's case or should be distinguished. Here's one example, but also look at the above examples to see how the writer has signaled that the case is similar or dissimilar.

> Michaels was not confined by unreasonable duress. **Unlike** the mourners in *Wilson* who risked giving up being able to bury their loved one, Michaels in our case didn't risk anything. In fact, his career could have improved from the publicity of leaving the Academy's holding room ....

C. Judiciously use analogies.

Be strategic. Do not robotically refer to a case or cases in every sentence. In fact, as strange as this may sound, you might write the first draft of your Application with *no* explicit case references—use just rule-based reasoning. Then, when you work on your second draft, find the places where a link back to a case or cases would be most logical and make the biggest impact on your reader. (Often, those places will jump off the page when you read over your first draft.) In those logical places, insert a phrase (or sometimes a sentence) referring back to the case or the aspect of a case that helps you make your point.

Here's a longer, more complex example of reasoning so you can see this principle of restraint in action:

> In our case, a court is likely to find that Mr. Vivek did not "operate" the vehicle because he was not in actual physical control of the vehicle and there was no risk of colliding with anything else. If the vehicle had been in Drive, **like the defendant's vehicle in *Wood***, then our client would have posed a risk of collision with another person, vehicle, or object. But our client's vehicle's transmission was not engaged, and his foot was not on the brake—ready to be released and start the car moving at any moment. So it did not pose a threat.
>
> Making the car a risk to others would require two intentional acts that Mr. Vivek was not capable of because he was unconscious. First, he would have had to apply enough pressure on the brake to free the shifter for movement. Second, while holding sufficient pressure on the brake, he would have had to move the shifter into a gear. Then, if those two things had happened, the vehicle could have posed a risk of colliding with someone or something. But that's not what happened in our case. **Unlike the threat of harm in *Wood* that was poised to happen at any moment because the vehicle's transmission was engaged**, there was no threat of harm in our case.

D. Make only meaningful comparisons or contrasts.

Be sure that your comparisons or distinctions with a case are meaningful. For instance, in the example below, imagine that the issue is whether a fictional auto-accident plaintiff (Smith) can prove that he suffered a "serious impairment of body function," which is a requirement for tort recovery under Michigan's no-fault law. In this context, it would be a given that every case you discuss involved a motor-vehicle accident of some sort. And that given wouldn't impact whether the injury was severe enough to meet the statutory threshold for recovery. So a case reference like this would *not* be helpful and, in fact, would probably distract the reader:

> As in *Jones*, the present case arose from an auto accident ....

As you see, this comparison is true and accurate, but it's superficial. It doesn't drive at the actual element at issue. Instead, it should help the reader appreciate why the *Jones* case supports the idea that Smith's injury was serious. So save your case references for meaningful points.

E. Compare similar things.

In other words, avoid false comparisons. A false comparison occurs when two things are compared in a way that is misleading because the items being compared are not sufficiently alike in relevant respects. This logical fallacy often arises when differences between the two things outweigh their similarities, leading to faulty conclusions. It's like comparing apples to oranges—just because they are both fruits doesn't mean they can be meaningfully compared in all contexts.

For example, if *Jones* is a case opinion, then you wouldn't want to compare *Jones* to a human being, right? Here are some examples of false comparisons to avoid:

> Like *Jones*, Smith suffered a bone fracture. [comparing a case, *Jones*, to a person, Smith]
>
> Like the plaintiff in *Jones*, the present case involves an injury that doctors could see and feel. [comparing a person (the plaintiff in *Jones*) to a case (your case)]

In those examples, we compared human beings to court cases. So we need to refine our writing to make sure that we have true, logical comparisons: a person to a person, a thing to a thing, or a case to a case. Here are some correct examples:

> Like the plaintiff in *Jones*, Smith suffered a bone fracture. [properly comparing a person to a person]
>
> Like the diagnosis in *Jones*, the diagnosis in the present case was supported by multiple radiological studies. [properly comparing a diagnosis to a diagnosis]
>
> Unlike *Jones*, this case does not involve more than one injury. [properly comparing a case to a case]

F. Address significant differences.

Nothing is more glaring in an analogy than when the reader thinks: "Mmmm. I don't think that those cases actually are similar, so I disagree with the writer." Undoubtedly, there will be differences in facts between a precedent case and the client's case, and most of those differences you may ignore. But sometimes there is a legally significant difference that goes directly to your point. Those differences you definitely should address soon after analogizing to that caselaw.

You can see in bold where the writer points out a difference, which maintains credibility with the reader, but then they neutralize it so it doesn't tank the entire analogy:

> Michaels was not confined by unreasonable duress. Unlike the mourners in *Wilson* who risked giving up being able to bury their loved one, Michaels in our case didn't risk anything. In fact, his career could have improved from the publicity of leaving the Academy's holding room. Michaels will likely argue that the chance of losing his career had the same force over him as the mourners' desire to bury their loved one. **But neither Michaels nor the Academy knew whether the paparazzi would take any interest. Even if they did, there's no such thing as bad publicity in Hollywood.**

And here's another example of dealing with significant differences:

> The defendant's conduct was extreme and outrageous. The extreme and outrageous conduct in *Haverbush* lasted over two years while, in our case, the conduct was one unwitting incident. **True, the time period over which the conduct occurred isn't a dispositive factor. In fact, the gravity of the one incident in our case is equal to or greater than the sum of incidents in *Haverbush*.** So the defendant's one act of exposing him to violent criminals is likely extreme and outrageous conduct.

G. Avoid bridges to nowhere.

All too often, the legal writer shifts the burden of analysis to the reader. The writer will make a loose connection between some facts and the law, but then not make the actual connection. Below, observe the bridge to nowhere in the penultimate sentence:

> The Martins displayed no malice toward their neighbors in erecting the fence. In *Jackson*, the defendant built a fence for malicious reasons—to block light from their neighbor's house. In Mrs. Jones's case, the defendant built the fence not out of spite but for the purpose of growing roses. Therefore, it serves a useful purpose in their rose competition hobbies. **In *Kefirchijk*, the defendant had a useful purpose for building a fence—protecting passers-by from bow-staff competitions.** Therefore, Mrs. Jones cannot prove that the Martins built the fence with malice.

When the reader comes across the bolded sentence above, they'll have to do the work of trying to figure out how that case with the bow-staff is similar to the client's case. Don't shift the burden of analysis to your reader.

Using those same facts, here's how to properly prove a point with an analogy:

> Mrs. Jones's lawsuit against her neighbors will likely fail because they did not build a spite fence. The Martins built their fence, not out of pure malice, but to grow their roses for competition. They have competed in rose growing for many years, so this is not a pretext for spiting their neighbors.
>
> The Martins' purpose of growing rose vines is similarly meaningful, instead of pretextual, like the purpose presented in *Winkelbaur*—their children's safety—and the purpose in *Kefirchijk*—the public's safety. Perhaps any defendant could get around a spite-fence lawsuit by coming up with any reason. If that's the case, then the defendants in *Winkelbaur* did just that, and the court was fine with it. What's clear, though, is that a long-term hobby of rose growing is a much more substantial reason than the vagueness of "safety."
>
> Therefore, a court is likely to find that the Martins did not build a spite fence because they did not act with malice.

Above, the first paragraph lays out the argument using rule-based reasoning. Then the second paragraph supports that reasoning with a couple of analogies that specifically compare a point from the caselaw to a point in the case at hand. And the analogy even deals with a weakness, that the purpose could be pretextual.

Remember to do the work of specifically explaining how a case is like or unlike your client's case.

10.8 Advice for the Best Reasoning

A. Be creative within the structure.

Students often say that legal writing is so disciplined that it takes all the fun out of writing. That statement is probably coming from a comparison of creative writing with little structure to legal writing with rigid and conventional structures. But there is ample room for creativity within the rigid structure.

Chris Coughlin, director of legal writing at Wake Forest University School of Law, explained it this way:

> Think of the poetry form of haiku, a Japanese form of unrhymed poetry that is always three lines long, with five syllables in the first line, seven syllables in the second line, and five syllables in the third. While the haiku is written in a **strict form**, the writer has **freedom within the substance** of the poem to be creative. Likewise, while the legal writer may use a preset organization structure, outstanding legal arguments **build bridges** between prior cases and new sets of facts, a skill that mandates creativity.

B. Explain cases consecutively; then apply them together.

Hopefully it goes without saying from all the examples above, but in the law, we synthesize all cases on the same topic or element, and then we apply them all. We don't explain a case and then apply it; explain another case on the same topic and apply it; and then explain yet another case on the same topic and apply it. Rather, consecutively explain all cases for your topic; and then apply all of that law to your facts. Attorneys write cohesively this way because all cases on the same issue are seen as one mosaic of law.

Yes	No
Explain Case 1: X-ray, MRI **Explain Case 2: Steth, EKG** **Apply *concepts* in Case 1 and Case 2**	**Explain Case 1** **Apply Case 1** **Explain Case 2** **Apply Case 2**

C. Actually apply the law to the facts; don't merely state conclusions or repeat facts.

The most pernicious risk of writing is to assume that the reader will infer from your words what you mean; instead, you must explicitly lay out each step of reasoning for your reader. Otherwise, the reader can think whatever they want about the facts you're stating. You actually want to control your reader's thoughts by explicitly stating each step in your thinking.

The example below is a C or C- answer on a law-school exam; or, if it were in a court brief, it's the type of analysis that makes a judge roll their eyes. After you spot the non-reasoning below, you'll see a better example after it.

> I: Did the employee engage in protected activity under the Whistleblower Protection Act, which would then make their employer liable for discharging them? The employee drafted but never sent an email to the *Detroit Free Press* complaining that their company was price gouging during the Covid-19 pandemic. The employee also downloaded and filled out but did not submit a complaint form from the Attorney General's office. When the company discovered the email, it deleted it and fired the employee.
>
> R: Employers may not discriminate against an employee who engages in protected activity. Protected activity is where an employee reports or is about to report a violation or a suspected violation of a law.

> A: The employee drafted but never sent an email to *Detroit Free Press* complaining that his company was price gouging during the pandemic. The employee also downloaded, filled out, but did not submit a complaint form from the Attorney General's office. When the company discovered the email, it deleted it, and it fired the employee.
>
> C: Thus, the employee did not engage in protected activity.

This might appear as sufficient reasoning, but this is merely repeating facts *without connecting them to the law*. In the Application section above, there should be application of law to fact—reasoning. But, instead, there are just facts. Stating just relevant facts is not legal reasoning. Instead, an attorney should explain how the facts satisfy or do not satisfy what the law demands.

Do not assume that your reader will do the analysis for you. Because everything else stays the same, here is just the Application section for the analysis above:

> A: The employee here did not **engage in protected activity** because they did not **report** a violation of law. At most, they composed an email and filled out a form. That's **preparing to report** but not actually reporting because they did not transmit or **communicate** the information to another person. And they likewise were not **about to report** because nothing in the facts shows that they were about to send the email or about to file the complaint.

See how the reasoning connects the law to the facts? It's now clear that the client's facts do not satisfy the elements of "protected activity" or "reporting."

Here's one more example of insufficient reasoning. See if you can't spot it:

> I: Was Daphne detained by coercion, an element required to prove false imprisonment? Daphne took her poodle to Derryl's house so Derryl could watch the poodle while Daphne was on vacation. They agreed on a price before the vacation. After the vacation, Daphne went to get her poodle from Derryl. She explained to him that she would pay him in a week after she got paid. Derryl demanded the payment immediately and would not return her poodle until she paid. Daphne waited at Derryl's house for several hours until Derryl finally relented and let her leave with her poodle.
>
> R: Personal coercion may amount to false imprisonment. (Rule from common-law case.)
>
> E: If a store employee detains a valuable item of a customer, then the customer has been personally coerced. Taking bed sheets worth $250 is taking a customer's valuable item. (From the *Clarke* case.)
>
> A: Derryl took Daphne's poodle away from her. We can assume that Daphne probably loved or at least liked per poodle.
>
> C: Therefore, Daphne has been personally coerced, which amounts to false imprisonment.

The thin analysis is found in the poodle's value, which isn't explained in the Application. The writer has just assumed the reader will understand that a poodle is valuable. Yes, we may make permissible inferences about dog ownership and whether an owner likes their animal. But the writer failed to connect the dots in the application between the law and the facts in any meaningful way. That is, they failed to use the facts to explain why Daphne's poodle is a valuable item.

Here's a solid example of applying the valuable-item rule to the poodle facts:

> A: Derryl took Daphne's poodle away from her. A poodle is an item of **value** both financially and emotionally. Any pure-bred animal like a poodle costs at least **several hundred dollars.** And any dog owner will obviously have an **emotional connection** to the canine friend; that is why people own animals. Some dog owners would even argue that a dog is **invaluable.** At least one celebrity even **cloned their dog** so they could continue to **enjoy** at least some characteristics of their former beloved dog. Further, combining the actual economic value with the emotional value of a poodle would definitely add up to more than the $250 bed sheets in *Clarke.* People can replace bed sheets, but they cannot replace the unique personality of their dear canine friend.

What's the lesson from this? You need to actually reason by connecting the law to the facts. Do not merely state relevant facts. Remedy this by following the reasoning techniques explained in sections 10.5 and 10.6.

D. Organize the Application by legal principles, not cases.

Don't formulaically address a different case in each paragraph of your Application section. That would be where the case dictates the structure of your Application. Letting the cases dictate the structure belies the fact that most cases have the same concepts in them, so it wouldn't make sense to address them one at a time; doing so would require you to repeat the same analysis in each paragraph.

Instead, let the concepts in the cases—the law—determine how you organize the Application.

Yes	No
Explain Case 1: X-ray, MRI Explain Case 2: Steth, EKG Apply *concepts* in Case 1 and Case 2	Explain Case 1: X-ray, MRI Explain Case 2: Steth, EKG Apply Case 1: X-ray, MRI Apply Case 2: Steth, EKG

Here is what you should not do:

> In the present case, Smith's fractured arm satisfies the "objectively verifiable" element of the statute's serious-impairment threshold. Our case is like the *Jones* case because Dr. Jackson saw Smith's fracture in two different radiological studies: traditional x-rays and an MRI. Because he could see the fracture on film, he did not need to rely on Smith's pain complaints to diagnose the injury.
>
> Our case is also like the *Thompson* case because the doctor there used a stethoscope and an EKG to diagnose the heart murmur. So, again, Dr. Jackson in our case did not need to rely on Smith's subjective complaints to verify the injury.

In the example above, the writer structured the Application around the two cases. But the law is organized around elements, definitions, and factors, so we must likewise structure our Application around those things. And besides, organizing around legal principles rather than cases avoids redundant arguments.

Organize your Application into logical paragraphs. A logical paragraph applies a separate element or subpart of an element. Each one should make a point that supports your answer—strive for *one main point per paragraph*. Your reader will appreciate the clarity of organizing the paragraphs by points of proof instead of by case.

Here is an example of a well-structured Application, starting with the topic sentence:

> In the present case, Smith's fractured arm satisfies the "objectively verifiable" element of the statute's serious-impairment threshold. Like the doctors using x-rays in *Jones* and the stethoscope and EKG in *Thompson*, in our case, Dr. Jackson saw Smith's fracture in two different radiological studies: traditional x-rays and an MRI. Because he could see the fracture on film, he did not need to rely on Smith's pain complaints to diagnose the injury.
>
> And just as the doctors in *Jones* supported their diagnosis by feeling the plaintiff's broken clavicle on palpation, Dr. Jackson based his diagnosis, in large part, on feeling "all the classic signs of a fracture" when he touched Smith's arm. So again, Dr. Jackson did not need to rely on Smith's subjective complaints to verify the injury. His diagnosis was based on objective medical tests and his physical exam of Smith. Thus, under *Jones*, the court will conclude that Smith's fracture was objectively verifiable, satisfying that element of the statutory definition.

In the above reasoning, each paragraph focuses on just one point of proof. The first paragraph focuses on using objective medical equipment to prove the injury. And the second paragraph focuses on a doctor's actual physical examination of the patient. In other words, organize your Application by concepts, not by cases.

E. Identify factors from caselaw and apply those.

In Chapter 9, Explain Caselaw, you learned about pulling factors out of several cases as a way to synthesize them. See 9.9(B)(3). Now, here in the chapter about reasoning, applying law to fact, this is a reminder to make sure you actually apply those factors. An example will help.

Suppose the rule provides that parents of a minor are responsible for the child's wrongful acts if the parents "know or have reason to know of the child's tortious propensities." You find the following cases applying the rule:

> *Case 1*: Parents held liable for injury deliberately caused by child who was 7 years old at the time of the event, and parents had seen him hurt others but had failed to intervene.
>
> *Case 2*: Parents not held liable for shooting by 17-year-old child who had been involved in vandalism and other property destruction, but there were no previous injuries to persons.
>
> *Case 3*: Parents not held liable for drunken rape by 17-year-old child who had history of substance abuse, but no history of injuring persons or property.
>
> *Synthesis with Factors*: Thus, it appears that courts are concerned with the age of the child; a younger child may be more under the parents' control than an older one. In addition, the courts consider the child's previous behavior and whether that behavior would put the parent on notice that the child was likely to commit harm. Finally, the courts consider the similarity of the acts committed by the child in the past to the acts involved in this action.

Once you have a synthesis paragraph, you can then coherently apply each of the main points in the synthesis paragraph to the facts. Remember to have just one point per paragraph, and begin each paragraph with a clear topic sentence that states the argument.

Or, as one last example of organizing your Application by legal point, imagine that you find one or more cases where the court has decided the issue the way you want your case to come out. And then you find one or more cases where the court has decided the case the other way. You compare your case to each group of cases to determine whether your case is more like those where the court said "yes" or more like those where the court said "no."

Your case involves a 14-year-old boy who beat a Jewish man severely with a baseball bat. The parents had caught him downloading hate literature, including anti-Semitic material, from the Internet. He had never physically harmed another person, although he was caught spraying swastikas on a synagogue.

Imagine that you find the three same cases above about parents being liable or not liable for their children's conduct. You would apply those cases by point like this:

Synthesis paragraph cohesively explains what cases have in common.

> Thus, it appears that courts are concerned with the **age** of the child; a younger child may be more under the parents' **control** than an older one. In addition, the courts consider the child's **previous behavior** and whether that behavior would put the parent on **notice** that the child was likely to commit harm. Finally, the courts consider the **similarity** of the acts committed by the child in the past to the acts involved in this action.

First argument based on the first factor, **age** and **control**.

> In our case, although the child was not as close to the **age** of majority as were the children in *Case 2* and *Case 3*, he was a **teenager** and much more likely to be beyond the **control** of his parents than was the seven-year-old in *Case 1*.

Second argument based on **previous behavior** and similar conduct.

> Furthermore, while the child in our case had **previously demonstrated** hateful feelings or attitudes toward Jews in his choice of reading materials, that alone is not likely to results in an inference that the parents should have known of his dangerous propensities.

This paragraph continues the second argument.

As you learned above, organize the Application by concept or factor, not by case.

> Like the children in *Case 2* and *Case 3*, he had a **history** of violence toward property, but the courts seem to say that more is needed to hold a parent liable when the child harms another person. Therefore, our case is more like those where the courts said that there was no liability, and the parents in our case are not likely to be held liable for their son's act.

F. Begin each paragraph with a topic sentence that states a legal argument.

Avoid two common mistakes when drafting arguments: avoid starting the argument paragraph by merely repeating fact and avoid merely repeating the law. Instead, start each paragraph in your application-of-law section with an argument.

Many novice attorneys begin a paragraph of argument by merely repeating law or fact. Neither alone is an argument. It's only the combination of law and fact that can be an argument. Merely stating what the attorney-reader already knows (the law or facts) is not helpful. Advance thought forward by stating something new—an argument.

Here is an example of a paragraph of argument that begins with mere fact. This is less effective:

> The release on the baseball ticket stated, "The holder assumes all risk and danger incidental to the game of Baseball ... and agrees that the ... Participating

> Clubs ... are not liable for injuries resulting from such causes." This language is insufficient at informing the reader of its effect because "not liable" doesn't explicitly explain that the right to sue has been waived. [continue argument]

This is more effective at conveying your argument because the topic sentence is actually an argument:

> The release language is insufficient at informing the reader of its effect because "not liable" doesn't explicitly explain that the right to sue has been waived. [continue argument]

Here's a less-effective example of writing a paragraph of argument by beginning by merely repeating the law:

> A release must inform the reader of its effect. The release on the baseball ticket stated, "The holder assumes all risk and danger incidental to the game of Baseball ... and agrees that the ... Participating Clubs ... are not liable for injuries resulting from such causes." The release's stated effect isn't immediately clear because "are not liable" does not explicitly inform the reader that they relinquished the right to sue.

This example is less effective because the argument doesn't emerge until the last sentence. That's way too late because your reader may have already skipped to the next paragraph by then. Here's how it should look:

> The release's stated effect isn't immediately clear because "are not liable" does not explicitly inform the reader that they relinquished the right to sue. "[A]re not liable" speaks to the effect on the defendant—the party who drafted the document. On the contrary, the subject in our release to the verb "are" is "Participating Clubs." But *Xu* speaks to making the effect clear on the reader—not the drafter.

Reciting facts is not reasoning:

> Chef Montenegro insulted Ms. Thompson by calling her "Chef Idiot." He also threw a plate in front of her and made her clean it up. Therefore, this element is satisfied.

This argument above only lists facts—it does not connect them to the element. It then concludes, leaving the reader to make the connection for the writer.

Likewise, simply stating a conclusion is not reasoning:

> Chef Montenegro intended to cause Ms. Thompson emotional distress because his actions were directed at her. Therefore, this element is satisfied.

This sample has the opposite problem—it mentions the relevant element, but doesn't use facts to explain the conclusion.

Here's an improved revision:

> Chef Montenegro intended to cause Ms. Thompson emotional distress when he directly insulted Ms. Thompson by calling her "Chef Idiot." He also targeted Ms. Thompson directly with his actions when he threw a plate in front of her and made her clean it up, which was humiliating. Therefore, this element is satisfied.

In this example, the arguments use facts and law and connect them together.

10.9 Four Annotated Examples of Applying Law

The four annotated examples that follow bring everything in this chapter together. Have a look.

Reasoning Example #1: How a Supreme Court Justice Reasons

Justice Antonin Scalia was one of the best legal reasoners of all time, so this chapter wouldn't be complete without at least one example from him. What you see on the next page is a small excerpt from one opinion. It's a good example of using multiple types of rule-based reasoning and analogical reasoning to prove that the conclusion is correct.

More than anything, notice how Justice Scalia mainly relies on common sense to apply the plain meaning of the elements to the facts. As you learned in section 10.5, that's called rule-based reasoning. Yes, he threw in a smidge of reasoning by analogy to caselaw, but his reasoning here is mainly rule-based.

Summers v. Earth Island Institute

555 U.S. 488 (2009)

[The issue before the Court was whether Bensman, an outdoor enthusiast, had standing to sue to stop the federal government from selling 238 acres of National Forest. To have standing to sue, Bensman must prove a "threat of suffering 'injury in fact' that is **concrete** and **particularized**; the threat must be **actual** and **imminent**, *not* **conjectural** or **hypothetical**."]

Bensman failed to allege that any particular timber sale or other project claimed to be unlawfully subject to the regulations will impede a **specific** and **concrete** plan of Bensman's to enjoy the National Forests. **The National Forests occupy more than 190 million acres, an area larger than Texas.**

There may be a **chance**, but **hardly a likelihood**, that Bensman's **wanderings** will bring him to a **parcel about to be affected** by a project unlawfully subject to the regulations. Indeed, without further **specification,** it is **impossible to tell** which projects are unlawfully subject to the regulations.

The allegations here present a **weaker likelihood** of **concrete** harm than that which we found insufficient in ***Lyons*** where a plaintiff who alleged that he had been injured by an improper police chokehold sought injunctive relief barring use of the hold in the future. We said it was **"no more than conjecture"** that Lyons would be subjected to that chokehold upon a later encounter. Here we are asked to **assume** not only that Bensman will **stumble** across a project **tract** unlawfully subject to the regulations, but also that the tract is **about to be** developed by the Forest Service in a way that harms his recreational interests, and that he would have commented on the project but for the regulation.

Accepting an intention to visit the National Forests as adequate to confer standing to challenge any Government action affecting any portion of those forests **would be tantamount to eliminating** the requirement of **concrete, particularized** injury in fact.

The first sentence is just the conclusion, as it should be. He **repeats** an element to show the connection to the law, but he also used a **synonym**, *specific*.

This **quantification** shows how unlikely it is that Bensman will be injured. Adds great perspective.

Note the many **synonyms** in this paragraph, and a factual **characterization**, *wanderings*, relate to a non-imminent, conjectural injury.

The **analogy** begins with a point that **repeats** an element and **quantifies** (*weaker likelihood*). This analogy both compares facts and applies the court's reasoning.

The **characterizations** here really make the point about how unlikely it is that Bensman will be injured by the sale. *Stumble* and *tract* show how small the chances are.

This last sentence uses an **implication** (cause-and-effect reasoning). Agreeing with the opposite side would, in Justice Scalia's mind, lead to blowing up the standing rule.

Reasoning Example #2: Applying One Element and One Case

In this short eMemo below, a law-firm's partner asked an associate to research whether their client could be liable for IIED, among other causes of action. The scenario was that a prosecutor was receiving death threats from criminals he had locked up. A friend of the prosecutor, our client, had dinner with the prosecutor at the prosecutor's house, took pictures with his phone while there, and posted them to X.

Unbeknownst to our client, the photos had coordinates for the prosecutor's home embedded in them. Our client immediately removed the photos from X, and the prosecutor was never harmed. But it gave the prosecutor quite a scare, especially because some websites archive everything on X, even if a user removes a post.

The annotations point out the rule-based reasoning and analogical reasoning.

Dear Boss,

Our client seeks legal advice regarding whether geotagging a photo of a person who is vulnerable to attack, a prosecutor facing death threats, could amount to intentional infliction of emotional distress (IIED). To file a claim of IIED in Michigan, a plaintiff must show "(1) extreme and outrageous conduct, (2) intent or recklessness, (3) causation, and (4) severe emotional distress." *Graham v. Ford*, 604 N.W.2d 713, 716 (Mich. Ct. App. 1999). The recklessness element, which is primarily at issue here, may be proved where a "reasonable person would know emotional distress would result." *Haverbush v. Powelson*, 551 N.W.2d 206, 210 (Mich. Ct. App. 1996).

In Michigan, at least one court has said that "a significant breach of trust" amounts to reckless conduct. In *Lewis*, a boyfriend videotaped sexual encounters with girlfriends without their consent. *Lewis v. LeGrow*, 670 N.W.2d 675 (Mich. Ct. App. 2003). The court held that these facts amounted to "reckless" conduct to satisfy the second element of IIED. *Id.* at 689–690. In coming to its conclusion, the court reasoned that this was reckless because secretly videotaping another during sex "is deceptive and a significant breach of trust." *Id.* at 690.

The reasoning properly begins with a transition and the global prediction in the first sentence. Then the first argument, lack of intention, is clearly stated.

In our case, a court is likely to find that geotagging a photo to a vulnerable person's home is not reckless. Our client's revealing the prosecutor's home's location was an honest mistake. He did not intentionally reveal the prosecutor's location; the lack of intention makes his act less reckless. So he may have been negligent, but not reckless. Geotagging is not on most people's minds when they take a photo with their phone, so it is hard to say that our client was reckless in doing the everyday act of posting a picture to an internet website. This honest mistake starkly contrasts the intentional act

The writer proves the conclusion with **characterizations** (*honest mistake; unintentional; negligent, not reckless; not on people's minds*). This is logical and persuasive because they do not fit within the meaning of *reckless*. Great job with rule-based reasoning!

Once the argument is explained with rule-based reasoning, the writer supports that with an **analogy to the facts** in the precedent case. The facts are distinguished to make the point that our client wasn't reckless.

to deceive in *Lewis* where the boyfriend, with full presence of mind and with intent, deceived women by surreptitiously recording the most intimate act a human does.

Moreover, our situation with the geotagged photo lacks the severe breach of trust in *Lewis*. Secretly videotaping the most intimate of acts and distributing them breaches one of the most sacred trusts humans put in each other. Contrast that with the trust of not identifying a person's location. They carry different values in our society, and, because of that, a court is likely to find that the prosecutor's friend was not reckless.

Of course, the prosecutor could argue that the breach of trust was more severe in our case because the consequences were so great: the criminals he put away were allegedly actively looking for him. The consequences in *Lewis* were embarrassment at most, but in our case the consequences could have been loss of life, kidnapped family members, or other horrible acts.

That's true, but the prosecutor's friend's actions just weren't as conscious as what happened in *Lewis*. To rise to the level of conscious breach of trust from *Lewis*, the friend would have had to think through several possible step: First, he would have had to be aware while taking the picture that the photo was geotagged. Second, he would have had to know that the prosecutor did not want that photo posted. Third, he would have had to know that the "bad guys" would know about geotagging. Fourth, he would have had to know that the "bad guys" had the knowledge to figure out the prosecutor's location from the photo. That's a lot of assumptions to get to the same severe level of breach of trust in *Lewis*.

For these reasons, a court is likely to find that the prosecutor's friend was not reckless.

Note how every paragraph begins with a strong argument. And there are no sentences of just *objective* fact or pure law. The writer is applying the law in every sentence.

This argument relies completely on both **(1) analogizing to facts in precedent and (2) applying the precedent's reasoning**, which make this a really solid argument.

If there is an obvious weakness in your analysis, you should address that. Neutralize such **counterarguments** by explaining why they're not going to be stronger than all the other arguments you've been making.

This paragraph is largely where the writer explains away the counterargument. It does so using **inferences** from the facts, **characterization** of fact, and **cause-and-effect reasoning**. In other words: **common sense**, which is the hallmark of rule-based reasoning. And the writer supports that reasoning with a brief analogy to a case.

Reasoning Example #3: Applying One Element and Three Cases

Starting on the next page, you'll find the annotated reasoning from a short office memo. In fact, it's the reasoning from the sample document in section 2.4. You can read the facts and law there. But the basic story, which actually happened, is that an actor tried to get into the Academy Awards. Because he didn't have a ticket, he was detained by security and taken to a "resolution center." He claims he was then falsely imprisoned there. The memo focuses on the element of **confinement**, and it illustrates that element with three Case Illustrations. To fully understand the reasoning, you may want to pop over to that sample memo and have a quick read before you see the annotated reasoning below.

Enjoy.

The reasoning properly begins with a transition and the conclusion in the first sentence. Then the first argument, Michaels's will wasn't overcome, is clearly stated. That first argument, by the way, is applying the implicit rule the writer culled from the three cases. The rest of the paragraph proves that argument.

"Free to leave" is a **characterization** that contrasts overcoming one's will to confining them. Then the next sentence is a **hypothetical** about having permission to leave yet being confined.

In our case, Michaels was probably not **confined** by unreasonable duress. Michaels's will was not overcome. In fact, the Academy employee said that Michaels was **"free to leave."** How could anyone reasonably argue that permission to leave would overcome one's will? Yes, that assertion was followed by a statement that the Academy attorney would contact Michaels, but that was **merely informing** Michaels of the next step; it was not a threat. Such a statement does not **create** the type of fear that persuades courts to find confinement. Michaels incorrectly assumed that he could stay and talk the employee out of turning his information over to the attorneys. So it was Michaels's **independent** choice to stay.

"Merely informing" is addressing a **counter-argument** by clarifying the facts with a **characterization.**

The point about creating fear uses **cause-and-effect** reasoning to make a point about the element.

The **characterization** *independent* contrasts—is an **antonym**—of the rule of overcoming one's will to confine them.

The writer addresses a reasonable counter-argument. The writer explains it using **characterization** and **implications** (cause and effect).

Michaels will likely argue that "free to leave" did not really mean that. The unspoken subtext, perhaps, was that he would face more trouble if he left without the employee's permission. Michaels's presence for **six hours** supports this argument, suggesting that "free to leave" really did not mean that Michaels was free to leave. After all, that is **almost an entire work day**, much **longer than** the entire Academy Awards ceremony. If the employee's job was to simply collect information of those who allegedly trespassed on the red carpet, he could have done it in about **15 minutes.** In light of that, six hours might suggest some force confined Michaels.

The writer is explaining another solid **counter-argument** using **quantification.** The bolded terms show that. The next paragraph neutralizes this argument.

"Uphill battle" is **quantifying** how high a bar the law is.

Despite these arguments, Michaels still has an **uphill battle** because the precedent on unreasonable duress sets a very high bar. Michaels's mild emotional confinement by the Academy employee pales in comparison to the severe emotional distress the victim in *Parrott* experienced; she who was so overcome by threat of FBI prosecution and public humiliation that she confessed to a crime she did not commit. Michaels, on the other hand, persisted in trying to talk the employee out of turning his name over to the attorneys. So his will was not overcome as he did not confess to trespass just to leave.

This **analogy** comparing fact from precedent to our case makes the point about how high the bar is. Before analogizing to precedent, first make a point; then support that point with the analogy.

This **analogy** by contrast proves just how different the current case's facts are from the precedent facts. The writer is also **applying the court's reasoning** about humiliation and FBI force.

The Academy had no real **leverage** or even **motive** to force Michaels to stay in the resolution center. He might argue that the duress came from fearing the negative consequences of having to face the paparazzi. He feared them so much that it was a relief when the employee finally let him avoid the paparazzi by exiting through the back door.

This is **applying the courts' reasoning** from several cases and the **implicit rule** the writer created from them.

The writer is addressing another likely **counter-argument.** The argument is based on the **inference** (shown by using *indicates* in the reasoning) that the Academy employee was abusing their authority. And they punctuate that with an **analogy** to precedent.

Michaels will likely read much into the employee's statement, "you've suffered enough," which he said right before letting Michaels out. This statement, combined with allowing Michaels to exit through the back entrance, **indicates** that the employee used his position of authority to control Michaels—similar to the funeral director's leverage in *Wilson*. Perhaps he did it to send a message to others who would try to get onto the red carpet without permission. Or perhaps he wanted to make an example of Michaels.

The writer rebuts the counterargument with this argument, which relies on an **inference**.

More likely, though, "you've suffered enough" **signals** that the employee felt sorry for the joke of calling the paparazzi and sympathized with the **stress** the paparazzi caused Michaels. But it was just that: stress, and nothing more. It certainly was not unreasonable duress. It is not as though there was an **angry mob** out front throwing rocks. Such threat of violence could cause unreasonable duress. The threat of severe injury from rocks pales when compared to paparazzi photos or video.

Stress is a reasonable **characterization** of what Michaels felt.

The angry-mob reasoning is using the technique of **hypothetical**. This text doesn't discuss that much, but it can be an effective way to support a conclusion.

Note how all the topic sentences in this sample reasoning all state an argument. Nowhere does the writer simply repeat law or fact. This paragraph begins with the argument that *severity* is lacking in our case. Then that is supported by an analogy to a case.

Wilson underscores that confinement by unreasonable duress requires a severity that is not present in this case. The mourners in *Wilson*, who physically could have left, stayed in the bank because the funeral director leveraged the burial of their loved one to keep them in the bank. Leaving would have meant foregoing one of our society's most solemn rights: to bury a loved one.

Note how the reasoning is organized by legal principle, not by case. In fact, the writer already referred to *Wilson* above for another argument.

Michaels, on the other hand, would have given up very little—if anything—by braving the paparazzi. Any airtime, even if somewhat negative, could have even helped his career. Many so-called stars, from Paris Hilton to Kim Kardashian, got their starts through publicized scandals. **So perhaps there is no such thing as bad publicity**. If Michaels was so concerned about the paparazzi, he could have avoided them by covering his head with his shirt or hand. Besides, the chances of this non-newsworthy event making it on air, the Internet, or in print was very slim.

Giving up very little is an **implication** that proves there was no confinement, and it's **applying the reasoning** from *Wilson*.

This is using a well-known idiom or maxim to **characterize** the facts. This shows how not severe the situation was; thus, Michaels's will was not overcome.

To top it all off, Michaels was not in a particularly **vulnerable state**. Unlike the teller employee who was questioned and threatened, the pregnant home owner who bought expensive furniture, or the family who just wanted to bury their deceased loved-one, Michaels was **in complete control** of his situation. He could have walked out the resolution center at any time with **very little to lose**.

This final paragraph focuses on an implicit rule from the cases about vulnerable victims. It uses rule-based techniques of **characterization, synonyms**, and **antonyms** to make the point. And then it also supports that reasoning with an **analogy** to two different precedent cases.

Therefore, Michaels was not confined by unreasonable duress.

Reasoning Example #4: Applying the Court's Reasoning

What you see below is an email memo. As you read the Case Illustration for *Xu v. Gay*, take note of the court's reasoning, which is emphasized with bold; and then see how the writer, which in this case was a law student, applied the court's reasoning, which is likewise emphasized with bold.

Madame Borofski,

Question

You asked whether your ballet studio's release of liability for your ballet studio is effective to insulate you from liability. The current release simply states: "I assume all risks of personal injury and acknowledge the hazards in an exercise program." One of your dancers recently suffered stress fractures that a podiatrist claims is a result of Ballet Lansing's overtraining the dancers.

Answer

A court would likely find that the ballet studio's release is not valid because the scope isn't clear or developed enough; thus, it's not valid to insulate the studio from liability.

Controlling Law

A release's language about the scope must "explicitly inform the reader regarding the effect of the release." *Xu v. Gay*, 668 N.W.2d 166, 171 (Mich. Ct. App. 2003) (citations omitted).

In *Xu*, a fitness-gym member signed the following waiver before dying while using a piece of exercise equipment: "Vital Power Fitness Center assumes no responsibility for any injuries and/or sicknesses incurred to me or any accompanying minor person as a result of entering the premises and/or using any of the facilities." *Id.* at 171.

The court held that this release was not valid because its scope was unclear; instead, a release must "explicitly inform the reader regarding the effect of the release." *Id.* at 173. The court reasoned that the effect is clear when the release's scope of (1) injuries, (2) responsible parties, and (3) rights waived is clear. *Id.* The court took issue with (2) and (3). As to **scope of parties**, the court stated that the signor must know that they are "solely responsible," meaning that the scope of possible liable parties is singular: just the signor. The gym release said who was not responsible (i.e., "[The gym] assumes no responsibility"), but it never positively said who was responsible.

And as to the **scope of rights**, the court said that the release must state that the signor has given up the right to sue for negligence. *Id.* There's nothing in the gym's release that would inform a reader about the scope of rights they're giving up, so the court said it was invalid for that reason as well. *Id.*

Thus, the court said that the release was invalid because the scope of parties responsible and rights waived was either vague or not present.

Application

In our case, a court would likely find that the ballet studio's release is not valid because the scope isn't clear or developed enough; thus, it's not valid to insulate the studio from liability. First, as to the **scope of parties** responsible, the release does positively say that the signor is responsible for injuries when it states, "I assume all risks of personal injury. . . ." But it's missing the "solely" aspect from the *Xu* opinion, that the reader alone bears the risk of injury. Simply saying "I assume" doesn't necessarily negate the fact that the ballet madame could also be on the hook. It does use broad language—*all*—, which would please the *Dombrowski* court, but in reference to *risks*, not the parties released from liability or the parties responsible for the injury.

Readers love cohesion between law and reasoning. See how the writer clearly applies the reasoning about **scope of parties** here? There's a great mix of rule-based reasoning and analogical reasoning in this paragraph.

Admittedly, reading "I assume all risks," which is a positive statement about **who is liable**, is more explicit than a negative statement like "[the gym] assumes no responsibility" in *Xu*. But, again, the court was concerned with the release clearly conveying and the signor understanding who has sole responsibility. The scope of who has sole responsibility must be clear. It cannot leave that open.

The reasoning about **scope of parties** continues here. And note how the writer applies the case and does not merely state fact or state rules of law.

If it's a close call on the first "effect" element from *Xu*, then the second one is much clearer. From nowhere in the one-sentence release would a signor understand (or know) the **scope of rights** they have given up, let alone a specific right to sue. There's no discussion of rights and no discussion of suing.

Here the writer applies the second bit of reasoning from the case above, **scope of rights**.

Recommendation

For these reasons, the ballet studio's release language likely will not insulate our client from liability.

10.10 Checklist for Applying Law

Structure

To organize the structure of each Application section, did you:

___ begin with a transition from explaining the law to applying the law?

___ state your prediction/conclusion after the transition?

___ state one to three Argument-and-Proof combos to prove the prediction/conclusion?

___ prove the argument with rule-based reasoning, analogical reasoning, and counter-analysis?

___ state an internal conclusion at the end?

___ organize the application by legal point, not by case?

Rule-Based Reasoning

To apply the plain meaning of the <u>element</u> to the <u>facts</u> and show that the facts do or do not fit within the meaning of the element, did you:

___ use common sense to explain whether the facts fall within the meaning of the element?

___ repeat the element's words and its definition?

___ use synonyms of the element and apply them to the facts?

___ use antonyms of the element and apply them to the facts?

___ characterize the client's facts and fit that within or outside the element's meaning?

___ quantify the client's facts to explain whether the element is met or not?

___ infer conclusions from the client's facts and apply them to the element?

___ identify implications in the client's facts to prove whether an element is met?

Analogical Reasoning

To support your rule-based reasoning, did you:

___ apply a precedent case's <u>reasoning</u> to the client's facts?

___ show that the client's <u>facts</u> are **similar** to or **different** from the facts in a precedent case?

___ where applicable, address substantive **differences** between the precedent and client's facts?

___ avoid bridges to nowhere?

Effective Application of Law

In your rule Application, did you:

___ apply the two-part test in 10.4(B) to each sentence of reasoning?

___ avoid beginning a paragraph by reiterating a rule or Case Illustration (i.e., you think you're doing an analogy, but you're really just repeating a rule or case)?

___ avoid shifting the burden of analysis to your reader and make them connect the dots?

Chapter Eleven

IREAC: Conclude and Recommend

11.1 The Skill

Attorneys cannot just apply the law to the client's facts; they need to go the distance by clearly stating the impact, the consequences of the conclusions drawn from the analysis. Thus, a legal writer can't merely conclude in a document, "Therefore, Mr. Colthorpe was negligent" and be done with it. Rather, they need to recommend the next steps for the case. Should we sue? write a letter? enter settlement negotiations?

In simple terms, at the end of the document, we need to answer this question: So what?

11.2 Conclusions Within an IREAC Packet

When writing about one subissue in one IREAC packet, you need to finish off the analysis with a clear statement of where you stand on whether the facts satisfy the element. For context, one IREAC packet is one paragraph in the law-school essay in 2.1. Or it's the entire Opinion Letter or eMemo in 2.2 and 2.3. Or it's just section A or just section B in the Full Office Memo in 2.5. You get the picture.

You can see in those documents that the writer wraps up each IREAC packet with an internal conclusion. It's called an "internal" conclusion because it's internal to just one IREAC packet as opposed to being a conclusion stated for the entire document.

They sound something like this: "Therefore, the intent element is met." "For these reasons, Sarah was subject to an adverse employment action." They simply state the conclusion on the element.

However, readers like to know where the analysis is headed early on, which is why the mantra "conclude early and often" works well here. You'll definitely need a conclusion at the end of each IREAC packet—it's the "C" after all—but you should also give a preview of your conclusion immediately after stating the issue and at the beginning of your Application section. For examples of this, refer to the chapters on issue statements (Ch. 6) and applying the law (Ch. 10), as well as the sample documents in Chapter 2.

11.3 Whole-Document Conclusion in Objective Analysis

In objective, predictive analysis like opinion letters and memos, the final section in the document should be titled Conclusion or Recommendations—something like that. Follow the sample documents you've been given to see what you should call it. Center and bold the heading, or otherwise format it like the other headings in the document at that same level.

After the heading, first state the crystal clear conclusion or prediction of your analysis in one sentence. This will be the broad conclusion, the answer to the broad issue stated at the beginning of the document.

Do not include any reasoning. This type of Conclusion section is *not* like a five-paragraph essay you were taught in high school and college where you summarize your points. Remember that, by this point in the memo, your reader has already worked through all the analysis. Now is not the time to rehash it. Rather, simply state the conclusion.

After stating the conclusion, write in a sentence or two what the next steps are for the client. Some of your options include:

- Given this conclusion, we should file a complaint on behalf of our client.
- We need to learn more facts about the following: [list the open factual questions].
- We need to call [party] and negotiate a settlement.
- We need to write a letter, demanding that [party] cease operations.

Observe recommendation sections in the objective sample documents in Chapter 2:

Opinion Letter — page 12, last full paragraph

eMemo — page 20, in the Recommendation section

Short Office Memo — page 33, in the Conclusion

Full Office Memo — page 49, in the Conclusion

11.4 Whole-Document Conclusions in Persuasive Analysis

We're talking about briefs here. The goal in the conclusory, final section is to remind the court about the conclusion you want them to come to and the relief you're seeking from the court.

Begin the section with a heading. The heading may be either Conclusion, Relief Requested, or even Conclusion and Relief Requested. Center and bold it, or otherwise format it like other headings in the document.

Then simply state what relief you're seeking from the court.

Do not rehash the analysis. And remember to capitalize *Court* when referring to the court you're currently writing to.

Here's an example from the Appellate-Court Brief on page 103:

> **Relief Requested**
>
> Defendant-Appellant American National Fire Insurance Company asks the Court to reverse the district court's grant of summary judgment in plaintiff's favor, and to order the district court to instead grant summary judgment on American National's behalf. In the alternative, American National asks the Court to remand the case for a trial on the disputed factual questions.

And here's an example from the state trial-court brief on page 69:

> **Relief Requested**
>
> For these reasons, Defendant Buffalo Wild Wings Grill & Bar requests that this Court enter an order granting Defendant's Motion for Summary Disposition, dismissing the Plaintiff's claims with prejudice, and award attorney fees and costs.

And, finally, you may want to compare the conclusion in the brief that responds to the one above. Here's how that opposing counsel wrote the Relief Requested on page 86:

> **RELIEF REQUESTED**
>
> For these reasons, Plaintiff Trout respectfully requests this Honorable Court to deny Defendant's Motion for Summary Disposition and award to him costs, attorney fees, and any other relief this Court deems equitable.

PART THREE

Storytelling Skills

Part 3 teaches the skill of formal storytelling, which you'll use in sophisticated opinion letters, formal memos, and court briefs.

Chapter Twelve

Tell a Story

12.1 Attorneys Are Storytellers

What do these things have in common: novels, TikTok videos, movies, music lyrics, music videos, a conversation with a friend, operas, memes, and caselaw? You guessed it: they all involve storytelling. Humans are programmed to tell and enjoy stories. They allow us to teach, persuade, inspire, love, hate, include, and exclude—to be human.

Attorneys tell stories in many different places: briefs, over the phone, memos, letters, emails, and open court. Our stories vary in length: a sentence in an email memo, a paragraph in an office memo, 500 words in a court brief, or a 20-minute oral argument. And we tell stories for many different reasons: explain caselaw in a brief; persuade a court during oral argument; or convince the firm's partners that your case strategy is sound. And the audience is just as varied: client, judge, jury, reader, or the firm's decision-makers. Regardless of where, why, how, or to whom—it all involves storytelling.

This chapter explains how to tell the legal story.

12.2 How to Tell a Legal Story

You already know how to tell a story; you've been doing it since you could first talk. So this chapter is really about learning how to be a bit more conventional about it in a legal setting to make sure that your reader understands the story and enjoys reading it. Do this by being mindful of four aspects:

- Content
- Context
- Organization
- Readability

If at any point you'd like context for writing a legal story using these four parts, you may want to peek at the sample documents in Chapter 2; you'll find a Statement of Facts in all of the documents except for the law-school essay, opinion letter, and eMemo.

A. Content

When telling a legal story, include the legally significant facts. These are the facts that directly relate to the elements of law. They are more than just relevant—they go directly to the elements at issue. You know a fact is significantly relevant if you're going to use it in the reasoning section where you apply law to facts.

Most of the facts in your Statement of Facts will be the legally significant ones. If the issue, for example, is whether someone had intent to commit a tortious battery, only facts like the person's physical movements and emotional state are legally significant. And, on the other hand, facts about the actual injury (split lip, broken nose, etc.) or the location of the battery (bar, church, parade, etc.) are not significant to deciding the issue of intent. So you will give lots of detail about the intent facts because the law has anointed them to be special.

1. Include the good, the bad, and the ugly.

Regardless of whether you're writing an objective memo or a persuasive brief, you must include both favorable and unfavorable facts. Attorneys lose credibility immediately when they omit facts that don't paint their client in the best light. Instead of shying away from unfavorable facts, you'll learn in section 12.4 below how to shape them and put them in a context that supports your client.

And, of course, for objective memos, it's especially important that you include all the significantly relevant facts—warts and all. The readers—who are often decisionmakers—need to make a decision about the case based on your analysis alone, so it needs to be real, accurate, and honest.

2. Include missing facts.

Yes, that probably sounds a bit odd: how can you include something that doesn't exist? But you can point out and should point out if there are no facts or thin facts relating to an element of law. Come right out and state what additional facts you need to thoroughly complete the story.

3. Avoid legal conclusions.

Do not be argumentative in your storytelling. It doesn't matter what type of document you're writing: do not state legal conclusions or arguments in your Statement of Facts. You aren't making arguments here—you are simply telling the reader what happened. Save your arguments for the Application sections.

For example, do not write: Their relationship ended when the divorce decree was entered. Write instead: The court entered the divorce decree on May 15, 2022. Stay objective.

If you have any words of the law in the Statement of Facts, you have veered from storytelling into the reasoning lane. Stay in your lane while storytelling.

4. Cite sources when needed.

In objective memorandums that are meant to stay within a firm, you generally do not need to cite a source for each fact.

In persuasive documents that you send to a court and other attorneys, you must cite a source for every fact. That means that nearly every sentence in the Statement of Facts will have a citation in it. Section 17.7 explains how to cite factual sources.

B. Context

1. Start with context.

The first paragraph, maybe even the first sentence, of any Statement of Facts must set the stage with (1) the area of law, (2) a broad issue hint, and (3) the main parties.

Here's an example from the Full Office Memo on page 44. The first two sentences introduce the area of law, the issue, and the parties:

> Plaintiff Chloe Peters sued Guss Giles for retaliation in relation to a sexual harassment complaint. Peters was employed at DORA Oil and Gas Exploration, LLC.

So the area of law is employment and discrimination law. The issue is whether Giles sexually harassed Peters. And we've been introduced to the main characters. All that in two sentences. Well done.

And here's an example from the Trial-Court Brief on page 66:

> This case arises from an incident where Troy Trout alleges that he slipped and fell on black ice outside the premises of Buffalo Wild Wings Grill & Bar.

In one brief, efficient sentence, the writer states the general issue (premises liability), the area of law (property, tort), and the main players.

In both of the examples above, they give broad contextual information that sets the stage for the rest of the story.

2. Give context for each fact along the way.

Then, after setting the stage, give context as the story unwinds at any plot point that requires it. But always balance including just enough contextual information with swamping the reader with too much detail.

These background facts are necessary to help the reader understand the legal story. Taking the battery example from above a bit further, whether the fight occurred in a church during a sermon, at a bar at 1 a.m., or during fireworks at a Fourth of July celebration will help the reader understand the situation. These contextual facts may not be directly significantly related to the issue of intent, but they will help the reader understand the story. So include just enough contextual information so the reader can understand the story.

You'll find that transactional issues often require less chronological storytelling and more contextual information. That's just the nature of the beast. But tort or criminal issues, on the other hand, favor more storytelling with significantly relevant facts and less contextual information.

3. Consider beginning with a separate Overview section.

Where you have a longer set of complex facts, more than two pages, you may want to consider writing an Overview section. This is where you begin the Statement of Facts with a heading (Overview) and then give a brief overview of the facts where you introduce the parties and legal story. Here's an example of that:

Statement of Facts

A. Overview

This case concerns Mitten Oil & Gas, Inc.'s release of oil from its well into groundwater without a permit. The groundwater accumulated in an aquifer, which then released oil-tainted groundwater through a spring and into the Black River. It is undisputed that the Black River is a "navigable water" that was used for many recreational purposes, such as kayaking and fishing, before the spill.

Following the spill, the Conservation Club sued Mitten Oil, alleging that it discharged a pollutant into "navigable waters" without the permit required under § 402 of the Act. Mitten Oil has moved for summary judgment under Rule 56, arguing that groundwater *itself* is not a "navigable water," and thus not subject to the Act. The Conservation Club now opposes that motion.

B. Mitten Oil & Gas's spilled oil pollutes the navigable Black River

Lee Adams was fly fishing for trout in the Black River last spring when he looked down and saw what appeared to be an oil film covering the river's surface....

This Overview did a great job of establishing context with (1) the area of law, (2) a broad issue hint, and (3) the main parties. Happy reader.

C. Organization

Readers most appreciate a story told in chronological order, but there may be times to organize the facts by topic or by people's perception.

Whatever you do, don't organize your Statement of Facts by document, piece of evidence, or witness. Organize it as a cohesive story that develops characters, explains the conflict, and resolves the conflict.

1. Chronologically organize the facts.

After you set up the story with a contextual introduction, tell the story in chronological order. You're telling a story, so tell it in logical order (usually chronological order). Do not change the facts. Do not assume anything.

Use signposts along the way to signal the chronology: Later, ..., After ..., Then, ..., While ..., Since .... That will cut down on confusion and keep your story coherent.

2. Consider topical organization for transactional issues.

You should prefer to write the facts chronologically; however, sometimes, especially with transactional issues, it may make sense to organize the facts by topic. Perhaps the transactional matter occurred in three stages of negotiation, drafting, and review, so you'd use these three topics to organize and give structure to the story.

If your Statement of Facts is more involved, like something more than two pages long, you should add topical point headings. Topical point headings are usually phrases instead of complete sentences like you see in briefs' persuasive point headings. Here are some topical point headings to give you an idea of how they can be used to guide the reader:

- Overview
- Negotiating the Contract
- Drafting the Contract
- Reviewing the Contract

3. Sometimes organize the facts by perspective.

You should tell a story from different perspectives only when parties disagree on the facts. Tell the story chronologically for the most part, but on the parts of the story the parties disagree about, tell it from each party's perspective. Then get right back to telling the next event in the timeline.

D. Readability

Your story must be enjoyable to read. Obviously, writing with proper punctuation and grammar is essential to high readability. Beyond that, consider these four tips to make reading your Statement of Facts enjoyable:

1. Obsess over sentence-to-sentence flow.

Writers use transition words and phrases to signal how ideas relate to each other. This makes it easier for readers to follow and understand the story. You can use transition words or phrases to:

- show timing or sequence (Later, More recently, Next)
- show that you're adding to a previous idea (And, Also, Additionally)
- show consistency with or similarity to a previous idea (Similarly, Likewise)
- show contrast with—or an exception to—a previous idea (But, However, Yet)
- reinforce or clarify a previous idea (Again, Indeed, In other words)
- signal a conclusion or a logical reaction/effect (Therefore, Thus, So)

You can learn more about this and see examples in the Readability section of Chapter 18 Revise and Edit, 18.6(B).

2. Use lots of paragraphs.

Paragraphs are crucial to giving the reader a break. If we don't provide a break to our readers, they'll give themselves one by skimming—especially if all they see are dense walls of text. Avoid textual monoliths by using several paragraph breaks on a page. Try for a minimum of three paragraphs per page to keep the reader going.

Besides, having several paragraph breaks creates more spots of emphasis on the page: the topic sentence of a paragraph is a place to shout about an important fact.

3. Use names, not labels.

You should use the names of the people in your case. So you wouldn't use labels like *plaintiff* or *customer* like you would when explaining caselaw in a Case Illustration. Yes, explain what each character's role is in the story, but consistently use their names throughout.

After stating a person's first and last name, you may then refer to that person by just their last name. And, if the context is right, you may refer to them by their first name, though be careful not to be accused of being overly personal with the parties.

This is proper:

> Hamish Abdullah won the lottery on March 8, 2024 .... Abdullah spent half the winnings on charity and put the other half in savings.

This is unnecessarily obvious:

> Hamish Abdullah (Abdullah) won the lottery on March 8, 2024 .... Abdullah spent half the winnings on charity and put the other half in savings.

So don't add a parenthetical shorthand reference when it's not needed.

For businesses, use the full name the first time, but you may use a shorthand reference after that, like this:

> TechnoWatch, Inc. employed Sam Spivey for five years .... But TechnoWatch is known for litigating their noncompete agreements.

You should include a parenthetical with a shorthand reference that you intend to use going forward only if *not* including it would be confusing. Above, you do not need to add *(TechnoWatch)* after the first mention of the company because there's hardly any difference between the two uses. But with a longer, more complicated name or with two closely related company names, you may need to add a shorthand reference:

> Thomson Reuters Corporation (Thomson) is based in Toronto, Ontario, Canada .... Thomson allegedly helped the U.S. government deport thousands of people illegally living in the United States ....

But, again, do that only when the name is long or to avoid confusion with similar names.

4. Consider using headings.

Even if you're not using topical organization, a set of descriptive headings can help the reader make sense of the story, especially when the Statement of Facts is longer than two pages. Emphasize major plot points in the story by creating a descriptive heading for each one. In the Appellate-Court Brief on pages 92 to 95, you can see an example of this. Notice how the headings alone help tell the story by emphasizing major plot points:

Statement of Facts

A. The Detroit Water-Plant Project

...

B. The July 2, 2020, Loss

...

C. Detroit Water's Claim for Liability Coverage

...

For different levels of headings, use the formatting rules explained in 5.4(G).

12.3 The Process of Writing the Story

Now you're going to see the process of putting the story's content, context, organization, and readability—what you learned about in 12.2—together using the case below. Invest a bit of time to understand the case, and then observe how an attorney puts together a Statement of Facts.

For this case, imagine that you work as general counsel for TechnoWatch, a company that reviews and rates new technologies. You need to determine if a new hire's noncompete agreement with a former employer, TechBeat, is valid. The new hire is Sam Spivey.

New employees sign noncompetes, and they basically say that when they leave the company that they're not going to compete against the company in a certain geographic area for a certain period of time. TechnoWatch competes with TechBeat, so violating the noncompete agreement could expose TechnoWatch and Sam Spivey to liability.

A. Understand the Elements at Issue

The first step to piecing the story together is to understand the elements of law at issue; those facts that directly relate to the elements of law will be the backbone of your Statement of Facts. No, the elements themselves don't actually appear anywhere in the story, but the elements tell you what facts are significantly relevant.

The controlling rule in our case is that a noncompete agreement will be valid only if it's "reasonable as to its duration, geographical area, and the type of employment or line of business." Mich. Comp. Laws Ann. § 445.774(a) (West 2024). Because of this rule, we must include facts relating to the length of time during which Spivey is not allowed to compete with his former employer, the geographic area of the limitation on competition, the type of business Spivey engaged in while at TechBeat, and what he'd do while at TechnoWatch. Now, keep in mind that the reader likely won't know the rule of law when they read the Statement of Facts, but as the writer, you need to understand the elements so you know what facts to include.

B. Cull the Facts from All the Sources

A client's story is often in many places: their own narrative, receipts, medical records, autopsy report, police report, evidentiary hearing transcript, interrogatories, emails, text messages, security-camera footage, and on and on.

Your job at this point is to weave a narrative from the various sources. Take one document at a time and include in your Statement of Facts the significantly relevant information that develops the characters, explains the conflict, and resolves the conflict. As you turn to a new document, figure out where it fits in the timeline, and then insert those facts into the right place.

Charting the information in a table or spreadsheet will help to make sense of it as you're reading it. Here's a sample chart for our TechnoWatch problem:

Source	Facts	Element of Law
Spivey's Employment Interview (You personally attended.)	• TechBeat's website reviews new tech • TechBeat's website averages 210,000 monthly page views • Total social-media engagements: 340,000 per month • TechBeat earns small amount of money from advertisers for every 1,000 page views • Spivey appeared on *Street Signs* and *Business Live* 28 times and has been on 3 times since leaving TechBeat • Spivey gained modest following while at *Detroit Free Press* • Spivey became very popular while at TechBeat with more than 120,000 X followers	• Type of employment • Geographic limitation (internet is without borders)
Spivey's Résumé	• Spivey interned at CNET from May 15 to August 5, 2015 • Spivey worked at *Novi Note*, a local newspaper, from April 18, 2016 to January 20, 2017 • Spivey worked at *Detroit Free Press* from January 25, 2017, to April 10, 2018 • Spivey worked at TechBeat from April 13, 2018, until October 18, 2024 • Spivey freelanced from October 18, 2023, to present, February 18, 2025	• Type of employment
Phone conversation with Spivey after TechnoWatch decision to hire him	• TechBeat required employees to have X and Instagram accounts, pushed users to TechBeat's website • Spivey currently has 140,000 X followers • Three of TechBeat's employees work remotely in other states	• Type of employment • Geographic limitation
Noncompete agreement	• Section A: "Employee, upon leaving employment, may not engage in any act that competes with TechBeat within 50 miles of TechBeat's headquarters in Ann Arbor, Michigan, for one year." • Section B: "Employee, upon leaving employment, may not solicit or induce any individual or client in an attempt to enter into any business relationship if it is competitive with any aspect of TechBeat's business for one year."	• Type of employment • Geographic limitation • Duration limitation

From that spreadsheet of information, which is organized by source and element of law, construct a chronological timeline of significant plot points. Use those plot points to organize your first draft. A timeline could be as simple as this:

2018: Sam signed noncompete agreement with TechBeat.	2018–2023: Sam worked for TechBeat for five years.	2023: Sam quit job and does freelance work.	2024: After 6 months, TechnoWatch tries to hire Sam.

C. Write the First Draft

Working from your chart, start to weave together the first draft of your Statement of Facts. Start with a brief sentence that lays out important contextual information. Then tell the story chronologically and briefly give contextual information as you go.

If you need to cite sources, now is the best time to throw in rough citations so you don't have to find them all later and go through the whole process again.

D. Revise the Draft

Revise the first draft for content, context, organization, and readability. See 12.2. Do as many revisions as you need to make reading it an informative and enjoyable experience.

E. Polish the Final Draft

Conclude by polishing the draft for grammar, punctation, sentence-to-sentence flow, and citation format. Chapter 18, Revise and Edit, may be a good reference.

With our TechnoWatch scenario, steps (A) through (E) above culminated in the Statement of Facts below. You can see how the writer went from the information in the chart above to this narrative. The margin annotations explain its content, context, organization, and readability.

Statement of Facts

This employment case is about whether Sam Spivey's proposed new employment at TechnoWatch, Inc. would violate his noncompete agreement with his former employer, TechBeat, LLC. Sam Spivey is a content creator who reviews new technologies. He posts his content on social-media sites like X and Instagram. TechBeat employed Spivey from April 2018 until October 2023 when he voluntarily left to become a freelance reviewer. TechnoWatch now in February 2024 wants to hire Spivey, but it's concerned that doing so may expose it to liability because Spivey signed a noncompete agreement with TechBeat.

> The story opens with broad **context**: *employment*, three main characters, and *noncompete agreement*.

> After a bit of context, the **content** in chronological order begins in earnest. The content is significantly relevant to the elements of law.

> This opening paragraph culminates with **context** about why this story matters.

The noncompete agreement with TechBeat contains two relevant clauses. Section A is titled "Covenant Not to Compete," and it prohibits Spivey from engaging in any aspect of TechBeat's business within a fifty mile radius of TechBeat for one year after leaving its employ. Under Section B, which is titled "Non-Solicitation Covenant," Spivey agreed that for one year after his employment with TechBeat he would not "solicit or induce any individual... in an attempt to enter into any business relationship if it is competitive with

> The story slows down a bit here to offer vital **context**, but that context is **significantly relevant to the elements** for a valid noncompete agreement.

> Even though this is a transactional issue, the **content** of the story is still **organized** chronologically: Spivey signed the non-compete soon after being hired at TechBeat. And these facts are very relevant to the legal story because most of the analysis will focus on whether this is "reasonable."

This detailed **content** may seem unnecessary, but these facts are used in the Application later in the document.

any aspect of TechBeat's business." This section contained no limitation on geographical scope.

TechBeat runs a news-and-reviews website, and their main office is physically located in Ann Arbor, Michigan, though they do have some employees who work remotely. Their website averages 210,000 page views per month, and their official social-media accounts, including their employees' accounts, average 340,000 single engagements per month.

Note how the writer makes the paragraphs **readable**. Each sentence flows to the next because they are connected using signposts, pronouns, and repeated information.

Most of TechBeat's income derives from advertisements that are sold on its website. The advertisers pay for ad inventory on TechBeat's website for every 1,000 views that its website generates. And it also generates income from its technology reviewers. They require all employees to maintain at least an X account and an Instagram account that are branded with TechBeat marketing, and they also require its employees to regularly post to the company's Facebook page. The strategy is that all the social media accounts, both the employees' and the official ones, drive business to TechBeat's website so it can generate page views.

The story continues with specific **context,** just enough to help the reader understand the story.

After a brief pause for context, the chronological story picks back up by relating more **facts** that are **directly related to the elements of law**.

While employed at TechBeat, Spivey created written and video content. Posts of just text to X or Instagram were not generally reviewed unless the posts were extraordinarily long, or they involved video. TechBeat had a team that reviewed all videos to check for accuracy and consistent messaging and brand. Before Spivey left, he had about 120,000 X followers. His high number of followers equaled the combined total of all other employees' X followers. Spivey sent about 20,000 Tweets while at TechBeat, and roughly 30% of Spivey's posts were personal in nature.

Adding **signposts** about time, like *during*, increases **readability** by helping the reader understand the **chronology**.

During his five years of employment with TechBeat, Spivey appeared on CNBC's *Street Signs* and Fox News Channel's *Business Live* 28 times. His appearances on these news programs continued after his departure from TechBeat.

Adding **signposts** about time, like *after*, help the reader understand the **chronology.**

Spivey continued to maintain his X account after he left TechBeat by changing the prefix of his X username. This allowed all of his X followers to automatically continue following his posts as a freelance reviewer. After his departure, Spivey's X followers increased to 145,000.

If every story has a beginning, a middle, and an end, this is the end of the **chronological** story.

TechnoWatch would now like to hire Spivey.

There you have it. Put a story together by first understanding the elements; second, culling the facts from several sources; third, writing the first draft; and then, fourth, polishing the final draft. All the while, you're mindful of content, context, organization, and readability.

That's what an objective Statement of Facts would look like. In 12.4, you'll learn how to convert that into a persuasive story.

12.4 Making a Story Persuasive

We're mainly talking about court briefs here, but this would also apply to demand letters and oral arguments—anywhere you need to tell a story to persuade. Court briefs always require a separate section where you tell the story that relates to the brief's issues. This differs from objective memos because the court is the primary audience instead of other lawyers in the firm or your client. And the goal is to persuade the court to give you what your client needs.

You can see what a persuasive Statement of Facts looks like in three different briefs on pages 60, 79, and 92 in Chapter 2. There's also an example below.

A. Why We Tell Stories in a Brief

You may wonder why you're learning about storytelling in law school. Here's why:

> Story is the strongest non-violent persuasive method we know. Tell me facts and maybe I will hear a few of them. Tell me an argument and I might consider it. Tell me a story and I am yours. That is why every persuasive enterprise from the Bible to television commercials relies on story.[1]

Did you catch the "non-violent" part? I doubt a judge would appreciate a violent overture, but they would enjoy a good story told well. And you just might end up changing the judge's mind if they're initially opposed to your request.

B. Use Six Techniques of Persuasion

Before you can apply the six persuasion techniques, you need to make sure you already have a grasp on context, context, organization, and readability—what you learned about in 12.2. Keep doing all of those great things while building your persuasive Statement of Facts. But, in addition to those things, apply the attorney's artistic touch of persuasion.

The craft of persuading through storytelling requires a lot of effort, but it will become easier with practice. Consider drafting your Statement of Facts using six persuasion techniques. And you may even want to think about and apply each technique in different stages; trying to think about all six at the same time is really difficult.

Without further ado, here are the techniques for adding a subtle gloss of persuasion to your storytelling:

(1) Theme
(2) First impression
(3) Character, conflict, and resolution
(4) Airtime
(5) Placement
(6) Ethos, logos, and pathos

1. David Ball, *Theater Tips and Strategies for Jury Trial* 66 (1994).

1. Weave in the case's broad theme.

At this point, you have the story down on paper. Now it's time to turn it into a persuasive tool. We start with theme. Weave the case's theme throughout the Statement of Facts.

As you review your first draft of the Statement of Facts, ask whether a judge could see the connection among all the substantive parts of your brief like the Question Presented, Introduction, and Argument section—whatever parts your particular court requires. The theme is the thing that cohesively connects these parts and focuses your arguments.

Decide what your major theme is for the brief. Then subtly work that theme into the Question Presented, Introduction, Analysis Preview, each argument point heading, each argument, argument proof, and the Conclusion. Note that it must be *subtly reflected*, not that it necessarily must be repeated verbatim in all of those sections. Sometimes subtlety is more impactful than overt statements.

Of course, we all know the *most* famous theme of all time: "If the glove doesn't fit . . . ." I bet you could finish that one! (If not, it's "If the glove doesn't fit, you must acquit.") That case theme is more than 30 years old, yet many still remember it.

Here are a couple of themes the author has used successfully:

> Sanders could not have breached a fiduciary duty to an investor because he was **frozen out of the business.** Because of this, he didn't have access to the financial records or the bank account.
>
> **No good deed goes unpunished**. Ms. Richter is a do-gooder that took care of her niece. Her niece stole Ms. Richter's identity and ran up the credit cards. We shouldn't punish Ms. Richter for her good deeds. So we ask this Court to order Chase, Inc. to release her from this obligation.

The theme must relate to the main element or rule implicated in the case. In a case about the Confrontation Clause, for example, the judge's decision may hang on whether there was an ongoing emergency. So you'd want to come up with a theme that goes to whether there was an ongoing emergency. In other words, first figure out what element or rule is primarily at issue. Then come up with a general theme that lines up with that element and leans toward the resolution you're seeking.

Here are a few typical topics for case themes:

Clear Legal Standard:

> This case is about the fundamental right to enforce a clear contractual promise—a right that cannot be undermined by vague assertions or unsubstantiated defenses.

This emphasizes that the opposing party's arguments fail because they do not align with established law or clear contract terms.

Fairness and Justice:

> At its core, this case presents a simple question: Will the Court allow one party to benefit from a contract while simultaneously denying the other the protections that contract affords?

This frames the case as one about fairness and mutual obligations, appealing to the court's sense of equity.

Accountability:

> The issue before this Court is not just about a technical breach—it is about holding parties accountable when they seek to avoid responsibility for their wrongful conduct.

Casting the opposing party's behavior as evasive or irresponsible compels the court to enforce accountability.

Public Policy:

> If this Court accepts the Defendant's argument, it would set a dangerous precedent, allowing parties to evade liability through loopholes, contrary to the principles of fairness and the protection of consumer rights.

Suggests a broader implication to the court's decision focuses on public policy and future consequences.

Narrative of Harm:

> This case is about a promise broken, trust betrayed, and harm inflicted—harm that this Court has the power to remedy by enforcing the law as written.

This highlights the emotional or practical consequences of the opposing party's actions, making the issue resonate beyond abstract legal doctrine.

Simplifying a Complex Case:

> While the legal issues in this case may appear complex, the underlying truth is straightforward: Defendant promised one thing but delivered another, and Plaintiff is entitled to the benefit of that bargain.

Cutting through all the fog can help a judge do their job; however, be careful not to minimize the importance of the judicial system by saying the outcome "is clear."

Unsavory Client Proxy for Heroic Virtue:

> Infringing one person's Fourth Amendment right weakens everyone's Fourth Amendment right, so we urge this Court to suppress this evidence for the good of all.

Oftentimes, it's difficult to make your client likeable because some unsavory facts are simply unescapable. No theme will make that client likeable. You can, however, make an unsavory client a proxy for a heroic virtue or dearly held belief.[2] The concepts, for example, in the Fourth Amendment about protecting privacy and not allowing the government to search our belongings willy-nilly are concepts that most Americans hold dear. So in a situation where you're trying to suppress evidence that would allow a known murderer to go scot-free, focus on the good to the greater society.

2. Create a good first impression.

The theme is something you can weave in all parts of a persuasive brief. Now let's focus on just the Statement of Facts. In particular, look at the first paragraph of your Statement of Facts—one of the few places you're assured to have the reader's focused, undivided attention.

2. Brian J. Foley and Ruth Anne Robbins, *Fiction 101: A Primer for Lawyers on How to Use Fiction Writing Techniques to Write Persuasive Facts Sections*, 32 Rutgers L. J. 459, 471 (2001).

Do not begin with character introductions. The excellent advocate John Bursch demonstrated this when he wrote this example of how not to begin a Statement of Facts:

> The parties in this action are Plaintiff/Appellant Automotive Industry Supplier, Inc. ("Automotive Supplier") and Defendant/Appellee Independent Spring Manufacturer Corporation ("Spring Manufacturer"). Spring Manufacturer is a supplier of spring components for the automotive industry. Automotive Supplier purchased springs sold by Spring Manufacturer and incorporated them into parts that it sold to Automotive Producer, Inc. ("Automotive Producer"). The springs failed, and, following a recall, Automotive Supplier brought this lawsuit against Spring Manufacturer, claiming breach of warranty, among other things.[3]

Cue the warm blanket, fuzzy socks, and recliner because your reader is now out for the count. If not entirely asleep, then they're bored and perhaps a bit confused by all the moving parts.

Instead, begin the Statement of Facts like this:

> This is a case of commercial betrayal that illustrates the wisdom of the Uniform Commercial Code's notice provision in Section 2-607. Appellant Automotive Supplier is seeking in this action to recover over $10 million from a supplier of about $50,000 worth of springs used in Automotive Producer vehicles. Automotive Supplier is pressing its claim even though it has never asserted—even in this litigation—that Spring Manufacturer defectively manufactured the parts.
>
> To the contrary, all parties agreed that the root cause of the problem with the springs was not some manufacturing mistake made by Spring Manufacturer, but a design change that Automotive Producer directed. Automotive Supplier never once suggested that Spring Manufacturer was responsible for this design change until filing this lawsuit, five years after the problem was discovered and nearly six years since the time of sale.[4]

This better example starts with a memorable theme and tells an engaging story as it develops the characters. Spend the rest of the Statement of Facts using the story to prove the theme. Don't actually repeat the theme, but use the facts to show the theme. Show, don't tell.[5]

3. *Develop characters, conflict, and resolution.*

The next focus for writing the Statement of Facts is to explain and shape characters, conflict, and resolution, the building blocks of storytelling.[6]

a. Character Development

When explaining the characters, be sure to include their needs and goals. This motivation will set up the second building block—the conflict. Conflict is when something prevents a character from reaching those goals.

Make your client as a character as likable as possible. If the most significantly relevant legal story doesn't make your client likeable, then consider adding some background facts to help the reader understand where your client is coming from. This requires getting to know your client

---

3. John Bursch, *Storytelling in Brief Writing*, Warner Norcross + Judd, https://www.wnj.com/Publications/Storytelling-in-Brief-Writing.

4. *Id.*

5. Something Bryan Garner preaches. Bryan Garner, *The Winning Brief*, Tip #89.

6. Foley and Robbins, *Fiction 101*, supra note 3, at 461.

and listening to them. "Lawyers should still dig up dirt, but they should be mindful of planting flowers about their own clients."[7]

Shape the narrative by filling in gaps around data points with permissible inferences. A character's needs, wants, and likeability may not be obvious from the naked data points. So attorneys make permissible inferences to fill in some of these gaps.

Below is a storyline with five objective data points. Think of a narrative that paints Sam in a good light. Pay attention to his needs, wants, and likeability.

Sam signed noncompete agreement with TechBeat.	Sam worked for TechBeat for five years.	Sam quit job and does freelance work.	After 6 months, TechnoWatch tries to hire Sam.	TechBeat claims this would violate noncompete agreement.

How do we make Sam likeable? How do we develop his motivations? If the narrative isn't controlled, a judge will look coldly at the noncompete agreement and come to a conclusion without regard for the human impact.

One possible narrative is that Sam is grateful for his time at TechBeat, but he was ready to move on, try something new after five years. He really thought he could make freelancing work, but it was too much of a struggle. So he's now ready to join TechnoWatch for something new and a steady income. (In other words, he didn't leave to directly compete against TechBeat.)

This makes Sam likeable because he's trying to do what's best for him, and he's been taken by the inspiring entrepreneurial spirit. That excitement is infectious. And it uses the conflict of person against Corporate America, which taps into the David-versus-Goliath pathos. So the reader almost wants to root for Sam.

Of course, any storyline we create with a client's character must be credible. It at least must pass the straight-face test: if you can't say it with a straight face in open court, then you'd better not write it in your brief's Statement of Facts.

b. Conflict

After explaining the characters, begin to explain the conflict, which is where a character can't get what they want or need.

Conflict is what drives the narrative. An interesting character can hold a reader's attention for only so long. But introduce a conflict, and things get really good.

Here's a list of typical conflicts in storytelling:

Person Against Person
Person Against Self
Person Against Nature
Person Against Society
Person Against Machine (Powerful Entity, Corporate America)
Person Against Principle
Person Against God
God Against Everybody

7. *Id.* at 469.

You can use these conflict themes in your brief writing. And, yes, there could be many overlapping and layered themes: the Quran and Bible, for example, contain a set of stories about Person Against God, Person Against Person, Person Against Self, Person Against Society, and God Against Everybody else—not just one type of conflict.

Think of a recent book or case you read. What kind of conflict was there? Or what was the conflict in a movie you loved?

In Marvel movies (you know, Black Panther, Ironman, Black Widow, Thor, or Loki), there's always the major theme of Person Against Machine or Person Against Person (a villain like Thanos). But there are always sub-themes like Person Against Self (Tony Stark fighting his demons) or Person Against Nature or Society (Doctor Strange fighting against time).

Sometimes, these sub-themes are better to highlight than the obvious themes. Here's your goal in a brief: "The knowledgeable advocate attempts to make the case bigger than the mere movement of money from one side of the room to the other. He tries to make his case stand for a principle that is important to the jurors, or rest on an emotional appeal that will move them."[8]

Which conflict theme you choose to go with in a brief should be carefully considered.

c. Resolution

"The key," for this third building block, "is for the judge to want to resolve the conflict in favor of your client; after all, it is the judge who writes the ending."[9] "In a lawsuit, the good person with the worthy goal should win."[10]

The resolution is something procedural: suppress evidence, dismiss the case, or change venue. But subtly explain the resolution as a solution to the conflict.

4. Adjust airtime for favorable and unfavorable facts.

At this point, you've cohered the facts around a theme and started with a favorable first impression. And the reader knows the characters, the conflict, and the resolution. The potential harm now is including too much detail or not enough detail.

Not all facts deserve the same level of detail—the same amount of airtime. Decide which relevant facts are the most favorable and give them more airtime (more detail) in the Statement of Facts and arguments. Contrariwise, decide which are the most unfavorable facts but include less detail. Plus, adjust their placement as explained in Step 6 below.

Should you leave out unsavory parts of the story because they make your client look bad? No way! If you do, the court will distrust you as soon as they read about those facts in the opposing brief. Instead, bring them up but surround them with a favorable context.

So shape the level of detail based on how favorable or unfavorable the facts are.

An example is in order. Start by reading two paragraphs from a Statement of Facts section. Imagine that you represent Rodent Relief, Inc., a manufacturer of rat poison. And the issue is whether your company's labels on rat poison bottles gave sufficient notice of their danger. With that in mind, read these two paragraphs and think about airtime:

---

8. *Id.* at 471.
9. *Id.* at 472.
10. *Id.*

Statement of Facts

Rodent Relief, Inc., is a Delaware corporation that manufactures and sells rat poison. Each of its products has a warning label that was approved by the Environmental Protection Agency. On May 23, 2009, Plaintiff purchased a package of Rodent Relief's "No More Rat" rat poison at her local ABC Hardware store. When she brought it home, she stored it in a cabinet under a utility sink.

A few days later, her two-year-old son, Josh, found the poison and ate some. He immediately began vomiting and showing signs of shock. Plaintiff called 9-1-1, and emergency personnel took Josh to Bigtown Hospital's emergency room. He was treated for acute poisoning and kept in the Pediatric Intensive Care Unit for three days. He was eventually released and has recovered fully.

Now here's the same two paragraphs but with notes about how to write it better:

Statement of Facts

Rodent Relief, Inc., is a Delaware corporation that manufactures and sells rat poison. Each of its products has a warning label that was approved by the Environmental Protection Agency. [**Slow down!**] On May 23, 2009, Plaintiff purchased a package of Rodent Relief's "No More Rat" rat poison at her local ABC Hardware store. [**Slow down!**] When she brought it home, she stored it in a cabinet under a utility sink.

A few days later, her two-year-old son, Josh, found the poison and ate some. [**Speed up!**] He immediately began vomiting and showing signs of shock. Plaintiff called 9-1-1, and *emergency personnel* took Josh to Bigtown Hospital's *emergency room*. He was treated for acute poisoning and kept in the Pediatric Intensive Care Unit for three days. He was eventually released and has recovered fully.

Give airtime to the most significantly relevant facts. Why state where your client is incorporated? It's irrelevant and worse: it reminds readers that your client, like many corporations, seeks advantageous laws by incorporating in Delaware. In other words, your client is now "just another corporation." Too many lawyers stick this type of thing in without thinking about its impact on readers.

The same is true for dates. Irrelevant dates distract readers, and they create red herrings. Readers will assume that your issue is time-sensitive and will resent you when they learn that it's not. Hey, don't forget who your client is. What's all this stuff about the child getting deathly ill—about this medical EMERGENCY—and going to the ER? How does that help your client? This writer slooooooowed down for the bad stuff. But we want to hit and run for the bad stuff. Slooooow down for the *good* stuff, like your client's compliance with the law and EPA approval.

And, finally, here is a much-improved version, one that subtly persuades the reader to agree with your overall theme. Compare this to the first example above:

Statement of Facts

Rodent Relief, Inc., manufactures and sells rat poison. Before it sells any new product, its Vice President, John Decker, submits the product's warning label to the Environmental Protection Agency for approval. Decker confirmed that he did so before Rodent Relief began selling its "No More Rat" product. The proposed label for No More Rat warned, in large, bold print, that swallowing the poison could be fatal and that the poison should be kept away from children:

Lots of **airtime** for the details about how conscientious your client is about following the law. The **theme** of proper labeling really stands out.

A one-sentence paragraph really emphasizes important information, giving it maximum airtime.

An even more effective technique of **airtime** is to let the opposing party lay out the detailed facts favorable to your case.

The writer gives much less **airtime** to the unfavorable facts about the actual injury. They're still included, but with less detail.

WARNING! Fatal if swallowed! KEEP AWAY FROM CHILDREN!

The label also bore a skull and crossbones.

The EPA reviewed and approved this label. Every package of No More Rat poison ever sold has had this EPA-approved warning label on it.

Jan Allred testified that she saw the warning label, including the skull and crossbones, when she looked over the No More Rat package at the hardware store before buying it. She said that she "assumed it could make a child sick but couldn't kill anyone." She explained that she thought the warning was "really just extra cautious to stop lawsuits—stuff lawyers wanted on there." She thought that "it would be okay under my utility sink with the cleaning stuff."

After Allred stored the poison beneath her sink, her two-year-old son, Josh, found it. He swallowed some of the poison and became ill. He was taken to the hospital, where he was treated and released after a few days. He has made a full recovery.

So give more airtime to favorable facts and less airtime to unfavorable facts.

5. Place favorable facts in prominent locations, and do the opposite for unfavorable facts.

Emphasize favorable facts by putting them in prominent positions in the Statement of Facts. Do these things to emphasize a favorable fact in prominent positions:

- Put the fact at the beginning of a paragraph.
- Put the fact at the end of a paragraph.
- Put the fact in a separate short paragraph.
- Put the fact in a separate one-sentence paragraph.
- Put the fact in a short sentence.
- Use active voice (actor goes before verb).
- Put the fact in the first few words of a sentence.

In contrast, do these things to de-emphasize an unfavorable fact:

- Surround an unfavorable fact with a favorable fact.
- Put the fact in a longer, more complex sentence.
- Use passive voice (actor omitted).
- Put the fact in a dependent clause.
- Put the fact in the middle of a paragraph.

Many of these techniques were used in the sample Statement of Facts above where the writer played up good facts and downplayed bad facts. Take another look at that example with an eye for placement of facts.

6. Use ethos, logos, and pathos to subtly persuade in the Statement of Facts.

Use *ethos* to persuade. Always be honest in telling the story; this includes how you characterize the facts, explain motivations, and infer from the facts. As explained above, include even unfavorable facts. You'll lose credibility by painting a rosy picture that is easily shattered by reading opposing counsel's brief. Readers also judge your credibility from your writing ability. At the very least, use proper punctuation and grammar.

Use *logos* to persuade by making sure that all the significantly relevant legal facts are included in the story. A simple cross check with the arguments should reveal whether the primary facts you're relying on in the arguments are also a part of the narrative in the Statement of Facts.

And don't shy away from using data and statistics in the Statement of Facts. Quantifying facts makes them more memorable, and they are more persuasive especially when you shape the quantification to help the judge feel that your proposed resolution is the best fit for the case. 10.5(G).

And, finally, weave *pathos* into the narrative. The briefest of facts will be emotional facts. Emotional facts are ones that evoke emotion in the reader. They may or may not be directly related to the issue. For instance, in a state where fault is not supposed to play a role in creating a divorce decree, a party may slip in that one party led a double life by concealing another family in a foreign country. In a no-fault divorce state, that is not legally relevant or significant, but it certainly will create a distaste for that party. That's an emotional fact.

But don't go overboard with emotional facts. As Scalia and Garner write, "It is reasonable to humanize your tort-plaintiff client by describing her as an 80-year-old widow. It goes over the top to emphasize that her deceased husband was a county judge."[11]

Other than highlighting parts of the story that evoke emotion, you can shape the use of emotion by weaving in inspired beliefs and using the client's point of view.

12.5 Example of a Persuasive Statement of Facts

Now we're going to take the six principles of writing persuasive facts from above and apply them to the objective Statement of Facts you read about in section 12.3. But the story has evolved. Back in section 12.3, we were in a scenario where you were in-house counsel for TechnoWatch, and you wrote an objective memo discussing our chances of being sued by TechBeat if we hired Sam Spivey. In the Statement of Facts, you focused on writing the significantly relevant facts chronologically and giving context all along the way. You also made sure to include the facts that related to the elements of issue: a noncompete agreement must be reasonable as to limitation of time, duration, and geographic area.

Fast forward a few months: TechnoWatch did indeed hire Sam Spivey based on your memo. Then, not surprisingly, TechBeat sued Sam and TechnoWatch. We're now writing a brief to the court to ask the court to dismiss the case because the noncompete agreement is unreasonable. That brief requires us to write a persuasive Statement of Facts.

So you take the Statement of Facts from the objective memo and transform it into a persuasive Statement of Facts. Maintain an air of objectivity, but also subtly persuade the court that your story proves that the noncompete is unreasonable. Of course, there's no mention of the law in the Statement of Facts. Instead, we let the story do the talking.

---

11. Antonin Scalia & Bryan Garner, *Making Your Case: The Art of Persuading Judges* 94 (West 2008).

A. The Thinking for the TechnoWatch Statement of Facts

Here's the thinking for the TechnoWatch case for the six persuasion techniques you just read about.

Theme

The theme needs to play to the law, and the law is that noncompete agreements are unreasonable if the limitations on duration and geography go too far given the type of business. Well, the type of business here is on the internet, so a physical geographic limitation doesn't make sense. Telling someone they can't do business within 50 miles is very different than saying they can't do their business anywhere on the Internet when that's the only way of doing business.

So the main theme here is that a geographical limitation on work doesn't make sense—is unreasonable—when the type of business is completely online. So we'll want to use words such as *Internet, global, worldwide, livelihood*, and *career* to weave the theme throughout the facts.

First Impression

We'll start the story at a place that sets the theme and makes Spivey look like a reasonable person who just wants to make a living.

Characters, Conflict, and Resolution

We'll develop Spivey's character as an interesting, successful tech reviewer who's excited about new possibilities.

And TechBeat will come off looking like a Goliath who cares more about money than individuals.

Airtime

We want to emphasize that the type of business involved is 100% Internet based, so we'll give extra detail about that. We also want to focus on Spivey as a likeable, self-made reviewer. If the reader can see that TechBeat didn't play a role in Spivey's success, that may help the reader "root" for Spivey.

Placement

We'll put the airtime facts about TechBeat's trying to end Spivey's online livelihood in prominent locations like at the beginning of a paragraph and in short sentences and paragraphs. And unfavorable facts, like the fact that Spivey's social-media followers gained while at TechBeat continued to follow Spivey after he left, we'll downplay in the middle of a paragraph.

Ethos, Logos, and Pathos

We'll maintain credibility by not taking any of the characterizations too far, and we'll maintain an air of objectivity.

We'll use logos in the form of data and statistics to tell a lot of the story, but we'll quantify facts to shape the narratives laid out above.

As for pathos, the narrative of David-versus-Goliath will hopefully evoke some emotion in our reader. We need to be careful we don't use emotion too much because judges will see right through that.

B. The Thinking Applied to the Persuasive Statement of Facts

The annotations below point out how we applied those persuasion techniques. One way to really see the persuasive elements is to compare this version of the story to the objective Statement of Facts in 12.3. One final note: A Statement of Facts in a brief must have citations to the sources. This example omits them so you can focus on just the story. Enjoy.

Statement of Facts

The story opens with the **theme**: global Internet businesses are trying to deprive the little guy of a livelihood.

This employment case is about whether a noncompete agreement for a global Internet business may deprive a former employee of their online livelihood. Sam Spivey reviews new technologies and posts his reviews to blogs, websites, and social media. That's what he did before joining TechBeat and what he did while at TechBeat from April 2018 to October 2023.

After the theme, the writer gives **context** with the main **characters**. And it establishes the **conflict**: David versus Goliath.

Note the prominent **placement** of favorable facts early in the paragraph and early in the Statement of Facts.

In 2023, Spivey left TechBeat because he wanted to take his career in a new direction. As a freelance reviewer, he tried innovative ways of connecting with people interested in tech. After six months of freelancing, he then joined TechnoWatch where he can both be more innovative but also rely on a steady income. TechBeat then sued to stop Spivey from doing any technology reviews.

The **theme** of this story is David versus Goliath. Spivey has always been a tech reviewer, but now Big Corp wants to stop him.

When Spivey started working for TechBeat in 2018, he signed an employment agreement. Two clauses are relevant today. Section A prohibits former employees from engaging in any aspect of TechBeat's global internet business within a fifty mile radius of Ann Arbor, Michigan, for one year after leaving its employ. Under Section B, former employees may not solicit anyone anywhere in the world to compete with TechBeat's online technology reviews.

This is an example of giving less **airtime** to unfavorable facts. The writer omits the clause heading "Covenant Not to Compete." Yes, the substance of the agreement is here to maintain credibility and not hide any significantly relevant details, but there's less detail about it.

This unfavorable information, the actual noncompete agreement, is explained in an honest way, but one that emphasizes the unreasonable aspects: an Internet business is global, so prohibiting someone from doing it effectively destroys their career. This is using **airtime** and **placement** to shape the facts.

This paragraph continues the **theme** of Tech-Beat being Goliath with lots of **airtime** for the company's size.

TechBeat runs a news-and-reviews website, and their main office is physically located in Ann Arbor, Michigan, though they do have some employees who work remotely. Their website averages 210,000 page views per month, and their official social-media accounts, including their many employees' accounts, average 340,000 single engagements per month.

This detailed **content** maintains objectivity by simply explaining what Tech-Beat does.

TechBeat makes money by sending customers to its website. Advertisers pay for ad inventory on TechBeat's website for every 1,000 views that its website generates. Its contingency of technology reviewers post tech reviews on the website. And they all post heavily to social media with the goal of sending customers to the flagship website to generate page views. They require all employees to maintain at least an X account and an Instagram account that are branded with TechBeat marketing, and they also require its employees to regularly post to the company's Facebook page.

This paragraph continues the theme by making the corporation all about money; this contrasts Spivey's narrative of the little guy just trying to do what he loves.

While at TechBeat, one-third of Spivey's social-media posts on his business accounts were personal. His post about his animals and love of being outdoors received thousands of engagements from viewers all around the world. The 120,000 X followers Spivey gained while at TechBeat continued to follow him after he left, but he also quickly gained 25,000 more in the few months of freelancing.

Note the strategic **placement** of favorable information. Most of Spivey's appeal was his personality, not the fact that he worked for TechBeat. In fact, he became more popular after leaving.

Note how the focus on worldwide followers supports the **theme** of the Internet being a global tool, so limiting Spivey's use of it destroys his livelihood.

During his five years of employment with TechBeat, Spivey appeared on CNBC's *Street Signs* and Fox News Channel's *Business Live* numerous times.

His appearances on these worldwide news programs continued after his departure from TechBeat.

The Statement of Facts ends with a brief procedural statement about the litigation.

TechBeat now claims that Spivey violated the noncompete agreement when he was freelancing and now while employed at TechnoWatch.

12.6 Citing Sources in the Statement of Facts

In persuasive documents like court briefs, cite a source after every sentence with a new fact in it. But once you cite a source for that fact, you don't need to cite it again anywhere else in the document.

Citing a source for each new fact in the Statement of Facts is crucial for establishing credibility and reinforcing the strength of your argument. Courts rely on attorneys to provide accurate, verifiable information, and by citing a source for every factual assertion, you demonstrate that your account is based on evidence rather than conjecture. This builds trust with the court, showing that the facts you present are not only reliable but also backed by the record or other authoritative sources, which helps frame your argument as well-founded and legally sound.

Additionally, citing sources strengthens your position by preemptively addressing any challenges to the accuracy of your facts. Opposing counsel is likely to scrutinize your Statement of Facts and may attempt to undermine your argument by disputing the truthfulness or relevance of key details. By meticulously citing your sources, you make it difficult for the opposition to argue against the validity of your factual assertions. This also helps avoid credibility issues, ensuring that the court focuses on the merits of your legal arguments rather than questioning the foundation of your case.

You can see examples of citing sources in the three briefs in Chapter 2.

And section 17.7, Citing Sources in the Statement of Facts, goes into great detail about creating correct citations.

12.7 Checklist for Telling a Legal Story

Content

In your Statement of Facts, did you:

___ include the most legally significant facts?

___ put into the narrative all the facts you use in the application-of-law sections later in the document?

___ write about even unfavorable facts?

___ for persuasive documents like court briefs, cite a source for every fact?

Context

In your Statement of Facts, did you:

___ begin with contextual information that introduces the parties and the broad issue?

___ give contextual, background information along the way as needed for the reader to understand the story?

Organization

When organizing your Statement of Facts, did you:

___ prefer to generally organize the facts chronologically?

___ where appropriate, organize the facts by each character's perception (i.e., where characters disagree on the facts)?

___ avoid organizing the facts according to which document you got them from?

Readability

To make the Statement of Facts enjoyable to read, did you:

___ consider using headings for longer, more complex factual statements?

___ use lots of paragraphs, averaging three to five per page?

___ use actual names instead of role designations like *plaintiff* or *customer*?

___ connect the sentences for smooth flow?

___ revise and edit your Statement of Facts multiple times?

Persuasive Facts

If your document is persuasive in nature, did you use the six recommended persuasion techniques?

Did you:

___ subtly hint at a *theme* throughout the facts?

___ create a good *first impression* in the opening sentence or paragraph?

___ develop the main characters, explain the conflict, and resolve it?

___ give more or less *airtime* to favorable and unfavorable facts?

___ use *placement* by putting favorable facts in more prominent places (i.e., topic sentences) and unfavorable facts in less obvious places (i.e., the middle of a paragraph)?

___ use ethos (maintain credibility), logos (data, facts, and stats), and pathos (emotion) to subtly persuade your reader?

Citations

In your brief's Statement of Facts (not usually in objective documents), did you:

___ cite a source after every new fact?

___ format the citations according to your professor's recommended citation manual (also explained in 17.7)?

PART FOUR

Document Orientation Skills

Readers are mainly interested in reading your analysis of the issue, the rules, the caselaw, how it all applies, and the conclusion, you know, IREAC. But readers also need to see the big picture of the document, and that's what document-orientation skills do.

Chapter 13, Title the Document, focuses on accurately titling documents so readers understand the document's purpose.

Chapter 14, Caption the Document, covers how to properly begin legal documents with a caption.

Chapter 15, Use Document Headings, ratches up the magnification by looking at document headings, which create sections within a document.

And, finally, Chapter 16, Preview the Analysis, teaches the art of succinctly summarizing the IREAC analysis packets in a paragraph or two.

Chapter Thirteen

Title the Document

13.1 The Skill

A reader should—at a glance—determine what the document is. So much of what we do in documents as attorney-writers is to quickly give the reader the information they need. We do this because our readers, who are often attorneys, are some of the busiest professionals around. For heaven's sake, they usually bill in six-minute increments, so we build in as many efficiencies as possible.

Titling the document is one such efficiency.

13.2 Title Formatting

Most of the time, format titles in your legal documents using "title capitalization."

Title capitalization is where the main words are capitalized, and the other words are not. According to *The Redbook: A Manual on Legal Style*, do not capitalize (1) an article (e.g., *a*, *an*, *the*); (2) a conjunction or preposition shorter than five letters (e.g., *and*, *of*, *for*); or (3) the word *to* (e.g., Motion to Dismiss). See § 2.10 in *The Redbook* for more examples.

13.3 Opinion Letters and eMemos

When writing an opinion letter or eMemo, find a natural place to title the document. For letters, this often occurs in the subject line after the address and before the salutation. For eMemos written in the body of an email, write the title in the subject line.

The subject line of an opinion letter or eMemo should succinctly describe the legal issue or question being addressed. It should include the topic, the relevant parties, or the specific transaction, and, if applicable, clearly indicate that the document is an opinion. If it's not an opinion, then give the gist of what you seek. Here are some examples of how the subject line might be written:

Opinion on Enforceability of Contract Between ABC Corp. and Clothing Ltd.

Opinion on Liability in Slip-and-Fall Incident at 123 Elm Street

Intellectual Property Rights in Patent Application No. 123456; Pendletons, Inc.

Opinion on Compliance with Environmental Regulations for Hades Project

Validity of Noncompete Clause in Employment Agreement; Spivey v. TechBeat

The key is to make sure the subject line clearly states the legal issue, is specific to the matter, and reflects the objective or persuasive nature of the document.

Edit the title for these factors:

- **Conciseness**: The subject line should be brief yet informative. It must immediately convey the core issue or matter being addressed without unnecessary detail.
- **Clarity**: Use precise language. For example, specify the transaction or issue by mentioning key parties or the specific legal concern.
- **Neutral Tone**: The subject line should reflect the objectivity of the opinion letter. Avoid subjective or overly emphatic phrasing. Even in persuasive documents like a demand letter, aim for a neutral tone to avoid unnecessarily riling up the reader.
- **Format Consistency**: Ensure the subject line adheres to the firm's or client's formatting preferences, including capitalization or style.

13.4 Motions and Briefs

The title of the brief plays a key role in signaling to the court the specific type of filing, which allows court staff, judges, and opposing counsel to quickly understand its purpose. In fact, the title you write on the document goes into the permanent record of the court in the docket system.

A. Where to Put the Title

In court documents, put the title immediately below the caption. You can see examples of court-document titles here:

Trial-Court Brief (Moving Party) — pages 58 (motion) and 59 (brief)

Trial-Court Brief (Nonmoving Party) — page 78

Appellate-Court Brief — page 88

But also be mindful of the main point of Chapter 3, Deconstruct Sample Documents. You'll know from deconstructing motions and briefs in your court if there's a different convention, like putting the title immediately below the judge's name on the right side of the caption.

B. Motions

Use this formula to write a motion title:

[Moving Party]'s + Motion + [Descriptive Title]

You can see the three parts in these examples:

- Plaintiff's Motion for Summary Judgment
- Defendant's Motion to Exclude Prior Convictions
- Defendants' Motion to Dismiss Case

1. Moving Party

As you likely gathered, the moving party is either going to be *Plaintiff* or *Defendant*. Yes, it needs to be in the possessive form because it's possessing the word *motion*. For singular party, add 's. Thus, *Plaintiff* becomes *Plaintiff's*. If there are multiple parties making the motion, then form the possessive by simply adding an apostrophe to the plural word. Thus, *Plaintiffs* becomes *Plaintiffs'* and *Defendants* becomes *Defendants'*.

Generally, do not include the parties actual names. Why? It can be really clunky, and it's not necessary. Check out the clunk here:

> Defendants Jerome Willow, Biloxy Samuelson, and Jeremy Hall's Motion for Summary Judgment

That's really clunky. This is so much cleaner:

> Defendants' Motion for Summary Judgment

The one exception is if the parties are represented by different attorneys, and only one party is making a motion. So, from the example above, let's assume that just Jerome Willow is making a motion for summary judgment. His motion title would look like this:

> Defendant Jerome Willow's Motion for Summary Judgment

Specifying just the one defendant will help avoid any confusion. But, again, do that only if one of several parties is motioning the court.

2. "Motion"

The title must include the word *motion* because, again, this title goes into the court's docket, and it must alert the docket reader to what the document is.

3. Descriptive Title

Finally, the motion title must describe in general terms the type of motion. Is it a motion for summary judgment? Is it a motion to suppress evidence? Is it a motion to sequester witnesses? Include something just to give the reader a gist. You do not need to include detail such as the specific rule you're operating under because that rule will be in the motion's text (the paragraph after the title).

C. Briefs

The brief's title changes depending on whether you're the moving party or the nonmoving party. The motion titles above apply only to the moving party; nonmoving parties do not file a motion. So if the defendant is making a motion for summary judgment, they will have a motion document and then a separate brief. But the nonmoving party, the plaintiff in this example, will file just a response brief and not a motion document. Thus, for briefs, you need to know how to title them based on whether you are the moving party supporting your motion or the nonmoving party opposing the motion.

Regardless of which side you're on, the title for the brief must include the title for the motion so the docket can reflect that the brief goes along with the motion. Examples below will help make this clear.

1. Moving Party

The title for the brief must be identical to the motion's title except you should add "Brief Supporting" before it. Here's the formula:

Brief Supporting [Motion Title]

or

Brief in Support of [Motion Title]

The older convention is to use "Brief in Support of," but modernly attorneys try to write as concisely and directly as possible. "Brief Supporting" is just two words whereas "Brief in Support of" is four words, yet they both say the same thing. Be concise.

Thus, the brief title supporting a motion would look like this:

- Brief Supporting Plaintiff's Motion for Summary Judgment
- Brief Supporting Defendants' Motion to Exclude Prior Convictions
- Brief Supporting Defendants' Motion to Dismiss Case

You can see examples of this in the sample Trial-Court Brief in Chapter 2. On page 58, you'll see the title for the motion, and then on page 59 the title for the brief is identical to the motion's title except that it adds *Brief Supporting*.

2. Nonmoving Party

If you're the nonmoving party, follow this formula:

[Plaintiff or Defendant]'s + Response to + [Motion Title]

That's right: just add *Plaintiff's Response to* or *Defendant's Response to* before the motion title. Here are some examples:

- Defendant's Response to Plaintiff's Motion for Summary Judgment
- Plaintiff's Response to Defendants' Motion to Exclude Prior Convictions
- Plaintiff's Response to Defendants' Motion to Dismiss Case

You can see examples of this in the sample documents on page 78 in the nonmoving party's response brief.

3. Moving Party's Reply Brief

In the salvo of litigation, the moving party files a motion and a brief; then the opposing party files a "response brief"; and then the original moving party may file a "reply brief." If you're tasked with writing a reply brief, which is basically just a rebuttal to the nonmoving party's brief, the title will look like this:

- Defendant's Reply to Plaintiff's Response
- Reply in Support of Motion to Dismiss

You can see that you have some leeway with a reply title.

13.5 Appellate Briefs

The title for an appellate brief often falls under one of three categories: "Brief for Appellant," "Brief for Appellee," or "Reply Brief," though the exact terminology might vary slightly depending on the court's rules. Here's a breakdown of each:

A. Brief for Appellant

If your client is appealing the lower court's decision, the title should indicate this by stating "Brief for Appellant." This shows that your client, the appellant, is seeking a reversal or modification of a decision from a lower court. Some courts may allow or require "Opening Brief of Appellant," so checking the court's specific guidelines is essential.

If there's just one appellant, then something simple like this is customary:

> Brief for Appellant

But if there are multiple appellants and you represent just one, then specify the particular appellate:

> Brief for Appellant American National Fire Insurance Company

Lastly, it's conventional in some courts to also include the trial-court designation of Defendant or Plaintiff, like this:

> Brief for Defendant–Appellant

or

> Brief for Defendant–Appellant American National Fire Insurance Company

or

> Defendant-Appellant American National Fire Insurance Company's Brief on Appeal

More than anything, follow your court's conventions (which you can often glean from sample documents).

B. Brief for Appellee

If your client is responding to an appeal initiated by the opposing party, the title should be "Brief for Appellee." This signals that the brief defends the lower court's decision and argues for its affirmation. In this case, the appellee is usually asking the appellate court to maintain the decision made in the lower court.

All the examples above apply to this as well, just swap out "Appellant" for "Appellee."

C. Reply Brief

If the appellant wishes to reply to the appellee's brief, the title "Reply Brief" is used. This is typically the appellant's chance to respond to arguments presented by the appellee and clarify any points raised in the opening brief. Most courts prefer specific language like "Reply Brief of Appellant" to avoid ambiguity.

Chapter Fourteen

Caption the Document

14.1 Captions for Memos

The rules in this section apply to office memos that are either going to be printed or attached as a document to an email. If you are writing an email memo (sometimes called an eMemo), you would not include this type of caption because it's integral to the emailing system.

This is what a memo's caption should look like:

Memorandum

To:	Lucy Van Pelt, Partner
From:	Charlie Brown, Summer Associate
Date:	March 31, 2025
Re:	Woodstock, Inc.; Client File No. 3-44; Possible Lawsuit for Breach of Employee's Noncompetition Agreement

Note how the information here lines up vertically; use tabs to get that look.

Memorandum should be the first word on the page. Center it. Emphasize it with bold typeface.

In the *To:* line, type the name of the person to whom you're writing the memo. Often, this is the partner in the law firm who gave you the assignment. But sometimes it may be your client or a group of people all working on a project. If the person you're addressing has a professional title within your organization, include that after their name and a comma, like this:

To: Penelope Amarswari, Managing Partner

In the *From:* line, type your name. Many firms also have the convention of the memo's author initialing the *From:* line either electronically or physically after printing it. If you print out the memo, initial it before filing it or giving it to another attorney. If you attach it as an email, use the Adobe initial function to digitally initial it. Because these Adobe features cost money, law-school classes often do not require you to digitally sign your documents.

After *Date:*, type the date you submit the memo.

In a memo caption, *Re:* stands for "regarding." It is commonly used to indicate the subject or topic of the memo, serving as a brief indication of what the memo is about. In the *Re:* line, usually include three pieces of information: client name, description of matter, and file number. The client's name is obvious. A description of the matter should be brief: "estate plan," "arson," "false imprisonment," for example. Your law firm will instruct you on the file number, but you should generally put the law firm's internal file number for sure. If the matter is also being litigated, you should put the court file number as well (e.g., 24-3487-NZ).

Also be sure to format the caption so it's aesthetically pleasing and easy to read. You can do this by vertically aligning the information after the colons. In the example above, *Lucy*, *Charlie*, *March*, and *Woodstock* are all vertically aligned. There are many ways to accomplish this, but the easiest is to simply put your cursor after the colon and tab over.

Finally, be sure to single-space the caption. You may add a bit of line space after each line (i.e., 6 points or so), but do not double space it. (See 18.4(D) about line spacing.)

That does it for memo captions.

14.2 Captions for Court Documents

All principal documents that you file with a court must include a court caption. The court caption tells the reader which matter it belongs to. As it applies to your writing in law school, you'll include a caption for complaints, answers, motions, and briefs.

The caption for the same case must be identical on all documents related to that matter. So the caption for a complaint, answer, and motion for the same case will be identical.

A. Observe Court Captions in the Wild

The best thing you can do when you're practicing law is to find a sample caption for the court you're litigating in, and copy that caption's parts. Of course, change the information so it pertains to your matter, but, at the very least, use the sample document to know what parts to include and generally how it should look.

For writing court documents, you may want to use the sample documents in Chapter 2:

Trial-Court Brief (Moving Party) — page 58

Trial-Court Brief (Nonmoving Party) — page 78

Appellate-Court Brief — page 88

B. A Caption's Parts

A court caption includes the following parts:

- Court
- Parties
- Case number
- Judge

Optionally, you may also include the attorneys' information.

The addition of lines and other formatting will change depending on the firm or institution you work for.

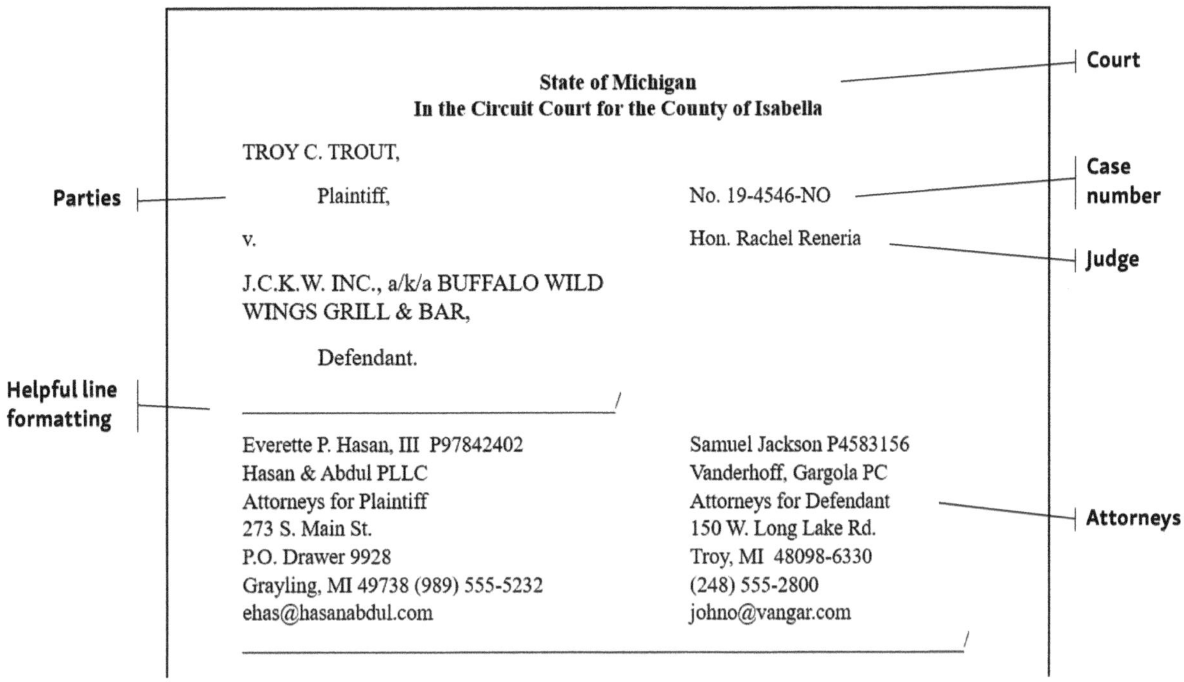

1. Court

At the top of the caption, which will be the very first thing the reader sees, state the court in which the matter is being heard. Center the court name and apply bold emphasis. Some writers use all caps, but that is becoming disfavored. In law school, default to not writing in all caps—but always follow what your professor tells you. And, finally, single-space the court information.

The first line is generally the state, and then the second line is for the actual court name and the county. Like this:

State of Michigan
In the Circuit Court for Isabella County

For federal matters, the first line is the general name of the court: United States District Court, United States Court of Appeals, or United States Supreme Court, and the second line is for the particular court, like this:

United States District Court
Central District of Florida

Some attorneys add "In the" before the first line and "for the" before the second line:

In the United States District Court
for the Central District of Florida

2. Parties

Below the court name, the caption gets divided into two sections. On the left, state the parties. Include the first name, middle initial, and surname. It's customary to write the actual names in all caps, but this is not necessary. You may either write them in all caps or capitalize just the first letter of each name.

Put a comma after the last party's name.

If the party names go onto a second or third line, make sure they are single-spaced.

After the party or parties for one side, write the party designation, which will be *Plaintiff* or *Defendant*. Pluralize it if there are multiple plaintiffs or defendants. And it's usually indented ½ inch.

Put a comma after the party designation.

The formatting is really important for the parties. Foremost, you need to have consistent line spacing between the parts. Note how in the example below that there are 8 points of space after each part:

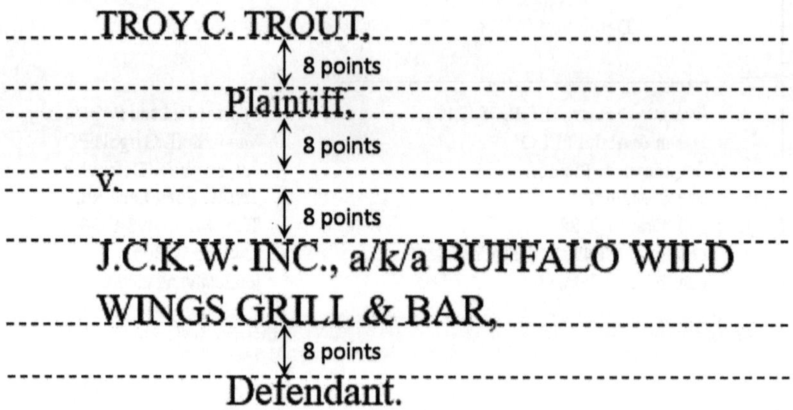

Having exactly 8 points is less important than having consistent spacing between the parts. You may have 10 or 12 points spacing between the parts—just keep it consistent.

Perhaps try this two-step method to ensure proper spacing. First, in your word processor, apply single-space formatting to the entire section in the caption where you write the party names. Second, use paragraph spacing after each paragraph to create the consistent line space between the paragraphs. You know where the line spacing button is in your word processor. For paragraph spacing, in Microsoft Word, go to the Layout tab on your menu, and you'll see *Spacing*, *Before*, and *After*. For Google Docs, use the Format menu.

3. Case Number

The court gives the person who files the original complaint to start litigation a case number. Use that case number in every caption for the same matter.

4. Judge

Below the case number, state the judge who presides over the litigation. It's customary to write the abbreviation *Hon.* for *honorable* before the judge's name. In cases with two judges, list both judges.

5. Attorney Information

Some courts require that the caption include the information of each attorney of record. This makes it easy for the court to communicate with the attorneys. Even if a court doesn't require it, many attorneys nonetheless include it as a courtesy.

Include the name, the law firm, a designation of which party the attorney represents, address, phone number, and email address. After the name, include the bar license number for that jurisdiction. You have to include the firm name because it is legally the responsible entity for the litigation. If your word processor tries to hyperlink the email address, turn that off.

6. Optional Formatting

You'll see a variety of formatting lines that help the reader's eyes make sense of where the parties end and begin. You can see some examples in the court briefs in sections 2.6, 2.7, and 2.8.

C. Word-Processing Hacks

Many attorneys and their administrative help use a table to keep the parties, court information, and attorney information separate. To do this, insert a table with two rows and two columns. That will create basically four quadrants. The beauty of using a table is that you can type the information in one quadrant, and it won't affect what's happening in the others. Like this:

STATE OF MICHIGAN
IN THE CIRCUIT COURT FOR THE COUNTY OF ISABELLA

Turn off these table borders using the instructions below.

Type the parties, party designations (i.e., *plaintiff* or *defendant*), and v. in this box. If you'd like to add formatting, it's customary to add an underline and then a forward slash at the bottom of this quadrant.	Type the court's file number and judge in this box.
Type the plaintiff's attorney's information here.	Type the defendant's attorney's information here.

You're probably thinking at this point that your caption doesn't look very professional. Just wait to apply the magic! That magic is to turn off the table's borders. You can right click in the table and turn off the borders with this button that appears in the pop-up ribbon: . Click on the down arrow and choose "No borders." You'll see the borders disappear. In Google Docs, go to Table Options and then Color, and turn the table borders white.

Chapter Fifteen

Use Document Headings

15.1 Why We Need Headings

When you are in a grocery store looking for, let's say, pickles, you will naturally look up to the signs at the end of each mile-long aisle. When you see a sign that says "condiments" or, better yet, "pickles," you know to turn down that aisle to grab your gherkins.

Well the same applies to legal documents. Readers use headings to make sense of the document and to know where to go to find what they're looking for. Most legal readers do not read an entire analytical document like an office memo or a brief from beginning to end; they will read just parts of the document. Or they may read it from top to bottom at one point, but then will want to return to it later for just a particular point or two. The headings will help them navigate the document.

So, then, headings speed up the comprehending process because they get the reader to their destination sooner. And, as you'll see with persuasive headings, they actually play a crucial role in conveying the substance of arguments.

15.2 Section Headings for a Whole Document

A. Reverse Engineer Your Document

You're probably reading this chapter because you've been asked to write a certain document like an office memo or court brief. The best advice about knowing what headings to include for your particular document is to get a sample document and identify its headings. Copy those same headings into the document you're writing. (This is applying the reverse-engineer skill explained in Chapter 3.)

If you're writing a memo for a law-school class, you will get a sample memo from your professor and copy the headings. Or imagine that you are writing a brief to be filed in court as a summer associate. The smartest way to figure out the headings is to find a brief filed in your court. Deconstruct it. And then reconstruct those same headings in your document.

B. Format the Whole-Document Headings

Along with observing what whole-document headings you need to include, notice how they are formatted. Typically, document headings are centered on the page and in bold emphasis. You can see what this looks like by taking a glance at the sample documents in Chapter 2.

Many legal documents, especially older ones, have headings in all-caps. This is okay, but all-caps is more difficult to read. You may use it, but use it only for short, descriptive headings; if you use it for complete-thought or full-sentence headings, you will make it more difficult for your reader to understand the idea.

One last note: Whole-document headings are typically not enumerated, but subheadings within a section usually are. Look, for example, at the Discussion section in the Full Office Memo on page 43. "Discussion" is not enumerated, but then the subsections are enumerated as A and B.

The sections below will take you through how to enumerate and format subheadings in the analysis part of your document.

15.3 Analysis Headings in Objective Documents

This section applies to just the main analysis section of an objective full office memo, something like the Discussion section. And, further, the advice in this section pertains only to a memo with multiple subissues. Generally, this happens when more than one element is at issue, so you'll have separate subsections under the Discussion heading, one subheading for each element at issue. Skim the sample memo on pages 43 to 49 for an example of subissues with headings.

A. Use a Heading for Each Element at Issue

Within the Discussion section of a Full Office Memo, you may have multiple elements at issue. As you learned in Chapter 4, you'll write up each subissue separately with an IREAC packet. The I of IREAC, the issue, will be signaled to the reader in the heading. The reader will know that's the issue because you would have pointed that out in the global Rule Foundation, the first substantive section in your Discussion.

Under that subheading, give a secondary Rule Foundation for just that element at issue, the R of IREAC; flesh that out with Case Illustrations, the E of IREAC; then apply all that law to the client's facts, the A of IREAC; and, finally, state an internal conclusion, the C of IREAC. That will complete addressing the first subissue.

Then write your second subheading for the next element at issue, and repeat the IREAC parts explained in the preceding paragraph.

See pages 43 to 49 for an example of this.

B. Enumerate Your Subheadings

Your subheadings should be enumerated. Typical enumeration schemes follow this convention: Roman numeral > Capital letter > Arabic numeral:

I. Heading

A. Subheading

1. Sub-subheading

2. Sub-subheading

B. Subheading

II. Heading

Or you could do something a bit more modern, which avoids Roman numerals: Capital letter > Arabic numeral > Lowercase letter:

A. Heading

1. Subheading

a. Sub-subheading

b. Sub-subheading

2. Subheading

B. Heading

Or you could create your own enumeration scheme. The main rules are that you need to, at the different levels, alternate between numerals and letters. For numerals, it's conventional to alternate between Roman and Arabic. And for letters, alternate between uppercase and lowercase.

The rules and examples in 5.4(G) for enumerating and formatting persuasive point headings likewise apply to headings in objective documents.

C. Use Typography to Show Hierarchy of Headings

In addition to using enumeration, you should also physically format the headings to show their hierarchical relationship to each other. See also 5.4(G). Changing the document typography visually alerts the reader to the relationship of the elements being discussed. Here are the guiding principles:

- Each heading, compared to the next, should have distinctive emphasis
- Subheadings should be indented compared to their parent heading

Emphasis in this context means applying bold, italics, or underlining to the text. You'll notice that the writer has already applied these guiding principles to the example headings immediately above.

D. Use Just a Descriptive Phrase

Finally, your headings in objective analysis documents should generally be just a descriptive phrase to orient the reader about the topic or element you discuss in that section. Thus, you may have a Discussion section that looks like this:

Discussion

[Global Rule Foundation]

A. **Objectively Manifested**

[Secondary Rule Foundation]

1. *Hearing Loss*

[Case Illustrations]

[Rule Application]

2. *Post-Traumatic Stress Disorder*

[Case Illustrations]

[Rule Application]

B. **Important Body Function**

[Secondary Rule Foundation]

[Case Illustrations]

[Rule Application]

C. **General Ability**

[Secondary Rule Foundation]

[Case Illustrations]

[Rule Application]

Instead of a short, descriptive heading, you could write a complete sentence that also signals your prediction, like this:

A. **Hearing Loss Is Objectively Manifested**

...

B. **Hearing Relates to an Important Body Function**

...

C. **Driver's General Ability Has Been Affected**

...

Attorneys usually do not opt for longer headings like these in objective analysis because it belies the nuance needed to address each element at issue. In other words, it's nearly impossible to accurately capture the conclusion from objective analysis in a short phrase.

So the best advice is to simply use short, descriptive phrases that alert the reader to the topic addressed in that subsection.

15.4 Analysis Headings in Persuasive Documents

You'll find everything you need to know about persuasive headings in Chapter 5. That chapter is all about coming up with arguments for a persuasive document like a brief or demand letter and then writing the arguments as concise persuasive point headings. See 5.4 in particular.

Chapter Sixteen

Preview the Analysis

16.1 Why You Should Preview Analysis

Let's say you meet someone you're interested in dating or at least getting to know better. What if at the moment you think about interacting with them, a note pops up in your mind's eye and tells you how the relationship will go. Maybe it'll say, "You will go on two dates, and then you'll both lose interest." Or, "You will eventually date for five years, and then he'll break your heart." Or, "You're going to get married, have 2.5 children, and live happily ever after."

That would be nice, but life doesn't work that way... unless you're a writer. Writers can preview what's to come at the beginning of the endeavor. That makes for a bad novel, but it's great for understanding legal analysis.

A preview at the beginning of your legal analytical document or at the beginning of an analysis section serves two purposes. First, it aids reader comprehension by removing suspense and giving your reader a quick understanding of the full argument that they're about to read. Second, it acts like a roadmap by giving the basic structure of the analysis to come.

Now, you're reading this chapter because your professor assigned it, probably along with instructions to write the "Brief Answer" or "Introduction" in a document. But keep in mind the greater goal for this assignment; it's not to learn how to write just the one document you're working on. Rather, it's to learn the skills needed to write *any* analytical document. So, in the future, when you're asked to write a Brief Answer, Introduction, Thesis, Overview, or Summary of Argument, you'll say, "I got this. It's just previewing my analysis."

16.2 Write the Preview Last

This may seem odd or ironic because the preview paragraph or section appears first in the document or in the analysis section. You won't know what to write, though, until you've finished the work of explaining the law and applying the law. Doing that will allow you to think through all the issues. Then you can—at the end of the writing process—summarize the law and analysis in the analysis-preview section.

You should jot down a little placeholder note to remind you to add the preview to your document once you're done writing the law and application-of-law portions.

16.3 One-Sentence Preview

Strive to beat the 30-second test when writing shorter, informal legal-analysis documents like opinion letters and eMemos. That test, which many experts write about, is to ensure that your reader understands the issue and answer within 30 seconds of beginning to read the document.

Start your timer, and then read the opening paragraph of this opinion letter, which is an excerpt from the Opinion Letter sample on page 11 of this textbook. Does it beat the 30-second test?

> Dear Sadie:
>
> It was a pleasure to speak with you last week. When we spoke, you reported that one of your former employees printed out and took LucyCo's password-protected customer list when he left the company. You asked for my opinion on whether that customer list is a trade secret. **The answer is no.**
>
> . . .

Definitely. The reader gains quick focus because they now know the issue and the answer within a moment of picking up the document. They can then better analyze the law and analysis to come.

Let's try one more. The example below is from the eMemo on page 19 of this text. Does it pass the 30-second test?

> Mr. Green,
>
> **Question**
>
> You asked me to research the elements for operating a vehicle while intoxicated and to analyze whether being passed out behind the wheel of a car while its engine is running with its transmission in Neutral is considered driving that vehicle.
>
> **Answer**
>
> The answer is no. Puntab Vivek, our client, was not driving the car because he was not in actual control of the vehicle, and it did not pose a threat to anyone.
>
> . . .

Indeed it does! Happy reader.

So that's the first principle of previewing the analysis in smaller documents: give a clear answer at the very beginning of the document.

As to its placement, it should go immediately after framing the issue, which you can see demonstrated in the two examples above.

You may choose to put the preview within a paragraph, like the first example above; this works well for shorter documents. Or you may put the preview in a separate section with its own heading, like you see in the eMemo excerpt; that works better for moderately longer documents.

Now, as to the answer itself, it should be just a short one-word or one-sentence answer to the issue statement. Anything longer than that would seem redundant of the analysis to come in the document.

And, sometimes, it may be helpful to preview the main reason behind the answer. The eMemo answer immediately above demonstrates what that looks like where the writer explains why Mr. Vivek wasn't "driving" the car.

Here are a few more examples of capturing the reason in a short sentence:

> Yes, a court is likely to find that Kaleb Munds accepted the risks of injury from a drone while skiing.
>
> No, you may not sue because the statutory time has passed.
>
> Yes, you will owe past taxes, but we can probably negotiate to reduce the amount by 25%.

Each of the three examples above clearly states the conclusion and gives the briefest of reasons. Because the analysis overall is short in these documents, the preview of it should likewise be short.

Above all, beat the 30-second test. You can't beat that test if the preview, the answer, isn't crystal clear. Here's a less-effective example of a one-sentence preview:

> Yes, the statutory period of limitations has expired.

What was that? Depending on your audience, there's a good chance the reader will not understand that. The words themselves do not carry much meaning for most folks. Plus, it begins with "yes" but then says that the time has expired. So which is it? May the client sue or not? If you are going to give a bit of reasoning, make sure the reader can understand it. This would make more sense: No, you may not sue because the statutory time has passed.

So be absolutely crystal clear what the answer is.

16.4 Standalone Preview

Longer, more complex analytical documents often require a standalone preview, complete with its own heading. If there's a 30-second test for informal documents, there's a 60-second test for these longer documents like a full office memo or brief. So the reader must understand the issue, answer, and reasoning within 60 seconds of picking up the document. The writer can go into more detail in these standalone previews because there's less chance of seeming redundant in such a long document.

A. Parts of a Standalone Preview

Regardless of the document you're writing, a standalone preview has these four parts:

(1) **Issue**: State the issue, conclusion, argument, or prediction, whichever fits the document.

(2) **Rule**: Explain the core governing rule of law in one sentence.

(3) **Reasoning**: Summarize the reasoning that occurs later in the document.

(4) **Conclusion**: State the conclusion, prediction, or relief requested.

You've no doubt astutely noticed that a standalone preview precisely follows the IREAC parts—except that it does not include caselaw examples. We give just the thirty-thousand-foot explanation here; leave the details like caselaw stories for the E of IREAC later in the document.

Each of these four parts happen very briefly. Keep your preview paragraph short—preferably four (or perhaps five) sentences. Readers like an overview, but if it gets too long and comprehensive, your reader will resent having to read what feels like the same thing—the same legal argument—twice.

Here's what these four parts look like in one type of standalone analysis preview from an objective full office memo:

Brief Answer

Conclusion

Rule

The bulk of this paragraph is **a summary of the reasons** that supports the conclusion.

Conclusion

Yes, a court will more than likely find that Peters has established retaliation. Retaliation requires an adverse employment action that was caused by the employee's complaint of sexual harassment. Giles interfered with Peters's ability to do her job when he took away her office keys and gave her busywork like cleaning the bathroom. These actions were caused by Peters's complaint because there was a short period of time, eight days, between the filing of the complaint and when Giles acted against her. Furthermore, Giles exhibited a retaliatory motive when he knowingly violated company policy in treating Giles poorly. Therefore, Giles did retaliate against Peters.

Does this beat the 60-second test? Definitely. Mission accomplished.

There are many more examples in the sample documents in Chapter 2. You should observe what these four parts of a standalone preview look like in those diverse documents, not just the one you're currently writing for a class. Here's where you can find the standalone analysis preview in the Chapter 2 sample documents:

Short Office Memo — Overview on page 28

Full Office Memo — Brief Answer on page 41

Trial-Court Brief (Moving Party) — Introduction on page 60

Trial-Court Brief (Nonmoving Party) — Introduction on page 78

Appellate-Court Brief — Summary of Argument on page 95

As a way to cement your learning, consider going to a couple of the standalone previews in the documents listed above and find the four parts (issue, rule, reasoning, and conclusion). More than any other thing you read in this chapter, using your observation skills will help you learn how to write an analysis preview.

1. Issue, Conclusion, or Prediction

Depending on the document, your reader either wants to know the issue or the conclusion very first. If your document, like a short office memo or full office memo, begins with a Question Presented or Issue Statement, then your analysis preview will come right after that, and you should begin with the conclusion—the answer to the stated question. In this way, the Issue Statement and the analysis preview work together to provide a summary of the case.

In persuasive documents like a brief, you should begin the analysis preview with a sentence or two that lays out the main issue and theme and then work your way to the conclusion by the end of the preview. It's a subtle form of persuasion.

2. Core Governing Rule

Give the one primary rule that the entire document's analysis hangs on. Do it in one sentence. And paraphrase it by putting it into accurate but easy-to-understand terms; yes, use the language of the elements, but make it understandable. You just need to give the reader a gist of the rule. You do not need to cite your law in the analysis preview because the reader knows that they're reading a summary of what's to come, and you're going to properly cite everything later in the document.

3. Summary of Reasoning

This is perhaps the most important part of the preview—the reasoning. You cannot write the preview until you've finished the explanation and application of law later in the document. The idea here is to summarize the reasoning that supports your conclusion—the analysis you write in the Application section.

After reading the preview, the reader should know the primary reasons that support your conclusion. And those reasons will include both a bit of law and a bit of the client's facts.

If you wrote your Application section well, the topic sentences to the paragraphs should state your primary reasons. Thus, you can merely take those topic sentences from the Application section and pop them into the analysis preview; then rework them so everything flows nicely, and call it a day.

4. Conclusion

Finish the standalone preview by clearly stating the conclusion. Or, if it's a persuasive document like a court brief, state the relief you're asking for.

B. Syllogistic Structure of a Standalone Preview

A standalone analysis preview follows the IREAC pattern for an important reason: it's based on Aristotle's syllogism from the 4th century BCE. There is logical power in putting that information in that order.

The deductive syllogism works like this:

(1) Major premise (i.e., the controlling rule of law)

— plus —

(2) Minor premise (i.e., the most relevant fact or facts)

— produces —

(3) Logical legal conclusion

In the law, we add an issue statement before these three substantive parts to orient and focus the reader.

You can learn much more detail about the syllogistic structure of legal analysis in section 4.3, IREAC Is Logical and Methodical.

C. Particular Standalone Previews

1. *Objective Full Office Memo*

There are two analysis previews in a standard office memo, which you likely already observed. The first is usually titled Brief Answer, and it comes right after the Issue Statement.

Here's an example of an analysis preview in a full office memo. You'll see that it comes directly after the issue has been framed.

Issue Statement

Under California law, did our client, the Academy of Motion Picture Arts and Sciences (the Academy), falsely imprison Donovan Michaels when (1) he mistakenly believed he could attend the Academy Awards ceremony, (2) the Academy's security escorted Michaels to a resolution center, (3) the Academy did not physically detain him, (4) but Michaels nonetheless did not leave because (5) an employee, at some point, called the paparazzi as a joke on Michaels, and (6) the employee emphasized the legal consequences Michaels could face?

Include the Brief Answer **heading**, centered and in bold.

Brief Answer

Begin with *No*, *Yes*, *Probably*, or *Probably Not*. Then state the **conclusion/answer**.

With many elements, it's helpful to focus your reader on what's at issue.

Most of the paragraph **summarizes the reasoning** that supports the conclusion.

Then give the core governing **rule**.

No, Michaels's suit against the Academy will fail because he was not confined. The tort of false imprisonment requires nonconsensual confinement of a person for an appreciable length of time. The only element at issue is whether Michaels was confined because he was not physically restrained. But in California, a person may be confined by fear or unreasonable duress. In the end though, a court would likely hold that Michaels was not confined because the situation was not so severe that his will was overcome, the Academy didn't use anything untoward as leverage to force him to stay, and Michaels wasn't especially vulnerable. Therefore, the Academy is not liable for false imprisonment.

Restate the **conclusion** to complete the syllogism.

You already learned about the four-part structure above: conclusion, rule, reasoning, conclusion. The only difference with a Brief Answer in a full office memo is that it's conventional to begin with a short one- or two-word answer: *Yes*, *No*, *Probably*, or *Probably not*. After this short one- or two-word answer, briefly state the conclusion in sentence form. Then state the core governing rule. Then give the reasons that support your conclusion—the facts with the law that led you to come to the conclusion that you did. In other words, the brief answer is a mini-application section or a summary of the main arguments.

2. Trial-Court Brief

In a brief, the analysis preview is often titled Introduction and appears in a standalone section. You need to make two slight modifications to this type of analysis preview. First, because it's a persuasive tool and the court is likely not aware of the case, the first couple of sentences do a bit more work than a typical analysis preview. They need to introduce the issue and the parties. Second, the Introduction in a brief must conclude by stating the relief you're requesting from the court. Here's an example of a good introduction:

Introduction

LuLu Corporation alleges that Fred Smith misappropriated a trade secret by printing off its customer list for use at his new business. To succeed, LuLu must prove that its customer list was, in fact, a trade secret. It cannot.

Start by orienting the judge to the **issue**, parties, and theme.

State the **conclusion** up front. This writer also chose to get right to the rub in this opening section.

State the **rule** in one sentence.

The Uniform Trade Secrets Act defines "trade secret" as information that outsiders cannot "readily ascertain[ ] by proper means." Here, it is undisputed that the general public can find all the names and contact information in LuLu's customer list by checking phone books, websites, and trade publications. So outsiders can readily ascertain this information through proper means. Thus, the customer list does not meet the Act's definition, and Mr. Smith is entitled to summary judgment.

Most of this paragraph **summarizes the reasoning** that applies the rule and supports the conclusion.

State the **relief requested** from the court.

3. Appellate-Court Brief

Federal Rule of Appellate Procedure 28 requires a summary of the argument in the appellate brief. The summary or preview gives the court a flavor of the case, acclimatizes them to the case and your arguments. And, what's more, it should create a blueprint for the argument section.

In an appellate-court brief, the analysis preview is often titled Summary of the Argument, but the particular title may be different based on the court. Still, it's just a preview of the analysis, so you need to state the issue/conclusion, the rule, the reasoning, and the relief requested. Here's an example previewing the analysis that might appear in an appellate brief:

Summary of Argument

The trial court erred in denying Ben Wallace's motion for summary disposition. To avoid summary disposition, Smith was required to show that he sustained a serious impairment of body function, which required proof that his injuries affected his general ability to lead his normal life. But Smith missed only two weeks of work and a few recreational activities after the accident, which was insufficient, as a matter of law, to show that his alleged injuries affected his ability to live his normal life. Therefore, this Court should reverse the trial court's decision and order the trial court to grant summary disposition in Mr. Wallace's favor.

This is the **conclusion** the writer wants the appellate court to come to.

Start the deductive syllogism, beginning with the major premise, meaning the **controlling legal rule**.

Now comes the minor premise, the application of law to fact. **Summarize your arguments.**

Finally, give your reader closure by stating the legal **conclusion**. Be sure to start with a transition word (*Therefore* and *Thus* work well) to help your reader appreciate, immediately, that closure has arrived.

16.5 Internal Analysis Preview

For longer documents like full office memos and court briefs, attorneys sometimes integrate a preview into one particular section of a document—not as a standalone section. If one section of analysis in your document is longer than three pages or is especially complicated, begin that section with an internal analysis preview.

We call this an "internal preview" because it's internal to one section, like the Discussion section of an objective memo or the Argument section of a brief.

It should be the very first paragraph or two in that section. In a long memo, it would be the first section immediately after the Discussion heading. For an example, look at the first paragraph of the Discussion section in the Full Office Memo on page 43. And in a brief, it will be the first section immediately after the Argument heading or the global point heading. You can see one in the wild in the appellate-court brief on page 96.

But it's the first thing in the section because it orients the reader by giving them an overview of what's to come.

Some documents may even have two analysis previews: one standalone at the beginning of the document and one integrated internally at the beginning of the primary analysis section. You may be wondering why a document would need two previews. The reason is that legal analytical documents are often used as a reference document where just one section gets read; they're not always read from cover to cover. One reader may be interested in just the high-level take of the case, so they'll read just the Question Presented and Brief Answer while another person in the firm may want the details, so they'll primarily focus on the Discussion section. So we give a preview twice.

The main concern with internal previews is that we don't overwhelm the reader with what may appear as repetitive information. After all, the second sentence in the preview paragraph teaches the controlling rule of law, and you're going to be teaching that in more detail in the Rule Foundation, which is the very next paragraph.

But it won't sound too repetitive if done well. Here's a little trick from Professor Mark Cooney for avoiding that feeling of repetition: consider using references to the parties to teach the law in that second sentence of the internal-preview paragraph. For example, instead of writing a pure rule of law ("The statute requires a plaintiff to prove that he or she suffered a serious impairment of a body function."), consider teaching that rule with references to the parties to your case. So if your appellate brief is about Smith's claim, consider stating that same rule this way: "To succeed, Smith had to prove that his broken clavicle was a serious impairment of a body function." Look back at the previous examples to see how that worked.

Below is an outline of a brief that summarizes the points above about an internal preview. This could just as easily be an objective memo because the same skills used to write one apply to the other. Here it is:

Argument

[Global Point Heading]

[Because this Argument section of my brief is longer than 3 pages, I'm going to include an **internal Analysis Preview** (issue, rule, application, and conclusion). I'll keep it brief, no more than four sentences. This will preview, broadly, the two arguments I have below.]

[Global **Rule Foundation** goes next. State the broad rules that apply to all the arguments to come. This is where you'd state all the elements or the broad controlling rule. If a particular rule or definition applies to just one argument, hold off, and instead state that in its respective argument section.]

I. State your first argument as a persuasive point heading here.

[Consider putting an **internal Analysis Preview** here if this one argument section will be longer than three pages. But make it very brief. If your sense is that it's going to be repetitive of what's to come, then do not include a preview here.]

[State a secondary **Rule Foundation** that pertains to just this one argument. You already stated the broad controlling rule or elements above. Now you can dive more deeply into just the one rule, element, or group of factors at issue in this one argument.]

[Explain caselaw with **Case Illustrations** that flesh out and give life to the rule, element, or group of factors explained immediately above.]

[**Apply the law** of the Rule Foundation and Case Illustrations to the client's facts.]

II. State your second argument as a persuasive point heading here.

[Consider putting an **internal Analysis Preview** here if this one argument section will be longer than three pages. But make it very brief. If your sense is that it's going to be repetitive of what's to come, then do not include a preview here.]

[State a secondary **Rule Foundation** that pertains to just this one argument. You already stated the broad controlling rule or elements above. Now you can dive more deeply into just the one rule, element, or group of factors at issue in this one argument.]

[Explain caselaw with **Case Illustrations** that flesh out and give life to the rule, element, or group of factors explained immediately above.]

[**Apply the law** of the Rule Foundation and Case Illustrations to the client's facts.]

16.6 Checklist for Analysis Preview

One-Sentence Preview

If your document contains informal analysis or is shorter like an opinion letter or eMemo, did you:

___ begin the document with a brief issue statement and answer, the answer being the analysis preview?

___ clearly state the answer in unambiguous terms?

___ optionally include a sentence that summarizes the main reason for the answer? Any more than that would be repetitive of the short analysis to come.

Standalone Preview

If your document requires a standalone analysis preview, did you:

___ write the preview last after you completed the explanation-of-law and application-of-law sections?

___ begin the standalone preview with an appropriate heading (e.g., Brief Answer, Introduction, etc.)?

___ include the issue, rule, summary of reasoning, and conclusion in that order (i.e., follow the syllogistic structure of deductive thinking)?

___ shape the *issue* and *conclusion* parts of the preview so they fit your particular document (e.g., the Brief Answer uniquely begins with a short one- or two-word answer)?

___ truly summarize the reasoning without merely repeating facts or stating a conclusion?

___ avoid citing sources of law, knowing that it will happen later in the document?

Internal Analysis Preview

If your document, like a full office memo or court brief, has an analysis section (e.g., Discussion or Argument) that is over three pages, did you:

___ begin that section with an internal analysis preview?

___ follow the rules above for a standalone preview, except an internal preview does not get its own heading?

___ if you have subsections, begin each subsection with a preview if the subsection is longer than three pages or contains complex analysis?

PART FIVE

Citing and Quoting Skills

Part 5 has just one chapter, but it will teach you just about all you need to know about citing and quoting the law.

Chapter Seventeen

Cite and Quote

17.1 Citation Rules

This chapter includes the most student-used citation information. The rules come from the *ALWD Guide to Legal Citation* and *The Bluebook*. The ALWD manual is cited along the way, but you can easily find the parallel in the Bluebook if you happen to use that. They both have the same rules.

At the outset here, we need to make one tiny point about periods before and after citations. Note that in your documents, you'd almost always insert a period after a citation before starting the next sentence. For simplicity (and because we can't be sure where you'll be citing) we've omitted that period in the examples in this chapter.

17.2 When to Cite

There are two broad rules for when you must cite authority in your legal analytical document:

(1) You must cite a source for every sentence of law the *first* time you mention the law, whether you quote or paraphrase it. But you are not required to cite successive references to the law you already cited.

(2) You must cite a source for every quotation. But once you cite a quotation, you don't need to use quotation marks or cite it unless you want to emphasize the authority of the phrase.

This means that your document's Rule Foundation will have a citation after every sentence.

As for Case Illustrations, every sentence of your Case Illustration needs a citation as well, like this:

> Threat of force can be inferred when an authority figure overcomes another's will. ***Parrott v. Bank of America*, 217 P.2d 89 (Cal. Ct. App. 1950)**. In *Parrott*, the defendant examined the plaintiff for three hours about a bank deposit and threatened to prosecute her unless she confessed to stealing it. ***Id.* at 95.**
>
> The court held that the actual physical force was not needed for false imprisonment because it can be fulfilled by taking away a person's freedom without any adequate complaint or authority, and it could be done by words or acts that the person fears to ignore. ***Id.*** The court reasoned that the jury could reasonably infer that there was a threat of force from an innocent person saying they would sign a confession. ***Id.***

In the case-illustration example above, the writer put a full case citation immediately after the topic sentence because that is the first time the writer stated that rule. And because it's the first time the writer has referenced that case, it needs to be a full citation. You'll learn more about the *Id.* citations below.

17.3 Full, Short, and *Id.* Citations

At the outset of this chapter, you need to know that attorneys have three different versions of any citation: full, short, and *Id.* A full citation gives the reader everything they need to find a source and understand its weight of authority. A short citation gives just part of a full citation. And an *Id.* just references the preceding citation.

Why the difference? Clutter on the page. It would be really annoying if every citation included the full-citation information. Let's look at that Case Illustration above but with full citations after every sentence:

> Threat of force can be inferred when an authority figure overcomes another's will. *Parrott v. Bank of America*, 217 P.2d 89 (Cal. Ct. App. 1950). In *Parrott*, the defendant examined the plaintiff for three hours about a bank deposit and threatened to prosecute her unless she confessed to stealing it. *Parrott v. Bank of America*, 217 P.2d 89, 95 (Cal. Ct. App. 1950).
>
> The court held that the actual physical force was not needed for false imprisonment because it can be fulfilled by taking away a person's freedom without any adequate complaint or authority, and it could be done by words or acts that the person fears to ignore. *Parrott v. Bank of America*, 217 P.2d 89, 95 (Cal. Ct. App. 1950). The court reasoned that the jury could reasonably infer that there was a threat of force from an innocent person saying they would sign a confession. *Parrott v. Bank of America*, 217 P.2d 89, 95 (Cal. Ct. App. 1950).

Ewww. Nobody wants to read that. So we use shorter citation versions when possible. Here are the rules for using full versus short citations:

(1) Give a full citation the first time you reference a *source*.

(2) Prefer to use *Id.* (because it's streamlined and beautiful) after giving a full citation.

(3) After giving a full citation, you may use a short citation at any time if you can't use *Id.*

(4) But if you're citing the immediately preceding citation, use *Id.*

You'll learn about the full and short citations below, but now's a good time to learn about the *Id.* citation, which may be new to you. In legal citation, *Id.* is an abbreviation from the Latin term *idem*, which translates to "the same." It is used to refer to the immediately preceding citation or source. When *Id.* is used in a legal document, it indicates that the citation being referenced is the same as the one mentioned directly before it. This abbreviation helps to streamline citations and avoid unnecessary repetition within legal writing, providing a concise way to refer back to a previously cited authority.

Id. is always italicized, and it always ends with a period: *Id.* And, guess what, that period must be italicized as well. Funky, right?

The example below shows how to properly use *Id.* The annotations in the margin will guide you through it:

This first paragraph is the Rule Foundation. The writer cites a case, *Parrott*, for the first time, so they properly give a full citation. Then the writer cites *Wilson* for the first time, also giving a full citation.

> Only the "threat of force" element is at issue. Threat of force can be inferred when an authority figure overcomes another's will. *Parrott v. Bank of America*, 217 P.2d 89 (Cal. Ct. App. 1950). Unreasonable duress could also be a threat of force. *Wilson v. Houston Funeral Home*, 50 Cal. Rptr. 2d 169 (Cal. App. 4th 1996).
>
> In *Parrott*, the defendant examined the plaintiff for 3 hours about a bank deposit and threatened to prosecute her unless she confessed to stealing it. *Parrott*, 217 P.2d at 95.
>
> The court held that the actual physical force was not needed for false imprisonment because it can be fulfilled by taking away a person's freedom without any adequate complaint or authority, and it could be done by words or acts that the person fears to ignore. *Id.* The court reasoned that the jury could reasonably infer that there was a threat of force from an innocent person saying they would sign a confession. *Id.*

In this second paragraph, the writer begins a Case Illustration. They cite the source, *Parrott*, but give a short citation because they already gave a full one above. The writer cannot use *Id.* here because *Id.* would refer the reader improperly to *Wilson*, the immediately preceding case.

The *Id.* citations in this final paragraph are all correct because they refer to the immediately preceding source, *Parrott*.

17.4 Citing Cases

ALWD Chapter 12 explains all you need to know about citing to caselaw. This section summarizes the most important aspects.

A. State Cases

1. Full Citations

Use a full citation the first time you cite a case.

After that, you'll use a short citation (see subsection 2 below), unless there's a sizeable gap since you last cited that case and you elect to "revive" the full citation.

Your professor will talk to you about two possible styles for citing cases: the so-called *parallel style* (citing both your state's official reporter and the West regional reporter) and the so-called *national default style* (which cites only West regional reporter). Your citation manual has complete instructions for both styles, with examples.

ALWD Rule 12.4 states that we should use the parallel style if our local court rules instruct. If you fall into this category, your full citation for a case must look like this:

Sherwood v. Walker, 66 Mich. 568, 33 N.W. 919 (1887)

Sherwood v. Walker,	66 Mich. 568,	33 N.W. 919	(1887)
title	official reporter	unofficial reporter	year decided

From this citation, we learn that Sherwood and Walker are the plaintiff and defendant, and the case title will reflect that, *Sherwood v. Walker*. Second, this case is printed in Michigan Reports. (*Mich.* is its abbreviation according to the tables and appendices in ALWD and Bluebook). The case is also printed in the North Western Reporter (*N.W.* is its abbreviation). Reporters are similar to statutory compilations in that the same authority is often published by both the government (official reporter) and a private publisher (unofficial reporter). Michigan Reports is the official, government-printed compilation, and North Western Reporter is the unofficial, regional reporter. Both reporters carry the same amount of weight.

We also learn from this citation's reporters that the case is printed in volume 66 of Michigan Reports, and the case begins on page 568 in that reporter. Likewise, the case is printed in volume 33 of the North Western Reporter, and the case begins on page 919 in that reporter.

Third, we also learn that *Sherwood* is from the highest court in Michigan because Michigan Reports collects and prints cases that are only from the Michigan Supreme Court. (The tables and appendices in ALWD and Bluebook cover that.)

And, finally, we know that the case is old! We can tell that from the year it was decided.

The citation tells us all this information in addition to being the case's address, the way to find this case. That is amazingly dense coding.

Here are two more examples:

> *Smith v. Jones*, 150 Mich. 350, 200 N.W.2d 400 (1989)
>
> *Pierce v. Joseph*, 175 Mich. App. 275, 260 N.W.2d 10 (1990)

Note that the full citations below include the pinpoint page numbers (in bold), which give your reader the exact pages, in both books, where you found the language that you've paraphrased or quoted. You'd use this full-citation style plus the pinpoint page number if you were both citing a case for the first time *and* wanted to give a pincite, like if you were quoting.

By the way, a shorthand reference for "pinpoint page number" is simply "pincite."

You can find the page numbers in online cases by following the instructions in 17.5. Here are the same full citations but with pincites:

> *Smith v. Jones*, 150 Mich. 350, **353**, 200 N.W.2d 400, **402** (1989)
>
> *Pierce v. Joseph*, 175 Mich. App. 275, **281**, 260 N.W.2d 10, **14** (1990)

So that's the parallel-citation style. If, on the other hand, your professor instructs you to use the default national citation style, you will cite to the regional reporter only and identify the court in the date parenthetical:

Sherwood v. Walker, 33 N.W. 919 (Mich. 1887)

title — unofficial reporter — court — year decided

And here are a couple more examples of the national-citation style:

> *Smith v. Jones*, 200 N.W.2d 400, 402 (Mich. 1989)
>
> *Pierce v. Joseph*, 260 N.W.2d 10, 14 (Mich. Ct. App. 1990)

(See Appendix 1 in the *ALWD Manual* for state court names and abbreviations.)

If you're merely identifying the case in the text rather than citing it as authority for a quotation or a point of law, then you can omit the pinpoint page numbers:

> In *Pierce v. Joseph*, 260 N.W.2d 10 (Mich. Ct. App. 1990), a building contractor agreed to construct a …

2. *Id.* Citation

After you have given the first, full cite, use a short form and pinpoint the page on which a quote or specific material appears.

As you learned above, use the *Id.* form if there is no intervening cite. And after *at*, give the pinpoint page number, which is 402 in this example:

> *Id.* at 402

If you're using parallel style, an *Id.* citation to *Smith v. Jones* from above would look like this:

Id. at 353, 200 N.W.2d at 402

pincite for official reporter — volume for *un*official reporter — pincite for *un*official reporter

3. *Short Citation*

If there *has* been an intervening cite, you can't use the *Id.* short form. Instead, you'd give more information, but much less than in a full citation. Include only the first-listed party from the case name (or the defendant's name in a criminal case), and cite to the regional reporter (assuming the national style):

> *Smith*, 200 N.W.2d at 401

If you're using parallel style, you must cite to both reporters, like this:

> *Smith*, 150 Mich. at 353, 200 N.W.2d at 402

Note that for short citations, as demonstrated immediately above, you must omit:

- the *v*,
- the defendant's name,
- the initial page numbers for both reporters, and
- the year in the parenthetical.

B. Federal Cases

1. *United States Supreme Court*

Cite to *only* the United States Reports (U.S.), the official reporter. If the U.S. cite is not yet available, cite to the Supreme Court Reporter (S. Ct.). See ALWD, Rule 12.2 and Appendix 1.

> *Mueller v. Allen*, 463 U.S. 388, 404 (1983)

2. United States Courts of Appeals

Cite to the Federal Reporter. Give the circuit number in the date parenthetical, which you'll find in ALWD Appendix 1(B) and 4.

Brock v. Richardson, 815 F.2d 121, 129 (6th Cir. 1987)

Cite the unnumbered District of Columbia Circuit and Federal Circuit as follows.

Davis v. Foster, 550 F.2d 100, 111 (D.C. Cir. 1989)

Rowe v. Hanes, 102 F.3d 200, 208 (Fed. Cir. 1995)

3. United States District Courts

Cite to the Federal Supplement. Give the state and the district in the date parenthetical, which you'll find in ALWD Appendix 4.

Kelly v. Bechtal Power Corp., 633 F. Supp. 927, 934 (S.D. Fla. 1986)

If the state has only one district, use D and the state abbreviation.

Verdolino v. Anderson, 12 F. Supp. 2d 205, 208 (D. N.H. 1998)

4. Short Forms of Federal Cases

The same rules for short state cases apply, but here's what the short forms look like:

Mueller, 463 U.S. at 397

Brock, 815 F.2d at 125

Id. at 125

C. Cases That Are Not Available in a Reporter

1. Slip Opinion

For a case that is not yet in a reporter, cite to the slip opinion. Give the docket number, the court, and the full date.

Mason v. Shoemaker, No. 88-1450 (Mich. Ct. App. June 10, 1997)

If you are quoting or directly paraphrasing when you first cite the case, give the page number in the slip opinion.

Smith v. Kroll, No. 89-1095, slip op. at 2 (Mich. Ct. App. July 8, 1997)

For later pinpoint cites, use a short form.

Smith, slip op. at 3

2. *Unreported Cases*

For unreported cases, those only published on LexisNexis or Westlaw, use the *ALWD Manual*, Rule 12.13.

For a full citation, include the title, the unique document number, and a parenthetical that includes the court abbreviation and exact date (month-day-year).

> *Goodyear Tire & Rubber Co. v. Moore*, No. 24536-05, 2005 WL 1611323 (Va. Ct. App. July 12, 2005)
>
> *Boedeker v. Larson*, No. 2134-04, 2004 Va. Ct. App. LEXIS 596 (Dec. 7, 2004)

Short citation looks like this:

> *Goodyear Tire & Rubber Co.*, 2005 WL 1611323 at *3
>
> *Boedeker*, 2004 Va. Ct. App. LEXIS 596 at *2

17.5 Find the Right Page Number in Cases Online

Whenever you quote, you must give a pinpoint page number to where the quote comes from. Even though attorneys nowadays research cases completely online, the citation system is still based on the print reporters. This makes it so the pagination is standard online and in print.

This means that Lexis, Westlaw, Bloomberg, Casemaker—whatever website you're using for research—has to insert the page numbers from the printed reporters in the library into the online opinion. This is why you may have noticed numbers inserted in your online opinion with a * preceding it.

If you're looking at a state case, one * means that it's the page number for the official reporter, if your state has one. And two ** before a number is the page number for unofficial (i.e., regional) reporters. If you are following ALWD's national style of citing cases, you will need only the page number for the unofficial, regional reporter, the one preceded by **. However, if you're using a parallel form of citation, then you need to cite both the official (one *) and the unofficial (two **) in the citation.

In the example from a random case about property law and a "right of way" on the next page, you'll see that the last word on page 208 in the regional reporter is *Pomerantz*. And the first word on page 209 is *is*. If you're looking for the pinpoint page number in the regional reporter, you'd cite page 208 or 209. And if you want to cite both pages, it would look like this: 208–209. Or you could shorten it like this: 208–09.

> owned by Vince and Paul and the ROW is attached to this opinion as an Appendix.
>
> In 2006, Audette purchased the property at 17 Fairfield Street, an inland parcel that lies approximately 200 yards from the ROW. As the Kubics concede, Audette holds an express easement allowing him to use the ROW to gain access to the lake. In addition, in 2007, Audette purchased a release deed for the ROW from Francesca Pomerantz. Audette claims that Pomerantz ****209** is an heir to the original developers (the Robinsons). [5]
>
> 2. The topography of the ROW. The ROW has three distinct ***292** portions. Beginning at Fairfield Street, the initial forty or so feet of the ROW are relatively flat. This is the area that lies between Vince's and Paul's homes. The middle section of the ROW drops relatively steeply until it flattens out again near the water.
>
> The current waterline of the eastern shore of the lake is approximately thirty feet westward of the

Now, if you're using a parallel case citation, then you need to also cite the official reporter. That is always designed by one *. So you'd cite to page 291, 292, or 291–292.

17.6 Citing Codified Law

A. State Statutes

See ALWD, Appendix 1 for the abbreviation of statutory compilations.

Note: The year in the parenthetical for state citations in the copyright year of the source you're looking at. So if you're researching in Westlaw or Lexis, then the copyright year is always the current year. If, however, you're researching statutes in a printed book, then you need to find the copyright year in the front of the book.

1. Full Citations

You are supposed to cite to the official code whenever possible. But you may cite to the unofficial code. The year refers to when the particular volume was published, the copyright year. Use the date on the spine of the volume, on the copyright page, or on the title page—in that order of preference. Rule 14.4(a).

Mich. Comp. Laws Ann. § 500.101 (West 2024)

2. Short Forms

After you have given the full cite, use a short form for a later cite. See Rule 14.5. You may cite just the section number. For example, the previously cited statute may be short-form cited as follows.

§ 500.101 [if there is an intervening cite]

Id. [if there is no intervening cite]

When discussing a statute in a memorandum or brief, you may adopt an informal reference that does not confuse the reader. For example, if you are writing about a statute that requires dogs to be kept on leashes, you could refer to it as "the statute" (if there is only one) or "the dog-leash statute."

B. Federal Statutes

1. Full Citations

You are supposed to cite to the official code whenever possible. See Rule 14.2.

26 U.S.C. § 3303 (1990)

But you may cite to the unofficial code if the official code is not readily available or does not contain the statute.

26 U.S.C.A. § 3303 (West 1993) [the cited material appears only in the bound volume]

2. Short Forms

Use the same short forms as for state statutes.

C. State Constitutions

To cite state constitutions, see Ch. 13 and Appendix 1(B). Here's an example of citing the Michigan constitution:

Mich. Const. art. IX, § 3

D. United States Constitution

To cite the federal Constitution, see Ch. 13.

U.S. Const. art. I § 9, cl. 2

U.S. Const. amend. XIV, § 2

You may not use a short form other than *Id.* for constitutions. But you may refer to the article or amendment by name (e.g., the Fourth Amendment) in general discussion.

17.7 Citing Sources in the Statement of Facts

A. Full Citation of Source Documents

In a court brief, you must cite a source for every single fact in your Statement of Facts.

Use Chapter 25 in ALWD as a guide. Rule 25.2 explains that your citations in the Statement of Facts will have these parts: (1) document name, (2) pinpoint reference, and (3) date.

Rule 25.2(a) is the second most important rule. It explains what words you should abbreviate. Abbreviate (1) any word in ALWD Appendix 3(G) and (2) any word of six letters or more, without causing confusion. Delete articles (*a, an, the*) and prepositions (*of, on, in,* etc.).

1. Document Name

Imagine that you need to cite a document titled Evidentiary Hearing Transcript because that's the source of a certain fact. The ALWD Guide has a rule specific for transcripts (25.4), but it follows the general rule for citing documents in the Statement of Facts. I'll apply Rule 25.2 here to demonstrate this generally applicable rule.

First of all, because the document actually has a title, we don't need to create a name for it. If your document doesn't not have a title, then create one that describes the document.

Once you've either identified a name or created one, you then need to follow the ALWD rules for a document name. First, in the name, don't use articles (*a*, *an*, *the*) and prepositions (*of*, *on*, *in*, etc.).

Second, abbreviate each word according to ALWD Rule 25.2(a). That rule requires that you abbreviate (1) any word found in Appendix 3(G) and (2) any word of seven letters or more. But the overriding rule is that you can't do anything that will cause confusion.

Let's apply these rules to our document name of Evidentiary Hearing Transcript. *Evidentiary* is not in Appendix 3(G). Yes, it's over seven letters, but there's no way to abbreviate it and not cause confusion with *evidence*. So we'll just leave it as it is.

Hearing is abbreviated in Appendix 3(G) as *Hr'g*.

Transcript is likewise abbreviated in Appendix 3(G) as *Tr.*

Putting it all together, we have this as the official document name for the citation: Evidentiary Hr'g. Tr.

2. Pinpoint Reference

Under 25.2(b), you need to include a pinpoint reference in the citation.

Most often, the pinpoint reference is simply a page number.

Or some documents enumerate the paragraphs. If that's the case, include a pilcrow (¶) and then the paragraph number, like this:

> Evidentiary Hr'g. Tr. ¶ 5

You can create the pilcrow on a Mac by using these keystrokes: Option + 7. And you can do the same thing on a PC with a number pad: Alt + 0182. On a PC, you can also find it on the Word menu: Insert > Symbol.

Some documents, like depositions have both page numbers and line numbers. Here's an example:

> Evidentiary Hr'g. Tr. 15:21–16:4

You may not be familiar with the weird series of numbers (15:21–16:4). The number before the colon is always the page number, and the number after the colon is the line number. So that second citation says that the material is found beginning on line 21 of page 15 and continues through to line 4 on page 16. Use that format any time your source document has line numbers.

3. Date

Under ALWD Rule 25.2(d), include the document's date only if failing to do so would cause confusion. If the document you're citing is the only one with that name, then you do not need to include a date. But if you have two documents with the same name (e.g., two depositions by the same person), then include the date to distinguish the documents.

When you do need to include a date, use Appendix 3 to abbreviate the words in the date.

B. Short Citations in the Statement of Facts

ALWD Rule 25.5 correctly notes that the modern trend is to use *Id.* for short citations, and that is exactly what you should do. But be sure to add a pinpoint reference to every *Id.* if the pinpoint reference is different than the immediately preceding citation. Thus:

> Evidentiary Hr'g. Tr. 15:21–16:4
> *Id.* at 17:22.
> *Id.* [for a fact on the same page and line]
> *Id.* at 15:2.

Remember that all three parts of *Id.* take italics: *I - d -* .

Sometimes you won't be able to use *Id.*, and you'll need to do a short form. A short form for court-document citation is to simply drop anything other than the title and pinpoint citation. Thus:

> Full citation: Evidentiary Hr'g. Tr. 15:21–16:4
> Short citation: Evidentiary Hr'g. Tr. 8:13

17.8 Citations for Direct Quotes & Paraphrases

A. Advice About Quoting

A. Prefer short quotes that contain just the decisive or controlling language.

B. Quotations must be exact. Any changes must be shown by ellipses or brackets.

C. Quotes must also be true to the original's meaning. Make sure you have not changed the meaning when you use ellipses or brackets.

D. Significant mistakes in the original should be followed by *sic* in brackets, but otherwise left as they appear in the original.

> The court said, "The statue [sic] does not apply to the plaintiff."
> *Smith*, 200 N.W.2d at 401.

B. Pinpoint Citation to a Case

Whenever you directly quote or paraphrase a source (except a statute), you must give the number of the page where the quotation or paraphrased material appears. With cases, if you have given the first, full citation earlier, you only need to use a short form.

> The court said, "Silence does not constitute acceptance of an offer." *Smith*, 200 N.W.2d at 401.

C. Pinpoint Citation in a First Reference to a Case

If you are quoting or paraphrasing directly from a page at the same time you are giving a first, full citation, then you must merge the pinpoint citation into the full citation.

> The court said, "Silence does not constitute acceptance of an offer." *Rogers v. Campbell, Inc.*, 447 A.2d 589, 595 (N.J. 1982).

D. Pinpoint Citation to More Than One Page

See Rules 5.3 and 5.4 for how to pinpoint more than one page. Notice the difference between material that runs continuously from one page to the next and material that is not continuous.

> *Smith*, 200 N.W.2d at 402–03 [The quote or other cited material appears continuously on pages 402 through 403 of the North Western Reporter.]
>
> *Smith*, 200 N.W.2d at 402, 403 [In the North Western Reporter, part appears on 402 and another part on 403.]

E. Block Quotations

Quotations of 50 words or more must be done in block style. Block quotations are disfavored because they usually don't get read, but sometimes they're unavoidable. Include one only when the language is significant and decisive.

If you write one in your document, follow these rules:

- Lead into the block quotation with a phrase that sets the expectation for what's in the quotation.
- Single-space the text.
- Indent the text 1/2" on each side.
- Use left or full justification.
- Do not use quotation marks.
- Put the citation outside of the quotation against the left margin.
- Make sure the line spacing before and after the quotation is the same.

Here is an example:

> The court set out different rules as follows:
>
> > Silence does not constitute acceptance of an offer. Since 1865, this has always been the rule in Michigan. The Restatement, on the other hand, follows the minority view. Under the minority view, silence may constitute acceptance if the offeree should have realized that the offeror might reasonably regard the silence as acceptance.
>
> *Smith*, 200 N.W.2d at 401. [Continue with paragraph or begin a new one.]

For more on paragraphing block quotes, see ALWD Rule 38.5(d), (e).

F. Quoting a Case Within a Case

If you quote language that a court quoted from an earlier case, you must generally provide attribution to the earlier case. See Rule 38.4(c).

> The court said, "It has always been the rule that 'a defendant does not have to retreat if he is within his own home.'" *Dyer*, 124 N.W. at 631 (quoting *State v. Gowdy*, 56 N.W. 546, 547 (Iowa 1905)).

Note: In this example, you are quoting from *Dyer*, which in turn quoted from *Gowdy* the words in single quotation marks. If the earlier case is not significant, you can do it like this:

> The court said, "It has always been the rule that 'a defendant does not have to retreat if he is within his own home.'" *Dyer*, 124 N.W. at 631 (citation omitted).

17.9 Leading into Quotations

A. Examples of Lead-Ins that Merge into the Quote

> The court said that "the exception to the rule does not apply in this case." *Smith*, 200 N.W.2d at 401.

> The court noted that earlier cases "did not impose a duty to retreat on those assaulted in their own homes." *Smith*, 200 N.W.2d at 401.

> The court said that "the rule has several exceptions." *Smith*, 200 N.W.2d at 401.

Note that your lead-in often ends with the word *that*, but not always. Either way, the lead-in will merge with the quote so that the quote is an integral part of your larger sentence. Also note that the quote begins with a lowercase letter and is not preceded by any punctuation (no comma or colon).

B. Examples of Lead-Ins that Merely Introduce a Quote: The Quote Itself Is a Complete Sentence Without the Lead-In

> The court said, "We will continue to follow the majority rule." *Smith*, 200 N.W.2d at 401.

> The court stated the general rule: "A person assaulted at home is not required to retreat before killing in self-defense." *Smith*, 200 N.W.2d at 401.

Note: Normally, you should write a lead-in to fit the quote. If the quote begins with a lowercase letter, try to follow the examples in part A, above. If the quote begins with a capital letter and makes a complete sentence, try to follow the examples you see here in part B.

Another note: In rare cases, you may not be able to write a lead-in that fits with the first letter in the quote. Then—and only then—you may change from capital to lowercase or vice versa to fit your lead-in. You must place the letter in brackets when you change it.

> The court said, "[W]e agree that a defendant should not be required to testify." *Smith*, 200 N.W.2d at 401.

In this example, the change is necessary to avoid an awkward double *that*.

17.10 Omissions & Alterations in Quotations

A. Using Ellipses to Show Omissions

An ellipsis is three spaced dots with a space before, between, and after the dots. It is used to show that you have omitted something from the original. See Rule 40.

Original:

> Silence does not constitute acceptance of an offer. Since 1865, this has always been the rule in Michigan. The Restatement, on the other hand, follows the minority view. Under the minority view, silence may constitute acceptance if the offeree should have realized that the offeror might reasonably regard the silence as acceptance.

Smith, 200 N.W.2d at 401.

(1) If you want to leave something out of the middle of a sentence, use just an ellipsis.

> The court said, "The Restatement . . . follows the minority view."

(2) If you want to leave something out before the end of a sentence, use an ellipsis and a period.

> The court said, "Silence does not constitute acceptance . . . ." *Smith*, 200 N.W.2d at 401.

Note: Because the omission is at the end of the quoted sentence, the sentence period follows the ellipsis. That's why there is a space before the first dot.

(3) If you want to leave something out after the end of the quoted sentence, (either the beginning of the next sentence or the entire sentence or more), you must use a period and an ellipsis.

> The court noted, "Silence does not constitute acceptance of an offer. . . . [T]his has always been the rule in Michigan." *Smith*, 200 N.W.2d at 401.

> The court acknowledged different views: "Silence does not constitute acceptance of an offer. . . . The Restatement, on the other hand, follows the minority view." *Smith*, 200 N.W.2d at 401.

Note that because the omission follows a complete sentence, the first dot is the sentence period. That's why there is no space before the first dot in these two examples.

(4) Do not use an ellipsis at the beginning of a quotation.

> The court noted that "this has always been the rule in Michigan." *Smith*, 200 N.W.2d at 401.

(5) Do not use an ellipsis at the beginning or end when you quote just a phrase.

> The court said emphatically that it "has always been the rule" that Michigan courts do not treat silence as acceptance of an offer. *Smith*, 200 N.W.2d at 401.

(6) Generally do not omit just a few words. For instance, the ellipsis in sentence 2 above is hardly worth the effort.

(7) However you do it, your quote must be grammatically correct. To test, read the sentence without the ellipsis—as if it was not there. The sentence still has to work grammatically.

B. Using Brackets to Show Alterations

Brackets can be used to change a letter from capital to lowercase or vice versa. Brackets can also be used to substitute words or letters or to insert information into a quote. Empty brackets are used to show that a letter has been deleted. See Rule 39.

Original:

"Because Jones repudiated the contract, he cannot recover for Smith's breach." *Smith*, 200 N.W.2d at 401.

(1) Using brackets to change a letter from upper case to lower case:

The court said that "[b]ecause Jones repudiated the contract, he cannot recover for Smith's breach." *Smith*, 200 N.W.2d at 401.

(2) Using brackets to substitute words:

The court said, "Because [the buyer] repudiated the contract, he cannot recover for [the seller's] breach." *Smith*, 200 N.W.2d at 401.

(3) Using brackets to substitute a letter:

The court said that if the buyer "repudiate[s] the contract, he cannot recover for [the seller's] breach." *Smith*, 200 N.W.2d at 401.

(4) Using brackets to insert information:

The court said, "Because Jones repudiated the contract [by refusing the goods], he cannot recover for Smith's breach." *Smith*, 200 N.W.2d at 401.

(5) Using brackets to show that a letter has been omitted:

The court indicated that if the buyer were to "repudiate[] the contract, he [could not] recover for [the seller's] breach." *Smith*, 200 N.W.2d at 401.

17.11 Signals Before Citations

You should always consider whether an introductory signal is needed before any given citation. The following is a sampling of the more commonly used signals. See Rule 35 for a complete listing.

A. No Signal

Provide no signal when the cited authority is the source of a quotation or supports your point directly.

The court stated, "The key element of the tort is extreme and outrageous conduct on the defendant's part." *Smith*, 200 N.W.2d at 401.

The primary inquiry is whether the defendant acted outrageously. *Smith*, 200 N.W.2d at 401.

B. *See* and *See Also*

Use the *see* signal if the cited authority clearly supports your point but does not say directly what you are saying. In other words, there is an inferential step between what the cited authority says and what you are saying. Use the *see also* signal to give additional support, especially after other authorities have been cited and discussed.

Because our client did not act intentionally or recklessly, she is not guilty of criminal contempt. *See Yellow v. Orange*, 100 F. Supp. 58, 60 (W.D. Mich. 1951) (noting that the crime of contempt requires a "guilty mind"); *see also Gold v. Brass*,

394 F.2d 42, 45 (9th Cir. 1971) (reversing contempt conviction because the defendant was "merely negligent"); *Silver v. Copper*, 285 F.2d 512 (D.C. Cir. 1968).

Note: Because the *see* and *see also* signals require an inferential step, an explanatory parenthetical can bolster the authoritativeness of your writing.

Another Note: Explanatory parenthetical information generally should be a sentence fragment. To structure them that way, you can begin the parenthetical information with a word that ends with the letters i-n-g. See Rule 37.3.

C. *Cf.*

Use the *cf.* signal when the cited authority says something different than you are saying but is sufficiently analogous to lend support. In other words, there is an inferential step between what the cited authority says and what you are saying—too big an inference to allow use of the *see* signal. Because of this larger inferential step, parenthetical explanations are strongly recommended when using the *cf.* signal.

> An employer might be subject to vicarious liability for some intentional torts, even intentional torts committed by employees acting outside the scope of employment. *Cf. Ellerth v. Burlington Corp.*, 435 U.S. 67, 75–77 (1998) (recognizing a limited range of vicarious liability for sexual harassment under civil rights law).

D. *E.g.*

E.g. means "for example." Use it to give one or more examples of support for what you are saying.

> Most states require that the defendant act intentionally or recklessly to be guilty of contempt. *E.g.* N.Y. Penal Law § 50 (McKinney 1980); Or. Rev. Stat. § 32 (1985); Utah Code Ann. § 12 (1981).
>
> A defendant, therefore, should not be guilty if he or she acted negligently. *See e.g. Yellow v. Orange*, 100 F. Supp. 58, 60 (W.D. Mich. 1951) (defendant "just careless"); *see also Gold v. Brass*, 394 F.2d 42, 45 (9th Cir. 1971) (defendant's act "merely inadvertent"); *Silver v. Copper*, 285 F.2d 512, 515 (D.C. Cir. 1968) (defendant's "mere oversight").

E. *But See* and *But Cf.*

To cite authorities that are contrary to what you are saying, use a signal introduced by *but*, such as *but see* or *but cf.*

> Either intentional or reckless disregard of a court order constitutes criminal contempt. *Gold v. Brass*, 394 F.2d 42, 45 (9th Cir. 1971). *But see Lead v. Pipe*, 512 F.2d 65 (10th Cir. 1980) (requiring intentional conduct for criminal contempt).

PART SIX

Editing Skills

One of the most satisfying skills of the attorney craft is making your writing enjoyable for the reader. That's what you'll learn about in Part 6.

Chapter Eighteen

Revise and Edit

18.1 Humans Write in Four Stages

Betty Flowers, a former university English professor and director of the Lyndon B. Johnson Library and Museum, taught that humans write in four stages. And she explains these four stages by the role or energy taken on for each one: (1) madman, (2) architect, (3) carpenter, and (4) judge.

The madman is full of ideas, writes crazily, even sloppily, and gets carried away by enthusiasm. This is what you may experience as you're researching the law for a writing project, and you have a slew of ideas come to you about what you should write. So you jot down notes and ideas in no particular order. This is the brainstorming phase of writing.

Now, it's important, as Professor Flowers taught, to keep the madman's nemesis at bay: the judge. The judge energy will slow things down to ensure that your first draft is grammatically correct. That's rubbish! Tell the judge to jump in a lake until you're ready for them.

After the initial brainstorming is done, you may have a yellow legal pad with circled ideas, or you have a document going on your laptop with several lines of text. Now the architect needs to come in and start giving structure to these ideas. The structure makes connections between the ideas. These ideas may begin as nonlinear, but they end up as an outline.

For attorneys, by the end of the architect phase, they'd have an idea of the main rules of law and which ones are at issue. And they'd have an outline of rules, caselaw, and arguments for each element at issue.

The carpenter then is ready to be hired. They come and write the first draft from an outline to complete sentences, paragraphs, and thoughts. Again, the carpenter is careful to not let in the judge because the judge likes to stop creativity. Hold them at bay at least until the first draft is done.

And, finally, after the first complete draft is inked, the judge's task is to make the document enjoyable to read. Look for problems. Revise and edit the draft. Work on transitions. Improve the grammar and punctuation. Write more concisely. You know, all the things that improve readability.

18.2 Be the Madman, Architect, and Carpenter for Each Part of the Document

You can't be the madman, architect, and carpenter for the entire document; that's just too overwhelming. Instead, be these types of writers for just one particular section at a time. So if you're writing an opinion letter, focus on writing just the issue and answer. Be the madman, architect, and carpenter. Then write the Rule Foundation. Be the madman, architect, and carpenter for just that. And so on.

Using the checklists in this textbook will help you write this first draft of each section.

Then, after all parts of the document are complete, bring in the judge to look at the entire document.

18.3 Be the Judge of the Entire Document

After you've written all the document parts, it's time to let the judge in and make your document enjoyable to read. The "judge" should focus on four areas:

- Typography
- Grammar
- Readability
- Citations

18.4 Apply Enticing Typography

Typography is the layout of the document. It includes line spacing before and after headings, first-line indents, and even font choice. More than anything, your document needs to have pleasing and consistent typography to maintain professional expectations. Follow these rules to do that.

A. Page Numbers

1. For all documents, use the same font and size for page numbers.

Make sure page numbers are in the same font and size as the rest of the document. You can use any professional typeface, but make sure it also gets applied to the page numbers. Once you change the font on one page number, Word automatically updates all other page numbers with the same font.

It's standard to put the page numbers in the footer. If, however, you have them in the header, make sure that you click the Different First Page box on the Header & Footer menu. That menu appears in Word, by the way, when you double-click into your header. Checking the box by Different First Page will make the page number on the first page disappear.

2. For court briefs, follow pagination conventions.

When a motion and brief are in one document, you need to follow these rules:

Motion:

- Insert page numbers only if it's more than one page
- If it's more than one page, insert Arabic page numbers
- Don't put a page number on the first page

Brief:

- Insert Roman page numbers from the first page until the Statement of Facts, but not including the Statement of Facts.
- Do not include a page number on the first page of the brief (so the first page number will be Roman numeral ii on the Table of Contents page
- Starting with the Statement of Facts, use Arabic page numbers

Properly doing that is a breeze once you know what you're doing. But it takes a minute to learn how to do that in Word. The best advice is to run this search in YouTube: "how to insert Roman and Arabic numbers in the same document."

B. Margins

Ensure that your margins are 1" all around. That's the standard setting in Word and Google Docs, but you should nonetheless check. The margins are likely to change after a block quotation and after indented headings. Especially check the margins after those two things.

C. Font

Use a standard font. Many serif fonts are acceptable. Serif fonts have little tails coming off of corners and ends of the letters. See the image from the *Merriam Webster Online Dictionary* to the right of this paragraph. Times New Roman, Georgia, and Cambria are typical serif fonts, while Calibri and Arial are commonly used sans serif fonts.

Use a standard size—typically 12 points.* Most sans serif fonts look better when used a little smaller—at 11 rather than 12 points. For this reason, many legal documents are written in 11 point Arial or Calibri. As a rule, avoid using a type size less than 11 points.

Use a consistent font, text size, and text color throughout your document. This may seem like a no-brainer, but it can often be an issue, especially when information is pulled from sources found on the Internet and pasted into the document. When this happens, the formatting from the source often remains. The result? The copied material could appear dark gray, or a different size or font.

To avoid bringing in foreign formatting, choose to paste without formatting.

Just to be certain, before you submit your document you should select the entire document using *Ctrl* + *A* or *Command* + *A* and then apply the same font, font size, and font color to the entire document.

---

* The text of this coursebook is set in 11 point Minion Pro.

D. Headings

Make sure you have consistent space before and after each heading in the document. Use the Paragraph Spacing feature in Word to adjust the space before and after each heading. You'll find this in Word under the Layout tab or in the Paragraph dialog box, which you can access by clicking on the arrow in the box:

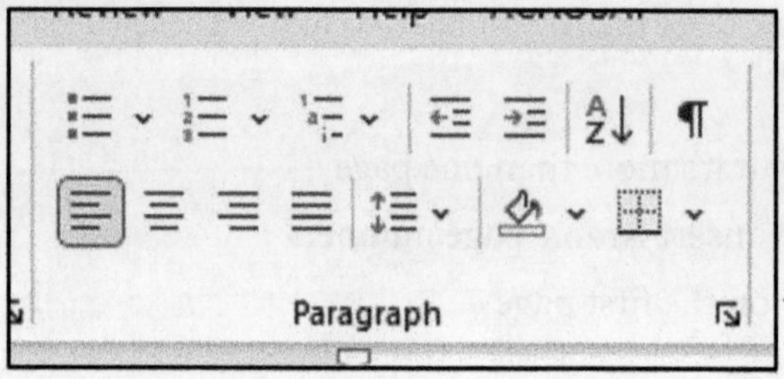

Arrow in the box

In Google Docs, you can adjust the space before and after paragraphs in the Format menu.

As a good guideline to follow, headings should have 18 points of line space above them, and 8 points of line space after them. Those amounts give the reader's eye a clear break so they know where one section ends and the next begins. You don't have to use these exact amounts in your own documents; just make them look nice. And be consistent throughout the entire document!

E. Paragraphs

There are two ways to alert your reader to when a new paragraph begins. Either use first-line indents or add space between the paragraphs. You must do one or the other to avoid this annoying format:

Relevant Caselaw

Confinement by unreasonable duress occurs when one's will is overcome. *Parrott v. Bank of America*, 217 P.2d 89, 95 (Cal. App. 2d Dist. 1950). In *Parrott*, bank managers accused a teller of stealing a customer's deposit. The bank managers questioned her for more than two hours, and they threatened her with an FBI investigation and to publicly humiliate her. As a result, she confessed to stealing the deposit even though she was innocent. A short time after the confession, the bank customer found the deposit at home.
The court held that the teller was confined during the questioning. *Id.* at 95. In support of this conclusion, the court mainly relied on the fact that an innocent person agreeing to sign a confession is evidence of force. *Id.*
The source of the duress may be when a person uses an invaluable possession as leverage. *Wilson v. Houston Funeral Home*, 50 Cal. Rptr. 2d 169 (Cal. App. 2d Dist. 1996). In *Wilson*, a funeral home director sent a limo to take a family to scheduled burial services. The driver, instead, took the family to a bank where the funeral director demanded full payment even though they had agreed to payment after the burial services. In the bank, he shouted, "Ain't nobody going nowhere until I get paid." *Id.* at 170. And for 45 minutes he tried to talk the widow into paying him. The court held that the family was confined by unreasonable duress because leaving the bank would have left their deceased loved one to an unknown fate. *Id.* at 174.

A paragraph begins here, but it's difficult to see that.

Another paragraph begins here, but it's likewise difficult to see that.

F. First-Line Indents

Ensure that first-line indents are consistent. If you don't have them, make sure no paragraph has them. If you do have first-line indents, make sure they are all the same. A standard first-line indent is either .38" or .5".

Indenting the first line of each paragraph clearly distinguishes each paragraph. Compare this to the example above:

Relevant Caselaw

Confinement by unreasonable duress occurs when one's will is overcome. *Parrott v. Bank of America*, 217 P.2d 89, 95 (Cal. App. 2d Dist. 1950). In *Parrott*, bank managers accused a teller of stealing a customer's deposit. The bank managers questioned her for more than two hours, and they threatened her with an FBI investigation and to publicly humiliate her. As a result, she confessed to stealing the deposit even though she was innocent. A short time after the confession, the bank customer found the deposit at home.

The court held that the teller was confined during the questioning. *Id.* at 95. In support of this conclusion, the court mainly relied on the fact that an innocent person agreeing to sign a confession is evidence of force. *Id.*

The source of the duress may be when a person uses an invaluable possession as leverage. *Wilson v. Houston Funeral Home*, 50 Cal. Rptr. 2d 169 (Cal. App. 2d Dist. 1996). In *Wilson*, a funeral home director sent a limo to take a family to scheduled burial services. The driver, instead, took the family to a bank where the funeral director demanded full payment even though they had agreed to payment after the burial services. In the bank, he shouted, "Ain't nobody going nowhere until I get paid." *Id.* at 170. And for 45 minutes he tried to talk the widow into paying him. The court held that the family was confined by unreasonable duress because leaving the bank would have left their deceased loved one to an unknown fate. *Id.* at 174.

Each of these first-line indents allows the reader to take a small break, and they signal a new topic.

Some writers prefer a more modern look. This modern look calls for squared off corners on the left side of each paragraph, which means that there are no first-line indents. To make it easy to distinguish between paragraphs, for this look, add a bit of extra line space between each paragraph.

Here's the modern look with six points of Paragraph Spacing after each paragraph:

Relevant Caselaw

Confinement by unreasonable duress occurs when one's will is overcome. *Parrott v. Bank of America*, 217 P.2d 89, 95 (Cal. App. 2d Dist. 1950). In *Parrott*, bank managers accused a teller of stealing a customer's deposit. The bank managers questioned her for more than two hours, and they threatened her with an FBI investigation and to publicly humiliate her. As a result, she confessed to stealing the deposit even though she was innocent. A short time after the confession, the bank customer found the deposit at home.

The court held that the teller was confined during the questioning. *Id.* at 95. In support of this conclusion, the court mainly relied on the fact that an innocent person agreeing to sign a confession is evidence of force. *Id.*

The source of the duress may be when a person uses an invaluable possession as leverage. *Wilson v. Houston Funeral Home*, 50 Cal. Rptr. 2d 169 (Cal. App. 2d Dist. 1996). In *Wilson*, a funeral home director sent a limo to take a family to scheduled burial services. The driver, instead, took the family to a bank where the funeral director demanded full payment even though they had agreed to payment after the burial services. In the bank, he shouted, "Ain't nobody going nowhere until I get paid." *Id.* at 170. And for 45 minutes he tried to talk the widow into paying him. The court held that the family was confined by unreasonable duress because leaving the bank would have left their deceased loved one to an unknown fate. *Id.* at 174.

You can play around with the space between the paragraphs until it looks good. But be consistent!

To add line spacing in Word, click on the Layout menu option, and you'll see options for spacing before and after paragraph. If you change the numbers but nothing changes on the screen, it's likely because the option "Don't add space between paragraphs of the same style" is turned on. Turn it off by clicking on the little arrow near "Paragraph" to get to the paragraph dialog box: .

G. Block Quotations

Make sure the line spacing before and after a block quotation is the same. Use a combination of (1) line spacing and (2) space after paragraph (explained above) to achieve that consistency.

(By the way, for the other rules of a block quotation, check out 17.8(E) in this book and ALWD 38.5.)

H. Spaces After a Period

Make sure that you have consistent spacing after each period. More and more, attorneys write with just one space after a period. But you may use two spaces after a period. Whichever format you choose, be consistent.

To check this, you may want to use the Find and Replace feature in your Word Processor. In the Find box, you can simply add a space or two and search for that. And then in the Replace box, you can add one space. (Literally, put your cursor in the Find box and tap the space bar.) That way, you can find any periods with two spaces after them and make sure they have just one. Or vice versa.

I. Prefer Curved Quotation Marks and Apostrophes

A really ugly detail that will annoy careful readers is when your quotation marks and apostrophes are formatted differently. Word processors default to formatting these in a "smart" or "curved" style. But when we paste from the Internet, especially websites like Westlaw, Lexis, or ChatGPT, the quotation marks and apostrophes come in as "straight."

The difference is subtle but noticeable:

"Shine" versus “Shine”

You should prefer to use curved quotation marks and apostrophes. To ensure that you do, when you're done writing your document, simply use the Find and Replace feature and replace them all in your document. Replacing them will make them all curved.

18.5 Use Guru Grammar

A reader is making assumptions about you based on your grammar. They're assuming how well you're educated and how intelligent you are. Besides that, using improper grammar highlights the incorrect usage and puts the substance of what you're trying to say on the backburner. So make your great thoughts shine by using proper grammar.

But there's a more important reason to use proper grammar: as attorneys, we are the protectors of language. There is no other profession that uses words more than attorneys do. Our very democracy requires words. An ordered civilization requires words. And the same words need to mean the same thing to all people. And because grammar and punctuation glues words together, we have to know their rules and follow them so all have access to the same meaning.

This is not meant to be a complete chapter on grammar and punctuation. You have many other great resources like *The Redbook* and *Core Grammar for Lawyers*. Instead, this section will focus on just the most important things to get right when writing legal documents:

- Avoid sentence fragments.
- Avoid run-on sentences.
- Quote correctly.
- Properly punctuate.
- Spell correctly.
- Properly format words as words.
- Know when to use *the plaintiff* versus *plaintiff*.
- Capitalize *court* only sometimes.

A. Avoid sentence fragments.

Sentence fragments stick out like a sore thumb. A sentence fragment is usually a complete sentence that cannot stand on its own because it begins with a word that makes it dependent. Words like *although*, *unlike*, *which*, *while*, and *when* at the beginning of a sentence make a sentence fragment.

Not this: Although she did fill out the form.

But this: Although she did fill out the form, she failed to sign it.

By adding "she failed to sign it," which is an independent clause, the entire sentence now works.

Not this: Unlike the plaintiff in *Shallal* who told multiple people about the violation.

But this: Unlike the plaintiff in *Shallal* who told multiple people about the violation, the employee in our case kept everything to herself.

Same thing: the sentence fragment is fixed in the second example above by adding an independent clause to it.

B. Avoid run-on sentences.

A run-on sentence is where the writer puts multiple sentences in one sentence without properly separating them.

Not this: She downloaded the complaint form, she filled out the complaint form.

But this: She downloaded the complaint form. She filled out the complaint form.

Not this: She downloaded the complaint form, however, she did not fill it out.

But this: She downloaded the complaint form; however, she did not fill it out.

A really pesky one is *however*. You cannot put it by itself or even with commas between two independent sentences in one sentence. You must use a hard stop before it like a period or semicolon. This applies only when there are two independent clauses in one sentence.

C. Quote correctly.

As a writer, you quote in two ways (leaving block quotations aside): a separate quotation or a merged quotation. A separate quotation looks like this:

> The court said, "Do it this way if you start at the beginning of a quoted sentence."

Use this when you want to quote a separate, complete sentence. The elements of a separate quotation are (1) attribution (e.g., "The court said"), (2) comma, (3) open quotation mark, (4) capital letter, and (5) end quotation mark outside the hard sentence stop. Observe these five elements in the example above.

And this is what a merged quotation looks like:

> The court said that "when the quote begins in the middle of the quoted sentence, use the word that and keep the small letter in the first word of the quotation."

Use this style most of the time because it's less intrusive to read and it highlights only the relevant portion of a quotation. The elements for a merged quotation are (1) no comma before the quotation mark, (2) open quotation, (3) a noncapital letter to begin the quoted material, (4) a closing quotation mark outside the hard sentence stop, and (5) the entire sentence—the writer's words and the quoted words—is one complete sentence.

D. Properly punctuate.

Here are a few of the more glaring problems to avoid:

- Use a comma to separate two sentences joined by *and*, *but*, or *so*.

  Do this: I'm sorry this took so long, but we had trouble finding the information.

  Do this: The court will probably not be this harsh, and it will consider all relevant factors.

  Do this: The court will probably not be this harsh and will consider all relevant factors.

- Use a comma after beginning a sentence with *in* or *on*.

  Not this: In *Debano-Griffin v. Lake County*, 828 N.W.2d 634 (Mich. 2013). The plaintiff complained to friends and family.

  You can't put a period immediately after the *In* clause. Instead, you need a comma to set off the *In* clause, which is a dependent clause, from the independent clause that begins with *The plaintiff*.

  Not this: In *Debano-Griffin v. Lake County*, 828 N.W.2d 634 (Mich. 2013) the plaintiff complained to friends and family.

  But this: In *Debano-Griffin v. Lake County*, 828 N.W.2d 634 (Mich. 2013), the plaintiff complained to friends and family.

- Properly form the possessive.

  For the singular possessive, add 's:

  Do this: Defendant's Motion for Summary Judgment

Do this: Jack Charles's obsession with fireworks in part proves his negligence.

Not this: Defendant Motion for Summary Judgment

For plural words, simply add ' (an apostrophe) at the end of the already pluralized word:

Do this: Defendants' Motion for Summary Judgment

Not this: Defendantses' Motion for Summary Judgment

Do this: The Charleses' obsession with fireworks in part proves their negligence.

Note how the Charles family has multiple people in it, so the plural form would simply be *Charleses*. We add *es* to singular words ending in *s* to form the possessive.

E. Spell correctly.

Most spell checkers will not pick up the following spelling errors, so you need to carefully read each word of your document aloud to find these mistakes:

- causal v. casual (attorneys usually need to write *causal*, but it comes out as *casual*)
- lead v. led (the past tense of *to lead* is *led* (e.g., This led the judge to one conclusion.))
- statute v. statue
- trial v. trail
- public v. pubic
- it's v. its (do you mean the contraction for *it is*, which is *it's*? Or do you mean the possessive *its*?)
- affect v. effect (*affect* is the verb form)

F. Properly format words as words.

When a word is used as a term, set it off with quotation marks or italics. The modern approach is to prefer italics:

Do this: *They* in that sentence is ambiguous because it could refer to *judges* or *attorneys*.

Not this: They in that sentence is ambiguous because it could refer to judges or attorneys.

Do this: They went back to the defendant's house after the bar crawl.

Do this: The legislature has not yet defined *serious impairment*, but courts have written much about the term.

Not this: The legislature has not yet defined serious impairment, but courts have written much about the term.

G. Know when to use *the plaintiff* versus *plaintiff*.

In a Case Illustration of a decided case, the best practice is to use a descriptive legal label instead of names (e.g., employee, business owner, invitee). But if you need to use party designations, you must use *the plaintiff* and *the defendant* consistently. You cannot use just *plaintiff* or even just *Plaintiff*. See 9.4(C)(3), 12.2(D)(3).

Everywhere else in a document, use names to discuss the case's parties. If using names creates confusion or ambiguity, then use their party designations, but as a proper noun: *Plaintiff* or *Defendant*.

So when writing about past cases, use *the plaintiff* or *the defendant*, but use *Plaintiff* or *Defendant* to refer to parties in the case at hand.

H. Capitalize *court* only sometimes.

The default rule is to not capitalize *court*. However, sometimes we do to show respect.

Capitalize *court* only

- when referring to the state or federal supreme court (e.g., "The Court [meaning the Michigan Supreme Court] held that . . . ") OR
- when writing a brief and referring to the court that will read the brief (e.g., "Defendant's respectfully ask this Court to grant the motion and award attorney fees.")

Here are the places in a document you're likely to apply these rules:

- **Case Illustration:** If the case you're writing about is the highest court in your jurisdiction, you need to capitalize *court* (e.g., "The Court held . . . ." "The Court reasoned . . . .")
- **Motion:** In a motion, you'll ask the court to grant a motion, so capitalize *court* to show respect to that court (e.g., "Defendant Daphne Annabelle asks this Court to order that this case be dismissed . . . .")
- **Brief:** In a brief, anytime you ask the court to grant your motion, capitalize *court*; this will be especially necessary in the Relief Requested (aka, Conclusion).

18.6 Ensure Rad Readability

You can increase your reader's enjoyment by improving the readability of your writing. Do that by

- connecting parts of the document,
- connecting sentences,
- eliminating legalese,
- quoting sparingly,
- preferring the active voice,
- preferring short sentences, and
- writing concisely.

A. Connect parts of the document.

Look at the big picture of your document, whatever kind it is. Is there a clear connection between the sections where you previewed the analysis, where you explained the codified law, where you explained the caselaw, where you applied the law, and where you gave suggestions? Your document is an entire ecosystem with all the parts working together.

Use topic sentences to begin almost every paragraph to connect the parts of a document. Taken together, each topic sentence should form an outline of your document. Highlight each one and ask yourself: *Does this state the main point of my paragraph?* That is, does it give the bottom line? (In a case analysis, that's the relevant decision or new rule from the case.) Does it help to transition from one idea to another? And, finally, does it connect to the document's other parts?

Remember that topic sentences should be specific and shouldn't be cluttered with cites or quotes.

B. Connect sentences.

Readers prefer fluent sentences without gaps between them. You can primarily achieve this by showing how sentences relate to each other. Writers use transition words and phrases to signal how ideas relate to each other. This makes it easier for readers to follow and understand the discussion. You can use transition words or phrases:

- **To add a point**: and, also, in addition, besides, moreover, what's more, too
- **To compare or expand**: similarly, likewise, in the same way
- **To introduce a conclusion**: so, therefore, thus, then, hence, it follows that, accordingly
- **To state a reason**: because, since
- **To show conflict**: but, on the contrary
- **To show contrast**: in contrast, whereas, on the other hand, rather
- **To concede a point**: granted, admittedly, of course, no doubt, even though, although, despite, it's true that
- **To return the thought to your point**: still, yet, even so
- **To restate (and reinforce) a point**: in other words, that is, again
- **To give an example**: for instance, for example, for one thing, such as
- **To sequence**: first, second, third; next, finally
- **To sum up**: to summarize, in short, in conclusion, all in all

C. Eliminate legalese.

Legalese takes the form of antiquated words that we no longer use in common speech. Legalese is not terms of art or even rarely used words like equipoise, pedantic, or supercilious. If those words precisely convey the meaning, then use them.

Avoid antiquated words that add -in or -by like *herein* and *hereby*. Certainly avoid *said* because nobody talks like that anymore.

Basically, if you're using an antiquated phrase just for the sake of feeling like you earned your law degree, you should strike it and prefer a more modern, familiar word.

D. Quote sparingly.

When in doubt, paraphrase. Paraphrasing the law and facts is much easier for your reader to understand. For more detail on this topic, see the section titled How Much of a Statute to Quote Versus Paraphrase under Explain Codified Law in section 8.2(D).

E. Prefer the active voice.

The active voice is when the **actor** (who is doing the action) comes first. Then the verb (the action) comes after the actor.

> During that play, I just dunked on Durant and Ibaka.
>
> And I got real emotional, real excited.
>
> It was unfortunate that James had to get hit, you know, with an unintentional elbow.
>
> And I hope he's okay.

The passive voice, on the other hand, is when (1) the verb comes first before **the actor** or (2) when the **actor** is unknown.

> The sheriff was shot by **me**.
>
> The sheriff was shot. ?
>
> I shot the sheriff.

Observe how with the first two examples, either the actor is last or is missing altogether. In the last example, the actor is before the verb, which is in proper active-voice form.

Why should you avoid the passive voice? It takes more time to figure out who is doing what and to whom or what. It's wordy. It can create awkward sentences. And it can cause your writing to seem flat and uninteresting.

Your word processor likely will flag the passive voice for you if you turn on the grammar function. In Word, you can find this under File > Options > Proofing.

But even better, write the first draft in the active voice by getting in the habit of writing in the order of actor > action.

F. Prefer short sentences.

Your sentences should average around 25 words per sentence. That means that you'll have some sentences with more and some with less. You can check the average length by turning on readability statistics in Word and then running Spelling and Grammar under the Review menu.

G. Write concisely.

Always strive to elide unnecessarily information from each sentence and paragraph.

Once you've established that you can't cut any more content, then look at your word and phrase usage to see if you're using more words than you need. Here are some quick tips for writing more directly:

- Use verbs more!

  Instead of nouns that require helping verbs, just use the verb form:

  make a determination > determine

  provide protection to > protect

  to effect settlement > settle

  render assistance > assist, help

  make inquiry < inquire, ask

  provide responses > respond

  So, if you see a phrase like "The parties are in agreement" in your document, you should change it to "The parties agree."

  One tip is to search your document for nouns ending in *ment*, *tion*, *ance*, *ence* and then turn those words into verbs and delete the former noun's helping verbs.

- Question every word

  Question every *of*. Do a search in your document using Ctrl + F for *of*. If you can rewrite a phrase or sentence to avoid *of* and overall improve the concision and directness, then you should.

  Avoid *because of the fact that*. This is a redundancy because after this phrase invariably the reader introduces a fact. Why not simply write "because" and then state the fact?

  Change *prior to* to *before*. Why not say something in one word instead of two?

  The same goes for *pursuant to*. Prefer *under*.

  Delete *in order* from your document because it adds no meaning.

18.7 Ensure Sightly Citations

Chapter 17 summarizes the Bluebook and ALWD Guide citation systems; go there for detail about how to cite sources. Here, instead, you'll find some brief advice on how to edit your citations.

The best advice about editing citations actually applies to when you're writing the first draft. Write your citations as you're initially compiling the document. That way you don't have to go back to each and every source when you're editing to add in the citations. And avoid using *Id.* in your initial drafts.

The reason for this is that during the revision stage when you're moving sentences and paragraphs around, you might end up with an *Id.* going to an unintended source.

But be sure to perfect your citations only after you're done editing.

A. Common Mistakes in Citations to Codified Law

Do not put a period after *Laws* because it's not an abbreviation.

Not this: Mich. Comp. Laws. § 38.873 (2024).

But this: Mich. Comp. Laws § 38.873 (2024).

Include the publisher's name in the parenthetical.

Not this: Mich. Comp. Laws Ann. § 38.873 (2024).

But this: Mich. Comp. Laws Ann. § 38.873 (West 2024).

Use the correct name for Lexis in the parenthetical. Use Appendix 1(B) in ALWD for more.

Not this: Mich. Comp. Laws Serv. § 38.873 (Lexis 2024).

But this: Mich. Comp. Laws Serv. § 38.873 (LexisNexis 2024).

B. Common Mistakes in Citations to Caselaw

Include only the regional (aka, unofficial) reporter, not the official one.

Not this: *Debano-Griffin v. Lake County*, 493 Mich. 167, 828 N.W.2d 634 (2013).

But this: *Debano-Griffin v. Lake County*, 828 N.W. 2d 634 (Mich. 2013).

Properly space the reporter abbreviation.

Not this: *Debano-Griffin v. Lake County*, 828 N.W. 2d 634 (Mich. 2013).

But this: *Debano-Griffin v. Lake County*, 828 N.W.2d 634 (Mich. 2013).

When citing U.S. Supreme Court cases, include only the official reporter.

Not this: *Rodriguez v. United States*, 575 U.S. 348, 135 S. Ct. 1609, 191 L. Ed. 2d 492 (2015).

But this: *Rodriguez v. United States*, 575 U.S. 348 (2015).

Never superscript ordinals in legal citations.

Not this: *United States v. Lott*, 954 F.3d 919 (6th Cir. 2020).

But this: *United States v. Lott*, 954 F.3d 919 (6th Cir. 2020).

Be sure to italicize just the case title and nothing else.

Not this: Rodriguez v. United States, *575 U.S. 348 (2015)*.

But this: *Rodriguez v. United States*, 575 U.S. 348 (2015).

Do not italicize the comma after the case title.

Not this: Rodriguez v. United States, 575 U.S. 348 (2015).

But this: *Rodriguez v. United States*, 575 U.S. 348 (2015).

In short citations to caselaw, omit the initial page number and any parenthetical.

Not this: *Debano-Griffin*, 828 N.W.2d 634 at 640.

But this: *Debano-Griffin*, 828 N.W.2d at 640.

Not this: *Rodriguez*, 575 U.S. at 355 (2015).

But this: *Rodriguez*, 575 U.S. at 355.

In short citations to criminal cases, use the defendant's surname as the shorthand reference.

Not this: *United States*, 575 U.S. 348.

But this: *Rodriguez*, 575 U.S. 348.

When using *Id.*, avoid all these mistakes.

Not this: Id, at 222.

Not this: *Id* at 222.

Not this: Id. at 222.

Not this: *Id.* at 222

Not this: *Id.* 222.

Starting from the top, always use a period in *Id.*, never a comma. Always italicize *Id.* Always use a period after the *Id.* citation to end the citation sentence. Always use *at* with an *Id.* citation. Here's the correct *Id.* citation:

Id. at 222.

Index

A